Life-Study
of
First John
Second John
Third John
Jude

Witness Lee

Living Stream Ministry
Anaheim, California

First Edition, December 1984.

Library of Congress Catalog
Card Number 84-82320

ISBN 0-87083-160-7

Published by

Living Stream Ministry
2431 W. La Palma Ave., Anaheim, CA 92801 U.S.A.
P. O. Box 2121, Anaheim, CA 92814 U.S.A.

Printed in South Korea

1 John

CONTENTS

vi

2 John

CONTENTS

3 John

CONTENTS

Jude

CONTENTS

LIFE-STUDY OF FIRST JOHN

MESSAGE ONE

A WORD CONCERNING THE WRITINGS OF JOHN

(1)

Scripture Reading: 1 John 1:2-3; 2:27; 3:9; 5:4, 18

With this message we begin the Life-study of the Epistles of John. We trust in the Lord to open up the Scriptures to us again and speak a fresh word to us all.

A REVELATION OF DIVINE THINGS

This message is an introductory word concerning the writings of John. John's writings include his Gospel, his three Epistles, and his Revelation. These writings occupy a particular and striking place in the full revelation of God in the Bible. In his Gospel, Epistles, and Revelation John writes of things that are mysterious. These things are mysterious because they are divine. Therefore, we need to see that John's writings are altogether a revelation of divine things. Here I would emphasize two words: revelation and divine.

The entire Bible, of course, is the holy revelation of God. The Bible was not written according to man's mind or according to human thought. Rather, the whole Bible is the divine revelation written in human language. Nevertheless, it is important for us to realize that this is especially true of John's writings, writings that are concerned with divine things.

Our Need for Revelation

Because John writes about divine things, it is necessary that these things be revealed to us. It is not possible for the natural human mentality to guess or infer what John's writings unveil to us. Whatever is revealed in the writings

of John is far beyond our human comprehension. Hence,
there is no room here for guessing or inference. Our
mentality cannot grasp, lay hold of, the divine things
revealed in John's writings. The Gospel of John, the three
Epistles of John, and the book of Revelation reveal matters
that are beyond our ability to imagine. We cannot even
conceive of these things, much less make inferences
regarding them. Because John's writings are of what is
divine, we cannot with our natural mentality imagine
what they contain. Only through divine revelation can the
divine things in John's writings be revealed to us.

As we read the writings of John, it is not adequate
merely to exercise our mentality. We need much prayer. We
also need to believe that today the divine Spirit is within
us, in our spirit. We should trust in this indwelling Spirit to
give us the revelation of the things contained in John's
writings, and also the wisdom to grasp, lay hold of, the
things we see in our spirit as a result of this revelation.
Like the Apostle Paul, we need to pray for a spirit of
wisdom and revelation: "That the God of our Lord Jesus
Christ, the Father of glory, may give to you a spirit of
wisdom and revelation in the full knowledge of Him" (Eph.
1:17). It is not sufficient simply to read John's writings or
meditate on them. Neither is it sufficient only to exercise
our natural understanding. When we come to the writings
of John, we should not trust in our reading, meditating, or
understanding. On the contrary, we should pray, "Lord, I
depend on You to grant me a revelation of what is
contained in these writings. Lord, I do not trust my natural
ability to understand Your word."

The entire book of Revelation is a revelation. This is
why it opens with the words, "The revelation of Jesus
Christ which God gave to Him" (Rev. 1:1). The word
"revelation" denotes the opening of a veil. Revelation is a
matter of opening a veil to show us something mysterious
hidden behind the veil. We all need such an unveiling.
Many marvelous divine things have been concealed, but
we may experience an unveiling and have these things
revealed to us.

Our Need for Understanding

Along with revelation, we also need understanding. We may see certain things, but we may not understand what we see. For example, suppose you visit a large factory and look at various kinds of machines. You see the machines, but you may not understand anything about them. Although the machines have been revealed to you, you still need understanding. The principle is the same with divine things. In addition to revelation, we also need wisdom for understanding. For this reason, Paul prayed for a spirit of wisdom and revelation.

Turning to the Mingled Spirit

The thought in John's writings is absolutely divine. These writings do not contain ethical teachings or philosophical concepts. On the contrary, these writings are filled with divine matters. The word "divine" denotes something that concerns God or that belongs to God. The things concerning God and belonging to God Himself are divine, and anything divine is mysterious. We are not able to grasp, to lay hold of, these mysterious things. God is real and infinite. How can we, mere human beings, comprehend Him? This is impossible. We do not have the capacity to comprehend God. But we thank Him that He created us with a spirit, and in His salvation He has regenerated our deadened spirit and has imparted His divine life into our spirit. He has even given us Himself as the life-giving Spirit to dwell within our spirit. Only in our regenerated spirit are we qualified to see a revelation of the mysterious things in the writings of John. Our human mentality is not qualified for this. There is no possibility of seeing such things with our natural mind. Thank the Lord that we have a regenerated spirit, even a mingled spirit, our regenerated spirit mingled with the divine Spirit. Therefore, we should turn to this mingled spirit and pray, "Lord, we trust in Your unveiling and in Your wisdom. We believe, Lord, that You want to show us something in John's writings. Lord, as You opened the veil to the Apostle John, open it again to us. Lord, we need the reopening of the

veil. Have mercy on us, and unveil the mysteries again.
Grant us the wisdom to understand and lay hold of what
You want to show us in the Epistles of John."

DIGESTING THE INFINITE GOD

We have pointed out that the word divine denotes
things that concern God and belong to God. Actually, this
word denotes God Himself. Hence, to say that the writings
of John reveal divine things means that they reveal God
Himself. As we come to the Epistles of John, it is not our
goal merely to learn things about God. We come to these
Epistles in order to see the things of God. We want to
grasp, receive, and even digest the things of God. How
great this is! Be impressed that it is not our aim in these
messages to have a Bible study. We are not endeavoring to
learn something related to religion or to study matters that
will help us to improve our behavior or uplift the standard
of our living. In these messages on the Epistles of John our
purpose is to see God, grasp God, receive God, and digest
God. When some hear about digesting God, they may be
bothered and ask how it is possible for God to be digested
by us. I can testify that I am very happy with this
expression "digest God." Daily I receive God and digest
Him. If I did not digest God, I would not be able to bear the
heavy burden that is upon me. Praise Him that through
digesting Him I can bear a heavy burden! Through the
digesting of the infinite God, I am what I am, and you are
what you are. The revelation of the divine things in John's
writings is given so that we may receive God and digest
Him.

SUPPLEMENTARY TO THE REVELATIONS
OF THE OTHER HOLY WRITINGS

A Supplement to the Synoptic Gospels

The revelation of the divine things in the writings of
John is supplementary to the revelations of the other holy
writings. This indicates that if the writings of John were
not in the Bible, something important would be lacking.

For example, the Gospel of John is a supplement to the synoptic Gospels, the Gospels of Matthew, Mark, and Luke. Without the Gospel of John, we could realize only that the Lord Jesus was a man who served God as a slave, as revealed in Mark, that He died on the cross to be our Savior, as revealed in Luke, and that He is the King, as revealed in Matthew. With the Lord as a slave, as the Savior and Redeemer, and as the King, we see His humanity. However, the Lord was God before He became a man. This means that in His Person He is of two aspects, a divine aspect and a human aspect. We may say that He has a twofold Person, for He is the God-man, God incarnate. He is God and also man. He is the real and complete God, and He is also a true and perfect man.

If we had only the first three Gospels, the synoptic Gospels, we would see only the aspect of the Lord's humanity, but not much of the aspect of His divinity. By this we realize the need for a supplement to the Gospels of Matthew, Mark, and Luke. The Gospel of John serves this purpose. This Gospel reveals that the man Jesus, the One who served God as a slave, who died on the cross to be our Redeemer, and who is the King of God's people, this One is the very God Himself. Because He is God, with Him there is no beginning and no genealogy. He is the eternal, infinite God.

The Gospel of John opens with the words, "In the beginning was the Word, and the Word was with God, and the Word was God" (John 1:1). The words "in the beginning" denote eternity past. In the beginning, in eternity past, was the Word. If John had not written this in his Gospel, we would never have imagined that our Savior was the eternal Word. What a marvelous revelation this is! Even with this revelation before us, we still may not be able to understand the true significance of the Word. Can you explain what the Word is? Do you know any books of ethics or philosophy that have such an expression as "in the beginning was the Word"? John says not only that the Word was in the beginning, but also that the Word was with God and that the Word was God. Then he goes on to

say, "In Him was life, and the life was the light of
men"(v. 4). We know from John 1:14 that this One, who
was the Word in the beginning, became flesh and tabernacled among us. In John 1:1, 4, and 14 we have Word,
God, life, light, and flesh. The wonderful Word, who is God,
became flesh. We may not regard the word flesh in a
positive way, but the Bible declares that the Word became
flesh. This is part of the revelation conveyed in John's
writings.

In John 1:14 we are told that the Word who became
flesh tabernacled among us. I appreciate the word "tabernacled." When the Word became flesh, He became the
tabernacle of God. We know from the book of Exodus that
the tabernacle in the Old Testament, a type of Christ, was
a mutual dwelling place for both God and man. God dwells
in the tabernacle, and we can enter this tabernacle to be
God's "roommate." I can testify that my roommate is the
very God who dwells in His tabernacle. My real dwelling
place is not my house; it is the tabernacle, the dwelling
place of God. This means that where God dwells, I dwell
also. How marvelous that the very Word who was with God
in the beginning became incarnate to tabernacle among
us!

John 1:14 says that the Word that became flesh and
tabernacled among us was full of grace and reality, and
also that the disciples beheld His glory. When we put verse
14 together with verses 1 and 4, we have the Word, God,
life, light, flesh, tabernacle, grace, reality (truth), and
glory. Then in John 1:29 we have the Lamb: "Behold, the
Lamb of God who takes away the sin of the world!" Are
you able to understand all these mysterious things? How
can the Word be God, and how can the life in the Word be
the light of men? How can the wonderful God Himself
become flesh, and how can the incarnated God, God in the
flesh, be the tabernacle? How can this tabernacle be full of
grace and reality? Furthermore, how can such an incarnated One also be the Lamb of God? Who would ever
imagine that in human history there could be a writing
containing such matters? This writing, the Gospel of John,

tells us of One who is the eternal Word and the very God, and tells us that in this Word there is life, that this life is the light of men, that He became flesh, that in the flesh He was the tabernacle, that when we come to this tabernacle we receive grace and truth and enjoy His glory, and that such a wonderful One also became a Lamb. A writing such as this is not merely human, and it is not something religious, moral, ethical, or philosophical. This is a writing containing a revelation that is altogether divine.

Many readers of the New Testament love the Gospel of Luke because it has many parables and presents the cases of sinners who are saved. However, we may love Luke because our view is limited, like that of a frog in a well. A frog in a well can see only a small circle of sky. But in the five books written by John the entire heaven is unveiled to us. When we see the revelation in the writings of John, we are lifted out of our "well."

John's writings not only lift us out of the well, but bring us to the heavens. In Revelation John could declare that he saw a door opened in heaven and that he beheld a throne set in heaven and One sitting upon the throne (Rev. 4:1-2). Eventually, John saw the new heaven, the new earth, and the New Jerusalem (Rev. 21:1-2). In a very real sense, the book of Revelation actually is not a book of prophecies; it is a book of revelation. In this book we are rescued from our low state and lifted up to the heavens. I hope that these messages will help you to be uplifted in this way. Then you will be able to testify, "No longer am I in a well with a narrow, limited view. Now I am in the heavens with a clear view of God's revelation." The purpose of John's writings is to uplift us and show us a revelation of mysterious, divine things.

A Supplement to the Other Epistles

As the Gospel of John supplements the synoptic Gospels, so the Epistles of John supplement the other New Testament Epistles. I have studied the writings of Paul and Peter, and I appreciate them very much. I have also studied the Epistles of James and Jude. I can testify that if we did not have the Epistles of John, we would sense a great loss. The Epistles of John are an important supplement to all the other Epistles.

A Supplement to the Entire Bible

Furthermore, the book of Revelation is a supplement to the entire Bible. Imagine what the Bible would be like if it did not include the book of Revelation. If such were the case, the Bible would be lacking a conclusion. What a great loss that would be!

COMPLEMENTARY TO THE
ENTIRE DIVINE REVELATION

John's writings are not only supplementary, but also complementary to the entire divine revelation. This means that the writings of John complete the Bible. His Gospel completes the Gospels, his Epistles complete the Epistles, and his Revelation completes the whole Bible. If we realize the importance of the writings of John, we shall surely thank the Lord for them. Praise the Lord for John's Gospel, Epistles, and Revelation!

SOME OUTSTANDING MATTERS IN FIRST JOHN
The Divine Life and the Divine Fellowship

In the Epistle of 1 John there are certain verses that I especially like. First John 1:2 and 3 say, "And the life was manifested, and we have seen and testify and report to you the eternal life, which was with the Father and was manifested to us. That which we have seen and heard, we report also to you, that you also may have fellowship with us, and indeed the fellowship which is ours is with the Father and with His Son Jesus Christ." In these verses, John says that the apostles report eternal life to us so that we may have fellowship with them. In what other writing can you find such a word? In the Epistle of 1 John we have the reporting of eternal life for the purpose of fellowship. This means that eternal life produces fellowship. When this life is reported, the result is the fellowship of the divine life. Therefore, in 1:2 and 3 we have the divine life with its divine fellowship.

The Anointing

First John 2:27 says, "And as for you, the anointing which you have received from Him abides in you, and you have no need that anyone should teach you; but as His anointing teaches you concerning all things, and is true, and is not a lie, and even as it has taught you, abide in Him." In this verse John says that the Lord's anointing teaches us concerning all things, and as it has taught us, we should abide in Him. The teaching of the anointing is altogether different from the knowledge of man's great teachers, including what is called the highest learning of Confucius. May we all have a full realization of the fact that the divine anointing within us is teaching us all the time and that we need simply to abide in the Lord according to the anointing.

The Divine Birth and the Divine Seed

Another marvelous verse is 3:9: "Everyone who has been begotten of God does not practice sin, because His seed abides in him, and he cannot sin, because he has been begotten of God." In this verse, John speaks of those who have been "begotten of God." John's writings emphasize the divine birth, our regeneration. It is a great wonder that human beings can be begotten of God, regenerated of Him. As believers in Christ, we have not only been begotten of our father—we have been begotten of God. Whoever is begotten of a human being automatically becomes a human being. In the same principle, whatever is begotten of a dog is a dog. The point here is that a certain kind of life will always beget that kind of life. I would not say that because we have been begotten of God, we are God. However, according to the Scriptures, we can say that because we have been begotten of God, we are children of God with the divine life and nature. God is our Father, and we are His children possessing His life and nature. Just as we have been begotten of our parents to have the human

life and nature, so we have been begotten of God to have
the divine life and nature.

According to 3:9, everyone who has been begotten of
God does not practice sin, because His seed abides in him.
To practice sin is to live in sin habitually. Because we have
been begotten of God, we do not practice sin. For example,
a cat practices mouse-catching because it has such a life.
However, a dog, having a different kind of life, does not
have that practice. Anyone who practices sin is not a child
of God. No one who is a child of God habitually lives in
sin.

The reason someone who has been begotten of God does
not practice sin is that God's seed abides in him. The seed
in this verse is God's life, which we received when we were
begotten of Him. This divine seed abides in every regenerated believer. How marvelous that God's seed abides in
us! What a tremendous revelation this is! I cannot say how
far this revelation goes beyond the teachings of Confucius
concerning the highest learning. Because we have been
begotten of God, His seed abides in us. Do you not have the
sense that there is something living and organic moving
and growing within you? Sometimes we can sense the
activity of this seed, and at other times we can sense that it
is blossoming.

In the parable of the sower in Matthew 13 we see that
the Lord Jesus came as a sower to sow Himself as the
divine seed into the human heart. Our heart is the soil
where the divine seed grows. This seed is nothing less
than God Himself. A wheat seed is wheat, and a carnation
seed is a carnation. In the same principle, God's seed is
God Himself. Through regeneration God has become an
organic life seed growing within us. Eventually, this seed
will blossom and bear fruit. Because this seed is divine, it
does not practice sin.

Begotten of God
and Not Touched by the Evil One

First John 5:4 says, "Because everything that has been
begotten of God overcomes the world," and 5:18 says, "We

know that everyone who has been begotten of God does not sin, but he who is begotten of God keeps himself, and the evil one does not touch him." When we put these verses together, we see that everything that has been begotten of God overcomes the world and that the evil one does not touch him. Later we shall see why 5:4 speaks of everything and 5:18 speaks of everyone. At present it is sufficient to see that everything that has been begotten of God overcomes the world and the evil one does not touch him.

Christians often complain about how strong the Devil is. But in John's writings there is a word telling us that we have been begotten of God and that the Devil does not touch us. The Devil knows that his efforts will be in vain if he touches one who has been begotten of God and who is keeping himself.

All these verses from 1 John are unique. We cannot find such verses in the writings of Paul or Peter. I would encourage you to spend some time to pray over these verses. I believe that if you pray over them, you will see something divine. I can testify that I have seen that eternal life has been reported to me, that I have a divine fellowship, that the divine anointing is within me, that I have been begotten of God, that I have the divine seed, and that I may be a person not touched by Satan. May we all see the marvelous revelation contained in these verses and be able to testify boldly concerning them.

LIFE-STUDY OF FIRST JOHN

MESSAGE TWO

A WORD CONCERNING THE WRITINGS OF JOHN

(2)

In this message we shall continue to give an introductory word concerning the writings of John. In the previous message we saw that John's writings are a revelation of divine things and that these writings are supplementary to the revelations of the other holy writings and complementary to the entire divine revelation. As we go on, we shall see that John's writings are mysterious to human understanding and all-inclusive concerning the Person of Christ.

MYSTERIOUS TO HUMAN UNDERSTANDING

The writings of John are mysterious. Matters such as the divine life and the divine fellowship (1:2-3), the anointing (2:27), and the divine birth (3:9) certainly are mysterious. Such things are mysterious because they are divine.

Have you ever realized that from the day you received the Lord Jesus, you have been a mysterious person? If a person is not mysterious, I doubt whether that one has been saved. Instead of asking others if they have been saved, we may want to check to see if they are mysterious.

We Christians are mysterious because we have the mysterious divine life with the mysterious divine nature. The divine life with the divine nature makes us mysterious beings. Do you know what a Christian is? A Christian is a person who is mysterious. Because we are mysterious, others should not be able to understand us so easily. Furthermore, because we are mysterious, sometimes we shall be misunderstood. In the church life and in our family life, there should also be an element of mystery. We are mysterious persons with the mysterious life of God.

ALL-INCLUSIVE CONCERNING THE PERSON OF CHRIST

Unveiling the Divinity of Christ Manifested in His Humanity

Toward the end of the first century, when the Apostle John was writing his Gospel, Epistles, and Revelation, there were already heresies concerning the Person of Christ. One heretical teaching was that Christ was God but not man, and another heresy was that Christ was man but not God. Other heretics denied that Jesus was the Christ. Because of such a situation, John was burdened to write concerning the Person of Christ in an all-inclusive way.

In John's writings we see that Jesus is the Christ and that the Lord Jesus Christ is both God and man. As we shall see, in chapter two of 1 John, the Apostle John deals with the heresy of the Cerinthians, those who separate Christ from Jesus and thus deny that Jesus is the Christ. When we come to chapter four, we shall see that John deals with the heresy of the Docetists, those who deny that Jesus Christ has come in the flesh. The writings of John reveal that Christ is all-inclusive, that Jesus is the Christ, and that He is both God and man.

Polemical against Heresies

In his writings the Apostle John was polemical, not against the law, circumcision, or Judaism, but against the heresies of the Gnostics, Cerinthians, and Docetists. The word "polemical" or "polemic" refers to the fighting for the truth by debating or disputing. A person who is polemical will debate strongly and sharply on behalf of the truth. He will fight for the truth and wage war for it. We need to follow John to be polemical against heresy.

We have pointed out that John was polemical against the heresies of the Gnostics, Cerinthians, and the Docetists. One source of these heresies was Greek philosophy.

As Paul was polemical in his writings against such matters as the law, circumcision, and Judaism, John was polemical against philosophical concepts that led to heresy.

Inoculating the Believers against All Heretical Doctrines concerning God and Christ

John's writings not only are all-inclusive concerning the Person of Christ and polemical against heresy, but they also inoculate the believers against all heretical doctrines (philosophies) concerning God and Christ. Such writings were needed not only for the first century but have also been needed throughout all the centuries. Even today in the twentieth century, we still need them. In the coming days they will still be a great help in keeping the truth concerning the Person of Christ and in preserving His believers in all the divine realities. We hope that these Life-studies may serve the same purpose.

If we do not see the revelation of the divine things contained in John's writings, we cannot be complete, mysterious, all-inclusive, or polemical. Futhermore, we shall not be properly inoculated against heresy. But if we see this revelation, we shall be mysterious, all-inclusive, and polemical, and we shall be inoculated against all heresies.

Here I would like to point out that the Trinity of the Godhead is revealed more fully in the Gospel of John than any other place in the Bible. We know from the Gospel of John that Christ was the very God in eternity (John 1:1) and that He became a man in time (John 1:14). His deity is complete, and His humanity is perfect. Hence, He is both God and man (John 20:28; 19:5), possessing both divinity and humanity.

As a man He was anointed by God with the Spirit (John 1:32-33; Matt. 3:16) to accomplish God's eternal purpose. Hence, He is the Christ, the anointed One (John 20:31).

Christ is the Son of God (John 20:31), who is the image of God (Col. 1:15), the effulgence of God's glory and the express image of His substance (Heb. 1:3), subsisting in the

form of God and equal with God (Phil. 2:6; John 5:18). As
the Son of God He came in the flesh with (Gk., *para*, from
with) the Father (John 6:46) and in the name of the Father
(John 5:43). Hence, He is called the Father (Isa. 9:6). He
was with God, and He was God in eternity past (John
1:1-2), not only coexisting but also coinhering with the
Father all the time (John 14:10a, 11a; 17:21). Even while
He was in the flesh on the earth, the Father was with Him
(John 16:32). Hence, Christ was one with the Father (John
10:30), working in the Father's name and with the Father
(John 10:25; 14:10b), doing the Father's will (John 6:38;
5:30), speaking the Father's word (John 3:34a; 14:24),
seeking the Father's glory (John 7:18), and expressing the
Father (John 14:7-9).

As the eternal God, Christ is the Creator of all things
(John 1:3), and as a man who came in the flesh (1 John 4:2)
with the physical blood and flesh (Heb. 2:14), He is a
creature, the Firstborn of all creation (Col. 1:15b). Hence,
He is both the Creator and the creature.

As the Sender and the Giver of the Spirit (John 15:26;
16:7; 3:34b), whom the Father sent in His name (the Son's
name, John 14:26), the Son, being the last Adam in the
flesh, became the life-giving Spirit through death and
resurrection (1 Cor. 15:45b; John 14:16-20), who received all
that is of the Son (John 16:14-15) to testify concerning the
Son and glorify the Son (John 15:26; 16:14), and who is the
breath of the Son (John 20:22). Hence, He is also the Spirit
(2 Cor. 3:17) to abide coexistingly and coinheringly with
the Son and the Father in the believers (John 14:17, 23) to
be the Triune God who is Spirit (John 4:24) mingled with
the believers as one spirit (1 Cor. 6:17) in their spirit (Rom.
8:16; 2 Tim. 4:22). Eventually, He became the seven Spirits
of God (Rev. 1:4; 4:5), who are the seven eyes of the Son, the
Lamb (Rev. 5:6).

I believe that many of these points will be puzzling to
those who hold to traditional systematic theology. For
example, how can the seven Spirits, who are the Spirit
of God, be the seven eyes of the Son, the Second of the
Godhead? If the Father, the Son, and the Spirit are

regarded as separate persons, how can the Third of the Godhead be the eyes of the Second?

Furthermore, in the Gospel of John the Lord Jesus said that He came in the Father's name. This is the reason that, according to Isaiah 9:6, His name is called the Father. When the Lord Jesus came, He also came with the Father. Have you ever thought that when the Lord Jesus came down from the heavens, He came with the Father? Some Christians may have the concept that when He came, He left the Father. But when the Lord Jesus came, the Father came also.

Moreover, the Lord said that He came to work in the Father's name. Who, then, was the One working, the Son or the Father? According to the Gospel of John, the Son came in the Father's name, He came with the Father, He came to work in the name of the Father, and He came to work with the Father. The Son did not do anything of His own will. Instead, He did the will of the Father. Likewise, He did not speak anything from Himself, but He spoke the Father's word. He also sought the Father's glory and expressed the Father.

The Son in John's Gospel is both the Sender and the Giver of the Spirit. But, eventually, He Himself became the Spirit. This Spirit is the seven Spirits of God, the seven eyes of the Lamb, the Son.

It certainly was foolish of Philip to say, "Lord, show us the Father and it suffices us" (John 14:8). To this request, the Lord Jesus replied, "Am I so long a time with you, and you have not known Me, Philip? He who has seen Me has seen the Father" (v. 9). Because the Lord Jesus came in the Father's name and with the Father, worked in the name of the Father and with the Father, did the Father's will, spoke the Father's word, sought the Father's glory, and expressed the Father, to see the Son was to see the Father.

If we see the revelation of the Trinity in the writings of John, we shall certainly become polemical. Those who are polemical cannot be political. However, even though we should be polemical in our fight for the truth, we still need to speak with others in a proper way.

THE FOCUS—THE MYSTERIES OF THE DIVINE LIFE

In His Gospel

The focus of John's writings is the mysteries of the divine life. In his Gospel the focus is the mystery of the manifestation of the divine life in the Person of Jesus. Life is invisible. Nevertheless, according to the Gospel of John, the divine life was manifested solidly, bodily, in the Person of Jesus. This is a mystery.

In His Epistles

In John's Epistles, especially in the first one, the focus is the mystery of the fellowship of the manifested divine life among the believers with God and with one another. This fellowship is mysterious. Although we are of different races, colors, and nationalities, we enjoy the one fellowship in the manifested divine life. We have a wonderful oneness among us. This is the mystery of the fellowship of the divine life.

In His Revelation

The Life Supply to God's Children

In the book of Revelation the focus is on Christ being the life supply to God's children for His expression, and the center of the universal administration of the Triune God. In chapter two of Revelation we see that we may eat of Christ as the tree of life in God's paradise and also as the hidden manna (vv. 7, 17). Furthermore, in Revelation 3:20 we see that we may feast with Him. The tree of life, the hidden manna, and the feasting with the Lord all indicate that Christ is our life supply. However, many Christians do not realize that Christ is our tree of life, our hidden manna, and our feast. But we have seen this revelation. We have seen in the book of Revelation that Christ is our life supply and that we may feed on Him as the hidden manna and as the tree of life and enjoy Him as our feast.

The purpose of enjoying Christ as our life supply is that we may be a lampstand shining Him forth. We in the churches are a lampstand constituted of the life supply of the Lord Jesus as the tree of life, the hidden manna, and the feast. This is mysterious, and it causes us to be mysterious.

The Center of the Universal Administration of the Triune God

Another mystery in the book of Revelation is that of Christ as the center of the universal administration of the Triune God. The people of the world may think that the world is under the rule of kings, presidents, and prime ministers. Actually, Christ is the King of kings, and the entire universe is under His administration. He is the real Administrator, and all earthly administrators are under His rule. The destiny of the world does not depend on human rulers. The world's destiny is in the hands of Jesus Christ, the King of kings.

John's writings cover an immense span reaching from eternity past to eternity future with the new heaven and the new earth and the New Jerusalem. In the first verse of his Gospel, John writes concerning eternity past, and in the last chapter of Revelation he speaks of the new heaven and the new earth, referring to eternity future. By this we see that John's writings cover the span from eternity past to eternity future. At present we are on the bridge of time leading us toward our eternal destiny. This also is divine and mysterious.

A CLEAR VIEW OF ETERNAL LIFE

I hope that in the coming messages we all shall have a clear vision concerning the extraordinary matter of eternal life. Not even the Gospel of John gives us as thorough a view of eternal life as does the Epistle of 1 John.

First John 1:1 and 2 say, "That which was from the beginning, which we have heard, which we have seen with our eyes, which we beheld, and our hands handled concerning the Word of life; and the life was manifested, and we have seen and testify and report to you the eternal life, which was with the Father and was manifested to us." Here we have a clear word regarding eternal life. The

following chapters of this Epistle define what this eternal
life is. As we shall see, 5:20 says, "And we know that the
Son of God has come, and has given us an understanding
that we might know Him who is true; and we are in Him
who is true, in His Son Jesus Christ. This is the true God
and eternal life." When we consider this verse in detail, we
shall see that "this" refers to the true God and Jesus Christ
in whom we are. This word includes the fact that we are in
this One, the true One. This implies that, in a practical
sense, eternal life is the very God in whom we are in our
experience. This surely is an experiential matter, not a
matter of doctrine or theology.

In between 1:1-2 and 5:20 we have the fellowship of the
divine life, the teaching of the anointing concerning the
Triune God, and the divine birth with the divine seed that
brings in all the divine virtues. We all need to see clearly
that eternal life is the Triune God whom we experience in
the fellowship of the divine life, according to the anointing,
and by the virtues of the divine birth with the divine seed.
I am burdened that we all see this vision. If we do not have
this basic and central view, we may see many other things
in the Epistles of John, but we shall nevertheless miss the
mark. Therefore, it is crucial that in these messages we see
from the Epistles of John what eternal life really is.

LIFE-STUDY OF FIRST JOHN

MESSAGE THREE

THE DIVINE LIFE

(1)

Scripture Reading: 1 John 1:1-2; 2:25; 3:15; 5:11-13, 20; John 1:4; 3:15-16, 36; 5:24; 6:47, 63; 8:12; 10:10, 28; 11:25; 14:6; Acts 11:18; Rom. 5:10, 17, 21; 6:23; Eph. 4:18; Col. 3:4; 1 Tim. 6:12, 19; 2 Tim. 1:10; Titus 1:2; Heb. 7:16; 2 Pet. 1:3; Rev. 2:7; 22:1-2, 14, 17, 19; Matt. 19:16, 29

In this message we shall begin to consider the divine life as revealed in 1:1 and 2. Then in a later message we shall go on to consider the fellowship of the divine life. The divine life and the divine fellowship are both of crucial importance. According to 1 John, first we have eternal life, and then we have the fellowship of the eternal life.

THAT WHICH WAS FROM THE BEGINNING

First John 1:1 says, "That which was from the beginning, which we have heard, which we have seen with our eyes, which we beheld, and our hands handled concerning the Word of life." This Epistle begins with the words "that which." The Apostle John uses the expression "that which" to open his Epistle and unfold the mystery of the fellowship in the divine life. The fact that he does not use personal pronouns here in reference to the Lord implies that what he intends to unfold is mysterious.

Paul's ministry is to complete the divine revelation (Col. 1:25-27) of God's New Testament economy, that is, the Triune God in Christ as the life-giving Spirit producing the members of Christ and building up the Body of Christ so that the Triune God may have a full expression—the fullness of God (Eph. 1:23)—in the universe. Paul's

writings were completed around A.D. 66. His completing
ministry was damaged by the apostasy preceding and
following his death. Then after a quarter of a century,
around A.D. 90, John's writings came forth. His ministry
was not only to mend the ministry of Paul that had been
broken, but also to consummate the entire divine revelation of both the Old Testament and New Testament, of
both the Gospels and the Epistles. In such a ministry, the
focus is the mysteries of the divine life. In his Gospel, as
the consummation of the Gospels, the mysteries of the
Person and work of the Lord Jesus Christ are unveiled. In
his Epistles (especially the first), as the consummation of
the Epistles, the mystery of the fellowship of the divine
life, which is the fellowship of God's children with God the
Father and with one another, is unfolded. Then in his
Revelation, as the consummation of the New Testament
and the Old Testament, the mystery of Christ being the life
supply to God's children for His expression, and the center
of the universal administration of the Triune God is
revealed.

In 1:1 John speaks of that which was "from the
beginning." This differs from "in the beginning" in John's
Gospel (1:1). In the beginning traces back to eternity past
before creation; from the beginning proceeds forward from
the creation. This indicates that John's Epistle is a
continuation of his Gospel concerning the believers'
experience of the divine life. In his Gospel he shows the
way for sinners to receive eternal life—by believing in the
Son of God. In his Epistle he points out the way for the
believers who have received the divine life to enjoy it in its
fellowship—by abiding in the Son of God. And in his
Revelation he unveils the consummation of the eternal life
as the believers' full enjoyment in eternity.

The phrase "from the beginning" is used twice in the
Gospel of John, eight times in this Epistle, and two times
in 2 John. In John 8:44; 1 John 1:1; 2:13, 14; and 3:8 it is
used in the absolute sense, but in John 15:27; 1 John 2:7, 24
(twice); 3:11; and 2 John 5, 6, it is used in the relative
sense.

EATING AND ENJOYMENT

John's writings are not mainly for study and understanding; they are primarily for the enjoyment of God's children. When you come to a feast, it is not your purpose to study the different courses of food. Study at such a time would frustrate you from the enjoyment of eating. In like manner, we should come to John's writings—to his Gospel, Epistles, and Revelation—regarding them as courses of a spiritual feast. When some hear this, they may wonder how we can say that John's writings are a feast. The answer is that no other writings in the Bible emphasize the matter of eating as much as John's writings do. Of course, Paul speaks about spiritual eating, but he does not speak about this as much as John does. One chapter in the Gospel of John, chapter six, is almost entirely devoted to eating. There the Lord Jesus says, "I am the bread of life" (vv. 35, 48). Then He goes on to say that He is the living bread and that if anyone eats of this bread he will live forever (v. 51); that unless we eat the flesh of the Son of man and drink His blood, we have no life in us (v. 53); that he who eats His flesh and drinks His blood has eternal life (v. 54) and abides in Him (v. 56); and that the one who eats Him will also live because of Him (v. 57), for he who "eats this bread shall live forever" (v. 58). To be sure, eating is strongly emphasized in chapter six of John's Gospel. To eat of the Lord as the bread of life is to feast on Him.

John also has much to say concerning eating in the book of Revelation. In Revelation 2:7 the Lord Jesus says, "To him who overcomes, to him I will give to eat of the tree of life, which is in the paradise of God." To eat of the tree of life is to enjoy Christ as our life supply. It was God's original intention that man should eat of the tree of life (Gen. 2:9, 16). But due to the fall of man the tree of life was closed to him (Gen. 3:22-24). Through the redemption of Christ, the way to touch the tree of life, which is God Himself in Christ as life to man, has been opened again (Heb. 10:19-20).

In Revelation 2:17 the Lord Jesus says, "To him who overcomes, to him I will give of the hidden manna."

Manna is a type of Christ as the heavenly food enabling God's people to go His way. The children of Israel ate of manna during their years in the wilderness (Exo. 16:14-16, 31). To partake of the hidden manna certainly is to enjoy Christ by eating Him.

Revelation 3:20 says, "Behold, I stand at the door and knock; if anyone hears My voice and opens the door, I will come in to him and dine with him and he with Me." In this verse "dine" means to take the principal meal of the day at evening. Here the Lord promises to dine with the one who opens the door to Him. To dine is not merely to eat certain foods, but it is to enjoy the riches of a meal. This dining may refer to the eating of the rich produce of the good land of Canaan by the children of Israel (Josh. 5:10-12).

These verses from the book of Revelation indicate that the Lord desires to recover the eating by God's people of the proper food as ordained by God and typified by the tree of life, the manna, and the produce of the good land, all of which are types of the various aspects of Christ as food to us. In his writings John definitely emphasizes the rich enjoyment of Christ by feasting on Him.

John also speaks of eating in the last chapter of Revelation. Revelation 22:1 and 2a say, "And he showed me a river of water of life, bright as crystal, proceeding out of the throne of God and of the Lamb in the middle of its street. And on this side and on that side of the river was the tree of life...." The tree of life is for God's people to receive and enjoy. For eternity all God's redeemed ones will enjoy Christ as the tree of life as their eternal portion. According to these verses, the tree of life is the life supply available along the flow of the Spirit as the water of life. Where the Spirit flows, there the life supply of Christ is found.

In Revelation 22:14 we have a promise concerning the enjoyment of the tree of life: "Blessed are those who wash their robes, that they may have right to the tree of life, and may enter by the gates into the city." This verse may be regarded as a promise related to the enjoyment of the tree of life, which is Christ with all the riches of life. Through

Christ's redemption, which has fulfilled all the requirements of God's glory, holiness, and righteousness, the way to the tree of life is opened to the believers. Therefore, those who wash their robes in the redeeming blood of Christ have the right to enjoy the tree of life as their portion.

All these quotations from John's Gospel and Revelation show the importance of eating in John's writings. This also indicates that his writings are mysterious, far beyond our natural understanding.

The writings of John can be compared to a Chinese feast consisting of many courses. It would exhaust our mentality to study all the courses of such a feast and their ingredients. You come to a feast not to study, but to enjoy the food by eating it. The principle is the same with John's writings. It is impossible for us to say how many "courses" are found in these writings. We need to come to John's writings for nourishment, that is, to eat and digest the spiritual food they contain.

THE WORD OF LIFE

Often before we partake of the main course at dinner, we are served an appetizer. In 1 John 1 the Apostle John also gives us an "appetizer." This appetizer is the Word of life. No doubt, John's intention is to serve us the divine life. But in order to stir up our appetite he serves us the Word of life as a spiritual appetizer. This is the Word mentioned in John 1:1-4 and 14, who was with God and was God in eternity before creation, who became flesh in time, and in whom is life. This Word conveys the eternal life and is the divine Person of Christ as an account, a definition, and an expression of all that God is. In Him is life, and He is life (John 11:25; 14:6). The phrase "the Word of life" in Greek indicates that the Word is life. The Person is the divine life, the eternal life, which we can touch. The "Word" mentioned here indicates that the Epistle is a continuation and development of John's Gospel (see John 1:1-2, 14).

If we could ask the Apostle John about the Word in 1:1, he would probably refer us to his Gospel. John 1:1 and 4 say that in the beginning was the Word, that the Word was with God and was God, that in this Word was life, and the life was the light of men. Furthermore, according to John 1:14, the Word became flesh and tabernacled among us, full of grace and truth and having the glory as of an only begotten from a father. In all these verses we have a definition of the Word. The Word is the very God. In this Word is life, and the life is the light we need. Then this wonderful One, God the Word, became flesh. This means that He became a man. As a man, He tabernacled among us. Actually, He was the tabernacle. Furthermore, this tabernacle becomes a mutual abode, in which both God and we may abide. Here in the tabernacle we enjoy grace, we receive the reality, and we see the glory. This is the Word of life mentioned in 1:1.

We have pointed out that the expression "the Word of life" actually indicates that the Word is life. This Word, who is the eternal life, became a man. As a man, He is the dwelling place as a mutual abode for both God and man. In this dwelling place we may enjoy Him as grace, receive Him as our reality, and behold His glory. This glory, which is the glory of God, has now become the glory of God's only begotten Son. Again I say, this Word is life, and this life is the expression of God. This means that the Word of life is God's expression.

BOOKS OF MYSTERIES

The writings of John are books of mysteries. In this Epistle, life, that is, the divine life, the eternal life, the life of God imparted into the believers in Christ and abiding in them, is the first mystery (1:2; 2:25; 3:15; 5:11, 13, 20). Issuing out of this mystery is another mystery, the mystery of the fellowship of the divine life (1:3-7). Following this is the mystery of the anointing of the Triune God (2:20-27). Then we have the mystery of abiding in the Lord (2:27-28; 3:6, 24). The fifth is the mystery of the divine birth (2:29; 3:9; 4:7; 5:1, 4, 18). The sixth is the divine seed (3:9). And the last is the water, the blood, and the Spirit (5:6-12).

EATING GOD AND EXPRESSING HIM

We should not spend too much time studying about the Word of life. Instead, we should eat the Word and enjoy it. We need to remember that John uses the Word of life as an appetizer to stir up our appetite. This appetizer, therefore, is for us to eat. However, our natural mind may want to inquire further and ask how this life expresses God. There is no need for us to make this inquiry. Rather, we need to eat the Word. Then we shall know how the Word of life can express God.

The kind of food we eat is reflected in our facial color. Suppose you do not eat well for some time. This may cause your face to have a very unhealthy appearance. But if someone has a healthy diet, this will be expressed in his facial color. By looking at his face you will know that he has been eating nourishing food, for the food he eats causes him to have a healthy appearance. The principle is the same with eating God. The more we eat God, the more we express Him.

Some Christians oppose the matter of eating God and ask how such a thing is possible. However, the concept of eating God, a divine thought, is absolutely according to the Bible, although religious people often miss it. They may prefer to worship God merely in an objective way, declaring that He is holy. But we would follow the Scriptures to partake of God and enjoy Him as our food. When you come to the dining table, you eat the food set before you. Likewise, when we come to the Lord, we should eat Him as our food.

The result of eating God is that we express Him. After we enjoy the divine life, we express the divine life. God is life, and the Word also is life. This Word speaks, defines, explains, and expresses God. God speaks for Himself. But He does not merely speak objectively from the heavens. He also speaks subjectively through us as a result of our eating of Him. Today our God speaks not only from the heavens; He also speaks through us, through our being. In what way does God speak through us? God speaks by our eating and enjoyment of Him.

In the early years of my ministry, most of my speaking was doctrinal. But today my speaking is mainly the expression of my enjoyment of the Lord. For many years I have been eating the Lord daily. Just as eating physical food makes me strong and active, so eating the Lord makes me strong and active in spirit. Spontaneously, as the result of enjoying God and digesting Him, I become very active in spirit.

Some may claim that it is heretical to teach that God can be digested by us. But I would say that it is heretical to deny that God is edible and that we can eat Him and digest Him. The Bible reveals that Jesus is the very God. Furthermore, according to John 6, we know that the Lord Jesus is edible. In this chapter He speaks clearly concerning our eating of Him. If we trace the thought backward from chapter six of John to chapter one, we shall see who Jesus is. The Jesus who speaks in John 6 concerning the eating of Him is the One who, in John 1, is the Word who was with God, who was God, and who became flesh. For the Lord Jesus to say that He is edible indicates that God Himself is edible. Therefore, we can boldly declare that our God is edible and that we can partake of Him, eat Him, and digest Him. When we eat God and digest Him, He speaks through us subjectively.

We may say that the food we eat and digest speaks for itself not objectively but subjectively; that is, our facial color indicates whether we have been eating nourishing food. The principle is the same with the Word of life as God's expression. The divine life is actually God Himself. When we eat God as life and digest Him, in our experience this life becomes the Word to define, explain, and express the very God we enjoy.

If we enjoy God as our nourishment, He will eventually become the constituent of our being. Dietitians tell us that we are what we eat. This means that the food we eat becomes the element or constituent of our being. For example, a person who eats a great deal of beef and drinks a great deal of milk eventually will be constituted physically of beef and milk. In a similar way, if we eat and drink of God day by day, we shall be constituted of God. Then the God of whom we have been constituted will express Himself from within us.

In what way is the God whom we eat and digest and of whom we are constituted expressed from within us? God is expressed in us by means of His attributes. God is love and light, and He is holy and righteous. When we eat and drink of God, we shall live Him as love, light, holiness, and righteousness. These divine attributes will become our virtues as the expression of God. How can we tell that someone has been eating and digesting God? We can tell this by the expression of God from within him. This expression of God is God's speaking. The human virtues that are produced through assimilating God with His divine attributes become the expression of God, and this expression is actually God's speaking.

This is the way we become God's testimony. A testimony is a matter of speaking or testifying. To become God's testimony means that the very God as the Word speaks Himself out from our being. This is the expression of the divine life.

THE WORD MANIFESTED SOLIDLY AND TANGIBLY

The Word in 1:1 is the eternal *Logos*, the expression of God. We know from John 1:1 and 14 that this Word, the Word of life, was incarnated and manifested in the flesh. Moreover, this Word was "from the beginning."

Let us read 1:1 once again, "That which was from the beginning, which we have heard, which we have seen with our eyes, which we beheld, and our hands handled concerning the Word of life." This verse indicates that the Word of life has been manifested solidly and tangibly, for the Word was heard, seen, held, and handled by the apostles. The sequence here is "have heard," "have seen," "beheld" (gazing with a purpose), and "handled," that is, touched by hands. These expressions indicate that the Word of life is not only mysterious, but is also tangible because of being incarnated. The mysterious Word of life in His humanity was touched by man, not only before His resurrection (Mark 3:10; 5:31), but also after His resurrection (John 20:17, 27) in His spiritual body (1 Cor. 15:44). At the time of John's writing there was a heresy that denied the incarnation of the Son of God (1 John 4:1-3). Hence, such strong expressions to indicate the Lord's solid substance in His touchable humanity were needed.

Toward the end of the first century the philosophical concepts of Gnosticism began to invade the church. One Gnostic concept was that matter was evil. Those who held this concept did not believe that Christ actually came in the flesh. To them, Christ was abstract, something like a phantom. This view of Christ is heretical. The Apostle John was burdened in his Gospel and Epistles to fight against this heresy. For this reason, in John 1:14 he purposely used the word "flesh." In John 1:1 he says that the Word was with God and was God. This is abstract and rather mysterious. But then John goes on to say that this Word became flesh. For the Word to become flesh is for the Word to become solid and tangible. Then in his first Epistle John points out that the apostles heard the Word of life and then saw, beheld, and handled this Word. The Apostle John even leaned upon the Lord's bosom. The expressions John uses concerning hearing, seeing, beholding, and handling the Word were an antidote to inoculate the believers against heretical teachings regarding the Person of Christ.

In one sense, the divine life is abstract and invisible. But in another sense the divine life is solid and visible, for the Word of life has been incarnated. The incarnated Word could be heard, seen, beheld, and touched.

The first Epistle of John is both a continuation and a development of the Gospel of John. In the Gospel of John we see how to receive the divine life by believing in the Lord Jesus. However, in John's Gospel we cannot see much concerning how to enjoy what we have received of the divine life. Therefore, in 1 John, the Apostle John gives us a continuation and development of his Gospel, showing us that after receiving the divine life we may enjoy the riches of the divine life. As we shall see in a forthcoming

message, it is through fellowship that we enjoy the riches
of the divine life.

LIFE-STUDY OF FIRST JOHN

MESSAGE FOUR

THE DIVINE LIFE

(2)

Scripture Reading: 1 John 1:1-2; 2:25; 3:15; 5:11-13, 20; John 1:4; 3:15-16, 36; 5:24; 6:47, 63; 8:12; 10:10, 28; 11:25; 14:6; Acts 11:18; Rom. 5:10, 17, 21; 6:23; Eph. 4:18; Col. 3:4; 1 Tim. 6:12, 19; 2 Tim. 1:10; Titus 1:2; Heb. 7:16; 2 Pet. 1:3; Rev. 2:7; 22:1-2, 14, 17, 19; Matt. 19:16, 29

LIFE AND THE WORD OF LIFE

First John 1:2 says, "And the life was manifested, and we have seen and testify and report to you the eternal life, which was with the Father and was manifested to us." In this verse "life" is a synonym for "the Word of life" in the preceding verse. Both life and the Word of life denote the divine Person of Christ, who was with the Father in eternity and was manifested in time through incarnation, and whom the apostles have seen and testify and report to the believers.

In 1:2 John says that the life was manifested. This manifestation of the eternal life was through Christ's incarnation, which John stressed strongly in his Gospel (John 1:14) as an antidote to inoculate the believers against the heresy which said that Christ did not come in the flesh. Such a manifestation, corresponding to the Word of life being touchable (1:1), indicates again the substantial nature of the Lord's humanity, which is the manifestation of the divine life in the New Testament economy.

THE ETERNAL LIFE

The life that was manifested is the eternal life. The word "eternal" denotes not only the duration of time,

which is everlasting, without end, but also the quality,
which is absolutely perfect and complete, without any
shortage or defect. Such an expression emphasizes the
eternal nature of the divine life, the life of the eternal God.
The apostles saw this eternal life and testified and reported
it to people. Their experience was not of any doctrine, but
of Christ the Son of God as the eternal life, and their
testimony and preaching were not of theology or biblical
knowledge, but of such a solid life.

We have pointed out that the eternal life is eternal not
only with respect to time, but also with respect to quality.
This life is also eternal with respect to its sphere. Therefore, the word eternal denotes three things: time, space, and
quality. As to the element of time, this life will last forever.
As to space, to sphere, this life is vast, unlimited. As to
quality, eternal life is perfect and complete, without defect
or shortage. The sphere or field of eternal life encompasses
the whole universe. Eternal life is so vast that it covers the
entire field of life. Whatever is in the field of life is
encompassed by this eternal life. Our human life, however,
is very different. Our life is not only temporary, but it is
also limited. But eternal life is neither temporary nor
limited; rather it is everlasting with respect to time and
unlimited with respect to space. Furthermore, our life has
many defects and shortages. However, the divine life, the
eternal life, has no defects and no shortages.

Indestructible

The eternal life is an indestructible life (Heb. 7:16).
Nothing can destroy or dissolve this life. It is an endless
life, being the eternal, divine, uncreated life, and the
resurrection life which has passed through the test of
death and Hades (Acts 2:24; Rev. 1:18). Satan and his
followers thought that they had terminated this life by
crucifying it. The religious leaders had a similar concept.
However, crucifixion gave this life the best opportunity to
be multiplied, to be propagated. Because this life is
unlimited, it can never be conquered, subdued, or destroyed.

The Life of God

Eternal life is the life of God (Eph. 4:18; 2 Pet. 1:3). We may say that this life is actually God Himself with the contents of divine love and divine light. And this life is of the Spirit of God (Rom. 8:2), especially when it becomes our life for our enjoyment.

The Son of God

Eternal life is also the Son of God. This life is not simply a matter or a thing; this life is a Person. The divine life is God Himself expressed in His Son. First John 5:12 says, "He who has the Son has the life." In our experience we know that eternal life is the Son of God Himself.

With the Father in Eternity

First John 1:2 says that eternal life was with the Father. The Greek word rendered "with" is *pros* (used with the Greek accusative case). It is a preposition of motion, implying living, acting, in union and communion with. The eternal life which is the Son was not only with the Father, but was living and acting in union and communion with the Father in eternity. This word corresponds to John 1:1-2.

The Father is the source of the eternal life, from whom and with whom the Son was manifested as the expression of the eternal life for those the Father has chosen to partake of and enjoy this life.

Instead of trying to analyze these aspects of eternal life, we should enjoy them as "courses" of a spiritual meal. Eternal life is the life of God, it is the Son of God, and it was with the Father in eternity. Here we have at least four courses for our enjoyment: God, the Son of God, the Father, and eternity.

Some may wonder how to enjoy all these marvelous courses. According to my experience, the best way to enjoy them is to pray-read the Word. For example, pray-read the words "the life of God" found in Ephesians 4:18. As you pray-read, you may say, "Oh, the life of God! Amen! Right now, I enjoy God, and I enjoy Him as my life. Hallelujah for God! Hallelujah for life! Hallelujah for the life of God! Hallelujah for the enjoyment of the life of God and for the enjoyment of God as life!"

Manifested to the Apostles

John says that the life which was with the Father was manifested to the apostles. The manifestation of eternal life includes revelation and impartation of life to men, with a view to bringing man into the eternal life, into its union and communion with the Father.

What was once hidden has been manifested to the apostles. John, one of the apostles, now opens to us the divine mysteries. If we eat the Word through pray-reading, we shall receive the benefit of the manifestation of eternal life.

Seen, Testified, and Reported to the Believers by the Apostles

The apostles saw eternal life, the life that was manifested, and then testified and reported this life to the believers. What they reported was not some theology or doctrine which they had heard and concerning which they had been taught, but the divine life, which they had seen and testified by their practical experiences. This divine life is a Person, the Son of God as the very embodiment of the Triune God to be our life.

Promised by God

The eternal life was promised by God. First John 2:25 says, "And this is the promise which He promised us, the eternal life." In the Gospel of John eternal life is promised in such verses as 3:15; 4:14; and 10:10. In Titus 1:2 Paul speaks of "the hope of eternal life, which God, who cannot lie, promised before times eternal." This promise of eternal life must be the promise made by the Father to the Son in eternity. It must have been that in eternity past the Father promised the Son that He would give His eternal life to His believers.

Released through Christ's Death

Eternal life was not only promised and manifested; it was also released through Christ's death (John 3:14-15). The divine life was concealed, confined, in Christ. But through His death this divine life was released from within Him.

Imparted to the Believers
through Christ's Resurrection

The eternal life that was released from within Christ through His death has been imparted into the believers through His resurrection. Concerning this, 1 Peter 1:3 says, "Blessed be the God and Father of our Lord Jesus Christ, who according to His great mercy has regenerated us unto a living hope through the resurrection of Jesus Christ from among the dead."

Received by the Believers
through Believing in the Son

The eternal life that has been released through Christ's death and imparted through His resurrection has been received by the believers through their believing in the Son. According to John 3:15-16 and 36, everyone who believes in the Son has eternal life.

Becoming the Believers' Life

After the believers receive eternal life, this life becomes their life (Col. 3:4). This is the purpose of God's salvation, that is, to make His life our life so that we may become His children, partaking of His divine nature to enjoy all that He is and to live a life that expresses Him.

The Believers Being Saved by Eternal Life
and Reigning in This Life

In Romans 5:10 Paul says, "For if, while we were enemies, we were reconciled to God through the death of His Son, much more, having been reconciled, we shall be saved in His life." Reconciliation to God through Christ has been accomplished already, but being saved in His life from so many negative things is still a daily matter. Day by day we may be saved in the eternal life.

In Romans 5:17 Paul goes on to say, "For if by the offense of the one death reigned through the one, much more those who receive the abundance of grace and of the gift of righteousness shall reign in life through the One, Jesus Christ." Having the divine life within us, we may be saved by this life and also reign in it. We can be kings ruling in the divine life over all negative things. For example, it may be difficult for us to rule our temper. Many of us would say, "Instead of ruling like a king over my temper, my temper has been ruling me." The reason many saints cannot rule their temper is that they do not enjoy eternal life. Do not make up your mind and strongly decide that from now on you will never lose your temper. That way does not work. Instead, forget about your temper and feast on this life. I would encourage you to mingle the calling on the name of the Lord with the pray-reading of the Word. If you do this, you will enjoy the Lord. As you enjoy Him, He will be the One reigning over all the negative things. Then as He reigns within you, you will reign in His reigning. This is the proper way to reign in life over your temper.

You cannot reign over your temper simply by learning the doctrines and teachings of the Bible. When some hear this, they may say, "You ignore Bible doctrine and uplift calling on the Lord and eating the Word. According to you, we can be overcomers by this calling and eating." I would reply by asking these ones how much they have been helped by doctrines and teachings to overcome their temper. Many of those who know the doctrines of the Bible still lose their temper again and again.

I would ask you to consider the situation among many of today's Christians. They may not be short of doctrine or Bible knowledge, but they are short of the calling on the name of the Lord and of the eating of the Word. We can testify that we are saved by calling on the Lord's name, and we are nourished by eating the Word.

When you are tempted to lose your temper, call on the

name of the Lord. Say to Him, "O Lord Jesus, save me from losing my temper!" It is even better to call on the Lord and pray-read the Word before you are tempted to lose your temper. If you are nourished through pray-reading the Word, the eternal life in you will reign as a king over negative things. In many cases this will even keep your temper from being stirred up. When you experience the reigning of the eternal life within you, your temper is put to death.

The Believers Laying Hold on Eternal Life

As believers, we should lay hold on eternal life. In 1 Timothy 6:12 Paul charges us to "lay hold on the eternal life to which you were called." In 1 Timothy 6:19 he urges us to "lay hold on that which is really life." This life is the eternal life. To lay hold on eternal life means that in everything—in our daily life, in our ministry, and in our jobs—we need to attach ourselves to the divine life and to apply the divine life to every situation, not trusting in our human life.

The Believers Inheriting Eternal Life in the Manifestation of the Kingdom

In Matthew 19:29 the Lord Jesus speaks of inheriting eternal life. To inherit eternal life is to be rewarded in the coming age with the enjoyment of the divine life in the manifestation of the kingdom of the heavens. Certain believers who have received eternal life enjoy it to some extent; however, they do not enjoy it to the proper extent. As a result, when the Lord Jesus comes back at the time of the manifestation of the kingdom, they will miss the enjoyment of the millennial kingdom. To miss the enjoyment of the divine life in the coming kingdom is to miss the enjoyment of eternal life during that dispensation.

The Believers Fully Enjoying Eternal Life in Eternity

In eternity all believers will fully enjoy eternal life. According to Revelation 22:1 and 2, in the New Jerusalem all the believers will enjoy the divine life as the flowing river and as the growing tree. Both the river and the tree are for our eternal enjoyment. For eternity, we shall enjoy this divine life (Rev. 22:14, 17, 19).

Eternal life is related to the present age, to the coming age of the kingdom, and to the eternal age. In the present age we receive the divine life and live the divine life. If we live this life according to the Lord's desire, we shall also enjoy the divine life in the coming age of the kingdom. Eventually, all believers will enjoy eternal life to the uttermost in the eternal age. However, if those who receive eternal life in this age do not live it properly but instead neglect it, then in the coming age, the age of the kingdom, they will miss the enjoyment of the divine life. By missing the enjoyment of eternal life in the kingdom age, they will learn certain lessons and be trained. Eventually they will be restored to the enjoyment of the eternal life. Then ultimately, in the eternal age, all believers will have the full enjoyment of the divine life.

LIFE-STUDY OF FIRST JOHN

MESSAGE FIVE

THE FELLOWSHIP OF THE DIVINE LIFE

Scripture Reading: 1 John 1:3-7

In previous messages we have considered the first of the basic matters in this Epistle—the divine life. Now we come to the second basic matter, and this is the fellowship of the divine life. Actually, the fellowship of the divine life is the topic of the entire Epistle of 1 John. In the Gospel of John Jesus Christ is revealed as the divine life for us to receive. When we believe in Him, He comes into us, and we have Him as life within. As the continuation of the Gospel of John, this Epistle shows us that after receiving the divine life, we may have the fellowship of life as the issue of the divine life. The fellowship of the divine life is the real enjoyment of the divine life. In other words, if we would experience the divine life, we need to pay close attention to the fellowship of this life.

In 1:3 John says, "That which we have seen and heard we report also to you, that you also may have fellowship with us, and indeed the fellowship which is ours is with the Father and with His Son Jesus Christ." Verse 1 speaks of "have heard" and then "have seen." Here it is vice versa. In receiving revelation, hearing is the basic thing. But in preaching, in reporting, seeing should be the base. What we preach should be what we have laid hold of and experienced of the things we have heard.

The apostles have heard and seen the eternal life. Then they report it to the believers that they may also hear and see it. By virtue of the eternal life, the apostles have enjoyed fellowship with the Father and with His Son, the Lord Jesus. They desire that the believers may also enjoy this fellowship.

THE ISSUE AND FLOW OF THE DIVINE LIFE

The Greek word for fellowship, *koinonia*, means joint participation, common participation. It is the issue of the eternal life, and is actually the flow of the eternal life within all the believers, who have received and possess the divine life. It is illustrated by the flow of the water of life in the New Jerusalem (Rev. 22:1). Hence, all genuine believers are in this fellowship (Acts 2:42). It is carried on by the Spirit in our regenerated spirit. Hence, it is called "the fellowship of the Holy Spirit" (2 Cor. 13:14) and "fellowship of [our] spirit" (Phil. 2:1). It is in this fellowship of the eternal life that we the believers participate in all the Father and the Son are and have done for us; that is, we enjoy the love of the Father and the grace of the Son by virtue of the fellowship of the Spirit. Such a fellowship was first the apostles' portion in enjoying the Father and the Son through the Spirit. Hence, it is called "the fellowship of the apostles" (Acts 2:42) and "the fellowship which is ours [the apostles']" in 1 John 1:3, a fellowship with the Father and with His Son Jesus Christ. It is a divine mystery. This mysterious fellowship of the eternal life should be considered the subject of this Epistle.

Fellowship is a common participation, a joint participation. Therefore, to have fellowship is to have a corporate participation in something. The fellowship of the divine life is the issue and flow of the divine life. Because the divine life is organic, rich, moving, and active, it has a particular issue, a certain kind of outcome. The issue, the outcome, of the divine life is the fellowship of life.

The fellowship of the divine life is clearly portrayed in Revelation 22:1. In this verse we see that in the New Jerusalem the river of the water of life flows out from the throne of God and of the Lamb. The throne of God and of the Lamb is the throne of the redeeming God, the Lamb-God. In Genesis 1:1 we have God, but in Revelation 22:1 we have God with the Lamb. In Genesis we have the creating God, but in Revelation we have the redeeming God. Out of this redeeming God as the source flows the river of water of life. The flow of the river of water of life is the fellowship of life. This means that fellowship is the outflow of the divine life from within the redeeming God.

According to the picture in Revelation, the river in the New Jerusalem flows downward in a spiral until it reaches the twelve gates of the city. By this we can see that the entire city of the New Jerusalem is supplied by the flow of this living water; that is, it is supplied by the fellowship of life. The fellowship of the divine life flows out of God and through His people in order to reach every part of the Body of Christ, which will consummate in the New Jerusalem.

THE FELLOWSHIP OF THE SPIRIT

The fellowship of the divine life, or the flow of the divine life, is the fellowship of the Spirit. Second Corinthians 13:14 says, "The grace of the Lord Jesus Christ, and the love of God, and the fellowship of the Holy Spirit be with you all." Here we see that the love of God is the source, that the grace of Christ is the course, and that the fellowship of the Spirit is the flow of the course. It is this flow that brings the grace of Christ and the love of God to us for our enjoyment. Therefore, the fellowship of the divine life is called the fellowship of the Holy Spirit.

BETWEEN THE BELIEVERS AND THE APOSTLES

The fellowship of the divine life is a fellowship between the believers and the apostles (1 John 1:3b; Acts 2:42). This means that there is a joint enjoyment of the Triune God among the believers and the apostles. The believers and the apostles need to have contact with one another. When there is the proper contact, there will be a two-way traffic, and this traffic is fellowship, a common participation. When we have this two-way traffic, we enjoy the divine life that is within us. This means that when we have fellowship, we have the enjoyment of the divine life.

The more of this two-way traffic we have, the better it will be. The more we contact the apostles, the more we shall enjoy the divine life. However, some may point out that the apostles are no longer with us. This is true, but we still have the writings of the apostles. Whenever we come to the apostles' writings, we may have the sense of being brought into fellowship with the apostles and enjoying the two-way traffic between us and them. Then in this traffic we enjoy the divine life together with them.

BETWEEN THE BELIEVERS AND THE FATHER
AND HIS SON JESUS CHRIST

The fellowship of the divine life is between the believers and the Father and His Son Jesus Christ. John says that first the believers have fellowship with the apostles through the divine life. Then he says that the apostles have fellowship with the Father and the Son. By this we see that fellowship joins the believers to the apostles and to the Father and the Son. Therefore, in this fellowship there is the full oneness of the divine life.

The flowing of electricity is a good illustration of the fellowship of the divine life. Electricity flows from the power plant into a building. The electrical current connects the power plant to the building. Furthermore, in a lighted ceiling of a particular room in the building, the individual lights are connected to each other by the flow of the electrical current. Apart from the flow of the current, the lights in the ceiling are separate. But through the flow of electricity, the lights are brought into a "fellowship" with one another, for they are all in the one flow of electricity. This is an illustration of the fact that the apostles and the believers enjoy fellowship together in the divine life.

THE FELLOWSHIP THE BELIEVERS HAVE
WITH ONE ANOTHER

In the divine life the believers have fellowship with one another (1:7; Phil. 2:1). As the electrical lights in the ceiling of a room have a current flowing within them, so we all have the divine current flowing within us. In this divine life and through this divine life we have fellowship for the enjoyment of the divine life. The more we have the divine life flowing within us, the more we enjoy the divine life.

In 1:3 only the Father and the Son are mentioned, not the Spirit, because the Spirit is implied in the fellowship.

Actually, the fellowship of the eternal life is the impartation of the Triune God—the Father, the Son, and the Spirit—into the believers as their unique portion for them to enjoy today and for eternity.

FOR FULL JOY

John goes on to say in 1:4, "And these things we write that our joy may be made full." Instead of "our," some manuscripts read "your." The apostles' joy is also the believers' joy because the believers are in the fellowship of the apostles.

Fellowship is the issue of the eternal life; and joy, that is, the enjoyment of the Triune God, is the issue of this fellowship, the issue of participation in the Father's love and the Son's grace through the Spirit. By such a spiritual enjoyment of the divine life, our joy in the Triune God may be made full.

We do not usually regard joy as a major item. But in this Epistle, joy is the third matter of major importance to be covered, coming after the divine life and the fellowship of the divine life. The divine life issues in fellowship, and fellowship issues in joy.

Are you a joyful Christian, or are you a sorrowful one? To be sorrowful may be an indication that you are out of the fellowship of the divine life. But if you are joyful, full of joy, you are in this fellowship.

The New Testament uses three words to describe our joy in the divine life. In addition to the word "joyful," the words "rejoice" and "exult" are used. Not only should we be joyful—we should also rejoice and exult. It is possible to be joyful and yet be silent. But in order to rejoice and exult we cannot remain silent. God's salvation makes us joyful and causes us to rejoice and exult. Therefore, when we gather together, we should be joyful. In the Old Testament God's people were full of joy when they came together for the feasts. In the Psalms they were even charged to make a joyful noise unto the Lord (Psa. 95:1; 98:4, 6). Religion does not like to hear a joyful noise, but God appreciates it. He likes to see that we are full of joy. Hence, the Apostle

John tells us that if we enjoy the fellowship of the divine life, we shall surely be full of joy. Furthermore, when we are full of joy, we shall rejoice and exult. We all should be such rejoicing and exulting Christians. Let us come to the church meetings joyfully because we enjoy the divine life in the divine fellowship.

ENJOYING GOD AS LIGHT

In 1:5 John says, "And this is the message which we have heard from Him and announce to you, that God is light, and in Him is no darkness at all." In addition to the three main things in the preceding verses—life, fellowship, and joy—a further message, which the apostles have heard from the Lord, is to announce to the believers that God is light. First we have the divine life, and then out of this we have the fellowship of the divine life. Fellowship issues in joy. When we are in this joyful element of the fellowship, we are in the light of God. Therefore, the sequence is life, fellowship, joy, and light.

In the preceding verses, the Father and Son are mentioned with clear words, and the Spirit is implied in the fellowship of the eternal life. Here God is mentioned for the first time in this Epistle, and He is mentioned as the Triune God—the Father, the Son, and the Spirit. This God, as revealed in the light of the gospel, is light.

The message that John and the other early disciples heard was, undoubtedly, the word spoken by the Lord Jesus in John 8:12 and 9:5 that He is the light. However, John says here that the message was that God is light. This indicates that the Lord Jesus is God and implies the essence of the divine Trinity.

The expression, "God is light," like "God is love" in 4:8 and 16, and "God is Spirit" in John 4:24, is used not in a metaphoric sense but in a predicative sense. These expressions denote and describe the nature of God. In His nature God is Spirit, love, and light. Spirit denotes the nature of God's Person; love, the nature of God's essence; and light, the nature of God's expression. Both love and light are related to God as life, which life is of the Spirit (Rom. 8:2). God, Spirit, and life are actually one. God is Spirit, and Spirit is life. Within such a life are love and light. When this divine love appears to us, it becomes grace, and when this divine light shines upon us, it becomes truth. John's Gospel reveals that the Lord Jesus has brought grace and truth to us (John 1:14, 17) that we may have the divine life (John 3:14-16), whereas his Epistle unveils that the fellowship of the divine life brings us to the very sources of grace and truth, which are the divine love and the divine light. His Epistle is the continuation of his Gospel. In his Gospel it was God in the Son coming to us as grace and truth that we may become His children (John 1:12-13). In his Epistle it is we, the children, in the fellowship of the Father's life, coming to the Father to participate in His love and light. The former was God coming out to the outer court to meet our need at the altar (Lev. 4:28-31); the latter is we entering into the Holy of Holies to contact Him at the ark (Exo. 25:22). This is further and deeper in the experience of the divine life. After receiving the divine life in John's Gospel by believing in the Son, we should go on to enjoy this life in his Epistle through the fellowship of this life. His entire Epistle discloses to us this one thing, that is, the enjoyment of the divine life by abiding in its fellowship.

God is Spirit. This refers to His Person. God is also love and light. Love refers to His essence, and light, to His expression. Both God's love and light are related to His life. This life is actually God Himself. Life is also the Spirit.

When this life was manifested, it came with grace and truth. When we received the Lord Jesus, we received life, and we now enjoy grace and truth. This life brings us back to God. First, God came to us so that we may receive grace and truth. Now we go back to the Father and contact Him as the source of grace and truth, and this source is love and light. Going back to the Father, we may enjoy love as the source of grace and light as the source of truth. Therefore, in the fellowship of the divine life, we are being brought back to God to enjoy love as the source of grace and light as the source of truth.

This understanding of love and light is not derived from human reasoning; it comes from the divine revelation in the Word. In this revelation we have a number of items for our enjoyment, comparable to many courses of a feast. We have God, the Spirit as the nature of God's person, love as the nature of God's essence, light as the nature of God's expression, the divine life, grace, and truth. When we have all these divine things, we are brought back to God the Father. When we are brought back to the Father, we meet Him and enjoy Him as love, which is the source of grace, and light, which is the source of truth. How marvelous that in the fellowship of the divine life we enjoy the divine light!

TO JOIN WITH THE APOSTLES
AND THE TRIUNE GOD
FOR THE CARRYING OUT OF GOD'S PURPOSE

In the fellowship of the divine life we join with the apostles and the Triune God for the carrying out of God's purpose. John's word in 1:3 indicates the putting away of private interest and joining with others for a certain common purpose. Hence, to have fellowship with the apostles, to be in the fellowship of the apostles, and to have fellowship with the Triune God in the apostles' fellowship is to put aside our private interest and join with the apostles and the Triune God for the carrying out of God's purpose. According to John's writings, this purpose is twofold. First, this purpose is that the believers may grow in the divine life by abiding in the Triune God (2:12-27) and, based upon the divine birth, live a life of the divine righteousness and the divine love (2:28—5:3) to overcome the world, death, sin, the Devil, and idols (5:4-21). Second, it is that the local churches may be built up as the lampstands for the testimony of Jesus (Rev. 1—3) and consummate in the New Jerusalem as the full expression of God for eternity (Rev. 21—22). Our participation in the apostles' enjoyment of the Triune God is our joining with them and with the Triune God for His divine purpose, which is common to God, the apostles, and all the believers.

When we enjoy the Triune God in the divine fellowship, we shall be brought into a situation where spontaneously we join ourselves to the apostles and the Triune God for a common purpose. God has a purpose, and the apostles work out God's purpose. By enjoying the divine life in the divine fellowship, we particplate in this purpose and its outworking.

The purpose God desires to fulfill through the apostles and also through us is first that the believers would grow in the divine life by abiding in the Triune God. Furthermore, God intends that, based upon the divine birth, the believers would live a life of the divine righteousness and the divine love to overcome the world, sin, death, the Devil, and idols. Second, God's purpose is that the local churches would be built up as the testimony of Jesus and that ultimately this testimony would consummate in the New Jerusalem. Therefore, God's purpose is to have every child of His grow in the divine life and live a life of righteousness and love to overcome all negative things. Then the local churches will be built up as the testimony of Jesus, and ultimately there will be the New Jerusalem as the eternal expression of the Triune God. This is God's purpose, and this is the burden of the apostles in their work. They have this purpose in common with God. Now we should join them in the fellowship of the divine life, and this enjoyment of fellowship in the divine life will usher us into the interests the apostles have in common with the Triune God. Along with the Triune God and the apostles, our purpose will be the believers' growth in life and their living a life of righteousness and love to overcome negative things so that the local churches may be built up and issue in the New Jerusalem as the consummate expression of the Triune God.

If we see what fellowship really is, we shall realize that fellowship is a great matter. However, for years we have understood fellowship to be merely a kind of enjoyment in the divine life. We have not seen that fellowship also involves a common interest. God does not supply us with enjoyment without a purpose. God is purposeful, and He has a purpose in giving us the enjoyment in the fellowship of His life. God's purpose is to feed us so that we may grow in the divine life and that with the divine birth as the basis we may live a life of the divine righteousness and divine love to overcome the evil one, the world, sin, and all idols. It is also God's purpose that the local churches may be built up as the testimony of Jesus. Eventually, this testimony will consummate in the New Jerusalem as the complete and eternal expression of the Triune God. This is the purpose of the fellowship of the divine life.

LIFE-STUDY OF FIRST JOHN

MESSAGE SIX

CONDITIONS OF THE DIVINE FELLOWSHIP

(1)

Scripture Reading: 1 John 1:5-7

In the foregoing messages we have considered two mysteries—the mystery of the divine life and the mystery of the divine fellowship. Although we have not covered these matters thoroughly, I believe that they have been somewhat opened to us and that we have at least received hints concerning how to delve into them further. In this message we shall begin to consider the conditions of the divine fellowship, that is, the terms that must be fulfilled in order to enjoy this fellowship.

If we would be in the divine fellowship, we need to fulfill certain conditions, terms, or obligations. Only then can we enjoy the divine fellowship. This matter of the conditions of the divine fellowship is revealed in the second half of chapter one and in the first half of chapter two (1:5—2:11). Only two verses speak of the divine life (1:1-2) and another two verses of the divine fellowship (1:3-4), whereas seventeen verses are related to the conditions of the divine fellowship. This indicates that, as far as we are concerned, the conditions of the fellowship are a very important matter.

The divine life and the divine fellowship are both on God's side. However, the conditions, the terms, the obligations, by which we can enjoy the divine fellowship are on our side. It is simple to receive the divine life and to be brought into the fellowship of the divine life. But it is not a simple matter to maintain this fellowship and remain in it. For this reason, the Apostle John does not pass over the conditions that must be fulfilled if we are to remain in the divine fellowship. As we shall see, there are two main conditions covered in 1:5—2:11: the confessing of sins (1:5—2:2) and the loving of God and the brothers (2:3-11).

The first condition of the divine fellowship involves both sin and sins. Sin and sins are a serious problem concerning our enjoyment of the divine fellowship, for they cause our fellowship with the Triune God to be frustrated and broken. Therefore, the Apostle John devotes a number of verses to confessing our sins. Before we consider these verses, I would like to bring to our attention some matters that will help us to understand John's writing concerning sin and sins.

INDWELLING SIN

According to the Bible, sin dwells within us, in our flesh. Romans 7:20 says, "But if what I do not will, this I do, it is no longer I that do it but sin that dwells in me." The word "dwell" here indicates that sin is something living. Anything that is not living, such as a chair, cannot dwell anywhere. For example, you would not say that a chair dwells in your home. In order for a certain thing to dwell in a particular place, that thing must be living and organic. Hence, the fact that sin dwells within us indicates that sin is a living entity.

The sin described in Romans 7 is personified. The activities of sin are those of a person. Sin takes occasion through the commandment and works coveting in us (v. 8). Furthermore, sin may deceive us and kill us (v. 11). According to Paul's word in verse 17, sin dwells in us and does certain things in us: "So now it is no longer I that do it, but sin that dwells in me." Moreover, Paul says that sin enters (Rom. 5:12), reigns (Rom. 5:21), lords it over people (Rom. 6:14), works death in us (Rom. 7:13), and is something that is quite alive (Rom. 7:9). Therefore, sin is not a lifeless element or substance. On the contrary, sin is a living thing that can dwell in us and do things against our will. This was the reason Paul could say that it was not he who did certain things, but sin that dwelt in him.

Some oppose us for teaching that sin dwells in our flesh

and that this sin dwelling in us is something personified. However, this teaching concerning indwelling sin and its activities is altogether according to the Scriptures. We cannot deny what Paul says in Romans 7 regarding sin.

SINS, THE FRUIT OF SIN

Of course, the Bible speaks both of sin and sins. Sins refer to trespasses, transgressions, and wrongdoings. For example, lying and stealing are sins. These sins are different from the sin that dwells in our flesh. Sins are deeds and activities, but sin is an evil element that dwells in our flesh.

The New Testament deals with the problem of sin by using both the word sin in the singular and the word sins in the plural. "Sin" refers to the indwelling sin, which came through Adam into mankind from Satan (Rom. 5:12). Sin is dealt with in the second section of Romans, 5:12 to 8:13 (with the exception of 7:5, where "sins" are mentioned). "Sins" refer to the sinful deeds, the fruits of the indwelling sin, which are dealt with in the first section of Romans, 1:18 to 5:11. However, the singular sin in 1 John 1:7 with the adjective "all" does not denote the indwelling sin, but denotes every single sin we have committed (v. 10), after we have been regenerated. Such sin defiles our purged conscience and needs to be cleansed away by the blood of the Lord in our fellowship with God.

THE SIN OFFERING
AND THE TRESPASS OFFERING

Our sin, the indwelling sin in our nature (Rom. 7:17), has been taken care of by Christ as our sin offering (Lev. 4; Isa. 53:10; Rom. 8:3; 2 Cor. 5:21; Heb. 9:26). Our sins, our trespasses, have been taken care of by Christ as our trespass offering (Lev. 5; Isa. 53:11; 1 Cor. 15:3; 1 Pet. 2:24; Heb. 9:28). After our regeneration we still need to take Christ as our sin offering, as indicated in 1 John 1:8, and as our trespass offering, as indicated in 1:9.

The Bible reveals that when the Lord Jesus was on the cross, He was made sin for us. Regarding this, 2 Corinthians 5:21 says, "Him who did not know sin He made sin on our behalf, that we might become God's righteousness in Him." Because the Lord was made sin for us, He condemned sin through His death on the cross. Romans 8:3 says, "God sending His own Son in the likeness of the flesh of sin and concerning sin, condemned sin in the flesh." Here we see that through the crucifixion of Christ, sin was condemned. For this reason, John 1:29 speaks of Him as the Lamb of God who took away the sin of the world, and Hebrews 9:26 says that Christ "has been manifested for the putting away of sin by His sacrifice." This means that Christ offered Himself for sin. As we consider these four verses, we realize that the Lord Jesus died on the cross to deal with sin, the very sin that dwells within us. He became sin, He condemned sin, He took away sin, and He was an offering for sin. Christ as the offering for sin is typified by the sin offering in chapter four of Leviticus.

As we have pointed out, we have not only the problem of sin in our flesh, but also the problem of the many sins we have committed. We have done many wrong things. For example, instead of honoring our parents, we may have despised them. This is sinful. We all have committed many trespasses, transgressions, offenses, and wrongdoings. All these are sins. When the Lord Jesus died on the cross to deal with our sin, He also bore our sins. First Peter 2:24 says, "Who Himself carried up our sins in His body onto the tree." This verse clearly indicates that Christ bore our sins. In 1 Corinthians 15:3 Paul declares, "Christ died for our sins." Moreover, in Hebrews 9:28 we are told that Christ was "once offered to bear the sins of many." By these verses we see that when the Lord was on the cross, He not only dealt with our sin, but also bore our sins. Therefore, He is both the sin offering and the trespass offering.

When we believed in the Lord Jesus, we received Him as our Redeemer. This implies that we received Him as our sin

offering and trespass offering. Receiving the Lord Jesus as
our Redeemer includes receiving Him as both the sin
offering and the trespass offering. Often we say that the
blood of Jesus cleanses us. This blood is the blood of the
sin offering and of the trespass offering. In 1:7 John
speaks of the blood of Jesus that cleanses us from all sin.
This is the blood of the Lord Jesus as both the sin offering
and the trespass offering. Now that we have believed in
Christ, we have Him as the Redeemer, the One who is our
sin offering and trespass offering. Therefore, both sin and
sins have been dealt with. We have been forgiven by God,
and we have been washed, cleansed, by the Lord's blood.
As we have pointed out, the blood of Jesus is the blood of
the sin offering and the trespass offering. We all have
believed in Christ and accepted Him as our sin offering
and trespass offering.

SIN NOT ERADICATED FROM OUR BEING

Now that we have been regenerated, do we still have sin
dwelling in us? Regarding this, there has been much
debate among Bible teachers. Years ago, there was a
strong teaching that claimed that sin has been eradicated
from believers. This is the teaching concerning the so-
called eradication of sin. Those who teach this use certain
verses in 1 John 3 and 5 as their basis: "Everyone who has
been begotten of God does not practice sin ... and he
cannot sin" (3:9), and, "Everyone who has been begotten of
God does not sin" (5:18). Those who follow the teaching of
eradication say that these verses prove that sin has been
rooted out of our being.

In 1933 I was told an interesting story by a brother who
once belonged to a group which taught the eradication of
sin. The leader of that group, a learned man, was very
strong in teaching the eradication of sin. One day this
leader took four young brothers to a park. Instead of buying
five tickets, the leader bought only two. Two brothers
entered the park using the two tickets. Then one brother
came out with the tickets and then entered the park again
with another brother. This was repeated until all five

brothers had entered the park using the same two tickets. The younger brothers were bothered by the fact that one who taught the eradication of sin could behave in such a way. They said to him, "What is this? Isn't this cheating? Isn't this sin?" The leader replied, "This is not sin; it is merely a weakness." The brother who related this incident to me could not accept that explanation. He knew there was something wrong. Eventually, he came to the church meetings and was made clear about the mistaken teaching concerning the eradication of sin.

The Bible does not teach that sin has been eradicated from our being. In 1:8 John says, "If we say that we do not have sin, we are deceiving ourselves, and the truth is not in us." To say that we do not have sin is to say that we do not have indwelling sin within our nature. This is something taught by the Gnostic heresy. The apostle is inoculating the believers against this false teaching. This section, 1:7— 2:2, deals with the believers' sinning after regeneration. This sinning interrupts their fellowship with God. If after regeneration the believers do not have sin in their nature, how could they sin in their conduct? Even though they sin only occasionally, not habitually, their sinning is an adequate proof that they still have sin working within them. Otherwise, there would be no interruption of their fellowship with God. The apostle's teaching here condemns today's teaching of perfectionism, the teaching that a state of freedom from sin is attainable or has been attained in earthly life. The apostle's teaching also annuls the erroneous teaching of the eradication of the sinful nature, which, by misinterpreting the word in 3:9 and 5:18, says that regenerated persons cannot sin because their sinful nature has been totally eradicated.

John says that those who say that they do not have sin are deceiving themselves, are leading themselves astray. To say that, because we have been regenerated, we do not have sin is self-deceiving. It denies the actual fact of our own experience and thus causes us to lead ourselves astray. We should not say that we no longer have sin. Sin remains in our flesh, in our sinful nature.

THE NEED FOR THE CONFESSION OF SINS

We have considered the question of whether or not as believers we still have sin in our nature. We have seen that we definitely have sin dwelling in us after regeneration. Now we need to consider a second question: Can we still commit sin after we are regenerated? Yes, a believer can still sin after he has been regenerated. In 2:1 John says, "My little children, these things I write to you that you may not sin. And if anyone sins, we have an Advocate with the Father, Jesus Christ the Righteous." John's words "if anyone sins" indicate strongly that we can still sin after we are saved.

Let us use as an illustration the matter of losing our temper. I do not believe that there is even one person who has never lost his temper after he was saved. Can you say that, during the time you have been a Christian, you have never lost your temper? Even if you have not lost your temper outwardly, what about inwardly? Even the single illustration of losing our temper is sufficient to make us clear concerning the fact that, even though we are believers, we can still sin and occasionally we do sin. Even though we have been saved and regenerated and are under the transformation of the Holy Spirit, it is still possible for us to sin. Since we can still sin after we are saved, we need to confess our sins (1:9). The confession of sins is the first condition of the divine fellowship.

THE MEANING OF FELLOWSHIP

In 1:6 John says, "If we say that we have fellowship with Him and walk in the darkness, we lie and are not practicing the truth." To have fellowship with God is to have an intimate and living contact with Him in the flow of the divine life according to the Spirit's anointing in our spirit (2:27). This keeps us in the participation and enjoyment of the divine light and divine love.

According to the context, "with Him" in verse 6 is with God. This is equal to "with the Father and with His Son Jesus Christ" (v. 3). Once again, this implies the divine Trinity.

THE DIFFERENCE BETWEEN
LIFE RELATIONSHIP AND FELLOWSHIP

It is very important for us to realize that the believers' relationship in life with God is unbreakable. However, their fellowship with Him is breakable. The former is unconditional; the latter is conditional. Once we have been regenerated, we are children of God, and we have a relationship in life with our Father. This life relationship is unbreakable. However, our fellowship with God is breakable.

We should not confuse our life relationship with God and our fellowship with God. Our relationship with God is based on life and has been settled once for all. But our fellowship with God is based upon the fulfillment of conditions and may fluctuate like the weather. Therefore, the life relationship with God has no conditions and is unbreakable. But our fellowship with God has certain conditions, it is breakable, and it may fluctuate. I hope that we all shall be clear concerning the difference between our relationship with God in life and our fellowship with Him.

LIFE-STUDY OF FIRST JOHN

MESSAGE SEVEN

CONDITIONS OF THE DIVINE FELLOWSHIP

(2)

Scripture Reading: 1 John 1:5-7

In the foregoing message we pointed out that the believers' relationship in life with God is unbreakable, but their fellowship with Him can be broken. The former is unconditional and has been settled once for all; however, the latter is conditional and may fluctuate. Let us now go on in this message to consider the first condition that must be fulfilled if we are to maintain the divine fellowship: the confessing of sins (1:5—2:2).

ABIDING IN GOD AS LIGHT

In 1:5 John says, "And this is the message which we have heard from Him and announce to you, that God is light, and in Him is no darkness at all." This verse speaks of God. In order to maintain fellowship with God, we need to abide in God. We have seen that in this Epistle there are seven mysteries: the divine life, the fellowship of the divine life, the anointing of the Triune God, abiding in the Lord, the divine birth, the divine seed, and the water, the blood, and the Spirit. Here we are concerned with the mystery of abiding. In the Gospel of John, the Lord Jesus said, "Abide in Me, and I in you" (15:4). Because He is the vine and we are the branches, we need to abide in Him. This revelation concerning abiding is a great matter and a crucial one. We all need to abide in God.

What does it mean to abide in God? Many years ago, I thought that to abide is merely to stay or remain. The Chinese version of the Bible uses the word "dwell." More than three hundred years ago, when the King James

Version was translated, in English the word "abide" did have the connotation of dwell. However, this connotation has largely been lost, and today the word abide primarily means to stay or remain. Actually, "dwell" is a more accurate rendering of the Greek. To abide in God, therefore, is to dwell in Him. Not only should we stay in God—we should dwell in Him. We should live, act, move, and have our being in God.

This thought corresponds to that conveyed by the word "walk" in verse 7, where we are told to walk in the light. The Greek word translated "walk" means to move, act, and have our being. As we remain in God, we should dwell in Him and have our being in Him. God is our true dwelling place, our home. Hence, wherever God goes, we should go with Him and in Him. Because God is our dwelling place, we need to dwell in Him.

We need to know not only who God is but also what God is. First John 1:5 tells us that God is light and that in Him is no darkness at all. The very God in whom we dwell is light. The first aspect of the first condition of maintaining our fellowship with God is to dwell in God as light. When the house in which we dwell is full of light, we also are in light, not in darkness. In a similar way, when we dwell in God, we dwell in light, for God is light.

If we do not dwell in God, our fellowship with Him will immediately be broken. Whenever we do not dwell in God, we are out of the divine fellowship. However, our life relationship with God is not broken. For example, whether a child's behavior is good or bad, he still has a relationship in life with his father. Whether a child stays at home or tries to run away, the relationship in life with his father remains unbroken. However, the child may not remain in fellowship with his father. There may be times when he does not want to be in the same room with his father or talk with him face to face. This is because the fellowship has been broken, although the life relationship remains. Our life relationship with God cannot be broken. But our fellowship with Him will be broken if we do not abide in Him as the divine light.

We have pointed out that Spirit is the nature of God's Person, love is the nature of God's essence, and light is the nature of God's expression. Light, therefore, is God's expression; it is God shining. Hence, when we dwell in God, who is the shining One, we are in light.

In 1:5 John says that in God there is no darkness at all. As light is the nature of God in His expression, so darkness is the nature of Satan in his evil works (3:8). Thank God that He has delivered us out of the satanic darkness into the divine light (Acts 26:18; 1 Pet. 2:9). The divine light is the divine life in the Son operating in us. This light shines in the darkness within us, and the darkness cannot overcome it (John 1:4-5). When we follow this light, we shall by no means walk in darkness (John 8:12), which according to the context (1 John 1:7-10) is the darkness of sin.

WALKING IN THE DIVINE LIGHT
VERSUS THE SATANIC DARKNESS

In 1:7a John says, "But if we walk in the light as He is in the light, we have fellowship with one another." To "walk" here means to live, behave, and have our being. We walk in the light, but God is in the light because He is light. "The light is the element in which God dwells (cf. 1 Tim. 6:16).... this walking in the light, as He is in the light, is no mere imitation of God,... but is an identity in the essential element of our daily walk with the essential element of God's eternal being: not imitation, but coincidence and identity of the very atmosphere of life" (Alford).

When we walk and live in the light of God, we have jointly the co-enjoyment of the Triune God and the co-participation in His divine purpose. The fellowship of the divine life brings us the divine light, and the divine light keeps us in the fellowship, that is, in the joint enjoyment of God and joint participation in His purpose.

In verse 6 John speaks of walking in darkness. To walk habitually in the darkness is to live, behave, and have one's being in the nature of Satan's evil works. According to 2:11, to walk in the darkness equals to practice sin (3:4, 8).

To walk in the divine light is not merely to dwell in this light; it is to live, move, act, do things, and have our being in the divine light, the light which is actually God Himself. When we dwell, live, and have our being in God, we walk in the divine light, which is the expression of God.

When the divine light shines, we see all the different truths, and these truths are realities. But when we do not have the divine light but are rather in darkness, we have the sense that everything is vanity and emptiness. I would ask you to consider your experience. When you are in the divine light, you can see the truth, the reality. For example, when you are in the light, God is a reality to you, and the divine life is also a reality. Furthermore, God's holiness, love, and grace are all realities to you. When we walk in the light, we see one reality after another. However, when we are in darkness, nothing is real to us. On the contrary, everything is empty, vain. When we are in darkness, we do not have any reality because we do not see anything. Instead of the sense of reality, we have the sense of emptiness and vanity.

When we dwell in God, we are in the fellowship. When we are in this fellowship, we are in light. Then as we walk in the light, Christ, the Spirit, the church, the Body, and the members of the Body are all real to us. We may testify and say, "Praise the Lord that I see Christ, the Spirit, the church, the Body, and the ground of the church! How wonderful! All this is real to me."

However, suppose a sister is offended by an elder. Although the elder had no intention of offending her, nonetheless something he said offended her because she is sensitive. Perhaps the elder said that all the sisters, no matter what their background may be, are fragile. This word offended the sister, and she said to herself, "I love the Lord very much, and I also love the church and am for the church. Why does this elder say that the sisters are fragile?" Because she is offended, the "switch" is turned off, and immediately she is in darkness. As a result, instead of enjoying the church life, she begins to be unhappy with the church. The church is no longer real to her, and she no longer cares about the church ground. She may say, "What is the church anyway? And what is the church ground? I don't care about the ground of the church." If she stays in darkness, she will eventually find that Christ, the Spirit, and the divine life are no longer real to her in her experience. She may say, "What is Christ? He is far away in the heavens. What is eternal life? This life doesn't mean much to me." This is an illustration of the fact that whenever we are in darkness, all the divine things become vain and empty to us.

Suppose after a period of time the sister who has been offended and is in darkness repents. The Lord is merciful and for no apparent reason, she turns to the Lord and says, "O Lord, forgive me." Immediately, the "switch" is turned on, and the light begins to shine again. Then this sister will experience the cleansing of the Lord's precious blood, and the divine things will become real once more.

Has this not been your experience? I can testify that I have experienced this a number of times. I know what it is to suffer from the "disease" of being in darkness and of being recovered to the fellowship in the divine life. From experience I know that when we are in the light, the divine things are real to us, but when we are in darkness, these things are not real to us.

If we would be in the divine fellowship, we need to abide in God as light, and we need to walk in the divine light. The divine light is versus the satanic darkness. The real issue here is not a question of right or wrong; it is a question of light or darkness. You do not need to consider whether what an elder says is right or wrong, but consider whether you are in light or in darkness. If you are in darkness, this indicates that you are out of the divine fellowship.

Light is the expression of God, and darkness is the expression of Satan. If we say, "I don't care for the church, and Christ is far away in the heavens— He is not in me," we are speaking lies, and these lies are the expression of

satanic darkness. In order to have the broken fellowship
recovered, we must condemn darkness. We may think that
we are right. But if we are in darkness, we need to confess
and say, "Lord, why am I in darkness? There must be
something wrong with me. Lord, even though I don't
realize in what way I am wrong, I know that I am wrong
because I am in darkness. Lord, I ask You to forgive me
and cleanse me." If we do this, light will come to us. I
speak of this from my own experience. A number of times I
realized that I was in darkness, although I did not know in
what way I was wrong. Therefore, I went to the Lord and
told Him that I was in darkness. As a result, the light
began to shine again.

Darkness may be compared to a stop sign on a street
corner. Darkness is a sign that we are wrong in some way.
Even if we do not know what is wrong, because we have
the sign of darkness within us, we need to confess our
situation to the Lord and say, "Lord, please forgive me.
Although I do not know where I am wrong, I still ask You
to forgive me. Lord, I sense darkness within me. I am
completely surrounded with darkness, and I cannot bear it.
Lord, because I am in darkness, I ask You to forgive me
and cleanse me with Your precious blood." If you confess to
the Lord in this way, light will come. Then the light will
show you in what matter you are wrong. If you confess
that matter to the Lord, you will receive more light. This is
the way to keep ourselves in God. This is also the way to
recover and restore the broken fellowship. If we take this
way, we shall maintain a proper fellowship in the divine
light.

PRACTICING THE DIVINE TRUTH
VERSUS THE SATANIC LIE

Let us read all of 1:6: "If we say that we have fellowship
with Him and walk in the darkness, we lie and are not
practicing the truth." To lie is of Satan. He is the father of
liars (John 8:44). His nature is a lie, and it brings in death
and darkness. With darkness is falsehood, the opposite of
the truth. The satanic darkness is versus the divine light,

and the satanic lie is versus the divine truth. As the divine truth is the expression of the divine light, so the satanic lie is the expression of the satanic darkness. If we say that we have fellowship with God, who is light, and walk in the darkness, we lie, we are in the expression of the satanic darkness, and we do not practice the truth in the expression of the divine light. This verse inoculates against the heretical teaching of the Antinomians, who teach freedom from the obligation of the moral law and say that a person may live in sin and at the same time have fellowship with God.

If we would maintain the divine fellowship, we must not only walk in the divine light, but also practice the divine truth, which is versus the satanic lie. The Greek word rendered "practicing" in 1:6 is *poieo*. This verb denotes doing things habitually and continually by abiding in these things. Hence, it is used in verse 6 in the sense of practice. This word is also used in 2:17, 29; 3:4 (twice), 7, 8, 9, 10, 22; 5:2; Romans 1:32, and various other places.

To practice the truth is to live the truth habitually, not merely to do it occasionally. To practice the truth is to do it constantly, continuously, unceasingly. This can be compared to breathing, which is constant, continuous, habitual. While we are speaking, we are breathing. There is no need for us to make up our minds to breathe or to try to energize ourselves to breathe, for breathing is natural and habitual. Hence, breathing is a practice. In a similar way, when we abide in God as light and when we walk in the divine light, we spontaneously practice the truth habitually.

Suppose a certain believer is in darkness. Because he is in darkness, whatever he does, whatever he practices, is wrong. He may try to go in a certain direction, but that will be wrong. If he tries to go in another direction, that also will be wrong. But if this believer is in the light, he will automatically practice the truth. He will live, behave, and talk to others in a proper way. This is to practice the truth.

If we are in the light, we shall see the church as a reality. We shall also see the Body and the members of the

Body as realities. We shall see that we are a particular member of the Body. But if we are in darkness, we may think that we are a great member of the Body, such as the shoulder, when actually we may be a small member, such as the little finger. This is another illustration of the fact that to be in darkness is to be in emptiness, vanity. But to walk according to what we see of the reality in the light is to practice the truth.

Often when we are in darkness we practice things that are nonsensical. For example, if a young person is in darkness, he may criticize an older brother in the Lord. This criticism is altogether nonsensical, for it is in darkness. This young person does not know what he is saying, and his criticism is vain and empty. He is not practicing the truth, because he does not see the truth.

It is when we are in the light that we see the truth. If we are in the light, whatever we do will be real. Not only shall we practice what is right and proper; we shall do what is real. This means that whatever we do is a reality. Habitually and automatically, we shall practice the truth, the reality. If we do this, we shall keep ourselves in the divine fellowship.

LIFE-STUDY OF FIRST JOHN

MESSAGE EIGHT

CONDITIONS OF THE DIVINE FELLOWSHIP

(3)

Scripture Reading: 1 John 1:5-7

We have seen that the believers' relationship in life with God is unbreakable, but their fellowship with Him can be broken. This means that our life relationship with God is unconditional, whereas our fellowship with God is conditional. The first condition of the divine fellowship is that of confessing sins (1:5—2:22). Related to this first condition are the matters of abiding in God as light, walking in the divine light, and practicing the divine truth. In this message we shall go on to consider the cleansing of the blood of Jesus, the Son of God.

CLEANSED BY THE BLOOD OF JESUS

In 1:7 the Apostle John says, "But if we walk in the light as He is in the light, we have fellowship with one another, and the blood of Jesus His Son cleanses us from all sin." In this verse we see that we walk in the light, but God is in the light, because He is light. When we walk in the light, which is God Himself, we have the co-enjoyment of the Triune God and the co-participation in His purpose.

When we live in the divine life, we are under its enlightenment, and it exposes, according to God's divine nature and through His nature in us, all our sin, trespasses, failures, and defects, which contradict His pure light, perfect love, absolute holiness, and excelling righteousness. At such a time we sense in our enlightened conscience the need of the cleansing of the redeeming blood of the Lord Jesus, and it cleanses us in our conscience from all sins so that our fellowship with God and with one another may be maintained. Our relationship with God is unbreakable, yet our fellowship with Him may be broken. The former is of life, whereas the latter is based upon our living, though it is also of life. One is unconditional; the other is conditional. This conditional one, our fellowship with God, needs to be maintained by the constant cleansing of the Lord's blood.

In verse 7 John says that the blood of Jesus cleanses us from all sin. The tense of the verb "cleanses" in Greek is present and continuous. This indicates that the blood of Jesus the Son of God cleanses us all the time, continuously and constantly. Cleansing here refers to the instant cleansing of the Lord's blood in our conscience. Before God, the redeeming blood of the Lord has cleansed us once for all eternally (Heb. 9:12,14), and the efficacy of that cleansing lasts forever before God, needing no repetition. However, in our conscience we need the instant application of the constant cleansing of the Lord's blood again and again whenever our conscience is enlightened by the divine light in our fellowship with God. This instant cleansing is typified by the purification of the ashes of the heifer for a water of separation (Num. 19:2-10).

In verse 7 John specifically says that the blood of Jesus cleanses us from all sin. The New Testament speaks of sin and also of sins. "Sin" usually refers to indwelling sin, which is dealt with in Romans 5:12 to 8:13. "Sins" refer to sinful deeds, the fruits of indwelling sin, which are dealt with in Romans 1:18 to 5:11. However, the singular sin in 1:7 with the adjective "all" does not denote indwelling sin; rather, it denotes every single sin we have committed since we have been regenerated. The sins we commit after regeneration defile our purged conscience and need to be cleansed away by the blood of Jesus in our fellowship with God.

When we are in the divine fellowship, we are in the light, and when we are in the light, we are exposed by the light. The divine light is much stronger than an x ray. This light exposes whatever is wrong in our being. As we walk in the light and practice the reality in the light, the light

shines within us, upon us, and through us. Exposed by this
shining, we realize that we are wrong in many matters. We
may see that we are wrong in our thoughts, emotions,
motives, and intentions. We may also see that we are
wrong with certain brothers and sisters. Because we are
exposed in this way, our conscience is condemned. In order
to deal with this condemnation in our conscience, we need
the cleansing of the Lord's blood. It is when we are in the
fellowship and under the light that we see our failures,
mistakes, wrongdoings, impure motives, and evil intentions. But at this very juncture, the blood of the Lord Jesus
cleanses us from every sin. As we have pointed out, the
tense of the Greek verb rendered "cleanses" indicates that,
when we walk in the light and are in fellowship with God
and with one another, the blood of Jesus cleanses us
constantly, unceasingly.

JESUS HIS SON

It is significant that in 1:7 the Apostle John speaks of
"the blood of Jesus His Son." The name Jesus denotes the
Lord's humanity, which is needed for the shedding of the
redeeming blood, and the title "His Son" denotes the Lord's
divinity, which is needed for the eternal efficacy of the
redeeming blood. Thus, the blood of Jesus His Son indicates
that this blood is the proper blood of a genuine man for
redeeming God's fallen creatures with divine surety for its
eternal efficacy, an efficacy which is all-prevailing in
space and everlasting in time.

The title "Jesus His Son" is also used by John as an
inoculation against the heresies concerning the Lord's
Person. One of the heresies insisted on the divinity of the
Lord by denying His humanity. The title Jesus as the
name of a man inoculates against this heresy. Another
heresy insisted on the humanity of the Lord by denying
His divinity. The title "His Son" as a name of the Deity is
an antidote to this heresy.

No other verse in the New Testament uses the expression "Jesus His Son." We have just pointed out that the
name Jesus refers to the Lord's humanity and that the title

"His Son" denotes His divinity. Jesus was a true man, a genuine human being, and the blood of Jesus was the blood of a real man. Because we are human beings, we need to be redeemed by human blood. In the Old Testament the blood for atonement was of animals, and was a type of the blood of Christ. However, animal blood could not actually redeem us, because we are human beings, not animals. As human beings, we need the efficacious blood of Jesus, the blood of a genuine man.

The Lord's divinity indicated by the words "His Son" is a guarantee, a surety, that the efficacy of the blood of Jesus will remain forever. The Lord's humanity qualifies Him to have the blood to shed for our redemption. His divinity insures the efficacy of the power of this redeeming blood. The efficacy of the cleansing blood of Jesus is insured forever by His divinity.

We have seen that when John wrote this Epistle, there were heresies concerning the Person of Christ. One kind of heretical teaching said that Jesus was divine but not human. A different kind of heretical teaching claimed that Jesus was human but not divine. With one short expression—"the blood of Jesus His Son"—John inoculates us against both kinds of heresies. The words "the blood of Jesus" indicate that Jesus was a genuine man, and the words "His Son" indicate that He is divine. The blood by which we are cleansed is the blood of a wonderful Person who has both humanity and divinity.

A CYCLE

In 1:1-7 we see a cycle in our spiritual life formed of four crucial things—the eternal life, the fellowship of the eternal life, the divine light, and the blood of Jesus the Son of God. Eternal life issues in the fellowship of the divine life, the fellowship of eternal life brings in the divine light, and the divine light increases the need of the blood of Jesus the Son of God so that we may have more eternal life. The more we have of eternal life, the more of its fellowship it brings to us. The more fellowship of the divine life we enjoy, the more divine light we receive. The more divine light we receive, the more we participate in the cleansing of the blood of Jesus. Such a cycle brings us onward in the growth of the divine life until we reach its maturity.

LIGHT VERSUS DARKNESS

In 1:5-7 John uses five important words: light, truth, darkness, lie, and sin. Light is the essence of God's expression. We may say that light is God expressed. When we walk in this light, truth will come forth, for truth is the issue of light. Light is the source of truth, and truth is the issue, the outcome, of light. Therefore, when we abide in the divine light and walk in the light, we practice the truth.

The lie is the essence of Satan, and darkness is the expression of the satanic essence. This darkness is related to sin. This is the reason that in these verses we have light, darkness, and sin. If we are not in the light, we are surely in darkness. When we are in darkness, we are deceived by the lie, which is the essence of Satan. Furthermore, since the lie and the darkness are related to sin, we are also involved with sin.

Let us remember that light is the essence of God's expression, and truth is the issue of this light. Lie is the essence of Satan, darkness is the expression of this essence, and this darkness is related to sin. When we are in the light, we practice the truth. But when we are not in the light, we are in darkness. When we are in darkness, we are deceived and are in a condition that is related to sin.

When we are in the light, we shall be exposed, and we shall see our sins. Then we need to confess our sins. As we confess our sins, spontaneously and continuously the blood of Jesus the Son of God will cleanse us from all sin.

When we are in darkness, we are in sin. Moreover, when we are in sin, our fellowship with God is broken. But if we are exposed by the light and confess our sins, our sins will be washed away, and our broken fellowship with God will be restored.

AN ANTIDOTE TO THE HERESY OF THE ANTINOMIANS

First John 1:6 may be regarded as an antidote to the

heretical teaching of the Antinomians. The word "Anti-
nomian" is an anglicized form of two Greek words: *anti*,
meaning against, and *nomos*, meaning law. The Antinomians were those who were against law, those who did
not care for the law. The Antinomians in John's time
taught freedom from the obligation of the moral law and
claimed that a person could live in sin and still have
fellowship with God.

In 1:6 John inoculates the believers against the heretical teachings of the Antinomians. Here John says, "If we
say that we have fellowship with Him and walk in
darkness, we lie and are not practicing the truth."
According to this verse, we cannot have fellowship with
God and at the same time walk in darkness. The satanic
darkness is versus the divine light, and the satanic lie is
versus the divine truth. As the divine truth is the
expression of the divine light, so the satanic lie is the
expression of the satanic darkness. If we say that we have
fellowship with God, who is light, and walk in darkness,
we lie, we are in the expression of the satanic darkness,
and we do not practice the truth in the expression of the
divine light.

In Galatians 5:13 Paul says, "For you were called to
freedom, brothers; only do not turn the freedom into an
occasion for the flesh...." Here Paul is telling us not to
misuse our freedom. In Galatians 5:1 Paul says, "For
freedom Christ has set us free; stand fast therefore and do
not be again entangled with a yoke of slavery." Then in
verse 13 Paul goes on to point out that we should not abuse
our freedom. Although we are free from the yoke of slavery
to the law, it is still necessary for us to be moral. This is
contrary to the heretical teaching which says that those
who are under grace have no obligation to keep the moral
law.

The Antinomians claim that we can still have fellowship with God even if we live in sin. John wrote 1:6 to
refute this false teaching. According to John's word, if we
say that we have fellowship with God and walk in
darkness, we take the way of the Antinomians. John

clearly indicates that in order to have fellowship with God, we need to deal with our sins by confessing them to God so that we may by cleansed by the blood of Jesus, God's Son.

TWO KINDS OF CLEANSING WITH THE LORD'S BLOOD

According to John's word in 1:7, the blood of Jesus cleanses us from all sin. Actually there are two kinds of cleansing with the Lord's blood. First, before God the redeeming blood has cleansed us once for all (Heb. 9:12, 14), and this cleansing lasts for eternity. The second cleansing is the instant and constant cleansing of the Lord's blood in our conscience. On the one hand, the Lord's blood washes our sin and sins in the presence of God. On the other hand, the same blood washes our sin and sins in our conscience. According to the typology in the Old Testament, the blood of the sacrifice was brought into the tabernacle and sprinkled in the Holy of Holies in the presence of God. This signifies the once-for-all washing of our sin and sins in the presence of God. The instant and constant cleansing of the blood is typified by the purification of the ashes of the heifer for a water of separation. The cleansing in 1:7 is not the eternal cleansing before God; rather, it is the continuous cleansing in our conscience. As we abide in the light, we are cleansed continually by the blood of Jesus.

We have pointed out that in 1:7 four matters—eternal life, the fellowship of eternal life, the divine light, and the blood of Jesus—form a cycle which we should experience in our spiritual life. First we have eternal life, and in this life we have fellowship. Fellowship brings in light, and under the shining of the light we experience the cleansing of the blood. Then the blood brings us more life, and with more life we have more fellowship. Then with more fellowship we have more light and more cleansing of the blood. This cycle of life, fellowship, light, and blood repeats itself again and again as we grow in life unto maturity.

LIFE-STUDY OF FIRST JOHN

THE DIVINE LIGHT AND THE DIVINE TRUTH

(1)

Scripture Reading: 1 John 1:5-7

In our Life-study of 1 John we need to insert at this point, as a parenthesis, some messages on the divine light and the divine truth. After these parenthetical messages, we shall consider further the conditions of the divine fellowship.

The divine light is the essence of God's expression. When God is expressed, the essence of that expression is light. What is the divine truth? The divine truth is the issue of the divine light. When the divine light shines in us, it becomes the divine truth, which is the divine reality. This means that when the divine light shines in us, we receive the divine reality. We may also say that the divine light brings us the divine reality.

THE DIVINE LIGHT

In 1:5 John says, "And this is the message which we have heard from Him and announce to you, that God is light, and in Him is no darkness at all." In verse 7 he speaks a further word concerning light: "But if we walk in the light as He is in the light, we have fellowship with one another, and the blood of Jesus His Son cleanses us from all sin." As we have indicated, the divine light is the nature, the essence, of God's expression and the source of the divine truth. This divine light shines in the divine life. Hence, if we do not have the divine life, we cannot have the divine light.

John 1:4 says, "In Him was life, and the life was the light of men." In Christ there is the divine life, and this life is the divine light. Therefore, life is light. When we have the divine life, we also have the divine light.

By this we can see that three matters are related: light, truth, and life. First, we need to learn to experience these matters and then learn how to present the truth regarding them to others.

KNOWING THE TRUTH, EXPERIENCING THE TRUTH, AND PRESENTING THE TRUTH

Among Christians today there is a great lack concerning the knowledge of biblical truths. Some know the truth, but their understanding is rather superficial. The goal of the Lord's recovery, therefore, is to recover all the biblical truths, all the biblical realities. As those who are in the Lord's recovery, we must realize that there is a desperate need for us all to have the full knowledge of the truth, the experience of the truth, and the skill to present the truth to others.

Suppose the parents of a certain young person in the Lord's recovery are opposing him. That brother should not be offended by his parents, and he should not argue with them. Instead, with a good spirit and a pleasant attitude, he should present the truth to his parents. Perhaps during a visit with them he may say, "Dad and Mom, let me tell you that light is the essence of God's expression and that truth is the issue of this light. Aren't you glad to hear about this? This light shines in the divine life, and the divine life is in Jesus Christ. Christ is even the life. The Lord Jesus says, 'I am the life.' When we are in this life, we have the shining of the divine light. Then as we are under this shining, we have the truth." Perhaps this brother's parents will accept his word, or they may reject it. But whatever the case may be, when he leaves them, he may want to say, "Dad and Mom, I need to go now. But I leave with you three 'diamonds'—life, light, and truth."

Many Christians are familiar with biblical terms, but they may not know the meaning of these terms. If you ask them concerning the meaning of light, truth, and life, they may answer that they do not know the meaning of these things. Therefore, we need to be able to present the precious truths regarding these matters to others. The need in the Lord's recovery today is that we all learn the truth, experience the truth, and develop the skill to present the truth to others.

The Lord's recovery spreads by means of the truth. Many of us can testify that we were not attracted to the Lord's recovery by a powerful and charming speaker. Rather, we were attracted by the truth. We were drawn this way by the presentation of biblical truth. For example, I know of one brother who was attracted by the presentation of how the first two chapters of the Bible, Genesis 1 and 2, and the last two chapters of the Bible, Revelation 21 and 22, reflect each other. Eventually, this brother was gained for the Lord's recovery by this truth. My goal in all the conferences and the trainings is simply to present the truths of the Bible.

I am glad to see that many of the young ones among us are eager to know the truth of the Word. After a period of time, these young people will be useful in the Lord's recovery. Those who are teen-agers at present will eventually be useful in spreading the biblical truths. Praise the Lord for the opportunity He has given us to be trained in the truths of the Bible!

THE EMBODIMENT OF THE DIVINE LIGHT

We have seen that the divine light is the nature of God's expression, that it is the source of the divine truth, and that it shines in the divine life. Now we must go on to see that the divine light is embodied in Jesus as God incarnate. Because He is the embodiment of the divine light, the Lord Jesus said, "I am the light of the world; he who follows Me shall by no means walk in darkness, but shall have the light of life" (John 8:12). He spoke a similar word in John 9:5: "While I am in the world, I am the light of the world." The divine light that issues in truth and shines in life is embodied in the Person of the Lord Jesus, who is God incarnate. This matter is deep and profound. I would encourage you to pray-read these verses in order to

touch the reality of these matters concerning the divine
light.

THE DIVINE TRUTH

The Meaning of Truth

In 1:6 John speaks concerning the divine truth: "If we
say that we have fellowship with Him and walk in the
darkness, we lie and are not practicing the truth." What is
truth? It is difficult to define truth. We may think that
truth in such a verse as 1:6 refers to sound or correct
doctrine. The word for truth in the Chinese language
means genuine doctrine. Many have a similar understanding of the English word "truth" and consider that, at
least insofar as it is found in the Bible, it means correct
doctrine.

In our daily conversation we may have a somewhat
different understanding of truth and regard truth as
meaning something that is true as opposed to something
false. For example, we speak of telling a true story.

If we would understand the meaning of truth in the
Bible, we need to go beyond the traditional and common
understanding of what truth is. The traditional view
concerning the truth in the Bible as correct doctrine is not
accurate, and the common denotation of the word should
not be applied to the word truth as found in the Bible.

The Greek word for truth is *aletheia*. In studying this
word, I consulted a number of lexicons and concordances. I
was especially helped by the article on truth in Kittel's
Theological Dictionary of the New Testament. Furthermore, I also considered all the verses in the New
Testament that use either the word *aletheia* or a related
word. After studying these verses in context and after
consulting the lexicons and concordances, I came to
certain conclusions regarding the meaning of truth in the
New Testament, and these conclusions are summarized in
the lengthy note on truth in 1:6 printed in the Recovery
Version of the Epistles of John. In this message we shall
consider only the first part of this note.

The Greek word *aletheia* means truth or reality (versus

vanity), verity, veracity, genuineness, sincerity. It is John's highly individual terminology, and it is one of the profound words in the New Testament. This word denotes all the realities of the divine economy as the content of the divine revelation, contained, conveyed, and disclosed by the holy Word.

God

According to the New Testament, truth is first God, who is light and love, incarnated to be the reality of the divine things—including the divine life, the divine nature, the divine power, the divine glory—for our possession, so that we may enjoy Him as grace, as revealed in John's Gospel (John 1:1, 4, 14-17).

Christ

Second, truth in the New Testament denotes Christ, who is God incarnated and in whom all the fullness of the Godhead dwells bodily (Col. 2:9), to be the reality of: a) God and man (John 1:18, 51; 1 Tim. 2:5); b) all the types, figures, and shadows of the Old Testament (Col. 2:16-17; John 4:23-24); and c) all the divine and spiritual things, such as the divine life and resurrection (John 11:25; 14:6), the divine light (John 8:12; 9:5), the divine way (John 14:6), wisdom, righteousness, sanctification, redemption (1 Cor. 1:30). Hence, Christ is the reality (John 14:6; Eph. 4:21).

The Spirit

Third, truth is the Spirit, who is Christ transfigured (1 Cor. 15:45b; 2 Cor. 3:17), the reality of Christ (John 14:16-17; 15:26) and of the divine revelation (John 16:13-15). Hence, the Spirit is the reality (1 John 5:6).

Now we can see that truth, *aletheia*, in the New Testament refers to God. Truth is God as the divine light and love incarnated to be the reality of all the divine things for our possession so that we may enjoy God as grace. This means that the very God is the truth, the reality, of the divine things for our possession. Therefore, we need to possess God as the reality and then enjoy

Him as grace. Hence, the divine reality is actually God
Himself. He is the reality of all the divine things.

Truth in the New Testament also denotes Christ as God
incarnate. Christ is the One in whom all the fullness of the
Godhead dwells bodily. As the embodiment of the fullness
of the Godhead, Christ, who is God incarnate, is the reality
of God and man, the reality of all the types, figures, and
shadows of the Old Testament, and the reality of all the
divine and spiritual things.

What is truth? What is reality? Reality is Christ as God
incarnate. Reality is Christ as the One in whom all the
fullness of the Godhead dwells bodily to be the reality of
God, man, the types, figures, and shadows, and all divine
and spiritual things. In the Old Testament we have many
types, figures, and shadows. Christ is the reality of them.
In the Bible we also read of many divine and spiritual
things, such as life, light, wisdom, and righteousness.
Christ Himself is the reality of all these things. Therefore,
when we read the word "truth" or "reality" in the New
Testament, we need to realize that it refers first to God and
also to Christ.

We have indicated that in the New Testament truth
denotes the Spirit, who is Christ transfigured and also the
reality of Christ and of the divine revelation. For this
reason, in 5:6, John says, "The Spirit is He who testifies,
because the Spirit is the truth."

It is surely worthwhile for us to study thoroughly the
meaning of truth in the New Testament. In this message
we have pointed out in a very brief way that truth, reality,
is God, Christ, and the Spirit. In the following message we
shall go on to consider other aspects of truth according to
the Word of God.

LIFE-STUDY OF FIRST JOHN

MESSAGE TEN

THE DIVINE LIGHT AND THE DIVINE TRUTH

(2)

Scripture Reading: 1 John 1:5-7

In this message we shall continue to consider the meaning of the word truth in the New Testament. We have pointed out that truth is God, Christ, and the Spirit. Therefore, truth is the divine Trinity. Actually the Three of the Trinity are all one reality.

THE WORD OF GOD

Having seen that truth is the Triune God, we may go on to point out that truth is also the Word of God as the divine revelation, which not only reveals but also conveys the reality of God and Christ and of all the divine and spiritual things. Hence, the Word of God also is reality (John 17:17).

The Word is the explanation of the Triune God. This means that the fourth aspect of what the truth is, the Word, is actually the explanation of the first three aspects of the truth, the Father, the Son, and the Spirit. Therefore, reality is God the Father, God the Son, God the Spirit, and also the divine Word.

THE CONTENTS OF THE FAITH

According to the New Testament, truth is also the contents of the faith (belief), which is the substantial elements of what we believe as the reality of the full gospel (Eph. 1:13; Col. 1:5). This is revealed in the entire New Testament (2 Cor. 4:2; 13:8; Gal. 5:7; 1 Tim. 2:4, 7b; 3:15; 4:3; 6:5; 2 Tim. 2:15, 18, 25; 3:7, 8; 4:4; Titus 1:1, 14; 2 Thes. 2:10, 12; Heb. 10:26; James 5:19; 1 Pet. 1:22; 2 Pet. 1:12).

The contents of the Word of God are also the contents of

our Christian faith. This is the objective faith, our belief.
The Word is the revelation and explanation of the Trinity,
and this Word has contents. In brief, these contents are the
contents of the New Testament and also the contents of
our Christian faith. Therefore, the contents of the New
Testament and of our Christian faith are also the truth, the
reality. This means that in the New Testament, reality
refers to the contents of our faith and to the contents of the
entire New Testament.

THE REALITY CONCERNING GOD, MAN,
AND THE UNIVERSE

In the Bible truth is also the reality concerning God, the
universe, man, man's relationship with God and with one
another, and man's obligation to God, as revealed through
creation and the Scripture (Rom. 1:18-20; 2:2, 8, 20).

If we would know the actual situation concerning God
and the universe, there is no need for us to guess or make
inferences. We simply need to come to the Scriptures, for in
the New Testament we have the truth concerning God, the
universe, and man. We also have the truth regarding
man's obligation to God and his relationship with God and
others. This truth is revealed partially in God's creation,
and it is revealed fully in the Scriptures. In God's creation
we can see certain aspects of the truth concerning God,
man, and man's relationship with God. Therefore, in the
New Testament the word truth is used to refer to these
matters.

GENUINENESS AS A DIVINE VIRTUE

In the New Testament the Greek word for truth,
aletheia, also denotes the genuineness, truthfulness, sincerity, honesty, trustworthiness, and faithfulness of God as
a divine virtue (Rom. 3:7; 15:8), and of man as a human
virtue (Mark 12:14; 2 Cor. 11:10; Phil. 1:18; 1 John 3:18) and
as an issue of the divine reality (John 4:23-24; 2 John 1;
3 John 1).

John 4:23 and 24 say, "But an hour is coming, and now
is, when the true worshippers shall worship the Father in

spirit and reality; for the Father seeks such to worship Him. God is Spirit; and those who worship Him must worship in spirit and reality." Some hold the concept that the word truth in these verses denotes the sincerity of God's worshippers. According to this concept, we should worship God not only in our spirit and with our spirit, but also worship Him in sincerity. This understanding is mistaken. In John 4:23 and 24 truth refers to the result, the issue, of God being reality to us. When we enjoy God as our reality, this enjoyment will have a certain outcome, and this outcome is truth, reality. Actually, this outcome of enjoying God as our reality is Christ coming forth from us. When we enjoy the Triune God—the Father, the Son, and the Spirit—as our reality, that is, when the divine Trinity becomes a reality to us for our enjoyment, this enjoyment issues in a certain kind of virtue. This virtue is the Christ experienced by us, the Christ who is the fulfillment of all the offerings.

WORSHIPPING GOD
WITH THE CHRIST WE HAVE EXPERIENCED

In Old Testament times the children of Israel worshipped God in a particular place—Jerusalem. When they went to Jerusalem to worship God, they could not be empty-handed. They were required to go to Jerusalem with offerings for the worship of God. All those offerings were types of Christ. Therefore, the children of Israel worshipped God in the place designated by God and with the offerings required by God. In typology the place chosen by God typifies the human spirit, where God's habitation is today (Eph. 2:22), and the offerings typify Christ.

In chapter four of John the Samaritan woman said to the Lord Jesus, "Our fathers worshipped in this mountain, and you say that in Jerusalem is the place where men must worship" (v. 20). The Lord Jesus answered, "Woman, believe Me, an hour is coming when neither in this mountain nor in Jerusalem shall you worship the Father" (v. 21). The Lord's answer indicates that the dispensation was changing. In Old Testament times God commanded

His people to worship Him in Jerusalem with the offerings. But the hour has changed, and now is the hour of the Spirit. Therefore, the Lord went on to say that God is Spirit and those who worship Him must worship Him in spirit, not in a certain place. This means that in the fulfillment of the typology, the human spirit replaces Jerusalem as the designated place. The Lord also told the Samaritan woman that the true worshippers must worship the Father not only in spirit, but also in reality. Reality here is the Christ whom we experience as the reality of all the offerings. Hence, Christ as the offerings is the fulfillment of the type of the sacrifices used in the worship of God. Today we need to worship God in our spirit and with the Christ whom we have experienced as the burnt offering, meal offering, peace offering, sin offering, and trespass offering.

We need to worship the Father with the Christ who is the fulfillment of the offerings that the children of Israel offered in their worship to God. This Christ is not the objective Christ; rather, He is the subjective Christ, the Christ whom we have experienced. The experience of Christ as the fulfillment of the offerings results in reality. This is the reality in John 4:23 and 24, the divine reality experienced by us and resulting in our virtue. This virtue also is reality.

Suppose two Israelites, one from the tribe of Judah and the other from the tribe of Dan, came to worship God. They both had to worship in Jerusalem, in particular, on Mount Zion, which was in the center of Jerusalem. They also had to worship God with certain offerings; they were not allowed to appear before Him empty-handed. For the proper worship of God they had to come to the place designated by God, and they had to bring their offerings. If they fulfilled these requirements, their worship of God would be proper.

According to the Old Testament, proper worship is not a matter of one's physical posture before God; that is, it is not a matter of standing, kneeling, or prostrating oneself. Proper worship in the Old Testament is a matter of coming to the right place—Mount Zion in Jerusalem—and with the right things—the offerings. After the offerings were presented to God, those who offered them could also enjoy them with God by eating a portion of them. Therefore, proper worship includes coming to the right place, presenting the offerings to God, and eating the offerings in the presence of God. This indicates that singing, praising, and praying are not the prerequisites for the proper worship of God. The prerequisites are the place God designates and the offerings God requires. After the offerings were offered to God at the place designated by God, they were enjoyed by the offerers in the presence of God and with God. According to typology, this is proper worship.

Now we need to understand how this typology is fulfilled by the proper worship in the New Testament. The proper place for us to worship God is in our spirit. Furthermore, when we worship God in spirit, we must worship him with the Christ whom we have been experiencing.

Do you know what the Christian life is? The Christian life is a life of daily experiencing the Christ we have received. The Christian life is a life of experiencing Christ all the time. This experience of Christ produces the offerings with which we worship God.

As Christians, we should daily experience Christ. Then we should come to the meetings of the church in spirit and with the Christ whom we have been experiencing in our daily living. In the church meetings we should worship God in our spirit and with the very Christ whom we have experienced as the offerings. We may offer Him as the sin offering or as the trespass offering. We may also offer Him as the burnt offering, as the meal offering, or as the peace offering. All these offerings are the Christ whom we experience subjectively.

This subjective experience of Christ is the issue of our enjoyment of the Triune God. When we experience Christ, we are actually enjoying the Father, the Son, and the Spirit. Hence, to experience Christ is to enjoy the Triune God. This enjoyment results in a reality that is very subjective and practical. On the one hand, this reality is

Christ in us; on the other hand, this is also our reality.

Suppose certain brothers in the church life are indifferent concerning Christ and idle with respect to the experience of Christ. As a result, they do not have any experience of Him. They have believed in the Lord's name and received Him, and that is all. They do not have any experience of Christ in their daily living. These brothers may be ethical and moral, not committing any gross sins. But because they do not have any experience of Christ in their daily living, when they come to the church meetings, they come empty-handed. They are not able to pray or give a word for the Lord. They may like to sit in the meeting and watch others function. This is an insult to God. This kind of worship is not only rejected by Him—it is condemned.

We should not come to God empty-handed. Whenever we come to Him, we should have something of the Christ we have experienced in our daily living. Do you know what God wants from us in our worship of Him? God wants the Christ we have experienced. His desire is that we worship Him with the Christ we experience day by day.

We have pointed out that in experiencing Christ we enjoy God the Father, God the Son, and God the Spirit. This enjoyment issues in a reality that we may call our personal reality. This personal reality is a matter of having Christ saturating our inner being. When we have this reality, we have Christ in our spirit, heart, mind, emotion, and will. This is the Christ whom we have experienced becoming our reality. Now we should worship God not only in our spirit, but also worship Him with this reality, which is the Christ we experience in our daily living. This is not only the divine reality for our enjoyment; this is also our human reality, our personal reality, which comes out of our enjoyment of the divine reality. This human reality is the issue of the divine reality which we enjoy daily. This is the proper understanding of reality in John 4:23 and 24.

The meaning of truth in John 4:23 and 24 has been either concealed or misunderstood. We have indicated that some Christians have been taught that to worship God in truth is to worship Him in sincerity. Years ago, I heard messages saying that we need to be sincere in our worship of God and that this sincerity is what the Lord Jesus meant by truth in these verses. For example, one may say to the members of a congregation, "You have come to worship God, but your heart is not here. If you are a businessman, your heart may be occupied with your business. This means that you are worshipping God without sincerity. When you worship God, you must forget about other things and worship Him with sincerity. For the worship of God, you need a sincere heart."

To interpret the word truth in John 4:23 and 24 as sincerity is to expound the Word of God in a way that is natural and religious. This interpretation is definitely not according to the divine revelation. The truth of the divine revelation here is that we need to worship God in reality, which is the issue of our enjoyment of the Triune God as reality. If we experience Christ daily, we shall enjoy the Triune God as our reality. This enjoyment will result in a virtue, and this virtue will become our human reality, a reality that is the outcome of the divine reality. Then we should worship God with this reality. This virtue is nothing less than Christ experienced by us, and this Christ is all the offerings. The Christ we have experienced is our sin offering, trespass offering, burnt offering, meal offering, and peace offering.

EXPERIENCING CHRIST AS THE OFFERINGS

As we have fellowship with the Lord in our daily life, we shall be in the light. In the light we see our sinfulness, and we realize that we are wrong in many matters. We may see that we are not right with our husband or wife or with our parents. Then in the light we confess our sins to the Lord, and we enjoy the cleansing of the Lord's precious blood. This is to experience Christ in a practical way as our Redeemer in our daily life.

Experiencing the Lord like this in our daily living, we should then come to the church meetings in our spirit and either offer a prayer or give a testimony of our experience. In our testimony we may say, "Dear saints, recently I was enlightened in my fellowship with God, and I saw that I was wrong in many matters and with certain persons. But I confessed everything to the Lord, and He cleansed me. Now I enjoy Him as my Redeemer and also as my sin offering and trespass offering." This is to offer Christ in the meeting as our sin offering and trespass offering. This is the way to worship God in our spirit with the Christ whom we experience.

As we continue to fellowship with the Lord in the light, we may realize that we should be absolute for God. However, we are not absolute for God, and of ourselves we cannot be absolute. In the course of our fellowship we may be further enlightened of the Spirit to realize that because we cannot be absolute for God, we need Christ as our life. He is the absolute One, and we need Him as our life so that we can live a life that is absolute for God. Spontaneously we may pray, "Lord Jesus, I cannot be absolute for God. But I thank You, Lord, that You are my life. You are absolute for God, and I believe that You can live such an absolute life for me and in me. Lord, I take You as my burnt offering to be my absoluteness." After you experience the Lord in this way, you may come to the church meeting with your experience of Christ. In the meeting you may offer up a prayer in which you present Christ to God as your burnt offering. In such a prayer you may say, "Lord Jesus, I should be absolute for God, but in myself I cannot be absolute. Lord, I thank You that You are my life. When You lived on earth, You were absolute for God, and now You are the One in me who is absolute for God. Lord Jesus, You are my burnt offering." This is to worship God in spirit with the Christ you experience as the burnt offering.

In your daily life, you may also experience Christ as the One feeding you with Himself as the bread of life. This is to experience Christ as your meal offering. Because you experience Christ in this way, You may come to the church meeting with Christ as your meal offering. Then either in prayer or in testimony you may speak concerning Christ as your daily food, as your meal offering.

If we experience Christ as the sin offering, the trespass offering, the burnt offering, and the meal offering, then we shall also experience Him as our peace offering. The peace offering is based upon and constituted of the sin offering, the trespass offering, the burnt offering, and the meal offering. If we experience Christ as these four offerings, certainly we shall enjoy Him as our peace with God and also as our peace with others.

Suppose a brother does not have peace in his married life and family life. If he experiences Christ as the sin offering, the trespass offering, the burnt offering, and the meal offering, he will also experience Christ as peace with his wife and children. Then this brother will be able to come to the church meetings with joy, and praise the Lord for being his peace. He will also be able to testify to the entire universe, including the angels and demons, that he is a peaceful person, a person enjoying peace to the uttermost. He will be able to testify that he has peace with God, with those in his family, with the Body, and even with everything in his environment.

Sometimes we become angry with the situation in our family life or in the church life. The reason for this anger is that we are lacking in the experience of Christ, and, as a result, we do not have Christ as our peace. But if we experience Christ daily as our sin offering, trespass offering, burnt offering, and meal offering, we shall have Christ as our peace in every situation. Then in the meetings of the church we shall be able to offer Christ as our peace offering.

When we come to the church meetings to worship God, we need to worship Him in our spirit. We should also worship God with the very Christ whom we experience day by day, with the Christ who has become our personal reality. In the sight of God, the Christ who is our personal reality is also our personal virtue. We have the highest human virtue, yet this virtue is not of ourselves. Rather, this virtue is the sweetness of the Christ whom we experience. This means that the Christ whom we experience daily becomes our personal virtue, with which we can offer God a pleasant, acceptable worship. When we come to worship God with such a Christ, God is happy with us.

Perhaps now we can understand that in the New Testament truth is not only the Triune God, the Word of God, the contents of the faith, and the reality concerning God, man, and the universe. Truth is also the genuineness, truthfulness, sincerity, honesty, trustworthiness, and faithfulness of God as a divine virtue and of man as a human virtue and as an issue of the divine reality. According to this understanding of truth, this divine virtue first belongs to God, and then through our experience of Christ this virtue also becomes ours. After the divine virtue is experienced by us, it becomes our virtue, a virtue that is an issue of the divine reality.

LIFE-STUDY OF FIRST JOHN

MESSAGE ELEVEN

THE DIVINE LIGHT AND THE DIVINE TRUTH

(3)

Scripture Reading: 1 John 1:5-7

In this message we shall continue to consider the meaning of the word truth in the New Testament.

THE TRUE STATE OF AFFAIRS

We have seen that truth is God, Christ, the Spirit, the Word of God, and the contents of the faith, the reality concerning God, man, and the universe, and the genuineness, truthfulness, and sincerity of God as a divine virtue and of man as a human virtue. In addition to these seven aspects of the truth, we need to see that truth in the New Testament denotes things that are true or real, the true or real state of affairs (facts), reality, veracity, as the opposite of falsehood, deception, dissimulation, hypocrisy, and error (Mark 5:33; 12:32; Luke 4:25; John 16:7; Acts 4:27; 10:34; 26:25; Rom. 1:25; 9:1; 2 Cor. 6:7; 7:14; 12:6; Col. 1:6; 1 Tim. 2:7).

Nearly all these eight aspects of the truth refer to the Triune God. The Triune God, who is the reality of everything, is revealed in the Word and conveyed to us by the Word. What is revealed in and conveyed by the Word is the content of our Christian belief and also the content of the New Testament. This content implies the real situation concerning God, man, the universe, man's relationship to God and to others, and our obligation to God. All these different realities are related to the unique reality, which is the Triune God Himself. Then through our experience of Christ this reality becomes our human reality, that is, it

becomes our human virtue with which we worship God.
Finally, truth refers to things which are true and real.

All the different realities revealed in the New Testament are related either directly or indirectly to the unique
reality—the Triune God. Therefore, for us Christians the
knowledge of what is true or real must come through our
experience of the Triune God.

THE DIVINE REALITY BECOMING OUR GENUINENESS

Of the eight matters we have covered concerning truth,
the first five refer to the same reality in essence. God,
Christ, and the Spirit—the divine Trinity—are essentially
one. Hence, these Three, being the basic elements of the
substance of the divine reality, are actually one reality.
This one divine reality is the substance of the Word of God
as the divine revelation. Hence, it becomes the revealed
divine reality in the divine Word and makes the divine
Word the reality. The divine Word conveys this one divine
reality as the contents of the faith, and the contents of the
faith are the substance of the gospel revealed in the entire
New Testament as its reality, which is just the divine
reality of the divine Trinity. When this divine reality is
partaken of and enjoyed by us, it becomes our genuineness,
sincerity, honesty, and trustworthiness as an excellent
virtue in our behavior to express God, the God of reality, by
whom we live; and we become persons living a life of truth,
without any falsehood or hypocrisy, a life which corresponds to the truth revealed through creation and the
Scripture.

The word *aletheia* is used in the New Testament more
than one hundred times. Its denotation in each occurrence
is determined by its context. For example, in John 3:21,
according to the context, it denotes uprightness (opposite
to evil—vv. 19-20), which is the reality manifested in a man
who lives in God according to what He is and which
corresponds to the divine light, which is God, as the source
of the truth, manifested in Christ. In John 4:23-24,
according to the context of this chapter and also to the
divine revelation of John's Gospel, it denotes the divine

reality becoming man's genuineness and sincerity (opposite to the hypocrisy of the immoral Samaritan worshipper—vv. 16-18) for the true worship of God. The divine reality is Christ who is the truth (John 14:6) as the reality of all the offerings of the Old Testament for God's worship (John 1:29; 3:14) and as the fountain of living water, the life-giving Spirit (John 4:7-15), partaken of and drunk by His believers to be the reality within them, which eventually becomes their genuineness and sincerity in which they worship God with the worship He seeks. In John 5:33 and 18:37, according to the entire revelation of the Gospel of John, truth denotes the divine reality embodied, revealed, and expressed in Christ as the Son of God. In John 8:32, 40, 44-46, according to the context of the chapter, it denotes the reality of God revealed in His word (v. 47) and embodied in Christ the Son of God (v. 36), which sets us free from the bondage of sin.

PRACTICING THE TRUTH

Here in 1 John 1:6 *aletheia* denotes the revealed reality of God in its aspect of the divine light. It is the issue and realization of the divine light in verse 5. The divine light is the source in God. Truth is its issue and realization in us. When we abide in the divine light, which we enjoy in the fellowship of the divine life, we practice the truth—what we have realized in the divine light. When we abide in the source, its issue becomes our practice.

I believe that after a period of time, perhaps another ten years, the truth in the Lord's recovery will be very prevailing. We do not care for numbers. But if several thousand saints can be trained with the truth, the prevailing truth will accomplish much for the Lord's purpose.

GOD REVEALED THROUGH CREATION

Let us now consider certain verses in the Epistles where the word truth is used. In Romans 1:18 Paul says, "For the wrath of God is revealed from heaven upon all ungodliness and unrighteousness of men who hold down the truth in unrighteousness." What is the truth in this verse? In order to answer this question, we need to read verses 19 and 20: "Because that which may be known of God is manifest among them, for God has manifested it to them. For the invisible things of Him from the creation of the world, being apprehended by the things made, are clearly seen, both His eternal power and divinity, for them to be without excuse." According to these verses, the truth in verse 18 means all that God is and all the things concerning God and His existence and the knowledge of them. Therefore, with Romans 1:18-20 as the basis, we may say that truth denotes the reality concerning God, the universe, and man. Because this truth has been manifested, man is without excuse.

Paul goes on to speak further concerning the truth in chapter two of Romans: "But we know that the judgment of God is according to truth upon those who practice such things" (v. 2). What is the truth in this verse? Truth here means the actual situation and condition of man. No doubt, it also refers to the truth in Romans 1:18-20, the truth concerning God's reality being manifested. Those who hold down this truth will one day be judged by God according to it.

In Romans 1:18 truth refers to what God is. According to Romans 1:19 and 20, this truth, this reality, can be known through God's creation. We need to hold to this truth. One day, God will judge according to this truth all those who hold it down.

In Romans 2:20 Paul goes on to say, "An instructor of the foolish, a teacher of babes, having the form of knowledge and of the truth in the law." The law here refers to the Mosaic law. In the Mosaic law there is a certain amount of the divine truth. All human beings should act according to this truth. Otherwise, God will judge them according to it.

I use these verses from the book of Romans to illustrate the fact that in the New Testament the word truth signifies different things. The point concerning the truth we have considered in Romans 1 and 2 is very different from the meaning of truth in the Gospel of John. According to the

Gospel of John, God is incarnated to be the truth, Christ is the truth of the divine life, and the Spirit is the truth, the reality, of Christ. All these matters, of course, concern the Trinity. But the truth in Romans 1 and 2 does not concern the Trinity. Rather, the truth in these chapters is related to what God is, as revealed through creation. Whatever is revealed concerning God through creation is a truth, a reality, and we need to hold on to this truth. Furthermore, truth in these verses from Romans denotes the reality concerning God, the universe, man, man's relationship with God and with others, and man's obligation to God, as revealed through creation and through the Scripture.

THE FAITHFULNESS OF GOD

In Romans 3:7 Paul speaks concerning a different aspect of the truth: "But if the truth of God abounded in my lie unto His glory, why still am I also judged as a sinner?" In this verse truth refers to the faithfulness of God. This, of course, is different from the meaning of truth in 1:18, where truth denotes the characteristic of God as revealed through the visible things in the universe. But in Romans 3:7 we have another matter concerning God— God's faithfulness.

How can we prove that the truth in Romans 3:7 denotes God's faithfulness? This can be proved by studying the context. Verses 3 and 4 say, "For what if some disbelieved? Shall their unbelief make the faithfulness of God of none effect? Certainly not! But let God be true and every man a liar, as it is written, That You should be justified in Your sayings and will overcome when You are judged." Notice that in verse 3 the word "faithfulness" is used. Then in verse 4 we have the adjective "true." Verse 4 indicates that God is true, faithful, in what He says; that is, God is faithful in His words. In verses 5 and 6 Paul continues, "But if our unrighteousness commends the righteousness of God, what shall we say? Is God unrighteous who inflicts wrath? I speak according to man. Certainly not! Otherwise how shall God judge the world?" These verses also are related to God's faithfulness. Then in verse 7 Paul goes on

to speak concerning the truth of God. According to the
context, therefore, truth here denotes God's faithfulness.
Instead of saying "the truth of God," Paul could have said,
"the faithfulness of God," since truth here equals faithfulness. This is the reason we interpret the word truth in
Romans 3:7 as denoting God's faithfulness.

Romans 15:8 says, "For I say that Christ has become a
servant of the circumcision for the truth of God, to confirm
the promises given to the fathers." In this verse truth also
denotes God's faithfulness. If we do not understand the
word truth in this verse as referring to God's faithfulness,
we shall not be able to understand this verse. Christ
became a servant of the circumcision for the truth of God, to
confirm the promises. This means that Christ became a
servant of the circumcision for the faithfulness of God, to
confirm the promises. Here Paul indicates that whatever
God has promised, He will fulfill. God fulfills His promises
because He is faithful. Once again, we see that truth in
Romans 3:7 and 15:8 refers to a particular virtue of God,
God's faithfulness.

THE HUMAN VIRTUE OF HONESTY

Mark 12:14 says, "And when they were come, they say
unto him, Master, we know that thou art true, and carest
for no man; for thou regardest not the person of men, but
teachest the way of God in truth: Is it lawful to give tribute
to Caesar, or not?" The Pharisees were trying to trap the
Lord Jesus by asking Him this question. Before they asked
the question, they said to Him that He was true and taught
the way of God in truth. Here "in truth" means in honesty.
Because the Lord was true and honest, He taught the Word
of God in honesty, not in falsehood. Therefore, in this verse
truth denotes the human virtue of honesty.

In 2 Corinthians 11:10 the word truth is again used to
denote a human virtue. In this verse Paul says, "The
truth of Christ is in me, that this boasting shall not be
stopped concerning me in the regions of Achaia." Here
truth denotes truthfulness, faithfulness, trustworthiness,
honesty. First, it denotes the faithfulness, the honesty, of

the Lord Jesus when He lived on earth as a man. Then it denotes this virtue as present in the living of the Apostle Paul. This virtue was an attribute of Christ. But since Paul lived by Christ, whatever Christ is became his virtue in his behavior. The important point for us to see is that in 2 Corinthians 11:10 truth denotes the human virtue of truthfulness, trustworthiness, faithfulness, and honesty.

First John 3:18 tells us to love in truth: "Little children, let us not love in word nor in tongue, but in deed and truth." Here truth denotes sincerity in contrast to tongue, just as deed is in contrast to word. In this verse the Apostle John is telling us to love in truth, in honesty. If we say that we love our brother, we should love him in deed and in truth. Otherwise, we shall love only in word or in tongue, but not in sincerity.

LOVING IN TRUTH AND KNOWING THE TRUTH

In 2 John 1 the Apostle John uses the word truth in two ways: "The elder to the chosen lady and to her children, whom I love in truth, and not only I, but also all those who have known the truth." First, John speaks of loving in truth. In this case truth denotes the revealed divine reality—the Triune God dispensed into man in the Son Jesus Christ—becoming man's genuineness and sincerity. Therefore, truth in this sense denotes a human virtue. However, this virtue is not produced by our natural being; rather, it issues from the enjoyment of the divine reality. This is the divine reality becoming our genuineness and our sincerity. In this verse John also speaks of knowing the truth. Here truth denotes the divine reality of the gospel, especially concerning the Person of Christ.

I use these verses as examples to point out our need to study all the verses in the New Testament that speak of the truth. Then with the help of the note on the word truth in 1 John 1:6, we can discern how this word is used in different verses. As 2 John 1 indicates, this word may be used in two different ways in the same verse. In each case, the denotation of the word is determined by the context. Therefore, to understand the meaning of the word truth in any particular verse, we need to study its context. As we have pointed out, the Greek word for truth, *aletheia*, is used in the New Testament more than one hundred times. By studying this word in its context, we shall be helped to have a proper understanding of truth in the New Testament.

LIFE-STUDY OF FIRST JOHN

MESSAGE TWELVE

CONDITIONS OF THE DIVINE FELLOWSHIP

(4)

Scripture Reading: 1 John 1:8-10

In this message we shall consider further the conditions of the divine fellowship.

LEADING OURSELVES ASTRAY

In 1:8 John says, "If we say that we do not have sin, we are deceiving ourselves, and the truth is not in us." To say that we do not have sin is to say that we do not have indwelling sin (Rom.7:17) within our nature. This is what the Gnostic heresy teaches. The apostle is inoculating the believers against this false teaching. This section, 1:7—2:2, deals with the believers' sinning after regeneration, which interrupts their fellowship with God. If after regeneration the believers do not have sin in their nature, how could they sin in their conduct? Even though they sin only occasionally, not habitually, their sinning is an adequate proof that they still have sin working within them. Otherwise, there would be no interruption to their fellowship with God. The apostle's teaching here also condemns today's teaching of perfectionism, that a state of freedom from sin is attainable or has been attained in the earthly life, and it annuls today's wrong teaching of the eradication of the sinful nature, which, by misinterpreting the word in 3:9 and 5:18, says that regenerated persons cannot sin because their sinful nature has been totally eradicated.

The Greek words rendered "we are deceiving ourselves" can also be translated "we are leading ourselves astray." To say that we do not have sin, because we have been regenerated, is self-deceiving. This denies the actual fact of our experience and causes us to lead ourselves astray.

Truth in verse 8 denotes the revealed reality of God, the real facts, conveyed in the gospel, such as the reality of God and all the divine things, which are all Christ (John 1:14, 17; 14:6); the reality of Christ and all the spiritual things, which are all the Spirit (John 14:17; 15:26; 16:13; 1 John 5:6), and the reality of man's condition (John 16:8-11). Here it denotes especially our sinful condition after regeneration under the enlightenment of the divine light in our fellowship with God. If we say we do not have sin after being regenerated, such a reality, the truth, does not remain in us; that is, we deny our true post-regeneration condition.

CONFESSING OUR SINS

In verse 9 John goes on to say, "If we confess our sins, He is faithful and righteous that He may forgive us our sins and cleanse us from all unrighteousness." Confession here denotes the confession of our sins, our failures, after regeneration, not the confession of our sins before regeneration.

God is faithful in His word (v. 10) and righteous in the blood of Jesus His Son (v. 7). His word is the word of the truth of His gospel (Eph.1:13), which tells us that He will forgive us our sins because of Christ (Acts 10:43), and the blood of Christ has fulfilled His righteous requirements that He may forgive us our sins (Matt. 26:28). If we confess our sins, He, according to His word and based upon the redemption through the blood of Jesus, forgives us, because He must be faithful in His word and righteous in the blood of Jesus. Otherwise, He would be unfaithful and unrighteous. Our confession is needed for His forgiveness. Such forgiveness of God for the restoration of our fellowship with Him is conditional and depends on our confession.

In verse 9 John speaks of both forgiveness and cleansing. For God to forgive us is for Him to release us from the offense of our sins. For Him to cleanse us is for Him to wash us from the stain of our unrighteousness.

"Unrighteousness" and "sins" are synonyms. All unrighteousness is sin (1 John 5:17). Both unrighteousness
and sins refer to our wrongdoings. Sins indicate the
offense of our wrongdoings against God and men; unrighteousness indicates the stain of our wrongdoings that we
are not right either with God or with men. The offense
needs God's forgiveness, and the stain requires His
cleansing. Both God's forgiveness and His cleansing are
needed for the restoration of our fellowship with Him that
has been broken so that we may enjoy Him in un-
interrupted fellowship with a good conscience void of
offense (1 Tim. 1:5; Acts 24:16).

OUR SINFUL CONDITION AFTER REGENERATION

Verse 10 says, "If we say that we have not sinned, we
make Him a liar, and His word is not in us." Verse 8 proves
that after regeneration we still have sin inwardly. Verse 10
proves further that we even still sin outwardly, though not
habitually. We still sin outwardly in our conduct because
we still have sin inwardly in our nature. Both verses
confirm our sinful condition after regeneration. In speaking of such a condition, the apostle uses the pronoun "we."
This indicates that he does not exclude himself.

The "word" in verse 10 is the word of God's revelation,
which is the word of reality (Eph. 1:13; John 17:17) and
which conveys the contents of God's New Testament
economy. It is synonymous with truth in verse 8. In this
word God exposes our true sinful condition both before and
after regeneration. If we say that we have not sinned after
regeneration, we make Him a liar and deny the word of His
revelation.

We have pointed out that verse 8 refers to indwelling sin
and that verse 10 refers to the act of sinning. Indwelling
sin is the sin we inherited through our natural birth. This
sin came into mankind through Adam, and now it dwells
in our nature. Even after we have been saved and
regenerated, sin remains in our fallen flesh. This is the
reason our body needs to be redeemed at the time of the
Lord's coming back. When the Lord Jesus comes back, our

body will be redeemed, transfigured, by the Lord's power (Phil. 3:21). This means that the Lord's power will change our body into a glorious body. Then indwelling sin will no longer be a part of us, for there will be no sin in our transfigured body. In verse 8 John says that if we say that, after we have been regenerated, we no longer have indwelling sin, we are deceived.

In verse 10 John tells us that if we say that, after we have been regenerated, we have not sinned, we make God a liar. The reason we make God a liar if we say that we have not sinned is that in His word of revelation, the Bible, He tells us clearly that we can still sin after we have been regenerated. But if we say that we have not sinned after we have been regenerated, we make God a liar. This means that the word of His revelation is not in us.

These verses indicate clearly that after regeneration we still have indwelling sin, and it is still possible for us to sin. We need to admit these facts. First, we must admit that, even though we have been regenerated, we still have sin dwelling in our flesh. If we neglect this fact, we shall be deceived and misled. As a result, we may indulge in sin.

In the past I heard of certain Christians who claimed that after they received the baptism in the Spirit and spoke in tongues, they no longer had sin within them. Yet in their experience they became involved in very sinful situations. They were deceived in thinking that because they had experienced the baptism of the Spirit they no longer had sin dwelling within them.

Even if you experience the baptism in the Holy Spirit and speak in tongues, the sinful nature is still within you. We should never believe that this nature has been eradicated. The sinful nature will remain in our flesh until the Lord Jesus comes back and by His divine power transfigures our fallen body.

We all need to admit that we have a sinful nature. I can testify that, as one who has been a Christian for more than fifty years, I have the deep conviction, the deep inner sense, that my sinful nature still remains. No matter how spiritual a believer may be, he still has indwelling sin in the flesh. We all need to realize this and admit it. This will keep us from being misled.

THE TEACHING CONCERNING SINLESS PERFECTION

In the past certain Christians have taught that a believer can reach the state of sinless perfection. I would not say that this teaching is heretical; however, this teaching is surely mistaken. Some who teach perfectionism use the Lord's word in Matthew 5:48 about being perfect as our heavenly Father is perfect. They also may misapply such verses as Hebrews 6:1 and 1 Corinthians 2:6. In these two verses the word "perfect" actually means mature or full-grown.

It is not correct to teach that we Christians may have a so-called second blessing and thereafter become sinlessly perfect. If we ever reach such a condition, we can maintain it only temporarily. Suppose one day you have a rich experience of the Lord early in the morning. As a result, for a few hours you may be sinlessly perfect. But then you may become careless again and fail the Lord.

Certain verses in the New Testament indicate that we can be perfect. The Lord's word in Matthew 5:48 about being perfect as our heavenly Father is perfect indicates that we can be perfect in this way. Otherwise, the Lord never would have spoken this word. However, it is a mistake to think that if we reach a state of perfection, we can remain in that state forever. Some believers have either exaggerated their experience of perfection or have gone too far in describing what they experienced. The point we are making here is that we should not think that we can reach a permanent state of perfection. We may be perfect today, but we may fall tomorrow. Before the Lord Jesus comes back to transfigure our body, we cannot be permanently in a condition of sinless perfection.

GOD'S FAITHFULNESS AND RIGHTEOUSNESS

We need to admit that after regeneration we still have sin; that is, we still have indwelling sin in our sinful nature. Because we still have sin within us, there is the possibility that we may sin. Whenever we sin, we need to confess. Then God will be faithful in the word of His new covenant to forgive us our sins. In the gospel, which is the new covenant, God promises that He will forgive us our sins because of the redemption of Christ. Therefore, if we confess our sins, God must be faithful to keep His word. If God would not forgive us, this would mean that He contradicts His own word. In such a case, God would not be faithful. However, we may have the assurance that as long as we confess our sins through the redemption of Christ, God must forgive us, for He must be faithful in His word.

In verse 9 John also tells us that God is righteous to cleanse us from all unrighteousness. Why must God be righteous to cleanse us in this way? God must be righteous to cleanse us from unrighteousness because He judged the Lord Jesus on the cross as our Substitute, putting all our sins upon Him. Because God has judged Christ for us, His blood is efficacious to cleanse us. Therefore, when we confess our sins through His blood, God has no choice but to forgive us. For example, suppose you owe an amount of money to a certain person. A friend of yours pays this debt for you, and the other party receives the payment. Now that party cannot righteously claim the payment from you, for the debt has already been paid. In a similar way, God has received payment for our sins through the death of Christ on the cross. Now whenever we confess our sins to God through the blood of the redemption of Christ on the cross, God must forgive us. In this matter He has no choice. He must be righteous.

God is faithful in His word, and He is righteous in His acts. In His word God must be faithful, and in His acts He must be righteous. Here we see the difference between faithfulness and righteousness.

FORGIVENESS AND CLEANSING

What is the difference between forgiving and cleansing? In order to know this difference, we need to know the difference between sins and unrighteousness. Sins refer to offenses, and unrighteousness is the mark, the stain, on our behavior caused by the committing of an offense. Whenever we sin, we commit an offense. This offense then becomes a stain on our behavior, and this stain is unrighteousness. For instance, suppose you buy two items, but you are charged only for one. If you pay for just one item, that will be an act of sinning against the store. With respect to the person who sold you the items, that is an offense. But with respect to your character, that is a mark of unrighteousness. For this reason, others would not say that you are sinful, but would say that you are unright-eous.

In a similar way, when we commit sins before God, with respect to God those sins are offenses. But with respect to us, they are stains of unrighteousness. We need to confess our sins. Then, on the one hand, God forgives our sins, our offenses. On the other hand, God washes away the mark, the stain, of our unrighteousness. This is the reason John in 1:9 speaks both of the forgiveness of sins and the cleansing from unrighteousness. The forgiveness of sins is actually the cleansing, the washing away, of the stain of our unrighteousness.

THE RESTORATION OF FELLOWSHIP

The writing of the Apostle John in these verses is tender and delicate. In verse 6 he says, "If we say that we have fellowship with Him and walk in darkness, we lie and are not practicing the truth." Then in verse 8 he goes on to say, "If we say that we do not have sin, we are deceiving ourselves, and the truth is not in us." In verse 10 he says, "If we say that we have not sinned, we make Him a liar, and His word is not in us." But in verse 9 John tells us, "If we confess our sins, He is faithful and righteous that He may forgive us our sins and cleanse us from all unright-eousness." God is faithful in His word to forgive our offenses, and He is righteous in His acts to cleanse away the stain of unrighteousness. Through God's forgiveness and cleansing, the offense is forgiven, and the mark is cleansed. The result is that our fellowship with God is fully recovered.

Fellowship with God is broken by sin and unrighteousness. But when sin is forgiven and the stain of unrighteousness is cleansed, our fellowship with God is restored. Once again we have the enjoyment of the divine life through our fellowship with the Father and the Son.

OFFERING CHRIST AS OUR SIN OFFERING
AND TRESPASS OFFERING

According to typology, the children of Israel had to offer the sin offering and the trespass offering. By presenting these offerings to God, they were actually making a confession to Him. The fact that they offered the trespass offering and the sin offering indicated that they realized they were sinful and that they had committed sins.

Some might argue that the types of the trespass offering and the sin offering in the Old Testament have nothing to do with us, since the Lord Jesus has come to be the fulfillment of all the offerings. Yes, the Lord Jesus is the fulfillment of the offerings. But what about your situation and condition as a believer in Christ? Do you not have sin within you? Do you not sometimes commit sin? What, then, should you do about indwelling sin and about the sins you commit occasionally? You need to confess that you still have indwelling sin and that you still commit sins, even though you do not sin habitually. To make such a confession to the Lord is to offer Christ to God as your sin offering and as your trespass offering.

Every day, and throughout the day, we need the Lord as our sin offering and trespass offering. I can testify that in my experience I need the Lord as my sin offering and trespass offering morning, noon, and night. I may have a pleasant time enjoying the Lord, but then a few minutes later I may be stumbled by something or someone.

GOD'S PROMISE AND OUR CONFESSION

Because we still have sin in us and because we still sin occasionally, we need to make confession to the Lord. We cannot say that we have no sin or that we have not sinned. Praise the Lord for the strong promise in verse 9 that if we confess our sins, God is faithful and righteous to forgive us our sins and to cleanse us from all unrighteousness. Therefore, we should not be bothered by indwelling sin, and, once we have made confession and received the Lord's forgiveness and cleansing, we should not be bothered by the sins we have committed.

The promise in 1:9 should never be misused as an encouragement to sin. This means that we should not think that we may go out to commit sin and then confess and receive the Lord's cleansing. This concept leads to Antinomianism, the concept that because we are under grace we are free from every regulation and can indulge in sin. As we shall see, in 2:1 John says, "These things I write to you that you may not sin." John wrote with the expectation that we would not sin. Nevertheless, we have the promise in 1:9 that if we do sin, we may be forgiven and cleansed, provided we make confession of our sin to God.

A BALANCED VIEW

I believe that we have seen a balanced view concerning the matter of sin after our regeneration. By now we all should be clear that after regeneration we still have sin in our nature and that it is still possible for us to commit sin. Do not believe that because you have been regenerated you no longer have sin in your nature or that you can no longer sin. This is a deception. Because we still have sin in our nature, it is always possible for us to sin. If you sin, you need to confess your sin to God. He has promised in His gospel to forgive us, and He will be faithful in His word. Furthermore, in redemption God judged Christ on our behalf. This means that He will not judge us for our sins if we confess them through the redemption of Christ. As the righteous God, He will surely cleanse us from our unrighteousness. In this way we may preserve our fellowship with Him and enjoy Him day by day.

We have pointed out that we should not believe that we

can be forever perfect before the Lord comes to transfigure our body. This is the mistaken concept concerning perfectionism. We believe that by the Lord's grace we can overcome and be perfect. However, this overcoming and perfection are not once for all. There is always a possibility that we may sin again. Therefore, we need to be in fear and trembling and on the alert lest we be damaged through the sin that dwells in our flesh. Day by day, we need to look to the Lord, pray, and be watchful. In case we fail and commit sin, we should make confession to the Lord. He will be faithful and righteous to forgive us and cleanse us by the blood of His Son, Jesus Christ.

LIFE-STUDY OF FIRST JOHN

MESSAGE THIRTEEN

CONDITIONS OF THE DIVINE FELLOWSHIP

(5)

Scripture Reading: 1 John 2:1-2

In this message we shall consider verses 1 and 2 of chapter two.

LITTLE CHILDREN

In 2:1 John says, "My little children, these things I write to you that you may not sin. And if anyone sins, we have an Advocate with the Father, Jesus Christ the Righteous." By using the expression "my little children" John was addressing all the believers regardless of age. The Greek word rendered "children" is *teknia*, plural of *teknion*, little child, diminutive of *teknon*, child, a word often used in addresses from elder to younger persons. "It is a term of parental affection. It applies to Christians irrespective of growth. Used in vv. 12, 28; 3:7, 18; 4:4; 5:21; John 13:33; Gal. 4:19" (Darby). The aged apostle considered all the recipients of his Epistle his dear little children in the Lord. In verses 13-27 he classified them into three groups: young children, young men, and fathers. Hence, verses 1-12 and 28-29 are addressed to all the recipients in general; verses 13-27 are addressed to the three groups respectively according to their growth in the divine life.

JOHN'S INTENTION

In 2:1 John tells the little children that he writes "these things" to them. These are the things mentioned in 1:5-10 regarding the committing of sin by the children of God, the regenerated believers, who have the divine life and participate in its fellowship (1:1-4).

John tells the recipients of this Epistle that he writes to them that they "may not sin." These words and the words "if anyone sins" in the following sentence indicate that the regenerated believers may still sin. Though they possess the divine life, it is still possible for them to sin if they do not live by the divine life and abide in its fellowship. In Greek the word "sins" here is an aorist subjunctive and denotes a single act, not habitual action.

In the words "that you may not sin" we see John's intention in what he writes concerning sin, the confessing of sins, and the receiving of God's forgiveness and cleansing. John's intention, his purpose, was that we would not sin. As he indicates in chapter one, if we sin, our fellowship with the Father will be broken. If we would maintain this fellowship, we need to keep ourselves from sinning. This is the main purpose of what John writes in chapter one of this Epistle.

In chapter one John shows us that we have received the divine life and that this life has brought us into the divine fellowship. In the divine fellowship we receive light, and now we should walk in the light as God is in the light (1:5,7). However, we need to realize that we still have the problem of indwelling sin, and regarding this sin we need to be on the alert. Even after our regeneration, the sin that came into the human race through Adam remains in our flesh. Although our spirit has been regenerated, God's life has been imparted into our spirit, and God's Spirit dwells in our spirit, nevertheless sin continues to dwell in our flesh. We need to admit the fact that we have dwelling in our flesh the sin that came into mankind through Adam. We also need to be on guard lest we commit sins. If we are not on the alert, we shall sin, and our sins will interrupt our fellowship with God. As a result of the breaking of our fellowship with Him, we shall lose the enjoyment of the divine life.

We may say that in chapter one we have a warning, a reminder, and a charge concerning our need to be on the alert. Yes, we have received the divine life, and the divine life is now our enjoyment, issuing in the fellowship with the Triune God. This is wonderful! But we need to realize that there is still the problem of indwelling sin. Because sin dwells in our flesh, there is always the possibility that our enjoyment of the divine life may be interrupted through the committing of sin.

If we do not realize that sin still dwells in our flesh but instead are deceived regarding this matter, we shall certainly sin. Then we shall lose the enjoyment of the divine life. Therefore, if we would remain in the enjoyment of the divine life and in the fellowship of the divine life, we need to realize that we have sin in our flesh and that sin is crouching, waiting for the opportunity to damage us, break our fellowship with the Triune God, and keep us from the enjoyment of the divine life received through regeneration.

Now we can see John's purpose in writing chapter one. Because he did not want the believers to lose the enjoyment of the divine life, he told them in 2:1, "I write to you that you may not sin." This was John's intention and also his expectation. Moreover, this word is also a warning and a reminder concerning the committing of sin.

AN ADVOCATE WITH THE FATHER

In 2:1 John says, "If anyone sins, we have an Advocate with the Father, Jesus Christ the Righteous." John did not have the confidence that the believers would always be able to keep themselves from sinning. He knew that even though we may be alert concerning the sin that dwells in our flesh, we may still sin. Therefore, he tells us that if we sin, we have an Advocate with the Father.

The Greek word rendered Advocate is *parakletos*, and it denotes one who is called to another's side to aid him, hence, a helper; one who offers legal aid or one who intercedes on behalf of someone else, hence, an advocate, counsel, or intercessor. The word denotes consoling and consolation, hence, a consoler, a comforter. Paraclete is its anglicized form. This word is used in the Gospel of John (14:16, 26; 15:26; 16:7) for the Spirit of reality as our

Comforter within us, caring for our cause or affairs. It is used here for the Lord Jesus as our Advocate with the Father, the One who cares for our case, intercedes on our behalf (Rom. 8:34), and pleads for us if we sin. This interceding and pleading is based upon His propitiation.

In chapter one John speaks concerning the redeeming blood of Christ that constantly cleanses us as we walk in the light. But in this verse John goes further to show us a Person, who is our Advocate with the Father. Hence, in the divine provision we have the blood of Christ and also the Person of Christ as our Advocate.

The Comforter in the Heavens and the Comforter in Our Spirit

As we have seen, "Advocate" is a translation of the Greek word *parakletos*. This word is formed of two words: the preposition *para* (used here as a prefix) and the word *kletos*. Put together, these words denote someone called to our side. The Greek word *parakletos* is used in the New Testament only by John. In his Gospel John says, "And I will ask the Father, and He will give you another Comforter, that He may be with you forever" (14:16). This indicates that while the Lord was with the disciples, one *parakletos*, one Comforter, was there with them. But this *parakletos* was about to leave. Thus, there was the need for another *parakletos*, another Comforter, to come. Actually, the first *parakletos* and the other *parakletos* are one. The One who is called "another Comforter" is now in us as the life-giving Spirit, and the One who was the first Comforter, the Lord Jesus Christ, is now in the heavens at the right hand of God.

We may use electricity as an illustration of these two Comforters. On the one hand, electricity is in the power plant. On the other hand, electricity has been installed into our homes. We may say, therefore, that with electricity there are two ends: one end in the power plant and the other end in our homes. As the electricity flows from the power plant, where it is stored, to our homes, where it is applied, these two ends are connected. We may compare the electricity in the power plant to the Comforter, the Lord Jesus, in the heavens, and the electricity in our homes to the other Comforter, the life-giving Spirit in our spirit. In the heavens we have the Lord Jesus Christ as our Comforter, and in our spirit we have the Spirit as another Comforter. However, these two are one. For this reason, the Greek word *parakletos* is used for both the Comforter in the heavens and the Comforter in our spirit.

In the Recovery Version we translate *parakletos* as Comforter in John 14:16 and as Advocate in 1 John 2:1. In John 14:26 and 15:26 this Greek word is also translated Comforter. Comforter is an appropriate translation of *parakletos* in John 14:16, for in this verse there is a certain feeling that this Paraclete comes to comfort the disciples in their sorrow caused by the Lord's leaving them. The Lord had told His disciples that He was leaving, and they were troubled by this. Therefore, in this chapter the Lord indicated to the disciples that they did not need to be sorrowful, for He would ask the Father to send them another Paraclete, another Comforter. Because the troubled disciples were in need of comfort, it is correct to render *parakletos* in John 14:26 as Comforter. This Greek word does imply the thought of comfort; it refers to one who helps us, serves us, stands by us, and goes along with us. Such a one surely is a comforter.

A Spiritual Attorney

It is also correct to translate *parakletos* in 1 John 2:1 as Advocate. According to the usage in ancient times, this Greek word may refer to a person who functions as an attorney, a legal advocate. The situation in 1 John 2:1 is different from that in John 14:16; it is a situation that requires an advocate or attorney. However, the word "attorney" does not seem fitting to use in the actual translation of the Word. Therefore, after much consideration, we selected the word Advocate.

The Advocate in 2:1 is actually a spiritual attorney. This *parakletos* stands beside us, like a nurse caring for us, and serves us. The *parakletos* is also a counselor. At school the students have a counselor to help them choose the right courses. Our *parakletos* also helps us in making choices. In his translation of 1 John 2:1 J. N. Darby uses the word "patron." In his note he explains that the word patron is used in the sense of a Roman patron, who maintained the interest of his client in every way. One function of a Roman patron was much like that of an attorney today. When we are in a particular kind of situation, we may give the entire matter over into the hands of an attorney. The attorney then takes care of our case. This is the function of our Advocate in 2:1.

Parakletos is an all-inclusive word. It implies the thought of helping and nourishing, the thought of counseling, and also the thought of consoling. It includes the concept of an advocate, an attorney, who takes care of our case.

With the Father

John tells us in 2:1 that we have an Advocate with the Father. The phrase "with the Father" is used also in 1:2. In each case the Greek word translated "with " is *pros*, with the accusative, a preposition of motion, implying living, acting, in union and communion with. The Lord Jesus as our Advocate is living in communion with the Father.

John's use of Father as the divine title here indicates that our case, which the Lord Jesus as our Advocate undertakes for us, is a family affair, a case between children and the Father. Through regeneration we have been born children of God. After regeneration, in case we sin, it is a matter of children sinning against their Father. Our Advocate, who is our propitiation, undertakes for our sinning to restore our interrupted fellowship with the Father so that we may abide in the enjoyment of the divine fellowship.

In the past I wondered why John told us that we have an Advocate with the Father. An advocate is someone involved in cases of law. We can easily see why we may need an advocate, an attorney, with the judge in a court of law. But why do we need an advocate with our Father? The answer to this question is that the "case" of our sins after regeneration is a matter involving the Father and the family "law court." Whenever we sin, we offend our Father. Our judge, therefore, is a Father-judge, our court is our spiritual home, and our case is a family matter. But we do have a member of our family, our elder Brother, the Lord Jesus, who is our Advocate with the Father. As our Advocate, our elder Brother takes our case. This is the reason John does not say that we have an Advocate with God, but says that we have an Advocate with the Father.

A child may have the mistaken idea that because his father loves him, he can do anything he wants at home with his family. Of course, this is not the case. Although our Father loves us, any sins we commit are an offense against Him. Yes, God is our Father. But if we sin, He will have a case against us. Therefore, in our spiritual family we sometimes need an Advocate.

In this verse we have two important titles—Advocate and Father. The title Father indicates that we are in the divine family enjoying the Father's love. The title Advocate indicates that we may be wrong in certain matters and need someone to take our case. Hence, in family life we need our elder Brother to be our Advocate who takes our case.

The truth in the Bible is always presented in a balanced way. The truth in this verse is also balanced. On the one hand, the title Father is a sign of love; on the other hand, the title Advocate is a sign of righteousness. For example, a father loves his child. But if the child misbehaves, the father will have a case against him, a case based on righteousness. Although the child is still loved by his father and will continue to be taken care of by him, the father has a case against the child and may need to discipline him. In a similar way, whenever we sin, the Father has a case against us. Therefore, we need a heavenly attorney. We need Jesus Christ, our elder Brother, to be our Advocate.

We have emphasized the fact that Christ is our Advocate with the Father. Please notice that John does not

say that we have an Advocate with God, or that we have
the Son with the Father. Rather, he tells us that if we sin,
we have an Advocate with the Father.

JESUS CHRIST THE RIGHTEOUS

According to John's word in 2:1 our Advocate with the
Father is Jesus Christ the Righteous. Our Lord Jesus is the
only righteous Man among all men. His righteous act
(Rom. 5:18) on the cross fulfilled the righteous requirement
of the righteous God for us and all sinners. Only He is
qualified to be our Advocate to care for us in our sinning
condition and restore us to a righteous condition so that
our Father, who is righteous, may be appeased.

Instead of saying "Jesus Christ the Righteous," we may
say "Jesus Christ, the right One." Jesus Christ certainly is
the One who is right, the right One, and only this right
One can be our Advocate with the Father. The reason we
have a problem and the Father has a case against us is
that we are the wrong ones. Because we are the ones who
are wrong, we need the righteous One to take care of our
case.

A PROPITIATION CONCERNING OUR SINS

In 2:2 John goes on to say, "And He is a propitiation
concerning our sins, and not concerning ours only, but also
concerning the whole world." The Greek word for propitiation here and in 4:10 is *hilasmos*. In 1:7 we have the blood
of Jesus; in 2:1 the Person of Christ as our Advocate; and
now, in 2:2 we have Christ as a propitiation concerning our
sins. Our Advocate, who shed His blood for the cleansing
of our sins, is our propitiation. This word "propitiation"
indicates appeasing or peacemaking. When a child is
wrong and his father has a case against him, there is no
peace between them. In such a situation, there is the need
of peacemaking and of appeasing the father. This peacemaking, this appeasing, is propitiation.

As an aid to understanding the word propitiation in 2:2,
it will be helpful to review what Paul says in Romans 3:25
regarding the propitiation-cover: "Whom God set forth a

propitiation-cover through faith in His blood, for the showing forth of His righteousness in respect of the passing by of the sins that occurred before in the forbearance of God." The Greek word for propitiation here is *hilasterion*. This word is different from *hilasmos* in 1 John 2:2 and 4:10 and *hilaskomai* in Hebrews 2:17. *Hilasmos* is "that which propitiates," that is, a propitiatory sacrifice. In 1 John 2:2 and 4:10 the Lord Jesus is the propitiatory sacrifice for our sins. *Hilaskomai* means "to appease, to reconcile one by satisfying the other's demand," that is, to propitiate. In Hebrews 2:17 the Lord Jesus makes propitiation for our sins to reconcile us to God by satisfying God's righteous demands on us. But *hilasterion* is "the place of propitiation." Therefore, in Hebrews 9:5 this word is used for the cover, the lid, of the ark (translated "mercy seat" in the King James Version) within the Holy of Holies. In Exodus 25:16-22 and Leviticus 16:12-16, the Septuagint also uses this word for the cover of the ark. The law of the Ten Commandments was in the ark, exposing and condemning by its righteous requirement the sin of the people who came to contact God. By the lid of the ark with the atoning blood sprinkled upon it on the day of atonement, the whole situation on the sinner's side was fully covered. Hence, it was upon this lid that God could meet with those who broke His righteous law without, governmentally, any contradiction of His righteousness, even under the observing of the cherubim that bore His glory overshadowing the lid of the ark. The propitiatory or expiatory sacrifice, which foreshadowed Christ, satisfied all the requirements of God's righteousness and glory. As a result, God could pass by the people's sin that occurred at that time. Furthermore, in order to show forth His righteousness, God had to do this. This is what is referred to in Romans 3:25. For this reason, Romans 3:25 uses the same word, *hilasterion*, to reveal that the Lord Jesus is the propitiation place, the propitiation-cover, whom God set forth for showing forth His righteousness by passing by the sins of the Old Testament saints, for, as the propitiatory sacrifice, He made the full propitiation on the cross for their sins and fully satisfied the requirements of God's righteousness and glory.

The Lord Jesus Christ has offered Himself to God as a sacrifice for our sins (Heb. 9:28), not only for our redemption but also for God's satisfaction. In Him as our Substitute, through His vicarious death, God is satisfied and appeased. Hence, Christ is the propitiation between God and us.

John says in 2:2 that Christ is the propitiation not only concerning our sins, but also concerning the whole world. The Lord Jesus as a propitiation concerning man's sins is for the sins of the whole world. However, this propitiation is conditional upon man's receiving it by believing in the Lord. Unbelievers do not experience its efficacy, not because it has any fault, but due to their unbelief.

LIFE-STUDY OF FIRST JOHN

CONDITIONS OF THE DIVINE FELLOWSHIP

(6)

Scripture Reading: 1 John 2:1-2

In this message we shall continue to consider 2:1-2.

In verse 1 John says, "My little children, these things I write to you that you may not sin. And if anyone sins, we have an Advocate with the Father, Jesus Christ the Righteous." We have seen that here John tells his little children, all the recipients of this Epistle, that his intention in writing was that they would not sin. But if anyone sins, we have an Advocate, a helper or counsel, with the Father, Jesus Christ the Righteous.

In verse 2 John goes on to say that Christ is "a propitiation concerning our sins, and not concerning ours only, but also concerning the whole world." As we have pointed out, the Lord Jesus Christ has offered Himself to God as a sacrifice for our sins, not only for our redemption but also for God's satisfaction. His vicarious death satisfied God and appeased Him. Hence, He is the propitiation between God and us. As the propitiation concerning man's sins, the Lord Jesus is for the sins of the whole world. However, this propitiation is conditional upon our receiving it by believing in the Lord.

THE BLOOD OF JESUS
AND THE ADVOCATE WITH THE FATHER

John's writing in this Epistle is tender and delicate. When I first read chapter one years ago, I was very happy. However, I did not understand why John added 2:1-2. It seemed to me that the problem of sin had been fully solved in chapter one, and I thought that these verses in chapter

two were not necessary. Later I came to appreciate the
importance of these verses.

According to chapter one of this Epistle, we have
received the divine life, and we are enjoying it in the
fellowship of life. In this fellowship we receive the divine
light, and in this light we practice the truth. But we still
need the warning concerning the sin that dwells in our
flesh. We need to be careful and on the alert regarding
indwelling sin.

Whenever we sin, we need to confess our sin to God. If
we confess our sins, God is faithful in His word to forgive
us our sins, and He is righteous in His redemption to
cleanse us from all unrighteousness. This is wonderful.
Nevertheless, as 2:1-2 indicates, we still need a Person, an
Advocate with the Father, to take care of our case. Because
we are not capable of handling the case ourselves, we need
a heavenly attorney.

In chapter one John speaks of the blood of Jesus, and in
chapter two, of our Advocate. Not only has God provided
the blood of Jesus Christ, which was shed for us so that we
may be forgiven and cleansed; God has also prepared
Christ as our Advocate. First, the Lord Jesus shed His
blood as the price of our redemption. Then after shedding
His blood, He becomes our Advocate, our heavenly
attorney, taking care of our case. How marvelous that our
Advocate pays our debt and takes care of our case!

The fact that Christ is our Advocate with the Father,
and not simply with God, indicates that our case which the
Lord undertakes for us is a family affair, a case between us
as the Father's children and the Father. Actually, our
Advocate is our elder Brother, the Son of the Father.

The divine family is full of love, but it is also full of
righteousness. Hence, there are regulations and also the
Father's discipline. We should never think that in the
Father's house we can be unruly. Our Father is orderly,
and His house should be much more orderly than a human
court of law. However, as children in the Father's house,
we are often naughty. We make mistakes, break the family
regulations, and offend the Father. For this reason, we

need the Lord, our elder Brother, to be our Advocate with the Father.

As the One who shed His blood for us, the Lord Jesus is the righteous One. He is right not only with the Father, but also right with us. The Lord is our Paraclete (the anglicized form of *parakletos*, the Greek word rendered Advocate). He comes alongside to help us, He serves us, He takes care of us, and He provides whatever we need. We were in need of the cleansing blood; therefore, He provided us with His own blood for redemption and cleansing. We also need someone to take care of our case. Therefore, He is now our Advocate, our *parakletos*.

THE DIVINE LIFE AS THE BASIC FACTOR OF OUR SPIRITUAL INHERITANCE

We who believe in Christ have been born of God and have become God's children. God is now our Father, and we are His children. Because we have been born of God, we have His life. God's life is divine, eternal, and indestructible. This life is the basic factor of the spiritual inheritance we have in God's salvation.

We may use our human life as an illustration. As human beings, through birth we have our natural life, our human life, as our basic inheritance. Any particular thing we inherit depends on our human life. When a person dies and thereby loses his human life, that is the termination of everything. He no longer has an inheritance. In the same principle, the divine life we have received through regeneration is our basic inheritance in God's salvation. Life, therefore, is crucial. The basic element of our spiritual inheritance is the divine life.

THE ENJOYMENT IN THE FELLOWSHIP OF THE DIVINE LIFE

We thank the Lord that we have the divine life and that this life moves, works, and acts in us. The moving of the divine life within us issues in fellowship. Hence, fellowship is the issue of the marvelous divine life we have received. In this fellowship we enjoy God, we enjoy the apostles, we enjoy the believers, and we enjoy the church and even the churches. All this enjoyment depends on the fellowship of the divine life, and this fellowship issues out of the divine life itself.

Although we have received the divine life and enjoy God, the apostles, the believers, and the church life in the fellowship of the divine life, we still need to be watchful concerning sin. Sin is not merely something on the surface that can be washed away. On the contrary, sin dwells in our flesh. According to Paul's word in the book of Romans, sin may deceive us, conquer us, and kill us. In particular, indwelling sin damages our fellowship.

If our fellowship is damaged through sin, we lose the enjoyment of God. We also lose the enjoyment of the apostles, the enjoyment of the believers, and the enjoyment of the church life. In other words, once we lose the fellowship, we lose the enjoyment of our entire spiritual inheritance. As a result, in a practical way we become the same as unbelievers. Unbelievers do not have God, and they have nothing to do with the enjoyment of the apostles, the believers, and the church life.

When we enjoy the fellowship of the divine life, we enjoy God, we enjoy the apostles, we enjoy the believers, and we enjoy the churches. What a wonderful enjoyment this is! But as soon as sin works within us and we commit sin, our fellowship is broken. Whenever our fellowship is broken, we lose the enjoyment of God, the apostles, the believers, and the church life. It is very important that we see this and have a proper realization concerning it.

DIVINE PROVISIONS

The Blood of Jesus and the Faithfulness and Righteousness of the Father

Even though we have been regenerated and have received the divine life to become children of the Father, we still must admit two things: first, that we still have sin in our flesh; second, that it is always possible for us to commit sin. Whenever we are under the divine light in fellowship and sense that we are wrong in certain matters or with certain persons, we must immediately confess our sins to our righteous Father. Our Father is ready to forgive us. Just as a human father, who has been offended by the behavior of his child, is ready to forgive the repentant child, so our divine Father is ready to forgive us. Once we confess our sins, our Father will be the faithful and righteous God to us. He is waiting to forgive us our sins and to wash away the stains of our offenses.

In 1:7 John says that "the blood of Jesus His Son cleanses us from all sin." Here we have the blood as a provision prepared for us. According to the tense of the Greek verb in this verse, the cleansing of the blood is present and continuous. The blood of Jesus the Son of God cleanses us all the time, continuously and constantly. The provision of the blood is ever available, and the cleansing of the blood is continuous. The blood is always ready for us to enjoy its provision.

In 2:1 John says, "My little children, these things I write to you that you may not sin." This indicates that John's intention was that the believers would not sin. We also should have this intention. We need to pray, "O Lord, keep me from sinning. Lord, preserve me in Your presence and in Your fellowship. Lord, deliver me continuously from sin." But no matter how much we may be on the alert concerning sin, it is always possible that we shall sin. Whenever we commit sin, we need to confess our sin to God. The provision of the blood is ready for our cleansing, and the Father is willing to forgive us our sins and to cleanse us from all the stains of our offenses.

Christ as Our Advocate and Propitiation

After covering these matters in chapter one, John goes on in chapter two to show us that the divine provision not only includes the blood of Jesus and the faithfulness of God, but also includes the living Person of Christ as our Advocate. As the One who shed His blood for us, this Person is now our heavenly attorney taking care of our case. He is qualified for this because He is the righteous

One, the One who is right with the Father.

In 2:2 John says that the One who is our Advocate with the Father is‾ also a propitiation concerning our sins. Whenever God's children offend the Father, the fellowship between them is broken. Furthermore, there is no peace; instead there is turmoil. Realizing the situation, the children should make confession to the Father, who is ready to forgive them and cleanse them. The cleansing blood has been provided, and the Father Himself is faithful to forgive and righteous to cleanse. But how can the peace between the Father and His children be restored? We may think that as long as there is forgiveness and cleansing, peace will come automatically. However, there is still the need for our Advocate to be our propitiation between the Father and us so that the Father may be appeased and that peace may be restored.

Let us once again use our human family life as an illustration. Often the mother in a family will be the one who appeases the father in behalf of the children. Suppose the children in a particular family offend the father, peace is lost, and now there is turmoil in that family. The children repent and confess their wrongdoings to the father, and he forgives them. However, the situation between the children and the father is still not altogether pleasant. At such a time, a wise mother will speak both to the children and to the father. On the one hand, she may say to the children, "Children, it is all right now. Your father has forgiven you." On the other hand, she may turn to her husband and say, "Isn't it wonderful that the children have repented and have confessed to you." As a result, the peace between the father and the children is restored through the mother's being the propitiation, the peacemaker.

THE RESTORATION OF FELLOWSHIP

In chapter one of 1 John we see that we have the blood to wash us and the Father's faithfulness and righteousness for our forgiveness and cleansing. Although our problem is solved through our confessing, through the cleansing of the blood, and through the Father's forgiveness and cleansing, we still need Christ as our Advocate with the Father and as our propitiation. He is the One who makes peace, the One who appeases the Father for us. As the appeasing One, He causes everyone involved, the Father and the children, to be happy and peaceful. Immediately, we have the enjoyment of the fellowship. This is the picture portrayed in these verses of John's first Epistle.

We need to be deeply impressed with all the divine provisions: the cleansing blood, the faithfulness of God, the righteousness of God, the Advocate, and the propitiation. With God we have the provisions of His faithfulness and righteousness, and with Christ we have the provisions of His blood and of Himself as our Advocate and propitiation. Day by day, we who have the divine life and the enjoyment of this life in fellowship need to be on the alert concerning sin. But if we sin, we should immediately make confession. Then we shall experience the effectiveness of all these provisions. We shall have the washing of the Lord's blood, the faithfulness and righteousness of the Father for our forgiveness and cleansing, and Christ as our Advocate and propitiation for the appeasing of the Father and the restoring of the peace between us and the Father. Through Christ as our Advocate and propitiation, we again have peace with the Father and we enjoy fellowship with Him.

LIFE-STUDY OF FIRST JOHN

MESSAGE FIFTEEN

CONDITIONS OF THE DIVINE FELLOWSHIP

(7)

Scripture Reading: 1 John 2:3-6

Before we consider 2:3-6, I would like to say a further word concerning propitiation. John says in 2:2, "He is a propitiation concerning our sins, and not concerning ours only, but also concerning the whole world." According to its biblical meaning, propitiation leads to enjoyment, for it ushers in fellowship between God and us. According to Paul's word in Romans 3:25, God has set forth Christ a propitiation-cover through faith in His blood. This indicates that Christ is not only the One who propitiates, but also that He is the place of propitiation. Christ as the propitiation place is the place where God and His redeemed people may converse, have fellowship, and enjoy one another.

In his first Epistle, John indicates that God's provision not only includes the blood of Jesus and God's righteousness and faithfulness, but also includes the Advocate who pleads our case with the Father and who Himself is our propitiation, our peacemaker. Christ Himself is actually the peace between God and us. This peace is the ground on which we and God may converse, have fellowship, and enjoy one another.

In the first section on the conditions of the divine fellowship (1:5-10), the problem that affects our fellowship is sin. If we sin, we need to confess. If we confess our sins, the blood of Jesus will cleanse us from our sins. Then in His faithfulness and righteousness, the Father will forgive us our sins and cleanse us from unrighteousness. Furthermore, our Lord Jesus Christ will be the Advocate with the Father to handle our case. Eventually, this precious One will be our propitiation and thus the base, the ground, where we enjoy God and have fellowship with Him and He with us.

We may use an example from family life as an illustration of how Christ as our propitiation restores pleasant fellowship between us and the Father. Suppose the children in a family offend their father by disobeying him. As a result, their fellowship with the father is broken. However, the children repent and confess to the father, and he forgives them. Nevertheless, the situation is still not altogether pleasant. Then the mother may come in as the peacemaker, as the one who helps all the parties to be peaceful and happy. She may even prepare something for the family to eat so that they may have an enjoyable time together. This is an illustration of what Christ does as our propitiation. After we confess our sins and are cleansed by the blood and forgiven by the Father, the Lord handles our case with the Father and then becomes the very enjoyment that appeases the Father. This is Christ as our propitiation.

As we consider this matter, we shall realize that this is not merely a doctrine but is something very experiential. From experience we know that when we confess our sins, we have the sense that the blood has cleansed us and that the Father has forgiven us. Immediately, there is also a sense of enjoyment. That enjoyment is Christ as our propitiation. It is by this enjoyment, by Christ as our propitiation, that we may converse with God and He with us, and that together we may enjoy Christ and have fellowship around Christ. Therefore, Christ is the enjoyment that is the propitiation with God for us. Eventually, He becomes the very ground of our fellowship with the Father. It is in this way that our fellowship, which is broken through sin, may be recovered. Praise the Lord that by the five provisions—the blood, God's faithfulness and righteousness, the Advocate, and the propitiation—we are restored to full fellowship with God!

THE SECOND CONDITION FOR MAINTAINING
THE DIVINE FELLOWSHIP

Verses 1 and 2 of chapter two are a conclusion to the word in 1:5-10 regarding our confession and God's forgiveness of our sins, which interrupt our fellowship with Him. That is the first condition of, the first requirement for, our enjoyment of the fellowship of the divine life. Verses 3 through 11 deal with the second condition of, the second requirement for, our fellowship with God—the requirement that we keep the Lord's word and love the brothers.

In verse 3 John says, "And in this we know that we have known Him, if we keep His commandments." It is significant that this verse begins with the conjunction "and." This conjunction used at the beginning of the sentence indicates that John is about to speak concerning another condition for maintaining our fellowship.

We have seen that the first condition of the divine fellowship is dealing with sin. If we do not deal with sin, sin will damage our fellowship. Therefore, in order to maintain our fellowship with the Father, we need to confess our sins. Not only is this true doctrinally, but it is also true according to our spiritual experience. From experience we know that in order to maintain our enjoyment of the divine life in fellowship, the first thing we must do is to deal with sin. Hence, dealing with sin is the first condition, the first requirement, of keeping ourselves in the fellowship of the divine life. Now that John is going on to consider the second condition, he begins verse 3 with the conjunction "and." This word points to another condition, another requirement, of maintaining the divine fellowship.

KNOWING GOD EXPERIENTIALLY

In verse 3 John says, "In this we know that we have known Him." The Greek word for know in this verse may also be rendered perceive. Here the meaning is to perceive not doctrinally but experientially, by keeping the Lord's commandments.

A more literal translation of the Greek words rendered "have known Him" would be "have come to know Him." This denotes that we have begun to know Him and still continue knowing Him till the present time. This refers to our experiential knowledge of God in our daily walk related to our intimate fellowship with Him.

Our knowing of the Lord has begun and is continuing. This continuous knowing of the Lord is an experiential knowing. If we know the Lord in this experiential way, surely we shall keep His commandments.

KEEPING HIS COMMANDMENTS

In verse 4 John goes on to say, "He who says, I have known Him, and is not keeping His commandments, is a liar, and the truth is not in this one." In this verse truth denotes the revealed reality of God as conveyed in the divine word, which reveals that our keeping of the Lord's commandments should follow our knowing of Him. If we say that we have known the Lord, yet we are not keeping His commandments, the truth (reality) is not in us, and we become a liar.

When I was young, I was bothered by the word "commandments" in these verses. I thought that this term always referred to the Ten Commandments of the Mosaic law, and I wondered why John here mentioned this law, telling us that we must keep the Ten Commandments. Actually, the commandments in this verse are commandments in the New Testament, not the commandments of the Mosaic law. These New Testament commandments are the commandments of the Lord Jesus given directly by Him, or the commandments given through the apostles. In the Gospel of John the Lord gave us the definite commandment to love one another: "A new commandment I give to you, that you love one another, even as I have loved you, that you also love one another" (John 13:34). This commandment to love one another was given by the Lord Jesus Himself. Hence, it is not a commandment of the Old Testament, but a commandment of the New Testament. Other New Testament commandments were given by the Lord Jesus indirectly through His apostles.

If we say that we know the Lord experientially in the New Testament way, then we should keep the New Testament commandments. But if we do not keep these commandments, this is a sign that actually we do not know Him, even though we say that we do. According to John's word in verse 4, if we say that we have known Him, yet do not keep His commandments, we are a liar, and the truth is not in us.

KEEPING HIS WORD

In verse 5 John continues, "But whoever keeps His word, truly in this one the love of God has been perfected. In this we know that we are in Him." Here "word" is synonymous with "commandments" in verses 3 and 4, for the word comprises all the commandments. "Commandments" emphasizes injunction; the "word" implies spirit and life as a supply to us (John 6:63).

The word in verse 5 is the totality, the aggregate, of all the commandments. No matter how many commandments there may be, as a whole these commandments are the word of the Lord. Hence, in verse 5 John speaks of keeping His word. By this he means keeping the word spoken either by the Lord Himself directly or spoken through the apostles.

THE LOVE OF GOD PERFECTED IN US

In verse 5 John tells us that in the one who keeps the Lord's word the love of God has been perfected. In this verse the Greek word for love is *agape*. This word denotes the love which is higher and nobler than *phileo* (see notes 7[1] and 7[2] in 2 Peter 1). Only this word with its verb forms is used in this Epistle for love. "The love of God" here denotes our love toward God, which is generated by His love within us. The love of God, the word of the Lord, and God Himself are all related to one another. If we keep the Lord's word, God's love has been perfected in us. It is altogether a matter of the divine life, which is God

Himself. God's love is His inward essence, and the Lord's word supplies us with this divine essence with which we love the brothers. Hence, when we keep the divine word, the divine love is perfected through the divine life by which we live.

The word "perfected" is very important. The Greek word for "perfected" is *teleioo*, meaning to complete, to accomplish, to finish. The love of God itself is perfect and complete in Himself. However, in us it needs to be perfected and completed in its manifestation. The love of God has been manifested to us in God's sending His Son to be both a propitiation and life to us (4:9-10). Yet, if we do not love one another with this love as it was manifested to us, that is, if we do not express it by loving one another with it as God expressed it to us, it is not perfectly and completely manifested. It is perfected and completed in its manifestation when we express it in our living by habitually loving one another with it. Our living in the love of God toward one another is its perfection and completion in its manifestation in us. Thus, others can behold God manifested in His love essence in our living in His love.

John concludes verse 5 by saying, "In this we know that we are in Him." The pronoun "Him" refers to the Lord Jesus Christ. The phrase "in Him" is a strong expression; it stresses that we are one with the Lord. Because we are one with the Lord, who is God, the loving essence of God becomes ours. It is supplied to us by the Lord's word of life for our walk of love so that we may enjoy the fellowship of the divine life and abide in the light (v. 10).

In our reading of verse 5 we may wonder whether the love of God here refers to God's love or to the love with which we love God. The Chinese Version speaks of our loving of God, or of the love with which we love God. But the English expression seems to indicate that John is referring to God's love.

If we consider the Greek text and also take care of the context, we shall realize that this expression in verse 5 denotes our love toward God. However, this love is generated by the love of God, which we enjoy. First we enjoy the love of God; hence, the love of God is our enjoyment. Then the love of God, which is enjoyed by us, produces in us a love with which we love God. This is the love of God becoming our enjoyment and producing within us a love for God. On the one hand, this is the love with which we love God; on the other hand, this love is produced by God's love, which is enjoyed by us.

Actually it is rather difficult to say whose love John is referring to in verse 5. We have seen that this love is God's love enjoyed by us and also that it is the love produced in us with which we love God. Love comes from God to us and becomes our experience and enjoyment. The result is that this love produces a love in us toward God. Therefore, this love comes from God, it passes through us, and it returns to God. What a wonderful, experiential love this is!

The love in verse 5 is both God's love for us and our love for God. This is God's love becoming our love through our enjoyment of the divine love. When God's love becomes our love, we have within us a love toward God. Through our experience of God's love, the love that comes from Him now returns to Him.

We have pointed out that in verse 5 John speaks of the love of God being perfected in the one who keeps His word. In itself God's love is absolutely perfect. There is no need whatever for God's love to be perfected, for it is already perfect and complete. However, God's love becomes the love with which we love Him, and this kind of love does need to be perfected. We love God by the love that is generated in us through our experience of the divine love. Although we may have this love and may love God with this love, our love is still very limited and far from perfect. Therefore, our love for God needs to be perfected. As we grow in the divine life, our love for God also will grow.

Our love for God actually is not our own love. It is still God's love, but it is God's love becoming our experience and producing a love in us for God. Through our experience and enjoyment of the divine love, we love God. Now this love needs to be perfected.

I believe that all of us in the Lord's recovery can say that we love God. But we still need to ask to what degree, to what extent, we love Him. Some of us may have a very high degree of love for the Lord, but this love is not perfect. I wish to emphasize the fact that in itself God's love is perfect. But the love that is produced in us through our experience and enjoyment of God's love needs to grow, increase, and be perfected.

In our study of 2:5 we may have two questions concerning the love mentioned in this verse: first, the question whether this love is God's love or our love; second, the question concerning why God's love needs to be perfected. I believe that by now we have the proper answer to both questions.

In this verse the love of God is not mentioned in an objective sense; rather, John speaks of God's love in a subjective sense. John is referring here to God's love becoming our enjoyment in order to produce a love in us for God. Hence, now we know that the love of God here refers to the divine love experienced by us and becoming our love for God.

Furthermore, we have come to see that this love needs to be perfected. God's love viewed in an objective sense does not need to be perfected. But in an experiential, subjective sense, the love of God does need to be perfected in us. The love with which we love God, the love produced by our enjoyment of God's love, certainly needs to be perfected. Our love toward God is not complete, perfect, absolute. No matter how much we love God, our love has not yet been perfected. Therefore, we need to have our love for God perfected, and have it perfected to the uttermost.

LIFE-STUDY OF FIRST JOHN

CONDITIONS OF THE DIVINE FELLOWSHIP

(8)

Scripture Reading: 1 John 2:3-6

In this message we shall continue to consider 2:3-6.

We have seen that 2:1 and 2 are a conclusion to the word in 1:5-10 regarding our confession and God's forgiveness of our sins. Confessing our sins is the first condition of our enjoyment of the fellowship of the divine life. According to 2:3-11, the second condition is that we keep the Lord's word and love the brothers.

A SIGN INDICATING THAT WE ARE IN THE LORD

In 2:5 John says, "But whoever keeps His word, truly in this one the love of God has been perfected. In this we know that we are in Him." The words "in this" in the last sentence refer to the matter of keeping the Lord's word and having the love of God perfected in us. The phrase "in Him" refers to our being in the Lord Jesus Christ. This is a strong expression, for it emphasizes the fact that we are one with the Lord.

If we read the context of these verses, we shall realize that it is an important matter to have a sign indicating that we are in the Lord. How can we prove that we are in the Triune God? What is the evidence that we are truly in Him? The first sign that we are in Him is that we know God experientially in our daily life.

When John speaks of knowing God (v. 3), he speaks of knowing Him not doctrinally but experientially, by keeping His commandments. We should not merely know in a doctrinal way that God is almighty and that He created the heavens and the earth. We need to know God experientially in a way that affects our daily living. Others may wonder why you do not participate in certain forms of worldly entertainment. The reason that you do not participate should be that you know God, that you know Him in His holy nature. Because God's holy nature does not allow you to participate in that form of entertainment, you refrain from doing so. Likewise, if we know God in His nature, this will affect the way we do our shopping. Knowing God in this way will also cause us to be sincere in relation to others. Because we know the Lord in His nature of sincerity, we would not be political. Therefore, the reason we behave ourselves and have our being in a particular way should not be merely that we follow the outward teachings of the Bible, but even the more that we know God's nature and character and live according to what God is.

Sometimes others may try to convince you that there is no need for you to be so strict in your living. They may tell you, for example, that there is nothing wrong with spending some time engaging in a certain kind of amusement. You may wish to answer them by saying, "I do not view this as a matter of right or wrong. My testimony is that I know my God. I have a living God dwelling within me, and I am in Him and one with Him organically. This means that His nature becomes mine and what He is becomes my constituent. As a result, I know Him subjectively and experientially. This is the reason I cannot conduct myself in the same way others do. Unbelievers do not have Him, and, of course, they do not know Him or experience Him. Do you know why I behave in the way I do? It is because I have Him, know Him, and enjoy Him. The Lord is not only my life—He is everything to me. I do not live according to certain regulations or requirements. This is a matter of the divine life within me. The Lord dwells in me, and I know Him experientially."

THE TASTE OF THE DIVINE NATURE

To be in the Lord Jesus Christ is to be one with Him organically. It is not to be one with Him merely in a doctrinal way. When we are organically one with the Lord, He is our life and even becomes our nature.

Every kind of life has its particular nature. With the nature of the divine life there is a certain taste. Because we have the Lord as our life and because we enjoy His nature, we also have the taste that comes with the divine nature. However, anyone who does not have the divine nature cannot have the divine taste. But because we have the taste of the divine nature, we simply cannot do certain things.

As an illustration of what we mean by the taste of the divine nature, we may consider what happens when something with a bitter taste is placed in the mouth of a baby. There is no need to teach the young one not to eat something bitter. As soon as a bitter-tasting substance is placed in a baby's mouth, he will spit it out. The child does not behave according to regulations learned from his mother. There is no need for a mother to teach her baby not to eat things that are bitter. In the life of her child there is a nature that rejects things that taste bitter. In a similar way, there is in the divine nature a particular taste that causes us to reject those things that are contrary to the nature of the One who lives within us.

KNOWING GOD SUBJECTIVELY

We do not know God merely in an objective, doctrinal way. It is in this way that the Jews know God. They know God objectively, apart from any subjective experience of Him. This means that they do not have any inner experience of the subjective God. But as those who have been born of God and who possess God's life, we know Him not merely objectively, but in particular we know Him subjectively and experientially.

Because we know our God in this way, we cannot speak certain things, do certain things, or go certain places. Others may even defame us and falsely accuse us. However, because we know God subjectively, often we shall not have any desire to vindicate ourselves or argue in our own defense. No matter what others may say, we know that we have the divine life. We have God within us as our life and nature. Eventually this indwelling One will be expressed in our character and conduct. It is in this way that we know God experientially, and this knowing is a strong sign that we are in Him and one with Him.

In our behavior and way of speaking, we should bear a sign that we are in God. We should not talk with others the same way that unbelievers do. If your husband or wife, your children, your neighbors, and your classmates or co-workers cannot see a sign that you behave yourself according to the experience of God, then there is a question whether you are truly in God or not. We thank the Lord that those in the Lord's recovery do have the testimony in their daily life that they are in God. We bear a sign that we are in God, even though at some times we are weak and fail Him. We thank the Lord that we have some evidence, some sign, in our daily walk that we are in God. This sign is an indication that we know the Lord experientially. Because we know Him experientially, spontaneously we keep His commandments.

ABIDING IN HIM

In 2:6 John goes on to say, "He who says he abides in Him ought himself also to walk even as that One walked." To be in Christ is the start of the Christian life. That was God's doing once for all (1 Cor. 1:30). To abide in Him is the continuation of the Christian life. This is our responsibility in our daily walk, a walk which is a copy of Christ's walk on earth.

Because God has put us in Christ once for all, we now must bear the responsibility to abide in Him. To abide in Him is actually to have fellowship with Him. On the negative side, this requires that we deal with our sins; on the positive side, this requires that we keep His word.

LOVING GOD AND THE BROTHERS

According to the context of these verses, the Lord's word here refers to His commandments. His commandments are to love God and to love the brothers. We love our begetting Father, and we love all His children, all those begotten of Him.

When we are abiding in the Lord, having fellowship with Him, our abiding in Him spontaneously issues in love for God and for the brothers. Therefore, the second condition, the second requirement, of fellowship is that we love God and the brothers.

The Greek word used for love in verse 5 is *agape*. This word denotes a love higher and nobler than that denoted by the Greek word *phileo*. Only *agape* with its verb forms is used in this Epistle for love. In this verse "the love of God" denotes our love toward God, which is generated by His love within us. The love of God, the word of the Lord, and God Himself are all related to one another. If we keep the Lord's word, God's love has been perfected in us. This is altogether a matter of the divine life, and this life is God Himself.

God's love is His inward essence, and the Lord's word supplies us with this divine essence, with which we love the brothers. The word itself is not this essence or substance. The word is what conveys this essence and supplies it to us. Therefore, the word supplies us with the very essence of God, which is the divine love. As a result, we have something substantial within us for us to participate in and enjoy. This means that eventually the essence of God's being becomes our enjoyment. Then out of this enjoyment there will be an issue—our love for God and His children.

NOT LOVING WITH OUR NATURAL LOVE

It should not be with our natural love that we love God and His children. On the contrary, our natural love needs to be put on the cross. We should love God and His children with the divine love, the love that is conveyed to us through the word of the Lord and that becomes our experience and enjoyment.

Many of today's Christians understand the Bible in a natural, religious, or ethical way. This is true in particular concerning the requirement to love God, the brothers, and

our neighbor. From the time I was a youth I heard about
loving the brothers and loving our neighbor. Today
Christians often talk about loving the brothers or about
loving our neighbor. Once when I was in Houston for a
conference, a lady came up to me after the meeting and
said strongly, "People in this country don't know to love
others. You should travel to different places and teach
Christians to love one another."

Yes, the Bible does tell us that we should love one
another and that we should love our neighbors as
ourselves. However, it is not God's intention to command
us to love others with our natural love. Instead, God
desires that we love Him and His children with the divine
love which we have enjoyed.

THE LOVE OF GOD BECOMING OUR LOVE

This is the reason verse 5 says that the love of God has
been perfected in us. On the one hand, this love is the love
of God; on the other hand, this love, having been
experienced and enjoyed by us, becomes our love for God
and the brothers.

How can our love for God be called the love of God? It is
because this love is not our love, but is God's love.
However, this is not the love of God as it is objectively; it is
the love of God experienced by us subjectively. This is the
love of God becoming our love through our experience and
enjoyment of Him. This love then becomes our love for God
and others.

God wants us to love Him with His love. He also wants
us to love His children, and even the whole world, with His
love. First we need to enjoy God's love and experience His
love to such an extent that it fills us, saturates us, and
becomes our very essence, causing us to be permeated with
the love of God. Then with this love we shall love God, we
shall love God's children, and we shall love all people. We
do not love them with our natural love; we love them with
the love of God we have experienced and enjoyed. Praise
the Lord for such a wonderful love! This is the love
revealed in the first Epistle of John.

This experience of the love of God is altogether a matter in the fellowship in the divine life. If we do not enjoy God in the fellowship of the divine life, we cannot have such a love.

LOVING OTHERS WITH THE LOVE OF GOD

If we experience the love of God, we shall have the deep realization that our natural love is one thing and that the love of God which becomes our love through experience is something very different. One difference between God's love and our natural love is that it is very easy for our natural love to be offended.

When we love others, we become involved with them. For this reason, it is often the case that those we love in a natural way eventually become our enemies. Because natural love may have such a result, those who are wise in a human way are slow and careful in loving others. They realize that if you love others in a foolish way, sooner or later that love will cause trouble. Many divorces and separations are the result of a foolish natural love that is easily offended and leads to enmity. For example, a certain man and woman may know each other only for a short time. In a quick way they get married. Then after only a little time has gone by, they may separate or get a divorce. At first they loved each other, but not too long after they were married they became enemies. This is the result of loving each other in a natural way. If they had never loved one another in a natural way, they would not have become enemies.

It is not very likely that you will regard as your enemy a person unknown to you that you see walking on the street. Those who become your enemies are often those whom you love in a natural way. This is why some exercise their human wisdom to be very careful in loving others. They realize that loving others in a natural way leads to problems. In order to avoid these problems, they are very slow in loving others.

The point I am making here is that we need to be careful not to love others by our natural love. Rather, our natural love should be put on the cross. We need to love others by the love of God we have experienced and enjoyed. If we experience God's love, we shall love God with this love. We shall also love the brothers with this same love. This kind of love does not cause trouble. May we all see that we need to love God and others with the divine love that has become our experience and enjoyment.

JOHN'S BASIC VOCABULARY

Thus far in these messages we have covered sixteen verses from 1 John, ten verses from chapter one and six verses from chapter two. In these verses we can see many items of John's basic vocabulary: the Word, life, the Father, the Son, fellowship, joy, light, truth, the faithfulness of God, the righteousness of God, confessing, forgiveness, cleansing, and the blood. All these matters are positive. On the negative side, we have sin, sins, unrighteousness, darkness, and lie. All these terms are found in chapter one. In chapter two we have the Advocate, the propitiation, the word or the commandment, and love. I encourage you to pray-read all these terms. The more we pray-read them, the more we shall realize how rich they are. Praise the Lord for the blood, the faithfulness of God, the righteousness of God, His forgiveness, and His cleansing! Praise Him for the Word, the life, the fellowship, the joy, the light, and the truth! Praise Him also for the Advocate, the propitiation, the word as the commandment, and the love of God!

LIFE-STUDY OF FIRST JOHN

CONDITIONS OF THE DIVINE FELLOWSHIP

(9)

Scripture Reading: 1 John 2:7-11

In this message we shall consider 2:7-11, the last portion of the first Epistle of John concerned with the conditions of the divine fellowship.

AN OLD COMMANDMENT

In verse 7 John says, "Beloved, I am not writing a new commandment to you, but an old commandment, which you had from the beginning; the old commandment is the word which you heard." The "old commandment" referred to here is the commandment given by the Lord in John 13:34: "A new commandment I give to you, that you love one another, even as I have loved you, that you also love one another." This commandment is the word the believers heard and had from the beginning.

In verse 7 the phrase "from the beginning" is used in the relative sense. We have pointed out that this phrase is used twice in the Gospel of John, eight times in this Epistle, and two times in 2 John. In John 8:44; 1 John 1:1; 2:13, 14; and 3:8, it is used in the absolute sense; whereas in John 15:27; 1 John 2:7, 24 (twice); 3:11; and 2 John 5, 6, it is used in the relative sense. John was not writing a new commandment to the believers; he was writing an old commandment, which they had from the beginning, that is, from the time the Lord Jesus was on earth and gave them the commandment to love one another. That old commandment is the word which they heard.

The commandment of the Lord is His word. This means that His commandment is not merely an injunction; the

Lord's commandment is also a word conveying the life supply. In John 6:63 the Lord Jesus said, "The words which I have spoken unto you are spirit and are life." Therefore, in 2:7 "the word" indicates the life supply. Whatever the Lord speaks is a word supplying us with life and spirit. What the Lord says may also be an injunction demanding that we do a certain thing. Nevertheless, as long as that injunction is something uttered by the Lord, something that proceeds out of His mouth, it is a word that supplies us with life. Therefore, whenever we take the Lord's word and keep it, we receive the life supply.

THE OLD COMMANDMENT BECOMING NEW

In verse 8 John goes on to say, "Again, I am writing a new commandment to you, which is true in Him and in you, because the darkness is passing away, and the true light already shines." The commandment of brotherly love is both old and new: old, because the believers have had it from the beginning of their Christian life; new, because in their Christian walk it dawns with new light and shines with new enlightenment and fresh power again and again.

The relative pronoun "which" in verse 8 is in neuter gender. It does not refer to "commandment," which is in feminine gender. It should refer to the fact that the old commandment of brotherly love is new in the believers' Christian walk. This is true in the Lord, since He not only gave it to His believers, but also renews it in their daily walk all the time. This is true also in the believers, since they have not only received it once for all, but also are enlightened and refreshed by it repeatedly.

In verse 8 John tells us that the darkness is passing away and that the true light already shines. The passing away of the darkness is its vanishing in the shining of the true light. The true light is the light of the Lord's commandment. Because this light shines, the commandment of brotherly love dawns in the darkness and makes the old commandment new and fresh throughout the entire Christian life.

Many who read verses 7 and 8 are bothered by what John says concerning an old commandment and a new commandment. In verse 7 he says that he is not writing a new commandment but an old commandment. But in verse 8 he says that he is writing a new commandment. How can an old commandment be a new commandment? Is the new commandment a commandment other than the old commandment, or is it the old commandment becoming new? If we read these verses carefully in context, we shall see that actually the old commandment and the new commandment are one. The reason for this is that the commandment is the word of the Lord, and the word of the Lord dawns as a new day dawns when the sun rises in the morning. When the sun rises, the shining of the sun swallows up the darkness. The darkness of night always vanishes with the shining of the morning sun. Here John indicates that the Lord's commandment, as His living word, shines as the dawning sun, and this shining swallows up darkness.

After any kind of human commandment has been given, it gradually becomes old. Human commandments are not living. Because these commandments are not living, they never dawn and they never shine. But the commandment given by the Lord is His living word. Because His commandment is His living word, this word shines. When this living word dawns in the darkness, it dawns with heavenly light. The shining of heavenly light makes old things new. In particular, it makes the old commandment new, fresh, and full of light.

Perhaps you are familiar with the principle that the shining of light indicates newness. Suppose you shut off the light in a room for a period of time. When you turn on the light again, you will spontaneously have the sense of newness. The shining of light brings us this sense of newness. Every time light shines it brings in a new situation.

Because human words are dead, they cannot shine and therefore cannot give us a new beginning. But the Lord's commandment, as His living word, always gives us a new beginning because His word shines anew and afresh again and again.

Many of us can testify that we have experienced the shining of the Lord's word in this way. For instance, in John 13:34 the Lord Jesus commands us to love one another. We can testify that many times this commandment has become new and fresh in our Christian life. Throughout the years we have been Christians, often this old injunction has become a fresh word to us. Whenever we contact the Lord and His old commandment dawns in our darkness, light shines. With this light there is newness. This is how the old commandment can be a new commandment. The old commandment becomes new because it is a word that is living and shining. This shining makes the old commandment new and fresh.

Now we can understand why the Apostle John says, "I am not writing a new commandment to you, but an old commandment. . . . Again, I am writing a new commandment to you." In these verses John seems to be saying, "I believe that what I am writing to you is shining upon you and swallowing the darkness. The darkness is now vanishing, passing away, in the shining of this new light."

TRUE IN HIM AND IN US

In verse 8 John says that the fact of the old commandment of brotherly love being new in the believers' Christian walk is true both in the Lord and in us. This is true in the Lord because He gave the commandment and because He renews and refreshes this commandment. This is true also in us because we not only have received the old commandment, but also have a new and fresh enlightening of this commandment. Under this enlightenment, we have the consciousness that this word is new and refreshing to us. This word even makes us new. Therefore, this is true in us because the darkness is vanishing and the true light is already shining.

What is this true light? This light is the light in the word of the Lord that is shining upon us. This shining can be compared to the dawning of a new day.

LIGHT AND DARKNESS

In verse 9 John continues, "He who says he is in the light and is hating his brother, is in the darkness until now." Light is the expression of God's essence and the source of truth. The divine love is related to the divine light. The divine love is versus the satanic hatred, which is related to the satanic darkness. Hating a brother in the Lord is a sign of being in darkness (v. 11). Likewise, loving a brother is a sign of abiding in the light (v. 10).

In chapter 1 of this Epistle John speaks about light and darkness with respect to the first condition of the divine fellowship. When in chapter two he speaks regarding the second condition, he also mentions light and darkness. Hatred is a sign that we are in darkness, whereas love is a sign that we are in the light.

In verse 10 John goes on to say, "He who loves his brother abides in the light, and there is no cause of stumbling in him." Abiding in the light depends upon abiding in the Lord (v. 6), from which issues love toward the brothers. Stumbling comes from blindness, and blindness comes from darkness.

Both conditions of the divine fellowship depend on the divine light. If we are not in the divine light, we are automatically through with the fellowship of the divine life. Whenever we are without light, we are automatically in darkness. Whenever light vanishes, darkness is present. Likewise, as long as we abide in the divine light, darkness vanishes.

The absence of the divine light is a strong sign that we are not in the divine fellowship. In chapter one, concerning the first condition of the divine fellowship, whether we are in light or darkness is determined by whether or not we deal with sin. If we sin, we are in darkness. But if we deal with sin by confessing it and experiencing God's forgiveness and cleansing, we shall be in the light. In chapter two, concerning the second condition of the divine fellowship, whether we are in darkness or light is determined by whether or not we love the brothers. If we hate, we are in darkness. But if we love, we are in the light. When we are in the light, we are then in the divine fellowship. But when we are in darkness, we have nothing to do with this fellowship.

In verse 11 John says, "But he who hates his brother is in the darkness and walks in the darkness, and does not know where he is going, because the darkness has blinded his eyes." In John 12:35 and 40, darkness is the issue of blinding; here it is the cause of blinding. Darkness brings in blindness, and blindness is the cause of stumbling. How is it possible for a Christian to be stumbled? A Christian may be stumbled by the blindness that comes from darkness. Darkness is the result of an interruption in our fellowship. Whenever our fellowship in the divine life is broken, immediately we are in darkness. This darkness causes blindness. Then it is easy for us to stumble.

MAINTAINING THE DIVINE FELLOWSHIP BY FULFILLING THE TWO CONDITIONS

In 1:5—2:11 we have the conditions of the divine fellowship. The first condition is the confessing of our sins, and the second condition is loving God and the brothers. In order to confess our sins, we need to realize that we still have sin dwelling in our flesh and that it is always possible for us to sin. Whenever we sin, we need to confess our sin. Our confession is based on God's provisions: the blood of Jesus, the faithfulness and righteousness of our faithful and righteous God, the Advocate, and Christ as our propitiation. Through these provisions we may enjoy the restoration of our fellowship. This restoration of fellowship is wholly based on propitiation. Actually, propitiation is itself the restored fellowship. With propitiation as the basis, we may converse with God, and He with us. We then have twoway traffic for a mutual enjoyment between us and God. This is the first condition for maintaining the divine fellowship.

We have emphasized the fact that the second condition is loving God and the brothers. In order to fulfill this condition, we need to know God continuously and experientially. It is not sufficient to know God once in a while, and we do not know Him once for all. We need to know Him experientially by continuously living in the divine life. Our daily life should be a life of knowing God constantly, for our life should be a life of living God. As long as we live God, we shall constantly know Him.

I can testify from experience that whenever I speak, I have the opportunity to know God. In giving a message my desire is to speak in God and with God. Sometimes, however, a certain word may be about to come out of my mouth. Then I realize that I need to swallow it, for the very God in whom and with whom I speak regulates what I say. I do not want to speak in myself but in God. I cannot tell you how much I have come to know God in the matter of my speaking. Whenever I speak, I know God. Speaking is always a golden opportunity for me to experience Him.

If we would experience and enjoy the divine love and have it become the love by which we love God and others, we need to know God experientially. This is the basic requirement for having the love of God become our love.

If we continually know God in an experiential way, we shall automatically keep the commandments of the Lord. When we know God, we keep the Lord's commandment. To keep the Lord's commandment means that we take His word. We have pointed out that the Lord's word is not merely a command or injunction; it is also a supply of life to us. The Lord's word always supplies life in our spirit. This can be proved by our experience. Whenever we receive the Lord's word and put it into practice, immediately we have the life supply within us.

The Lord's word is different from the Mosaic law. The Mosaic law is an injunction with demands and require-ments, but without any supply. However, whatever the Lord commands us in the New Testament is a supplying word. His life supply backs up His commandment. His commandment is not merely an injunction requiring us to do something; it is also a word that always supplies whatever it demands. The Lord's word even supplies us with the Lord Himself as life and as the Spirit. Therefore, we may experience Him and enjoy Him. If we know Him, we shall keep His word. By keeping His word we enjoy His supply.

When we keep the Lord's word and receive His supply, the love of God will be perfected within us. This means that as we receive the supply of the Lord's word, the love of God becomes our enjoyment, and this enjoyment issues in a love for God and the brothers.

If we would fulfill the second condition of the divine fellowship—the requirement that we love God and the brothers—we must know God. If we know Him, we shall keep His word. If we keep His word, we shall receive His supply of life. Then the love of God will be perfected in us. Our experience and enjoyment of God's love will issue in a love for God and the brothers. This is the fulfillment of the second requirement for maintaining the divine fellowship.

The two conditions of the divine fellowship involve sin on the negative side and love on the positive side. On the negative side, we need to deal with sin; on the positive side, we need to exercise ourselves to love God and the brothers. Therefore, sin must be dealt with, and love must be perfected. If we deal with sin and exercise ourselves to love God and the brothers, we shall fulfill the conditions of keeping ourselves in the fellowship of the divine life.

LIFE-STUDY OF FIRST JOHN

CONDITIONS OF THE DIVINE FELLOWSHIP

(10)

Scripture Reading: 1 John 2:3-11

In these messages on the conditions of the divine fellowship, we have seen that there are two conditions or requirements for maintaining this fellowship. The first requirement, described in 1:5—2:2, is the confessing of sins. The second requirement, described in 2:3-11, is the loving of God and the brothers. Therefore, if we want to maintain our fellowship with God, we need to deal with sin, and we need to love God and love the brothers.

In verses 9 and 11 of chapter two John says that the one who hates his brother is in the darkness and walks in the darkness. In verse 10 he says, "He who loves his brother abides in the light, and there is no cause of stumbling in him." In these verses John emphasizes loving the brothers. My burden in this message is to consider why John indicates that the last requirement for maintaining the divine fellowship is that of loving the brothers.

THE GOAL OF THE DIVINE FELLOWSHIP

In order to understand why loving the brothers is the final term, condition, or requirement of the divine fellowship, we need to understand what is the purpose of the divine fellowship. What is the goal of the divine fellowship? In this fellowship we enjoy the riches of the divine life, but for what purpose do we enjoy these riches in this fellowship? The enjoyment of the riches of the divine life in the divine fellowship is for the church life. It is of crucial importance for us to see that the goal of the divine fellowship is the church life.

The Fellowship of the Apostles

In 1:3 John says, "That which we have seen and heard we report also to you, that you also may have fellowship with us, and indeed the fellowship which is ours is with the Father and with His Son Jesus Christ." In this verse the pronouns "we" and "us" refer to the apostles. The apostles have seen and heard the eternal life. They report this to the believers so that the believers may have fellowship with the apostles. Because the fellowship described in 1:3 was first the portion of the apostles in enjoying the Father and the Son through the Spirit (2 Cor. 13:14), it is called the fellowship of the apostles (Acts 2:42) and "the fellowship which is ours" (the apostles'). The apostles are the representatives of the church. Hence, whenever the New Testament speaks of the apostles, the church is implied, for the apostles represent the church. This principle will still be in effect in the New Jerusalem. Concerning the New Jerusalem, Revelation 21:14 says, "And the wall of the city had twelve foundations, and on them twelve names of the twelve apostles of the Lamb." The apostles represent all the saints in the church. Because the apostles represent the church and because the fellowship of the divine life is called the fellowship of the apostles, we may say that this fellowship is for the church life.

The Fellowship of the Spirit

In 1:3 John says that the fellowship which the apostles have is the fellowship with the Father and with His Son Jesus Christ. Therefore, this fellowship involves the apostles and also the Father and the Son. Only the Father and the Son are mentioned here, not the Spirit, because the Spirit is implied in the fellowship. However, elsewhere we are clearly told that this fellowship is "the fellowship of the Holy Spirit" (2 Cor. 13:14). The divine fellowship is a fellowship of the apostles, the representatives of the church, and also a fellowship between these apostles as the representatives of the church and the Father and the Son. The fact that the divine fellowship is also a fellowship of the Spirit means that this fellowship is carried out by the

Spirit. This fellowship is not merely *with* the Spirit; it is also *of* the Spirit. This means that it is the Spirit's fellowship and that this fellowship is carried out by the Spirit.

We have just pointed out what it means to say that the divine fellowship is the fellowship of the Spirit. Actually, the Spirit Himself is the fellowship. This means that the fellowship is not only carried out by the Spirit, but also that the Spirit is the fellowship that is carried out.

Once again we may use electricity as an illustration of the divine fellowship. Electricity flows from the power plant into the church meeting hall. As a result, when the switch is on, all the lights in the ceiling have "fellowship" in the current, the flow, of electricity. It is the current of electricity that carries out this fellowship. However, it is more accurate to say that actually the current itself is the fellowship. If there were no electrical current, there would not be any fellowship. The current of electricity is the fellowship of electricity, and this fellowship includes the power plant, the meeting hall, and the lights.

Today the divine fellowship is the apostles' fellowship. This means that it is the fellowship of the church. This fellowship is also the fellowship of the believers with the apostles. Furthermore, it is the fellowship of the apostles and the believers with the Father and the Son. Because this fellowship is carried out by the Spirit, it is called the fellowship of the Spirit.

Fellowship for the Church Life

We all need to realize that this divine fellowship is altogether for the church life. This fellowship is not merely for our enjoyment, experience, supply, nourishment, and edification. Ultimately, this fellowship is for the church life.

A LIFE OF BROTHERLY LOVE

Because the divine fellowship is for the church life, there is not only the need for us to confess our sins, but also the need for us to love the brothers. For the maintaining of the fellowship, to confess our sins is not adequate. In order to maintain the divine fellowship, we need to love the brothers. The reason for this is that the church life is a corporate life, a life that involves the brothers. If we lose our brotherly love and if we no longer love one another, what will become of the church life? The answer is that the church life will disappear. Where there is no brotherly love, the church life is finished. Actually, brotherly love is the church life.

In the past we have viewed the church life from different angles and have presented various definitions of the church life from these different angles. Now we need a definition of the church life that is in line with the angle of brotherly love. We all need to learn a new term to describe the church life—a life of brotherly love. Do you know what the church life is? The church life is a life of brotherly love.

I can testify that in the church life in the Lord's recovery we surely experience brotherly love. In particular, I can testify that we enjoy brotherly love during the semi-annual trainings. During the days of the training, brotherly love is especially evident and prevailing, and saints from many different countries enjoy this brotherly love together. It seems that the more international we are, the more brotherly love we experience and enjoy.

Recently we had a conference in Stuttgart, Germany. At that time we all were in an international atmosphere. The saints who attended that conference spoke different languages, and the hymns were sung in all the languages. Whenever I heard a hymn sung in these different languages, I was beside myself with joy in the Lord. The brotherly love was so prevailing that it seemed that in a sense, there was no need for translation. The atmosphere of brotherly love was marvelous. This brotherly love is the church life.

The church life involves saints of different races, countries, languages, and nationalities. All colors are represented in the church life: black, white, yellow, brown, and red. We praise the Lord that together we enjoy true brotherly love!

I wish to emphasize the fact that the divine fellowship is for the church life. This fellowship must be maintained by brotherly love. On the one hand, brotherly love is the result, the issue, of the divine fellowship; on the other hand, brotherly love is a condition, a term, of the divine fellowship. Therefore, brotherly love is both a condition for this fellowship and its result.

KNOWING THE LORD EXPERIENTIALLY

We ourselves cannot produce a love that is both the condition and the issue of the divine fellowship. The only way for us to have such a love is to know the Lord experientially and continually. This is the reason John says in 2:3, "And in this we know that we have known Him, if we keep His commandments." This refers to our experiential knowledge of God in our daily walk, a knowledge related to our intimate fellowship with Him.

KEEPING THE LORD'S WORD

In 2:4 John goes on to say, "He who says, I have known Him, and is not keeping His commandments, is a liar, and the truth is not in this one." According to 2:3 and 4, knowing the Lord involves keeping His commandments. Then in verse 5 John speaks of keeping His word. The "word" in verse 5 is synonymous with "commandments" in verses 3 and 4. "Commandments" emphasizes injunction; the "word" implies spirit and life as a supply to us (John 6:63).

To take the Lord's word simply means to receive His divine supply. This supply is always contained in the Lord's word and is conveyed to us by His word. Therefore, the Lord's word is a channel through which the divine supply of life reaches us. For example, electricity flows from the power plant into a building through wires. We may say that the wires are the container of electricity and the means through which it is conveyed from the power plant into a building. The word of the Lord can be compared to such an electrical wire. As electricity comes from the power plant into a building by passing through

the wires, so the heavenly electricity flows into us through
the channel of the Lord's word.

We all must come to know the Lord experientially. In
our knowing of Him, we need to take His word in order to
receive His supply. Because the Lord's word is the channel
that brings us the divine supply, we need to take His word
into us in a living way. This is the reason I encourage you
to pray-read the Word of God.

LIGHT AND LOVE

The divine supply that comes to us through the Word
has a particular expression, and this expression is the
divine light. Whenever we receive the Lord's word into us,
the essence of the divine supply comes in with light as its
expression. When the supply comes, light comes with it.
From experience we know that whenever we receive the
Lord's word, we have light. Light is the essence of God's
expression. In the light, that is, in the essence of God's
expression, we have love as the essence of God's being.
This is the way to enjoy the love of God. We receive the
Word, and light comes. Whenever light comes, love is
spontaneously present.

With this love which we enjoy in the divine light, we
first love God. We love Him not by our own love, by our
natural love, but by His own love which we experience and
enjoy. Moreover, when we love God, we also love every one
begotten of Him. This means that when we love the
Father, we love His children. Therefore, in this way we
love the brothers. Because we love the brothers, we
spontaneously have the desire to participate in the church
life. In particular, we want to be in the meetings of the
church.

When we receive the Lord's word through pray-reading,
we receive light. Then in the light we have love for God
and for all the saints. However, if we do not receive the
Word and thus are not in the light with the love, we may be
rather indifferent toward the saints and toward the church
life. Should we meet a brother in the Lord, we may not
even have the desire to greet him warmly. But when we

receive the Word and are in the light, spontaneously we experience God's love. We have the strong sense within that we love the Lord. Then if we meet a brother, we shall have the feeling that he is lovable and that we love him. Our response to him will be a response of love. Instead of being cold or indifferent, we shall have a genuine feeling of warmth toward him.

LOVE, FELLOWSHIP, AND THE CHURCH LIFE

In order to have the fellowship that is for the church life, we need brotherly love. If we would have this love, we need to know the Lord experientially. As those who know the Lord, we need to take His word again and again. When we take the Word, we receive light. In this light we spontaneously have love. This love is a strong indication that we also have the Lord Himself, for love is the essence of God's being. As light is the nature of God's expression, love is the nature of God's being. This means that when we have God's love, we actually have God Himself. With this love, the divine love experienced and enjoyed by us, we love God and His children. When we have this love for God and for the children of God, we have the church life. As we have pointed out, this love actually is the church life.

Love is both a condition of the divine fellowship and the result of experiencing this fellowship. The love that issues from the divine light, the light that comes when we receive the Lord's word in our knowing of Him, is the very fellowship that is for the church life. May we all have this love, the love of God, perfected in us so that we may maintain the divine fellowship for the church life.

LIFE-STUDY OF FIRST JOHN

MESSAGE NINETEEN

THE TEACHING OF THE DIVINE ANOINTING

(1)

Scripture Reading: 1 John 2:12-27

The Epistle of 1 John is composed of three main sections: the fellowship of the divine life (1:1—2:11), the teaching of the divine anointing (2:12-27), and the virtues of the divine birth (2:28—5:21). In the foregoing messages we have covered the first section of this Epistle and the first basic matter revealed in this book—the fellowship of the divine life. In this message we come to the second section and to the second basic matter—the teaching of the divine anointing.

THE DEFINITION OF THE ANOINTING

The fellowship of the divine life is divine and mysterious. However, the divine anointing is even more mysterious. It is very difficult to give an adequate definition of the divine anointing. The anointing is the function of the all-inclusive, compound, life-giving Spirit, who is the processed Triune God. In this definition we can see the different elements, or ingredients, of the anointing. The anointing is the function, the moving, of the compound ointment.

The first mention of the anointing in the Bible is in Exodus 30. In that chapter we have a revelation of the compound ointment that was used to anoint the tabernacle and the priesthood.

In principle, John's writings are based on what is written in the Old Testament. For example, in his Gospel John uses the word "tabernacled" in 1:14 and the phrase "Lamb of God" in 1:29. Furthermore, John 1:51 refers to Jacob's dream about the heavenly ladder at Bethel.

Moreover, many of the signs in the book of Revelation can be found in the Old Testament. In the same principle, John's first Epistle is based on the Old Testament. In keeping with this principle, the word "anointing" used by John in chapter two refers to the ointment in Exodus 30. In the Life-study of Exodus, Messages 157-163, we considered the basic elements of the compound ointment and the measure of these elements. The ointment in Exodus 30 is a full type of the all-inclusive, compound, life-giving Spirit, who is the processed Triune God. The anointing is actually the function, the moving, of such a Spirit.

The anointing is very mysterious, but it is also real and experiential. Instead of using the noun "ointment," John uses the verbal noun "anointing." This word refers to the moving of the all-inclusive Spirit within us. If we carefully read 2:12-27, we shall realize that the anointing is actually the personification of the all-inclusive, compound, life-giving Spirit, who is the processed Triune God.

THE DIVINE TRINITY

First John 2:12-27 is a section concerning the divine Trinity according to the believers' growth in life. In these verses the Trinity is covered in a very positive and meaningful way. But if we do not have a spiritual and heavenly view of these verses, we shall not see that the Trinity is covered here. The teaching of the divine anointing concerns the divine Trinity, but this teaching is according to our growth in life. This means that the more we grow in life, the more we shall be concerned with the Trinity.

The entire New Testament is structured with the Trinity. In Ephesians, for example, every chapter is structured with the Trinity. Second Corinthians 13:14 says, "The grace of the Lord Jesus Christ, and the love of God, and the fellowship of the Holy Spirit be with you all." This verse at the very end of 2 Corinthians indicates that the whole book of 2 Corinthians is concerned with the grace of Christ, the love of God, and the fellowship of the Holy Spirit. We also see the Trinity in the book of Revelation:

"Grace to you and peace from Him Who is, and Who was, and Who is coming, and from the seven Spirits Who are before His throne, and from Jesus Christ, the faithful Witness, the Firstborn of the dead, and the Ruler of the kings of the earth" (1:4b-5a). Here we see that the mysterious book of Revelation opens with the Trinity, for in this book also the Trinity is the basic structure.

I wish to emphasize the fact that the divine Trinity is the basic structure of the entire revelation in the Bible. If the divine Trinity were removed from the Scriptures, there would not be any reality of the divine revelation in the Scriptures.

In 1 John only sixteen verses are devoted to the mysterious, all-inclusive, compound anointing (2:12-27). If we study these verses carefully and get into the depths of them, we shall see that the divine Trinity is here, and that the Trinity is covered according to the growth in life of the believers.

A POLEMICAL SECTION

These sixteen verses are also very polemical. These verses are the most polemical section of this Epistle. We have already mentioned that John's writings are polemical, for he was fighting against heresies, including Gnosticism, Cerinthianism, and Docetism. These heresies were related to the Person of Christ, and they caused damage and confusion to the church life. Therefore, it was necessary for the Apostle John to be polemical and to fight against these heresies, inoculating the saints against the poison of the heresies concerning the Person of Christ.

In these sixteen verses John gives a word regarding the deep truth of the Trinity. But John's way of writing is based on the growth in life of the believers. For this reason, John classified the believers into three groups: children, young men, and fathers.

LITTLE CHILDREN

In verse 12 John refers to the recipients of this Epistle as "little children." This is a general address and does not refer to any specific class of believers. As we have already mentioned, according to verse 1 of chapter two, the aged Apostle considered all the recipients of his Epistle his dear little children in the Lord. We shall see that later in verses 13 through 27 John writes to the young children, young men, and fathers. But here he addresses all the believers as little children, no matter what their spiritual age may be. On the one hand, all the believers are God's children. On the other hand, in the church life God's children were also John's children.

John considered the believers his children, not his students or his followers. To be a student is a matter of knowledge, and to be a follower is a matter of participating in a certain activity. But the word "children" indicates life. In this Epistle John refers to the believers in a way that indicates life. John did not even say "my dear children." Instead, he used the more intimate expression "little children."

Sometimes an elderly parent will refer to his mature son as his child. For example, a man may be in his eighties and his son, in his sixties. Nevertheless, the father may still refer to his son as his child. This is a sign of a tender, intimate relationship. In this Epistle, John, an elderly father, addresses all the believers as little children. Writing in an intimate manner, he says, "I write to you, little children...." This term of address also indicates that in writing these verses John is concerned with the believers' growth in life.

THE FORGIVENESS OF SINS

In verse 12 John says, "I write to you, little children, because your sins have been forgiven you because of His name." The forgiveness of sins is the basic element of God's gospel (Luke 24:47; Acts 5:31; 10:43; 13:38). Through this, the believers who receive Christ become the children of God (John 1:12-13).

John realized that forgiveness of sins is a basic factor in our becoming God's children. In verse 12 John tells the little children that their sins have been forgiven because of the Lord's name. They have believed in this precious name and have received the forgiveness of sins. The forgiveness of sins is the first basic element in the gospel. If we believe in the name of the Lord and call on His name, the first blessing we receive is the forgiveness of sins. Through forgiveness, we have been justified and have become the children of God. Regeneration, therefore, is based on the forgiveness of sins. This is the reason the Apostle John regards forgiveness of sins as the basic factor in addressing the recipients of this Epistle as little children.

THE FATHERS

In verse 13 John goes on to say, "I write to you, fathers, because you have known Him who is from the beginning. I write to you, young men, because you have overcome the evil one. I write to you, young children, because you have known the Father." Now we see that some of John's little children are fathers, others are young men, and others are young children.

The fathers are those believers who are mature in the divine life. They are classified by the apostle as the first group among his recipients. These believers are fathers because they "have known Him who is from the beginning." The words "have known" are in the perfect tense. This denotes that the state produced continues. These mature believers *have known;* therefore, they *know* all the time. Such living knowledge is the fruit of the experience of life.

John says that the fathers have known Him who is from the beginning. Here "from the beginning" is used in the absolute sense. The One who is from the beginning is the eternal, preexisting Christ, who is the Word of life from the beginning (1 John 1:1; John 1:1). Knowing in the way of life such an eternal Christ is the characteristic of the mature and experienced fathers, who were not and could not be deceived by the heresies that claimed Christ was not eternal. As the eternal, preexisting One, Christ existed from eternity. This eternal One existed before all created things came into existence. Truly He is the eternal and preexisting One.

Here John does not say that the fathers know the Son of God or Jesus Christ. Rather, he says that they have known the One who is from the beginning; they have known Christ as the eternal, preexisting One. This knowing is a matter of experience, not merely a matter of doctrinal knowledge. If we would know Christ as the eternal, preexisting One, we need to experience Him. The Apostle John did not ascribe this qualification to the young ones. It was to the fathers that he ascribed the qualification of knowing through experience the One who is from the beginning.

Among us there are some fathers, those who have come to know the Lord through their experience of Him. To know the Lord in this way of experience takes many years. This is the qualification of those who can be called "fathers." The criterion that determines who is a father is the experiential knowledge of the Lord as the eternal One, a knowledge that is gained through the life course of many years.

THE YOUNG MEN

In verse 13 we also have the second category of believers—the young men. These are the believers who are grown up in the divine life. One characteristic of these grown-up and strong young believers is that they overcome the evil one. This is possible because the young men are nourished, strengthened, and sustained by the word of God which abides in them and operates in them against the Devil, the world, and its lust (vv. 14b-17).

Overcoming the evil one is a strong evidence that a believer has grown to be a young man. I can testify that in the church life today there is a group of young ones who overcome the evil one and also overcome evil things.

THE YOUNG CHILDREN

The third category of believers mentioned by John is that of the young children. These are the believers who have just received the divine life. They are classified by the apostle as the third group of recipients.

John says that the young children have known the Father. The Father is the source of the divine life, of whom the believers have been reborn (John 1:12-13). To know the Father is the initial issue of being regenerated (John 17:3, 6). Hence, such an experiential knowledge in the youth of the divine life is the basic qualification of the young children, who are the youngest in John's classification.

Just as a child of a human father knows his father, so the young children in the divine life know their Father. The New Testament tells us that we have received the Spirit of sonship, in which we cry, "Abba, Father." All the young children know their Father; they know the One who has begotten them with the divine life.

In verse 13 John says, "I write to you, young children." Here the Greek word is *egrapsa,* have written; in other manuscripts, it is *grapho,* write. Although *egrapsa,* according to more recent manuscript discovery, is more authentic, *grapho,* which is taken by the King James Version and J. N. Darby's New Translation, is more logical according to the context. The Apostle in this verse addresses his writing to each of the three classes of his recipients, all in the present tense. In the following verses, verses 14 through 27, he addresses each of the three classes again, but all in the aorist tense (v. 14 to the fathers and young men; v. 26, see also v. 18, to the young children).

A CONFIRMING WORD

In verse 14 John continues, "I have written to you, fathers, because you have known Him who is from the beginning. I have written to you, young men, because you are strong, and the word of God abides in you, and you have overcome the evil one." Although the Greek word rendered "have written" is aorist, it does not indicate that any previous epistle was written by the apostle to the recipients. It means that he repeats what he has written to them in the preceding verse to strengthen and develop what he has said. By repeating certain matters, John confirms what he has already written.

In verse 14 John again refers to the fathers as knowing

Him who is from the beginning. Because the fathers are full of experience, there is no further advancement.

Concerning the young men, in verse 14 John not only says that they have overcome the evil one, but also says that they are strong and that the word of God abides in them. This word, ending with "abides in you," strengthens the word "you have overcome," which was written in the previous verse to the young men. Many among us are strong young men who have overcome the evil one and who have the word of God abiding in them. Through the word of God that abides in them, they are strengthened, nourished, sustained, and invigorated.

We have seen that in verse 13 John addresses the fathers, the young men, and the young children, and that in verse 14 he again addresses the fathers and the young men. Where is John's second address to the young children? It is in verse 18: "Young children, it is the last hour, and even as you heard that antichrist is coming, even now many antichrists have come; whereby we know that it is the last hour." Here "young children" refers to the young children in verse 13 as the third class of recipients. In the verses that follow John goes on to speak to the young children concerning the anointing.

DEGREES OF GROWTH IN LIFE

We have seen that in 2:12-27 John writes concerning the divine Trinity according to the believers' growth in life. First, he addresses all the believers as his little children, those whose sins have been forgiven because of the Lord's name. Then John goes on to speak to the fathers, those believers who are mature in the divine life. Through the divine anointing, these believers have known Him who is from the beginning, that is, the eternal, preexisting Christ who is the Word from the beginning. The young men are the believers who are grown up in the divine life. Through the divine anointing, they have overcome the evil one. Furthermore, they are strong and the word of God abides in them. Another characteristic of the young men is that they do not love the world. The young children are the believers who have just received the divine life. Through the divine anointing, they have known the Father. They have also heard that antichrist is coming. But they have an anointing from the Holy One and they know all things.

The fathers, young men, and young children have different degrees of the growth in life. John's classification of the believers is according to their spiritual age, not according to any other criterion. Some are fathers, and others are young men or young children. The use of these terms indicates strongly that these verses in particular were written by the Apostle John based upon the growth in life.

ENJOYING THE HEAVENLY MELODY

The fact that John's writing is based on the believers' growth in life should cause us to realize that if we would understand the Trinity, especially as the divine Trinity is covered in this portion, we must be in the process of the growth in life. This means that we must be in the line of life. If we are not in the line of life pursuing the growth in life, we shall not be able to understand anything concerning the divine Trinity.

When the Triune God as revealed in this portion is ministered to believers who are not growing in life, they do not have any understanding or appreciation of what they hear. But when this is ministered to the seeking ones who are growing in life, they can understand what is ministered and are helped by it. They appreciate the "music" that is "played" concerning the Triune God. They are very responsive when we speak concerning the all-inclusive, compound, life-giving Spirit, who is the processed Triune God. However, those Christians who are not in the line of life and who are not growing in life may wonder what we mean by such terms as all-inclusive, compound, life-giving, and processed. Praise the Lord that we have the all-inclusive, compound, life-giving Spirit, who is the processed Triune God, living, moving, and working within us! When we hear the heavenly melody regarding this wonderful Triune God, we rejoice, and we are very happy in the Lord.

LIFE-STUDY OF FIRST JOHN

THE WORLD AND THE THINGS IN THE WORLD

Scripture Reading: 1 John 2:15-17

In this message we shall consider 2:15-17, verses concerned with the world and the things in the world. In these three verses John defines the world and the things in the world.

The word in 2:15-16, strictly speaking, is not to the fathers nor to the young children; it is a word given to the young men. Of course, whatever is written in the holy Word is written for all of God's children. Nevertheless, according to the context of chapter two, these verses are written specifically to the young men, to those who are strong, who have the word of God abiding in them, and who have overcome the evil one.

THE DEVIL'S MASKS

In the first section of this Epistle, the section concerned with the fellowship of the divine life (1:1—2:11), we saw that sin and sins damage our fellowship. In the second section of this Epistle we see two other negative things: the world and antichrist. In verses 13 and 14 John also mentions the evil one. However, this evil one, Satan, the Devil, does not appear directly here. Instead, he wears the masks of the world and of antichrist. No one would love the Devil if he were to appear directly. But everyone loves the world. The world is Satan's mask that he uses to deceive us and cheat us. In this section of 1 John, the problem is not with the Devil; it is with the world as the Devil's mask.

For those who love material things according to their lustful desires, Satan will appear wearing the mask of the world. But for those who are religious and care for things that are religious, philosophical, or doctrinal, Satan will come with another mask—the mask of antichrist with his heretical teachings.

The anointing that we have within us enables us to deal with the masks of the world and of antichrist. The young men need to confront the mask of the world. For this reason, the word concerning the world is written to the young men. What is the main problem faced by the young children, the youngest ones in the church life? This problem is the problem of heresy, the mask of antichrist. The antichrists do not consider themselves antichrists, but claim that they are for Christ. This claim, however, is a pretense, a falsehood, a deceit. Therefore, John points out that such ones are antichrist; they are not for Christ. Although they bear the name of Christ, this is a pretense. Whereas the young men in the divine life should overcome the world, the young children need to beware of antichrist. These two negative things—the world and antichrist—are found in the second section of this Epistle.

A DEFINITION OF THE WORLD

In verse 15 John says, "Do not love the world, neither the things in the world. If anyone loves the world, the love of the Father is not in him." The Greek word for world, *kosmos,* has more than one meaning. In Matthew 25:34; John 17:15; Acts 17:24; Ephesians 1:4; and Revelation 13:8, it denotes the material universe as a system created by God. In John 1:29; 3:16; and Romans 5:12, it denotes the fallen human race corrupted and usurped by Satan as components for his evil world system. In 1 Peter 3:3 it denotes adorning, ornament. Here, as in John 15:19; 17:14; and James 4:4, it denotes an order, a set form, an orderly arrangement, hence, an ordered system (set up by Satan, the adversary of God), not the earth. God created man to live on the earth for the fulfillment of His purpose. But His enemy Satan, in order to usurp the God-created man, has formed an anti-God world system on this earth by systematizing men with religion, culture, education, industry, commerce, and entertainment through men's fallen nature in their lusts, pleasures, pursuits, and even in their indulgence in living necessities, such as food, clothing, housing, and transportation. The whole of such a satanic system lies in the evil one (1 John 5:19). Not loving such a world is the ground for overcoming the evil one. Loving it just a little gives the evil one the ground to defeat us and occupy us.

In verse 15 John says that if we love the world, the love of the Father is not in us. The love of the Father here is our love toward Him generated by His love within us. We love Him with the love by which He has loved us.

It is important for us to understand the different meanings of the word *kosmos* in the New Testament. We have pointed out that this word is used to denote the material universe, the fallen human race corrupted and usurped by Satan, and the anti-God world system set up by Satan in order to usurp the man created by God for the fulfillment of His purpose. It is the last mentioned denotation of *kosmos* that applies to 2:15. In this verse the world refers to the anti-God world system formed by Satan. Every thing, every one, and every matter have been systematized by the evil one, the adversary of God, and made a part of his world system.

In such a situation, where shall we go? The answer is that we need to go to the Triune God. Only the Triune God has not been systematized by Satan. Along with going to the Triune God, we also need to go to the Word of God. Therefore, since every thing, every one, and every matter have been systematized by Satan, we need to flee to the Triune God and His Word. God's Word is our refuge, our protection.

OVERCOMING THE EVIL ONE

According to the context, the young men have overcome the evil one, the one who formed this anti-God system, the one who has systematized all things, all persons, and all matters. How can the young men overcome this evil one? They can overcome him because they have the word of God abiding in them. The Word of God is also their refuge, stronghold, and fortress. Day by day, the young men need to stay in the Word of God. We know from our experience that when the word of God abides in us and we stay in the Word as our refuge, we are protected from the evil one.

In 5:19 John says that the whole world system lies in the evil one. Not only has this evil one systematized everything, but the entire system lies in him. We may use a patient in surgery as an illustration of the world lying in the evil one. In surgery, a patient is anesthetized and lies on the operating table. The surgeon is then able to operate on the patient, and the patient has no consciousness of what is happening. This is a picture of the whole world lying under the hand of Satan. Those in the world are unconscious of the fact that they are lying on the "surgery table" of the evil one and that he is "operating" on them.

NOT LOVING THE WORLD

In verse 15 John charges us not to love the world or the things in the world. He tells us that if we love the world, the love of the Father is not in us. Not loving the world is the ground for overcoming the evil one. However, if we love the world, this will give the evil one the ground to occupy us. Whenever we open ourselves to the world, to Satan's anti-God system, we lose the battle against him.

THE THINGS IN THE WORLD

In verse 16 John speaks concerning the things in the world: "Because all that is in the world, the lust of the flesh, and the lust of the eyes, and the vainglory of life, is not of the Father, but is of the world." The lust of the flesh is the passionate desire of the body; the lust of the eyes is the passionate desire of the soul through the eyes; and the vainglory of life is the empty pride, boast, confidence, assurance, and display of material things of the present life. These are the components of the world.

The Lust of the Flesh

The lust of the flesh, the passionate desire of the body,

is mainly related to the body. Because the fruit of the tree of knowledge of good and evil has entered into the human race, our body became fallen and corrupted. Adam and Eve, our first parents, partook of the fruit of the tree of the knowledge of good and evil. As a result, an evil element came into the human race, and now this element is in our physical body. From experience we know that an evil, satanic element dwells in man's nature.

Asceticism is an attempt to deal with the lust of the flesh. However, asceticism is not effective in dealing with the passionate desire of the body. In certain Christian writings we can see the element of asceticism. For example, we can find asceticism in the famous book, *The Imitation of Christ*. Some Christian teachings concerning bearing the cross actually bring in asceticism. In the four Gospels the Lord Jesus clearly spoke concerning the cross. However, we should not confuse the genuine bearing of the cross with asceticism. No matter to what extent people may mistreat their body by following ascetic practices, asceticism will not work in dealing with the lust of the body.

The Lust of the Eyes

In verse 16 John also speaks about the lust of the eyes. We have pointed out that the lust of the eyes is the passionate desire of the soul through the eyes. When the fruit of the tree of the knowledge of good and evil came into the human body, the body became flesh. Because the body encompasses the soul, the soul fell under the influence of the fallen body. As a result, our soul also has been corrupted. Therefore, the soul, our psychological being, has become lustful due to the influence of the fallen body.

The fallen soul and body now work together. Our body influences our soul, and our soul influences our body. The body and the soul work together whenever we do something sinful. Because of this mutual operation of body and soul, it is difficult to say whether it is the body or the soul that takes the initiative to commit sin. Therefore, on the one hand, we have the lust of the flesh; on the other hand, we have the lust of the eyes. Apparently, the lust of the eyes is simply part of the lust of the flesh. Actually, this refers to something within our body. Our eyes are lustful because our soul is lustful. The lust in our eyes, therefore, comes from our soul.

The Vainglory of Life

In verse 16 John also mentions the vainglory of life. We have seen that the vainglory of life is the empty pride, boast, confidence, assurance, and display of material things of the present life. Here the Greek word rendered "life" is *bios,* a word that refers to physical life, and also to the present life. It differs from the Greek word *zoe* used in 1:1-2, a word that refers to the divine life.

In the New Testament three Greek words are used for life: *zoe,* which refers to the divine life, the life of God; *psuche,* which refers to our human life, our soulish or psychological life; and *bios,* which refers to physical life. The Greek word *bios* also denotes the present life. Hence, the vainglory of life means the vainglory of the present life. Whatever takes place in human society is the present life. With this present, earthly life there is vainglory. This vainglory includes empty pride, boast, confidence, assurance, and display of material things.

THE CONTENTS OF THE SATANIC SYSTEM

We have seen that the world in 2:15 denotes an evil, satanic, anti-God system that is constituted of the things created by God. Satan has used these things to form his system. However, these things are not the contents of the satanic world system. This system comprises the lust of the flesh, the lust of the eyes, and the vainglory of the present life. For example, God has created different kinds of food. Without food we cannot survive. However, Satan uses food to form a satanic system. This does not mean, however, that food is part of the contents of Satan's evil system.

Farming and industry are also necessary for human life. It would be impossible for us to survive without farming and industry. Satan has utilized farming and industry in forming his evil system. But these things in themselves are not the contents of the world system formed by Satan. What, then are the contents of the satanic system? The contents of this system are the lust of the flesh, the lust of the eyes, and the vainglory of life.

It is not easy to differentiate between the things, matters, and persons used by Satan to constitute his evil system and the actual contents of this world system. Your car and house may be used by Satan to constitute the anti-God world. But neither your car nor your house is part of the contents of Satan's evil system. I would emphasize again that the contents of Satan's system is the lust of the flesh, the lust of the eyes, and the vainglory of this present life.

We may use owning a car as an illustration of the difference between something used by Satan to form his system and the actual contents of this system. How can a car be utilized by the enemy of God to form his evil system? The car itself is not a problem and is not the content of Satan's system. The problem is with the lust of the flesh, the lust of the eyes, and, in particular, with the vainglory of the present life. If it were not for man's vainglory, a car would not become a problem. However, many people like to buy an expensive car in order to make a display. In their case, the car they drive is used for vainglory. In this country a car is a necessity. The problem, therefore, is not with the car itself; the problem is with the lust of the eyes and the pride of life. When you consider a certain kind of car, you may desire to have it. Some may think about a certain car day and night. The car is not wrong—the persons are wrong. The problem is not with the car they need; the problem is with the lust of the flesh, the lust of the eyes, and the vainglory of life.

As further illustrations, we may also refer to our need for clothing and housing. A dwelling place is a necessity, and clothing also is a necessity. Once again, the problem is not with the house or the clothes; these are not the actual contents of the world system. The problem is with the lust of the flesh, the lust of the eyes, and the vainglory of life, for these are the contents of Satan's evil system.

TWO TRINITIES

According to the Bible, the world is against the Father (v. 15), the Devil is against the Son (3:8), and the flesh is against the Spirit (Gal. 5:17). On the one hand, we have the divine Trinity—the Father, the Son, and the Spirit. On the other hand, we have an evil trinity—the world, Satan, and the flesh. If we enjoy the divine Trinity, we shall have nothing to do with the evil trinity.

THE FATHER AND HIS WILL

In verse 17 John goes on to say, "And the world is passing away, and its lust, but he who practices the will of God abides forever." As the world is against God the Father, so the things in the world (v. 15), which are its lust, are against the will of God. On the positive side, we have the Father and His will. On the negative side, we have the world and all the things in the world. The world is against the Father, and the things in the world are against the will of the Father.

According to John's word in verse 17, the world is passing away and its lust, but he who practices the will of God abides forever. To practice the will of God is to do the will of God habitually and continually, not merely occasionally. The world, its lust, and those who love the world are passing away. But God, His will, and those who do His will abide forever.

LIFE-STUDY OF FIRST JOHN

MESSAGE TWENTY-ONE

EXPERIENCING THE TEACHING OF THE ANOINTING CONCERNING THE TRIUNE GOD

Scripture Reading: 1 John 2:18-23

A WORD TO THE YOUNG CHILDREN

In 2:13 the Apostle John writes a very simple word to the young children, those believers who are very young in the divine life: "I write to you, young children, because you have known the Father." In verses 18 through 27 John writes a much longer word to the young children in order to confirm what he has already written to them. On the positive side, this further word is concerned with the anointing; on the negative side, it is concerned with the antichrists. In verse 18 John says, "Young children, it is the last hour, and even as you heard that antichrist is coming, even now many antichrists have come; whereby we know that it is the last hour." The words "young children" here refer to the young children in verse 13 as the third class of the recipients of this Epistle. Verses 18 through 27 emphasize the knowledge in life (vv. 20-21) and strengthen the word, "because you have known the Father," spoken to the young children in verse 13.

In verse 20 John speaks to the young children concerning the anointing: "And you have an anointing from the Holy One, and you all know." The anointing is the moving and working of the indwelling compound Spirit, which is fully typified by the anointing oil, the compound ointment, in Exodus 30:23-25 (see Life-study of Exodus, Messages 157-163). This all-inclusive life-giving Spirit from the Holy One entered into us at the time of our regeneration and abides in us forever (v. 27). It is by this Spirit that the

young children have known the Father (v. 13) and know
the truth (v. 21).

John's word to the young children concerning the
anointing has much to do with their growth in life. John's
word here also indicates that all the saints in the church
life need to receive the teaching of the anointing.

THE ANOINTING TEACHING US
CONCERNING THE TRINITY

If you read verses 18 through 27 carefully, you will see
that the teaching of the anointing is mainly a matter of
teaching us the mystery of the Trinity. For years, I have
been giving messages on the teaching of the anointing. In
those messages I emphasized the fact that the anointing
teaches us concerning all things, that is, concerning
everything in our daily Christian life. In this message I
would like to consider the teaching of the anointing in the
more restricted sense of the anointing teaching us all
things concerning the Trinity. In other words, in this
message I am concerned not with the broader application
of the principle, but with the proper interpretation of the
teaching of the anointing according to the context of these
verses. The more I consider these verses in context, the
more assurance I have that it is absolutely accurate to say
that the teaching of the anointing concerns the things of
the Trinity.

THE ELEMENTS OF THE COMPOUND OINTMENT

We have seen that the anointing is the moving of the
all-inclusive, compound, life-giving Spirit, who is the
processed Triune God. This Spirit is the fulfillment of the
type of the compound ointment revealed in Exodus 30. In
this compound ointment there are a number of different
elements which are the ingredients of the ointment. Just as
paint may have a number of different elements, so the
anointing Spirit also has different elements. These elements
include the processed Triune God and His activities. The
Triune God has passed through incarnation, human living,
crucifixion, resurrection, and ascension. These are the

steps in His activity. All these steps have become elements of the compound, life-giving Spirit. Therefore, the anointing Spirit is actually a compound of the Triune God and His activities. The anointing Spirit includes divinity and humanity, the divine nature and the human nature. Such a compound Spirit includes incarnation, human living, crucifixion, resurrection, and ascension. All these are elements of the compound Spirit typified by the compound ointment in Exodus 30.

The anointing is actually the moving of the ointment, and the ointment is a compound. Oil, however, is not a compound, for it contains a single element. The compound ointment, on the contrary, contains a number of different elements. In the compound Spirit we have the Father, the Son, the Spirit, divinity, humanity, incarnation, human living, the effectiveness of Christ's death, the power of His resurrection, and His ascension. The anointing is the moving of this compound Spirit with all His elements. Only this anointing, only the moving of this compound Spirit, can teach us the Triune God.

Paint is the best illustration of the compound ointment. What is the best way to know the elements of a particular paint? The best way is to buy a can of that paint and apply some paint to a piece of furniture. By applying the paint, you will be taught concerning the elements of the paint. This means that only the paint itself can teach you what the paint is. Apart from the paint there is no way for you to learn about the elements of the paint. In a similar way, it is by applying Himself to us as the "paint" that the compound Spirit teaches us concerning the Triune God and His activities. We also may say that the elements of the compound Spirit teach us the various matters concerning the Triune God and His activities. The anointing Spirit is the composition of the Triune God with all His activities, and now this compound Spirit teaches us concerning the things of the Trinity.

THE SUBJECTIVE TEACHING OF THE ANOINTING

Only through the Triune God becoming the anointing

Spirit can we be taught concerning the Triune God and His activities. This kind of teaching is not objective; rather, it is very subjective. The Triune God has become the anointing Spirit and His anointing is now within us. This subjective anointing, the moving of the composition of the Triune God with all His activities, can now teach us the things concerning the Triune God and His activities. Therefore, it is such an anointing that teaches us the things concerning the Triune God.

The Triune God has been compounded not only with the elements of His Person—divinity, the Father, the Son, and Spirit—but also with the elements of His activities—incarnation, human living, crucifixion, resurrection, and ascension. All these elements have been compounded to become the compound Spirit whose anointing teaches us concerning the things of the Trinity.

BAPTIZED INTO THE TRIUNE GOD

The revelation in the Bible concerning the Triune God is very experiential. For instance, in Matthew 28:19 the Lord Jesus said to His disciples, "Go therefore and disciple all the nations, baptizing them into the name of the Father and of the Son and of the Holy Spirit." In his *Word Studies in the New Testament* M. R. Vincent says that the name in Matthew 28:19 is equivalent to the Person. Hence, to baptize people into the name of the Father, the Son, and the Spirit means to baptize them into the Person of the Triune God. Just as a human name denotes a human person, the divine name denotes the divine Person. To baptize people into the name of the Triune God is to put them into the Person of the Triune God.

Vincent says also, "Baptizing *into* the name of the Holy Trinity implies a spiritual and mystical union with Him." The preposition "into" implies an organic union between us and the Triune God. To be be baptized into the Person of the Triune God means to be placed into an organic union with Him. As those who have been baptized into the Person of the Triune God, we are now organically one with the Triune God, and He is organically one with us.

THE TRIUNE GOD TEACHING US CONCERNING HIMSELF

The Triune God, who is now organically one with us, is teaching us concerning Himself. This teaching is subjective and experiential. Day by day, as we are in the organic union with the Triune God, we enjoy Him, we experience Him, and we live in Him, with Him, and by Him. This living is a constant teaching of the things concerning the Triune God. We can testify that we certainly enjoy the Triune God in our daily life.

We may use eating food as an illustration of learning the things of the Triune God in the way of enjoying and experiencing Him. The best way to know a certain kind of food is to eat that food. If you eat the food, you will be taught concerning the food by the very food you eat. This is not merely an objective lesson concerning food; it is a subjective knowing of the food through experience. The more you eat a particular food, the more you will come to know it. This knowledge is not doctrinal; it is experiential. In a similar way, we come to know the Triune God by enjoying and experiencing Him. It is impossible for us to know the Triune God merely by doctrine. But we can know Him by enjoying and experiencing Him.

When the Triune God becomes our enjoyment and experience, His moving is the anointing within us. This understanding enables us to give a proper definition of the anointing: the anointing is the moving of the Triune God becoming our inward enjoyment and experience.

KNOWING THAT THE FATHER, SON, AND SPIRIT ARE ONE

According to the Bible, we teach that the Father, the Son, and the Spirit are one. Isaiah 9:6 says that a Son has been given to us, yet His name is called the everlasting Father, or the eternal Father, or Father of eternity. This matches the Lord's word concerning Himself and the Father recorded in the Gospel of John. The Lord Jesus said that He, the Son, came in the name of the Father (John 5:43). The Lord never said of Himself that He was the Son and the Father. But He did say that He was the Son coming in the Father's name. In chapter fourteen of the Gospel of John the Lord also says that if we see Him, we see the Father (v. 9). Furthermore, in this chapter the Lord says that He is in the Father and the Father is in Him (vv. 10-11). So He says in John 10:30 the Father and the Son are one. When we confess Him, we also have the Father (1 John 2:23). Furthermore, He is also the Spirit (2 Cor. 3:17). When we have Him dwelling in us, we also have both the Father and the Spirit. Do you not have the Lord Jesus in you? Surely you do. Do you not also have the Father and the Spirit in you? You certainly have also both the Father and the Spirit in you. This means that the Father, the Son, and the Spirit are all in you. How many, then, do we have within us? From experience we know that we have only One within us. This One who dwells in us is the Triune God, the Father, the Son, and the Spirit.

THE TRIUNE GOD BECOMING
OUR EXPERIENCE AND ENJOYMENT

We need to be impressed with the fact that the anointing is the moving of the Triune God enjoyed and experienced by us. The moving of the Triune God within us who becomes our enjoyment and experience is the anointing. The anointing here in chapter two of 1 John refers to our experience of the Triune God. It is this experience that teaches us the things concerning the Trinity.

John's word concerning the anointing here was written to the young children, to those who are the youngest in the divine life. Even the youngest believers have experienced the Lord within them. They can testify from their experience that the One who lives in them is the Father, the Son, and the Spirit.

THE "TASTE" OF THE TRIUNE GOD

We need the proper experience of the Triune God. From the "taste" in our experience we know the things concerning the Trinity. For example, how do you know whether sugar tastes sweet or bitter? The way to know is to taste a little of it. The taste will teach you whether it is bitter or sweet. In a similar way, our experience, our taste, of the Triune God will teach us concerning Him.

John's intention in 2:18-27 is to warn the young children about the antichrists and their heretical teachings. In these verses John seems to be saying, "Do not listen to all these false teachings about the Person of Christ. You have a Teacher within you, and this Teacher is the anointing. Do not give heed to what the antichrists say, but listen to your experience of the Triune God's moving as the anointing within you." Praise the Lord for the experience of the teaching of the anointing concerning the Triune God!

LIFE-STUDY OF FIRST JOHN

MESSAGE TWENTY-TWO

THE ANOINTING

Scripture Reading: 1 John 2:20-27

THE ANOINTING AND THE TRUTH

In this message we shall consider 2:20-27. Verse 20 says, "And you have an anointing from the Holy One, and you all know." This verse speaks not of the ointment but of the anointing. The word "anointing" denotes something experiential that is taking place within us. The anointing is the moving and working of the indwelling compound Spirit. This all-inclusive life-giving Spirit from the Holy One entered into us at the time of our regeneration and abides in us forever (v. 27).

Verse 20 says at the end, "you all know." Some manuscripts read, "you know all things." I believe that the proper rendering should be "you know all," not "you all know."

In verse 21 John says, "I have not written to you because you do not know the truth, but because you know it, and because no lie is of the truth." In this verse the word "truth" is used twice. If we consider verses 20 and 21 together, we shall realize that the anointing surely must have something to do with the truth. Verse 20 says that we have an anointing, and verse 21 says that we know the truth. In this verse the truth is closely related to the anointing. Actually the anointing is the moving and working of the truth, which is the reality of the divine Trinity, especially of the Person of Christ (vv. 22-25).

The knowing in verse 21 is the knowing by the anointing of the indwelling and life-giving Spirit. This is a knowledge in the divine life under the divine light, an inner knowledge initiated from our regenerated spirit indwelt by the compound Spirit, not mental knowledge exercised by stimulation from without.

DENYING THE FATHER AND THE SON

In verse 22 John goes on to say, "Who is the liar if not he who is denying that Jesus is the Christ? This is the antichrist, who is denying the Father and the Son." The statement that Jesus is the Christ is related to the truth, and the truth is related to the anointing. These three matters are all related to one another. First we have the anointing, then the truth related to the anointing, and then the statement that Jesus is the Christ related to the truth.

Verse 22 indicates that the antichrist is the one who denies the Father and the Son. After speaking of Jesus being the Christ, John speaks concerning the Father and the Son. This indicates that the Father and the Son are related to Jesus being the Christ.

In these three verses we have four crucial matters: the anointing, the truth, Jesus being the Christ, and the Father and the Son. The anointing teaches us the truth, the truth is that Jesus is the Christ, and Jesus being the Christ is a matter that includes the Father and the Son. According to verse 22, to deny that Jesus is the Christ is to deny the Father and the Son. If we deny that Jesus is the Christ, this means that we deny the Father and the Son. This indicates strongly that Jesus, Christ, the Father, and the Son are one.

ENJOYING CHRIST AND GROWING IN LIFE

Here I would like to point out that when we speak of these matters, we are not fighting for doctrines. However, we are fighting for the genuine experience of Christ so that Christians may enjoy Christ in order to grow in life.

Not many today teach concerning Christian growth in the proper way. What is emphasized among Christians is growth in knowledge. But the New Testament teaches us that we need to grow in life. As newborn babes, we should desire to drink the milk of the Word so that we may grow in life (1 Pet. 2:2).

From experience we know that to grow in life is to grow by the ingredients of what the Lord is as our nourishment. We need to take this nourishment into our being as food and then assimilate it. The Lord Jesus told us definitely that He is our food. In John 6:35 He said, "I am the bread of life." For the Lord to be bread to us means that He is our food. In John 6:57 the Lord Jesus said that he who eats Him will live because of Him. The food by which we live is also the food by which we grow. If we do not grow by the food we eat, how can we live by it? Children grow by what they eat. Then they live by it. Hence, when the Lord Jesus said that he who eats Him will also live by Him, this implies both living by Him and growing by Him.

In the Lord's recovery we are wholly for the experience of the growth in life. This growth in life depends on our enjoyment of the Lord Jesus in a subjective way. If the Lord were not the Spirit, He could not be subjective to us, and He could not be our life. If the Lord could not be our life, then He could not be our nourishment.

Many Christians today emphasize objective teachings concerning the improvement of character and behavior. These teachings are ethical and are comparable to the teachings of Confucius. The teachings in the New Testament, however, are different. The New Testament teaches that after being processed through incarnation, human living, crucifixion, and resurrection, the Triune God becomes the all-inclusive life-giving Spirit in order to enter into our being to be our life and also our life supply so that we may live and grow by Him. This is the central line of the New Testament revelation.

The Lord Jesus declared that He is life. In John 14:6 He said, "I am . . . the life." If He were only on the throne in the heavens, how could He be our life? This would be impossible. In order for Christ to be our life, He must be the Spirit living within us. It is crucial that Christians experience Christ as their subjective life. We are fighting not for doctrines, but for the Christian experience of Christ as life.

THE HERESY OF CERINTHUS

We have pointed out that, according to verses 21 and 22, the truth is that Jesus is the Christ. However, this truth was denied by certain heretics who said that Jesus was not the Christ. Denying that Jesus is the Christ is the heresy of Cerinthus, a first century Syrian heresiarch of Jewish descent, educated at Alexandria. His heresy was a mixture of Judaism, Gnosticism, and Christianity. He distinguished the maker (creator) of the world from God, and represented that maker as a subordinate power. He taught adoptionist Christology (Adoptionism), saying that Jesus became Son of God by exaltation to a status that was not His by birth, thus denying the conception of Jesus by the Holy Spirit. In his heresy he separated the earthly man Jesus, regarded as the son of Joseph and Mary, from the heavenly Christ, and taught that after Jesus was baptized, Christ as a dove descended upon Him. Then He announced the unknown Father and did miracles, but at the end of His ministry Christ departed from Jesus, and Jesus suffered death on the cross and rose from the dead, while Christ remained separated as a spiritual being, and will rejoin the man Jesus at the coming of the Messianic kingdom of glory. This heresy denied that Jesus is the Christ. According to John's word, anyone who denies that Jesus is the Christ is the antichrist. Cerinthus was an antichrist, and his followers also were antichrists.

In verse 22 John says that the antichrist denies the Father and the Son. To confess that Jesus is the Christ is to confess that He is the Son of God (Matt. 16:16; John 20:31). Hence, to deny that Jesus is the Christ is to deny the Father and the Son. Whoever so denies the divine Person of Christ is an antichrist.

JESUS, CHRIST, THE FATHER, AND THE SON

The fact that to deny Jesus being the Christ equals denying the Father and the Son implies the thought that Jesus, Christ, the Father, and the Son are all one, all of whom are the elements, the ingredients, of the all-inclusive compound indwelling Spirit, who is now anointing the believers all the time. In this anointing, Jesus, Christ, the Father, and the Son are all anointed into our inner being.

In verse 22 John indicates that to deny that Jesus is the Christ is equal to denying the Father and the Son. Here John regards Jesus, Christ, the Father, and the Son as one. Surely Jesus and Christ are one. But if we deny that Jesus is the Christ, we deny the Father and the Son. This indicates strongly that the Father and the Son are one with Jesus and Christ. Since the Father and the Son are one with Christ and since Jesus and Christ are one, Jesus, Christ, the Father, and the Son are all one.

We all have heard that Jesus is the Christ, but have you ever heard that, according to 2:22, Christ is both the Father and the Son? We need to be impressed with the fact that here John says that to deny that Jesus is the Christ is to deny the Father and the Son. However, some claim that we should say only that Christ is the Son, not that Christ is both the Father and the Son. Nevertheless, in this verse John indicates that if we deny Christ, we deny both the Father and the Son. If Christ were only the Son and not also the Father, how would denying Christ mean that we deny both the Father and the Son? According to this understanding of Christ, to deny Christ would only mean to deny the Son, and this denial would have nothing to do with the Father. But John says that if someone denies Christ, he denies first the Father and then the Son.

In verse 23 John continues, "Everyone who denies the Son does not have the Father either; he who confesses the Son has the Father also." Since the Son and the Father are one (John 10:30; Isa. 9:6), to deny the Son is to be without the Father, and to confess the Son is to have the Father. To deny the Son here refers to the heresy that denies the deity of Christ, not confessing that the Man Jesus is God.

In verse 23 John first says that anyone who denies the Son does not have the Father either. If the Son and the Father were not one, how could those who deny the Son not have the Father? In this verse John goes on to say that he who confesses the Son has the Father also. Whoever denies the Son has neither the Son nor the Father. But whoever confesses the Son has both the Son and the Father. Both the negative side and the positive side of this verse indicate that the Son and the Father are inseparable. Because the Father and the Son are one, we cannot separate the Son from the Father nor the Father from the Son.

I would call your attention to the words "either" and "also" in verse 23. John says that whoever denies the Son does not have the Father *either*. Then he says that whoever confesses the Son has the Father *also*. These words indicate that the Father and the Son are one and inseparable. Therefore, to deny the Son is to deny both the Son and the Father, and to confess the Son is to confess both the Son and the Father.

THE WORD OF LIFE ABIDING IN US

Verse 24 says, "As for you, that which you heard from the beginning, let it abide in you. If that which you heard from the beginning abides in you, you will abide both in the Son and in the Father." "That which you heard from the beginning" refers to the Word of life—the eternal life which the believers heard from the beginning (1:1-2). Not to deny but confess that the Man Jesus is the Christ, the Son of God (v. 22) is to let the Word of the eternal life abide in us. In so doing we abide both in the Son and in the Father, and we are not led astray by the heretical teachings concerning Christ's Person (v. 26). This indicates that the Son and the Father are the eternal life for our regeneration and enjoyment. In this eternal life we have fellowship with God and with one another (1:2-3, 6-7), and in it we have our being in our daily walk (2:6; 1:7).

In verse 24 John says that if we let that which was from the beginning, that is, the Word of life, abide in us, we shall abide both in the Son and in the Father. This indicates that the Word of life is actually the Son and the Father.

Notice that here John speaks of our abiding in the Son and in the Father. In John 15:4 the Lord Jesus says, "Abide in Me and I in you." This verse speaks of a mutual abiding: we abide in the Lord, and the Lord abides in us. But in 2:24 John refers to the Word of life abiding in us, and says that if the Word of life abides in us, we abide in the Son and in the Father. By this we see that the Word of life is actually the Lord Himself. According to John 15:4, when we abide in the Lord, the Lord abides in us. Here it says that when the Word of life abides in us, we abide in the Son and in the Father. Once again, John puts the Father and the Son together as one, for the Father and the Son are one.

THE FATHER AND THE SON BEING ONE

The New Testament does not separate the Father and the Son. Especially in the Gospel of John we see that the Son is always one with the Father. The Son came in the name of the Father (John 5:43). Furthermore, the Son did not do His own work and will, He did not speak His own word, He did not seek His own glory, and He did not express Himself (John 4:34; 5:30; 6:38; 7:18). Rather, He always did the Father's work and will, spoke the Father's word, sought the Father's glory, and expressed the Father. The Son was one with the Father and could not be separated from the Father, neither could the Father be separated from the Son. Hence, in this Epistle John emphasizes strongly the fact that if we have the Son, we have the Father. But if we do not have the Son, we do not have the Father. This indicates that the Father and the Son truly are one (John 10:30).

ETERNAL LIFE

In verse 25 John continues, "And this is the promise which He promised us, the eternal life." The singular pronoun "He," referring to both the Son and the Father in the preceding verse, indicates that the Son and the Father are one. As far as our experience of the divine life is concerned, the Son, the Father, Jesus, and Christ are all one. It is not that only the Son and not the Father is the eternal life to us. It is that Jesus being the Christ as the Son and the Father is the eternal life to us for our portion.

According to the context of verses 22 through 25, the eternal life is just Jesus, Christ, the Son, and the Father. All these are a composition of the eternal life. Hence, the eternal life is also an element of the all-inclusive, compound, indwelling Spirit who moves within us.

A DIVINE COMPOUND

The eternal life in verse 25 is the Word of life, and the Word of life is Jesus, Christ, the Father, and the Son. Here we have six matters: Jesus, Christ, the Father, the Son, the Word of life, and eternal life. From the Bible, especially from 1 John, we know that Jesus is the Christ, that Christ equals the Father and the Son, and that this One is also the Word of life and the eternal life.

Together Jesus, Christ, the Father, the Son, the Word of life, and eternal life are a divine compound. All these six are elements that have been compounded into a single ointment. In Jesus we have humanity, with the Father we have divinity, and with Christ we have the anointed One. With Jesus we have the incarnation, with Christ we have the resurrection, and with the Son we have life. Therefore, with these elements we have all the ingredients of the compound ointment: divinity, humanity, incarnation, crucifixion, resurrection, and life.

If we study these verses in 1 John along with the record of the elements of the compound ointment in Exodus 30, we shall see that all the elements in Exodus 30 are found in these verses. To be sure, here we have the olive oil, the myrrh, the cinnamon, the calamus, and the cassia. We also have the numbers five and three (see Life-study of Exodus, Messages 157-163).

In chapter two of 1 John we certainly have the compound ointment, the all-inclusive Spirit. However, here we do not have the ointment merely in an objective way; instead, we have the subjective anointing, that is, the subjective moving and working of the ointment. This subjective anointing is the processed Triune God experienced by us. Furthermore, this anointing teaches us concerning the processed Triune God. For example, if someone should say that Christ is not in us, we should reply, "From my experience of the anointing I know that Jesus Christ is in me." Moreover, if someone should try to teach you that the Father, the Son, and the Spirit are three separate Persons, you may say, "I don't have three separate Persons within me. From my experience of the anointing I know that I have only One in me, and this One is the Father, the Son, and the Spirit."

AN ILLUSTRATION OF THE ONENESS
OF THE FATHER, THE SON, AND THE HOLY SPIRIT

In Matthew 28:19 the Lord Jesus gave this charge to His disciples: "Go therefore and disciple all the nations, baptizing them into the name of the Father and of the Son and of the Holy Spirit." However, when the apostles carried out this charge in the book of Acts, we are not told that they baptized the believers into the name of the Father, the Son, and the Holy Spirit. Rather, in Acts we are told that the believers were baptized into the name of Jesus Christ (Acts 2:38). This indicates that the name of Jesus Christ equals the name of the Father, the Son, and the Holy Spirit. This indicates that Jesus Christ is the Father, the Son, and the Holy Spirit. The apostles knew that Jesus Christ was equal to the Father, the Son, and the Spirit. Therefore, they carried out the Lord's charge to baptize the believers into the name of the Father and of the Son and of the Holy Spirit by baptizing them into the name of Jesus Christ. This is an illustration of the fact that the Father, the Son, and the Spirit are one. This is the Triune God, and we are in Him. To be in the Triune God is also to be in the divine compound, the compound ointment, which is the all-inclusive Spirit.

LIFE-STUDY OF FIRST JOHN

MESSAGE TWENTY-THREE

THE TEACHING OF THE DIVINE ANOINTING

(2)

Scripture Reading: 1 John 2:20-27

In the previous message we pointed out that according to 2:20-27 the Father and the Son are one. It is absolutely correct to say that the Son is not separate from the Father, nor the Father from the Son. However, there is still a distinction between the Three of the Godhead, a distinction between the Father, the Son, and the Holy Spirit.

JESUS AND CHRIST

The Lord is both Jesus and Christ. Although there is no separation between Jesus and Christ, there is a distinction between these two titles Jesus and Christ. The name Jesus means Jehovah our Savior or Jehovah our salvation. The title Christ means the anointed One. The name Jesus mostly denotes the Lord in His humanity, in His incarnation, human living, and crucifixion. The title Christ denotes the Lord as God's anointed One and especially what He is in resurrection and ascension. Jesus and Christ both refer to the same Person. Although this Person is inseparable, there is nevertheless a distinction between the two titles Jesus and Christ.

THE FATHER AND THE SON

Although the Son and the Father are one, we should not say that there is no distinction between the Father and the Son. There is a distinction between the Father and the Son, but there is no separation. When the Father is present, the Son is present also. Likewise, where the Son is, there the Father is also. The Father and the Son cannot be separated. For this reason, in verse 23 John says that whoever denies the Son does not have the Father either, and that he who confesses the Son has the Father also.

Whenever we speak about the Trinity, we need to be sober and careful with our definitions and illustrations. We have seen from 2:20-27 that Jesus, Christ, the Father, the Son, the Word of life, and eternal life all are one. However, there is still a distinction between them. We have already pointed out that Jesus and Christ refer to the same Person. Nevertheless, there is a distinction between the name Jesus and the title Christ. We should not say that they denote the same thing, for the denotations are quite different. Because our Lord is rich and all-inclusive, He needs different names and titles to describe Him. Therefore, He is Jesus and He is also Christ. As Jesus He is Jehovah our Savior, and as Christ, He is God's anointed One.

There should not be any doubt in us that the Father, the Son, and the Spirit are truly one and are one God. Although we believe in the Trinity, we definitely do not believe in three Gods. Tritheism, the belief in three Gods, is heresy, and we must condemn it. Although God is one, there is a clear distinction between the Father, the Son, and the Spirit in the Godhead.

THE TWOFOLDNESS OF THE TRUTH
CONCERNING THE TRINITY

The truth of the Triune God is twofold; that is, it has two sides or two aspects, the aspect of one and the aspect of three. The twofoldness of the truth concerning the Trinity is embodied in the word triune. This adjective is actually a Latin word composed of two parts: tri-, meaning three, and -une, meaning one. The word "triune," therefore, means three-one. On the one hand, our God is uniquely one; on the other hand, He is three. In the aspect of God's being one, there is no separation between the Father, the Son, and the Spirit. But in the aspect of God's being three, there is a distinction between the Father, the Son, and the Spirit. The Lord Jesus said, "I am in the Father, and the Father is in

Me" (John 14:10). Because the Father and the Son are mutually in each other, They cannot be separated. But there is still a distinction between the Father and the Son.

Concerning the Trinity we should not drift to either of two extremes, to the extreme of emphasizing the three or the extreme of emphasizing the one. Some Christians have gone to the extreme of emphasizing the three to the neglect of the one. Others drift to the extreme of the one and neglect the three. We need to be balanced. In order to be balanced we need to emphasize both aspects of the Trinity—the aspect of the three and the aspect of the one. Because in the foregoing message we pointed out that the Father and the Son are one, in this message I would like to say a balancing word that although the Father and the Son are one, there is still a definite distinction between them. In the sense of distinction, the Father is the Father, the Son is the Son, and the Spirit is the Spirit. Although there is a distinction between the Three of the Godhead, the Three nonetheless are still one.

In *The Principles of Theology* W. H. Griffith Thomas says the following:

> The term "Person" is also sometimes objected to. Like all human language, it is liable to be accused of inadequacy and even positive error. It certainly must not be pressed too far, or it will lead to Tritheism. While we use the term to denote distinctions in the Godhead, we do not imply distinctions which amount to separateness, but distinctions which are associated with essential mutual co-inherence or inclusiveness....
>
> While, therefore, we are compelled to use terms like "substance" and "Person," we are not to think of them as identical with what we understand as human substance or personality. The terms are not explanatory, but only approximately correct, as must necessarily be the case with any attempt to define the Nature of God.

I especially appreciate Griffith Thomas' word that the term "Person" must not be pressed too far "or it will lead to Tritheism," the belief in three Gods. In the same principle, when we say that the Father, the Son, and the Spirit are all one, we should not press this too far, or we will fall into another kind of error. Some have used sunlight as an illustration: the sun is the Father, the ray is the Son, and the shining is the Spirit. Another illustration is that of ice, water, and vapor, with these three respectively representing the Father, the Son, and the Spirit. Such illustrations may be used for temporary help; they should not be pressed too far or they will lead to error.

THE ANOINTING AND THE TRUTH

Let us now go on to consider again 2:20-27. Verses 20 and 21 say, "And you have an anointing from the Holy One, and you all know. I have not written to you because you do not know the truth, but because you know it, and because no lie is of the truth." In verse 20 John speaks of the anointing, and in verse 21 he speaks of the truth. No doubt, the truth in verse 21 is related to the anointing, and the anointing points to the truth.

In verse 22 John continues, "Who is the liar if not he who is denying that Jesus is the Christ? This is the antichrist, who is denying the Father and the Son." This indicates clearly that if we deny that Jesus is the Christ, we deny the Father and the Son. This also indicates that Christ is the Father and the Son.

ABIDING IN THE FATHER AND THE SON

Verses 23 and 24 say, "Everyone who denies the Son does not have the Father either; he who confesses the Son has the Father also. As for you, that which you heard from the beginning, let it abide in you. If that which you heard from the beginning abides in you, you will abide both in the Son and in the Father." Some who disagree with our understanding of these verses may say, "These verses mean that the Son is the way. In John 14:6 Jesus said that He is the way and that no one comes to the Father except through Him. These verses in 1 John mean that if we do not have the Son as the way, we shall not be able to reach the Father as the destination. Therefore, to deny the Son is to deny the way, and this results in not having the Father as the destination." However, according to verse 24, if we take the Son as the way to reach the Father, eventually we reach both the Son and the Father. In this verse John speaks of abiding both in the Son and in the Father. It may sound logical to say that Christ as the Son is only the way for us to reach the Father as the destination. Therefore, if we do not take the way, we shall not arrive at the destination. If we take the way, we shall reach the destination. However, here it says that if we take the way, we shall have not only the destination, but we shall have both the destination and the way. Here John indicates that we shall abide not only in the destination but also in the way, that is, both in the Son and in the Father. This proves that both the Son and the Father are the destination. Not only is the Father the abiding place, but the Son is also. This means that the Son is both the way and the destination, both the way to enter into the dwelling place and the dwelling place itself.

ETERNAL LIFE

In verse 25 John goes on to say, "And this is the promise which He promised us, the eternal life." In this verse John does not say, "They promised us"; he says, "He promised us." The singular pronoun "He" in this verse refers to both the Son and the Father in the preceding verse. This indicates that the Son and the Father are one. As far as our experience of the divine life is concerned, the Son, the Father, Jesus, and Christ are all one. It is not that only the Son and not the Father is eternal life to us. It is that Jesus being the Christ as the Son and the Father is the eternal divine life to us for our portion. The point we are emphasizing here is that the antecedent of the pronoun "He" is the Son and the Father and that this indicates that the Son and the Father are one.

THOSE WHO LEAD THE BELIEVERS ASTRAY

Verse 26 says, "These things I have written to you concerning those who are leading you astray." This verse indicates that this section of the Word is to inoculate the believers with the truth of the divine Trinity against the heresies concerning Christ's Person. The Greek words rendered "leading you astray" can also be translated "deceiving you." To lead the believers astray is to distract them from the truth concerning Christ's deity and humanity by deceiving them with heretical teachings concerning the mysteries of what Christ is.

THE INWARD TEACHING OF THE ANOINTING

In verse 27 John says, "And as for you, the anointing which you received from Him abides in you, and you have no need that anyone should teach you; but as His anointing teaches you concerning all things, and is true, and is not a lie, and even as it has taught you, abide in Him." I would call your attention to the pronouns "Him" (used twice) and "His." As was the case in verse 25, these pronouns refer to both the Son and the Father. This use of singular pronouns proves strongly that the Son and the Father are one.

It is significant that in these verses the pronoun "they" is not used with respect to the Father and the Son. Rather, John uses singular pronouns to refer to both the Son and the Father. Nevertheless, the expression "in the Son and in the Father" (v. 24) points to a distinction between the Son and the Father. If there were no distinction, there would be no need for John to say, "abide both in the Son and in the Father." Although there is a distinction between the Son and the Father, there is no separation, because the Father and the Son are one. Therefore the Father and the Son are distinct but inseparable.

In verse 27 John says, "You have no need that anyone should teach you." Concerning the indwelling of the divine Trinity (John 14:17, 23), we do not need anyone to teach us. By the anointing of the all-inclusive compound Spirit, who is the composition of the divine Trinity, we know and enjoy the Father, the Son, and the Spirit as our life and life supply.

According to verse 27, the anointing of the all-inclusive compound life-giving Spirit teaches us concerning all things. This is not an outward teaching by words, but an inward teaching by the anointing through our inner spiritual consciousness. This teaching by the anointing adds the divine elements of the Trinity, which are the elements of the anointing compound Spirit, into our inner being. It is like the repeated painting of some article: the paint not only gives color; its elements are also added to the thing painted, coat upon coat. It is in this way that the Triune God is transfused, infused, and added into all the inward parts of our being so that our inner man may grow in the divine life with the divine elements.

According to the context, "all things" refers to all things concerning the Person of Christ related to the divine Trinity. The teaching of the anointing concerning these things keeps us that we may abide in Him (the divine Trinity), that is, in the Son and in the Father (v. 24).

In this verse John also says that the anointing is true. The anointing within us of the compound Spirit as the composition of the Triune God who is true (5:20), is a reality, not a falsehood. This can be proved by our actual and practical experience in our Christian life.

John concludes verse 27 with an exhortation to abide in the Triune God. The Greek word translated "abide" is *meno*, a word that means to stay (in a given place, state, relation, or expectancy); hence, abide, remain, and dwell. To abide in Him is to abide in the Son and in the Father. This is to remain and dwell in the Lord (John 15:4-5). It is also to abide in the fellowship of the divine life and to walk in the divine light (1 John 1:2-3, 6-7), that is, to abide in the divine light (1:10). We should practice this abiding according to the teaching of the all-inclusive anointing so that our fellowship with God (1:3, 6) may be maintained.

LIFE-STUDY OF FIRST JOHN

MESSAGE TWENTY-FOUR

THE ANOINTING AND THE ANTICHRISTS

Scripture Reading: 1 John 2:18-27

In this message I would like to give a further word on the teaching of the divine anointing. We have seen that the teaching of the anointing concerning the divine Trinity is according to the believers' growth in life. We have also seen that the teaching of the divine anointing is for our abiding in the Triune God.

FELLOWSHIP AND THE ANOINTING

The fellowship of the divine life depends on the anointing. This means that maintaining the fellowship of the divine life depends on abiding in the Lord and in the light. To abide in the Lord and in the light is equal to abiding in the Triune God.

The Triune God reaches us as the Spirit. If God were only the Father and the Son, He would not be able to enter into us. It is only as the Spirit that the Triune God can enter into our spirit. The word "anointing" in 2:20 and 27 refers mainly to the Spirit, not primarily to the Father or the Son. Actually, the ointment is the Spirit, and the anointing is the moving of this ointment. When we speak of the anointing, we mean the Triune God reaching us as the Spirit. When the Triune God comes into our spirit, He is the life-giving Spirit. This life-giving Spirit, who dwells in our spirit, is now moving and working within us. This moving is the anointing.

The anointing has much to do with our abiding in the Lord. We enjoy the fellowship of the divine life so that we may abide in the Lord. This abiding is altogether a matter of the Lord as the Spirit dwelling in our spirit. This is the reason that immediately after the first section, which is

concerned with the fellowship of the divine life, John goes
on in the second section of this Epistle to speak of the
teaching of the divine anointing. Apart from the anointing, we cannot abide in the Lord. If we do not abide in the
Lord, we cannot maintain the fellowship. Furthermore, if
we do not maintain the fellowship, we cannot enjoy the
riches of the divine life. We may also say that to enjoy the
riches of the divine life, we need to maintain the
fellowship; to maintain the fellowship, we need to abide in
the Lord; and in order to abide in the Lord, we need to take
care of the inner anointing, which is the moving of the
indwelling Spirit in our spirit.

DENYING THE PERSON OF CHRIST

In verse 18 John says, "Young children, it is the last
hour, and even as you heard that antichrist is coming,
even now many antichrists have come; whereby we know
that it is the last hour." An antichrist differs from a false
Christ (Matt. 24:5, 24). A false Christ is one who pretends
to be the Christ in a deceiving way, whereas an antichrist
is one who denies Christ's deity, denying that Jesus is the
Christ, that is, denying the Father and the Son by denying
that Jesus is the Son of God (vv. 22-23), not confessing that
He has come in the flesh through the divine conception of
the Holy Spirit (4:2-3). At the time of the Apostle John,
many heretics, like the Gnostics, Cerinthians, and Docetists, taught heresies concerning the Person of Christ, that
is, concerning His divinity and humanity.

In verse 19 John goes on to say, "They went out from
us, but they were not of us; for if they had been of us, they
would have remained with us; but they went out that they
might be manifested that they all are not of us." These
antichrists were not born of God and were not in the
fellowship of the apostles with the believers (1:3; Acts 2:42).
Hence, they were not of the church, that is, not of the Body
of Christ. To remain with the apostles and the believers is
to remain in the fellowship of the Body of Christ.

In verse 22 John says, "Who is the liar if not he who is
denying that Jesus is the Christ? This is the antichrist,

who is denying the Father and the Son." To confess that Jesus is the Christ is to confess that He is the Son of God (Matt. 16:16; John 20:31). Hence, to deny that Jesus is the Christ is to "deny the Father and the Son." Whoever so denies the divine Person of Christ "is the antichrist."

THE ANOINTED ONE, THE ANOINTING ONE, AND THE ANOINTING

To deny that Jesus is the Christ is related to denying the anointing. However, due to the problem of language, we may not realize that Christ is related to the anointing. The Greek word for Christ is *Christos*, which means the anointed one, and the Greek word for anointing is *chrisma*. Both words are derived from the same root. Now we must go on to see that Christ as the anointed One becomes the anointing. Because He is the anointed One, He has an abundance of ointment with which to anoint us. Eventually, the anointed One becomes the anointing One. In fact, He even becomes the anointing. To deny that Jesus is the Christ is to deny that Jesus is the anointed One. Moreover, to deny the anointed One means to deny the anointing. Therefore, to deny the *Christos* is to deny the *chrisma*. Whenever someone denies that Jesus is the *Christos*, that one denies that Jesus is the anointed One. This is equal to denying the anointing, for after the anointed One enters into us, He becomes the anointing.

In 2 Corinthians 1:21 Paul says, "But He who firmly attaches us with you unto Christ and has anointed us is God." Because we have been attached by God to Christ, the anointed One, we are spontaneously anointed with Him by God. Christ has been anointed with the divine ointment, and the ointment that is upon Him now flows to us. This is pictured in Psalm 133, which says that the anointing oil flows from the head of Aaron to his beard and even to the skirts of his priestly robe. This indicates that Christ has an abundance of the anointing oil. God has poured the ointment upon Him. Through that anointing Christ has received the ointment, and eventually He, the anointed

One, became the anointing One. When He entered into us as the anointed One, He became the anointing One in us. Actually, the anointing that dwells in us is the anointed One becoming the anointing One and also the anointing. To reject this anointed One is to reject the anointing. Whenever someone denies that Jesus is the anointed One and thereby denies that He is the anointing One, this person also denies the anointing. Now we need to see that to deny the anointing is to be anti-anointing, the accurate meaning of the title antichrist. Antichrist, therefore, means anti the anointing.

According to verse 22, the antichrist is the one who denies that Jesus is the Christ. To deny that Jesus is the Christ is to deny that He is the anointing One. This is also to deny the anointing and thereby to be anti-anointing. What is the antichrist? The antichrist is someone who is anti-anointing. Furthermore, according to verse 22, to be an antichrist, to be anti-anointing, is to deny the Father and the Son. We may not be anti the anointing in this way, yet we have to admit that often we disobey this inner anointing.

God's intention is to work Himself into us as our life and our everything to make us His counterpart for the expression of Himself. In order to accomplish this, it was necessary for God to pass through the process of incarnation, human living, crucifixion, and resurrection. When He entered into resurrection, He became the compound, all-inclusive, life-giving Spirit. This Spirit is actually *Christos*, the anointed One, becoming the life-giving One. When we believed in the Lord Jesus, we received Him into us. The One we received is the anointed One, who through death and resurrection has become the anointing One. Furthermore, this anointing One is the all-inclusive indwelling Spirit. As soon as we believed in Him, He as the Spirit entered our spirit. Now He is within our spirit to anoint us, to "paint" us, with the element of the Triune God. The more this "painting" goes on, the more the element of the Triune God is transfused into our being. This is the anointing, which is the reality of the entire New Testament.

THE EFFECTIVENESS OF THE CROSS
AND THE REALITY OF RESURRECTION

This crucial and central matter of the anointing has been neglected by many Christians. Today many have a religion with doctrines and regulations, but they neglect the inward teaching of the anointing of the all-inclusive Spirit. Some teach concerning the cross. However, they may have only the doctrine of the cross; they may not have the life-giving Spirit imparting the effectiveness of the cross of Christ into their being. We may try to reckon ourselves dead. But we may do this without having the effectiveness of Christ's death imparted into our being through the anointing Spirit. Apart from the Spirit, reckoning ourselves dead is merely a vain practice. Years ago, I tried to follow this practice, but I found out that it did not work.

Christians today may also teach about resurrection. Although they teach the doctrine of resurrection, they may not have the reality of Christ's resurrection wrought into them through the life-giving Spirit. The life-giving Spirit is the reality of Christ's resurrection. The doctrine of Christ's resurrection cannot impart its reality into our being. This can be done only through the life-giving Spirit, who is actually the resurrected Christ Himself living in us. The doctrine is not the reality. It is the resurrected Christ Himself as the life-giving Spirit who is the reality of His resurrection. It is not sufficient to have the doctrine. We need the life-giving Spirit as the reality of the doctrine. Realizing this, in 1958 I began to give message after message saying that merely the doctrine of Christ's death and resurrection is vanity; only the Spirit can convey the effectiveness of Christ's death and the reality of His resurrection into us. If we realize this, we shall see that many of today's Christians have merely the doctrine without the Spirit.

THE LIFE-GIVING, ANOINTING SPIRIT

All that God is, all that God has, and all that God has attained and obtained, are included in the life-giving

Spirit. This life-giving Spirit is the compound Spirit as the ointment anointing us. In this anointing we have God with all His attainments in a living, substantial way. We should not have God merely in an objective, doctrinal way. We should have the subjective God, a God who is substantiated in our spirit through, by, in, and with the all-inclusive Spirit.

Because the all-inclusive Spirit is neglected and even ignored by many Christians today, certain believers are, in a sense, anti- the anointing ignorantly. They may worship the Father and believe in the Son in an objective way, believing in Him as the One who is the Lord far away in the heavens, but not caring for Him subjectively as the anointing Spirit who has come into their being and is now dwelling in them. Instead of caring for such a living and subjective Christ, some actually oppose the truth that Christ today is the life-giving Spirit who lives in the believers. This means that they are anti the Christ who is the indwelling, life-giving, anointing Spirit.

MANY ANTICHRISTS

Due to the influence of traditional teaching, many think that the term "antichrist" refers only to the man of lawlessness in 2 Thessalonians 2 and to the beast in Revelation 13. However, the term antichrist is not used in either of these chapters. The title antichrist should not be applied merely to the man of lawlessness and the beast. According to 1 John, the antichrists are those who are anti Christ, the anointed One, as the Son of God. Actually, in the New Testament the man of lawlessness is not called the antichrist. This title is found only in the Epistles of 1 and 2 John, where it is used to refer to those who deny that Jesus is the Christ, that is, those who deny that Jesus is the anointed One, as the Son of God. According to 1 John chapter two, whoever denies Christ in this way is an antichrist. "Antichrist," without the article, in verse 18 denotes the category, not a particular antichrist. Hence, "many antichrists" are mentioned in the following clause.

EXPERIENCING THE ANOINTING

The anointing Spirit within is the consummation of the Triune God, and in this Spirit there are the elements of divinity, humanity, human living, crucifixion, and resurrection. He is the all-inclusive Spirit comprising all that God has accomplished, attained, and obtained. This Spirit is now the anointing One within us.

First, Christ was the anointed One. Then as the anointed One, He became the anointing One who dwells within us to anoint us. However, most Christians either neglect this or are ignorant of it, and some actually oppose this truth. We thank the Lord that, by His mercy, we are experiencing and enjoying the wonderful anointing of the all-inclusive Spirit within us.

PAINTING OTHERS WITH
THE LIFE-GIVING SPIRIT

I am encouraged by the fact that many saints in the Lord's recovery, especially the young people, are enjoying this anointing. I expect that in the years to come the saints will go forth to preach and teach the wonderful, divine mysteries that are unknown to so many believers today. Many of us will be able to anoint others with the compound Spirit, applying this divine "paint" to them. If we would do this, we need to be "painted" persons, those who are saturated with the anointing. We should be those on whom the paint is "wet," always having a fresh application of the divine paint. Because this painting is taking place all the time, the paint on us should never dry. Then as such painted persons, we should go forth to paint others with the compound, all-inclusive, life-giving Spirit.

LIFE-STUDY OF FIRST JOHN

MESSAGE TWENTY-FIVE

THE VIRTUES OF THE DIVINE BIRTH
TO PRACTICE THE DIVINE RIGHTEOUSNESS

(1)

Scripture Reading: 1 John 2:28—3:10a

In previous messages we have covered the first two
sections of this Epistle: the fellowship of the divine life
(1:1—2:11) and the teaching of the divine anointing (2:12-
27). In this message we come to the third section: the
virtues of the divine birth (2:28—5:21). The sequence here is
very significant. First, John shows us that in the divine
life there is the enjoyment of fellowship, and in this
fellowship we enjoy the teaching of the anointing. Following this, John writes concerning the virtues of the divine
birth. According to 2:28—3:10a, the virtues of the divine
birth are for the practice of the divine righteousness.

THE BEGETTING ONE AND THE COMING ONE

First John 2:28 says, "And now, little children, abide in
Him, that if He is manifested, we may have boldness and
not be put to shame from Him at His coming." The
pronoun "Him" in this verse refers to the Father and the
Son. This means that "Him" actually refers to the Triune
God. Hence, to abide in Him is to abide in the Father, the
Son, and the Spirit.

The pronoun "He" in the phrase "He is manifested,"
according to the context, must refer to the Son. This
understanding is supported by the phrase "at His coming,"
found at the end of the verse. Here John is saying that if
the Son is manifested, we may have boldness and not be
put to shame from Him at His coming.

In verse 29 John continues, "If you have known that He

is righteous, you know also that everyone who practices righteousness has been begotten of Him." "He" here denotes the Triune God, the Father, the Son, and the Spirit, all-inclusively, because it refers to "He" and "Him" in the preceding verse, which denote the coming Son, and it also denotes "Him" in this verse, referring to the Father who has begotten us. This indicates strongly that the Son and the Father are one (John 10:30). The pronoun "He" refers both to the Son who is coming and to the Father who has begotten us. It is the Father, not the Son, who has begotten us, but it is the Son, not the Father, who is coming.

In this verse "He" as a pronoun serves two purposes, referring both to Him (the Son) who is coming and also to Him (the Father) who has begotten us. Are the Father and the Son one or two? The best answer to this question is to say that They are two-one. He is both the One who will come and the One who has begotten. As the begetting One, He is the Father; and as the coming One, He is the Son.

ABIDING IN HIM

In 2:28 the Apostle John says, "And now, little children, abide in Him." The word that begins in 2:13, to the three different classes of recipients, ends in verse 27. Now verse 28 returns to all the recipients. For this reason, the address is again to the "little children," as in verses 1 and 12.

The word addressed to the three groups of recipients in 2:13-27 concludes in the charge to "abide in Him" as the anointing has taught us. In this section, from 2:28 through 3:24, the apostle continues to describe the life that abides in the Lord. It begins (2:28), continues (3:6), and ends (3:24) with "abide in Him."

As we have pointed out, here the pronoun "He" refers definitely to Christ the Son, who is coming. This, with the preceding clause, "abide in Him," which is a repetition of the clause in verse 27 involving the Trinity, indicates that the Son is the embodiment of the Triune God, inseparable from the Father or the Spirit.

In verse 28 John says that if we abide in Him, "we may have boldness and not be put to shame from Him at His coming." The Greek words translated "at His coming" literally mean "in His presence" (*parousia*). John's word about not being put to shame indicates that some believers who do not abide in the Lord (that is, do not remain in the fellowship of the divine life according to pure faith in Christ's Person), but are led astray by the heretical teachings concerning Christ (v. 26), will be punished by being put to shame from Him, from His glorious *parousia*.

KNOWING THAT HE IS RIGHTEOUS

In verse 29 John twice uses the word "know": "If you have known that He is righteous, you know also that everyone who practices righteousness has been begotten of Him." The first use of the word know is a translation of the Greek word *eideta*, from *oida*, perceived with a conscious knowledge, a deeper inward seeing. This is for knowing the Lord. But the second use of the word "know" is a translation of the Greek word *ginoskete*, from *ginosko*, the outward objective knowledge. This is for knowing man.

The word "righteous" in verse 29 refers to the righteous God in 1:9 and Jesus Christ the Righteous in 2:1. In this word to all the recipients, beginning from 2:28, the apostle turns his emphasis from the fellowship of the divine life in 1:3—2:11 and the anointing of the divine Trinity in 2:12-27 to the righteousness of God. The fellowship of the divine life and the anointing of the divine Trinity should have an issue, that is, should issue in the expression of the righteous God.

KNOWING THAT EVERYONE
WHO PRACTICES RIGHTEOUSNESS
HAS BEEN BEGOTTEN OF GOD

According to John's word in verse 29, if we know that God is righteous, we "know also that everyone who practices righteousness has been begotten of Him." To practice righteousness is not merely to do righteousness occasionally and purposely as some particular act; it is to do righteousness habitually and unintentionally as one's common daily living. It is the same in 3:7. This is an automatic living that issues from the divine life within us, with which we have been begotten of the righteous God. Hence, it is a living expression of God, who is righteous in all His deeds and acts. It is not merely outward behavior, but the manifestation of the inward life; not merely an act of purpose, but the flow of life from within the divine nature we partake of. This is the first condition of the life that abides in the Lord. It is all due to the divine birth, which is indicated by the word "has been begotten of Him" and the title "children of God" in 3:1.

John's writings on the mysteries of the eternal divine life place much emphasis on the divine birth (3:9; 4:7; 5:1, 14, 18; John 1:12-13), which is our regeneration (John 3:3, 5). It is the greatest wonder in the entire universe that human beings could be begotten of God, and sinners could be made children of God! Through such an amazing divine birth we have received the divine life, which is the eternal life (1 John 1:2), as the divine seed sown into our being (3:9). Out of this seed all the riches of the divine life grow from within us. It is by this that we abide in the Triune God and live the divine life in our human living, a life that does not practice sin (3:9), but practices righteousness (2:29), loves the brothers (5:1), overcomes the world (5:4), and is not touched by the evil one (5:18).

ABIDING IN THE TRIUNE GOD
AND THE DIVINE BIRTH

First John 2:28—3:10a indicates that we can abide in the Lord. We have pointed out that certain pronouns used in these verses indicate that to abide in the Lord is actually to abide in the Triune God.

It is not a simple matter for us to abide in the Triune God. How can human beings abide in God? To abide in God is different from walking with Him. Genesis 5 tells us that Enoch walked with God. But what does it mean to abide in Him? Here John does not speak of walking with God, but speaks of abiding in God. To abide in God means to dwell in Him. We may find it rather easy to understand what it means to abide with God or dwell with God. But according to the natural mind it seems that it is impossible for human beings to dwell, to abide, *in* God.

Abiding in the Triune God is a matter that involves the divine birth. The third section of this Epistle emphasizes the divine birth. We have the words "begotten of Him" in 2:29 and the phrase "begotten of God" in 3:9; 4:7; 5:1, 4, and 18. By this we see that John repeatedly refers to our divine birth. In order for us to dwell in God, we need to realize that we have had a divine birth, that we have been born of God. Through this divine birth we have received the divine life, which is the divine seed. How wonderful that a divine seed has been sown into our being and that we have been born of God!

When a child is born of his parents, he automatically has a human life. We may say that this human life came from the sowing of a human seed, that the child's being came from a human seed. This seed means a great deal to a child's living, for it causes him to be different from any kind of animal. Because a newborn child has a human seed, the child can dwell in humanity. He has been born of humanity, and he has a human life from that seed. Therefore, it is easy for the child to remain, abide, dwell, in humanity. Actually, for a child to dwell in humanity is natural, spontaneous, and automatic. He can abide in humanity because he has had a human birth and possesses a human life from the human seed.

Suppose someone commanded a dog to abide in humanity. A dog may pretend for a little while to stand upright like a human being. But eventually he will go back to standing on four feet and spontaneously live according to the dog nature within him. Because a dog has not had a human birth, he does not have the human life, the human seed, to enable him to abide in humanity.

Do you know what makes it possible for us to dwell in the Triune God? We can dwell in Him because we have been born of Him. It is the wonder of wonders that human beings can be born of God. Although God is divine and we are sinners, we have nevertheless been born of the divine Being. Nothing could be greater than this.

This divine birth is not merely a doctrine or something
experienced psychologically. On the contrary, this birth
has actually taken place organically in our spirit. In John
3:6 the Lord Jesus says, "That which is born of the Spirit is
spirit." Praise the Lord that we have experienced such a
birth! This divine birth brings us a divine life, and the
divine life is the divine seed which is now in our being. In
this divine life we spontaneously abide, dwell, in the
Triune God.

We are already dwelling in the Triune God. There is no
need for us to exercise ourselves to dwell in Him since we
are already in Him. However, we need to be careful not to
allow this abiding in the Triune God to be interrupted.

We have been born of God, and God's seed abides in us.
By this seed we are in God and can abide in God. There is
no need for us to do anything. But we should not let our
abiding in Him be interrupted. This is the reason John
charges us again and again to abide in Him.

In 3:24 John says that we know that He abides in us, by
the Spirit whom He gave to us. This indicates that the
Lord's abiding in us and our abiding in Him is altogether
in the Spirit.

SATURATED WITH THE ALL-INCLUSIVE SPIRIT

Because we have been born of God and because His life
as a divine seed abides in us, we can abide in Him. As we
abide in Him, He saturates us. Of course, John does not use
the word "saturates." But if we experience what is written
in this section of 1 John, we shall realize that what John
speaks of actually involves being saturated with the
Triune God. The Triune God is not a theory or theology; He
is the living Spirit, the anointing. Therefore, when we
abide in the Triune God, He as the all-inclusive, compound,
indwelling, life-giving Spirit will saturate us, and we shall
be soaked with Him.

The more we are anointed with the Triune God, the
more we are saturated with Him. Let us use as an
illustration a piece of cloth that has paint applied to it. The
more the paint is applied to the cloth, the more the cloth

soaks the paint in until it is saturated with it. Eventually, the entire cloth will be saturated with the paint. The anointing is a divine painting. We have seen that the anointing is the moving within us of the compound, all-inclusive, life-giving, indwelling Spirit, who is the processed Triune God. Just as paint is composed of different elements, so this anointing, the processed Triune God, includes a number of different elements: divinity, humanity, incarnation, human living, crucifixion, and resurrection. All these elements have been compounded into the all-inclusive Spirit, who is the divine paint with which we are being painted. Now this Spirit is within us anointing us, painting the elements of divinity, humanity, incarnation, human living, crucifixion, and resurrection into our being until we are saturated with them.

My burden is to show the children of God that the Christian life is not a matter of religion or doctrine. The Christian life is altogether a matter of being saturated with the all-inclusive Spirit. This saturation cannot be accomplished by doctrine or theology. This is possible only through the processed Triune God, who is the all-inclusive Spirit.

Many Christians do not have a proper understanding of the Spirit. Some regard the Spirit merely as a force; others claim that the Spirit is in the believers to represent the Father and the Son. Such an understanding of the Spirit is far off from what is revealed in the Bible. In this kind of teaching concerning the Spirit there is no place for the elements that are included in the life-giving Spirit. According to this kind of understanding, at most the Spirit is merely a force or power or a representative of the Father and the Son. Those who hold this concept concerning the Spirit do not realize that according to the Bible the Spirit is the ultimate consummation of the processed Triune God. Many elements have been compounded into this one Spirit. Hence, when this indwelling Spirit anoints us, He saturates our being with all the elements of the processed Triune God. It is in this way that we are regenerated, transformed, and glorified.

Doctrine cannot regenerate us, and theology cannot transform us. Doctrine may be compared to a menu. When you go to a restaurant, you may read the menu. However, your purpose is not to study the menu—your purpose is to eat a nourishing meal. The menu cannot transform you by nourishing you. Only the food you eat can do this.

Suppose a person is undernourished and as a result has a pale complexion. The way to improve his complexion is not to apply cosmetics. To do this would be like doing the work of a mortician. The proper way is to feed him with nourishing food day by day. Eventually, this food will cause an inner transformation, an organic, metabolic change, that will be expressed in a healthy complexion. In the same principle, our transformation can be brought about only by the Spirit, not by doctrine. However, many Christians today care for doctrine and not for life in the Spirit. There are not many Christians who care for the experience of the divine life in the regenerated spirit. We need to be impressed with the fact that in this section of 1 John the experience of the divine life is a matter of the Spirit of God in our spirit.

In 2:28—3:10a we see that we have a divine birth. Through this divine birth we have received the divine seed. Now it is possible for us to dwell in God, and we need to dwell in Him. When we dwell in the Triune God, He saturates us. This is not a matter of correction or regulation—it is a matter of saturation. Referring to the illustration of the cloth and the paint, our being saturated with the Triune God is like the cloth having paint applied to it until it is thoroughly saturated with the paint. Our God today is the anointing, the divine paint. What we have within is not only the ointment but the anoint*ing*, not only the paint but the paint*ing*. As this painting takes place within us, it saturates us until we are soaked with the paint. Eventually, we shall be thoroughly saturated and permeated with the paint. This certainly is not a matter of religion, doctrine, theology, or teaching. This is a matter of the Triune God as the compound, all-inclusive, life-giving, indwelling Spirit in our spirit continually anointing us.

Through this anointing the very fibers of our being will be saturated with all that the processed Triune God is.

BECOMING THE EXPRESSION OF THE TRIUNE GOD

As the result of being saturated with the Triune God, we become His expression. Because we have been saturated with Him, we express Him. In a sense, after the cloth has been saturated with the paint, it becomes the paint and expresses not itself but the paint with which it has been saturated. Likewise, as the result of being thoroughly saturated with the Triune God, we shall express Him. In particular, because God is righteous, when we express Him, we shall express His righteousness.

PRACTICING RIGHTEOUSNESS HABITUALLY

We have seen that the word "practices" in 2:29 means to do something habitually and continually. In 2:29 John speaks not merely of doing righteousness but of practicing righteousness, that is, of doing righteousness continually and habitually as a way of life. A dog, for example, habitually, continually, and unintentionally stands on four legs. For a dog to try to stand upright on two legs and walk like a man would not be a practice but an attempt to act like a human being. Likewise, an unbeliever may do something righteous for a particular purpose. However, as children of God, we practice righteousness spontaneously, habitually, automatically, continually, and without a purpose. This means that we do not purposely intend to do righteousness; rather, we practice righteousness because this is the living of the divine life that is within us. Because we abide in the righteous God and He is saturating us with what He is, we express His righteousness by living a righteous life unintentionally and habitually.

May we all be deeply impressed with the fact that through the divine birth we have received the divine seed. Now through this divine seed we can dwell in our God. As we dwell in Him, He will saturate us with what He is. Because He is righteous, we shall continually express the

divine righteousness by practicing righteousness habitually and unintentionally. This is to practice the divine
righteousness by virtue of the divine birth.

LIFE-STUDY OF FIRST JOHN

MESSAGE TWENTY-SIX

THE VIRTUES OF THE DIVINE BIRTH TO PRACTICE THE DIVINE RIGHTEOUSNESS

(2)

Scripture Reading: 1 John 2:28—3:10a

In the Epistle of 1 John there are three main sections: the fellowship of the divine life (1:1—2:11), the teaching of the divine anointing (2:12-27), and the virtues of the divine birth (2:28—5:21). The sequence of these sections indicates that the fellowship of the divine life and the teaching of the divine anointing bring us into the virtues of the divine birth.

In the third section we see how much enjoyment we receive from the divine birth. In particular, this enjoyment is related to the virtues of the divine birth. The divine birth brings in many virtues. Only by the fellowship of the divine life and by the teaching of the divine anointing can we experience and enjoy all the virtues imparted to us through the divine birth. According to 1 John, the first of these virtues is to practice the divine righteousness. Therefore, the title of this message is "The Virtues of the Divine Birth to Practice the Divine Righteousness."

THE DIVINE BIRTH AS THE BASIS

The practice of the divine righteousness has a basis, and this basis is the divine birth (2:29; 3:9; 4:7; 5:1, 4, 18). Through this birth we have received the divine life as the divine seed. We may say that this seed is the "capital" for our Christian life. In order to live a Christian life, we need such capital; that is, we need the divine life sown as the divine seed into our being through the divine birth.

The divine birth brings us the divine seed, and through

this seed we partake of the divine nature for our growth in the divine life. A certain kind of life will always have a particular nature, and this nature is for growth. Because we have been born of God, we have the divine life. Within this divine life there is the divine nature. Now we are partaking of and enjoying this divine nature (2 Pet. 1:4) for us to grow in the divine life. This is the basis for the practice of the divine righteousness, the divine love (3:10b—5:3), and the overcoming of all negative things (5:4-21).

THE DIVINE LIFE AS THE MEANS

We have seen that the divine birth is the basis. Now we must go on to see that the divine life is the means. First, the divine life is the means for us to abide in the Triune God. If we did not have the human life, we could not abide in humanity. Likewise, if we did not have the divine life, we could not abide in the Triune God. But because we have the divine life, by this life we can abide in the Triune God.

By the divine life as the means we can also live this life in our human living. This means that we can live a life that practices the divine righteousness, loves the brothers, and overcomes all negative things.

THROUGH THE ABIDING IN THE DIVINE FELLOWSHIP ACCORDING TO THE DIVINE ANOINTING

We can practice the divine righteousness through the abiding in the divine fellowship according to the divine anointing (2:27-28). Through this abiding we first enjoy God as light (1:5, 7; 2:10), and then we enjoy Him as love (4:8, 16). Light and love are deeper than truth and grace. Light is the source of truth, and love is the source of grace. Through abiding in the divine fellowship according to the divine anointing, we not only receive truth and grace, but we also enjoy light as the source of truth and love as the source of grace.

With the divine birth as the basis, the divine life as the means, and through the abiding in the divine fellowship according to the divine anointing, we can practice the divine righteousness. Let us now go on to consider the practice of the divine righteousness.

PRACTICING THE DIVINE RIGHTEOUSNESS

A Charge to All Believers

In 2:28 John says, "And now, little children, abide in Him, that if He is manifested, we may have boldness and not be put to shame from Him at His coming." This word is addressed to the "little children," that is, to all the believers (2:1). This charge begins (2:28), continues (3:6), and ends (3:24) with "abide in Him." If we abide in Him, we may have boldness and not be put to shame from Him at His coming, at His *parousia*. This means that at His coming back we shall not be put to shame from His glory. But if we do not abide in the Triune God, continually living the divine life, then at the Lord's coming back we shall suffer shame, which will be a kind of discipline exercised upon us. Then we shall be kept away from His glory.

Knowing and Practicing

In verse 29 John continues, "If you have known that He is righteous, you know also that everyone who practices righteousness has been begotten of Him." The first mention of the word "known" in this verse is the translation of the Greek word *eidete*, from *oida*, which means perceive with a conscious knowledge, a deeper inward seeing. We need to know in such a way that God is righteous. If we perceive this, then we shall know that everyone who practices righteousness has been begotten of God.

Practicing righteousness is a matter that is habitual and unintentional as a common daily life. Hence, to practice the divine righteousness is to do righteousness habitually and unintentionally as our daily living. However, if we do righteousness intentionally with a purpose, that is not a matter of our common daily life. Rather, it is to behave in a political way. Someone may do righteousness with a purpose of gaining a position or a name for

himself. That is to behave in a political way. But we
Christians, as children of God, should be saturated with
the righteous God so that spontaneously we live a life that
practices righteousness habitually and unintentionally.
Instead of doing a particular act of righteousness for a
certain purpose, we practice righteousness as our common
daily life. This is an issue of the fellowship of the divine
life and the anointing of the divine Trinity. Furthermore,
this is an expression of the righteous God. Through
abiding in the righteous God, we are infused and saturated
with Him. Then our living becomes an expression of the
righteous God with whom we have been infused and
saturated. This righteous God then becomes our righteous
living, our daily righteousness. This practice of righteousness is not merely outward behavior, but the manifestation of the inward life. As we have pointed out, this is not
an act done for a purpose; it is the flow of life from within
the divine nature of which we partake.

Seeing What Manner of Love
the Father Has Given to Us

First John 3:1 says, "See what manner of love the
Father has given to us, that we should be called children of
God; and we are. Because of this the world does not know
us, because it did not know Him." This verse is included in
the passage which goes from 2:28 through 3:3. This
passage is one paragraph on the righteous living of God's
children.

In 3:1 John refers to the divine birth and to the
begetting Father. Of the Triune God implied in 2:29, the
Father is particularly mentioned. He is the source of the
divine life, the One of whom we have been born with this
life. The love of God is manifested by sending His Son to
die for us so that we may have His life and thus become
His children (4:9; John 3:16; 1:12-13). The sending of His
Son is for begetting us. Hence, the love of God is a
begetting love, particularly in the Father.

The word "children" in 3:1 corresponds to "begotten of
Him" in 2:29. We have been begotten of the Father, the

source of life, to be the children of God, the Owner of the children. We partake of the Father's life to express the Triune God.

In 3:1 John says, "Because of this the world does not know us, because it did not know Him." The Greek word rendered "because" may also be translated on this account or for this reason. For the reason that we are the children of God by a mysterious birth with the divine life, the world does not know us. The world is ignorant of our regeneration by God; it does not know us, because it did not know God Himself. It was ignorant of God, so it is also ignorant of our divine birth.

Realizing That the Children of God Have a Great Future

In 3:2 John goes on to say, "Beloved, now we are children of God, and it has not yet been manifested what we shall be. We know that if He is manifested, we shall be like Him, because we shall see Him even as He is." Since we are the children of God, we shall be like Him in the maturity of life when He is manifested. To be like Him is "what we shall be." This has not yet been manifested. This indicates that the children of God have a great future with a more splendid blessing. We shall not only have the divine nature, but shall also bear the divine likeness. To partake of the divine nature is already a great blessing and enjoyment; yet to be like God, bearing His likeness, will be a greater blessing and enjoyment.

The pronoun "He" in 3:2 refers to God and denotes Christ, who is to be manifested. This not only indicates that Christ is God, but also implies the divine Trinity. When Christ is manifested, the Triune God will be manifested. When we see Him, we shall see the Triune God; and when we are like Him, we shall be like the Triune God.

In verse 2 John says, "We shall be like Him, because we shall see Him even as He is." This means that by seeing Him we shall reflect His likeness (2 Cor. 3:18). This will cause us to be as He is.

Verse 2 indicates that the children of God have a great future. However, I have heard some saints say that they do not have a future. These saints need to realize that they have a great future with splendid blessings. Our future is indicated by the word "it has not yet been manifested what we shall be." What we shall be is a divine mystery. Because it is such a mystery, it must be something great. We are not able to imagine what our future will be. The fact that our future has not yet been manifested indicates that it will be wonderful. Although it has not been manifested what we shall be, we know that when the Son is manifested, we shall be like the Triune God.

Purifying Ourselves

In 3:3 John continues, "And everyone who has this hope in Him purifies himself, even as that One is pure." The hope spoken of here is the hope of being like the Lord, the hope of bearing the likeness of the Triune God. Our expectation is that we shall be like Him.

Verse 3 says that because we have this hope, we purify ourselves. According to the context of this section, from 2:28 through 3:24, to purify ourselves is to practice righteousness (3:7; 2:29), to live a righteous life that is the expression of the righteous God (1:9), the righteous One (2:1). This is to be pure without any stain of unrighteousness, even as that One is perfectly pure. This also describes the life that abides in the Lord.

Not Practicing Lawlessness

In 3:4 John says, "Everyone who practices sin practices also lawlessness, and sin is lawlessness." To practice sin is not merely to commit sin as occasional acts, but to live in sin (Rom. 6:2), to live a life which is not under the ruling principle of God over man.

No one who is a child of God practices sin habitually. We may sin occasionally, but we do not practice sin habitually. For instance, if someone has the practice of lying continually, this is a sign that he probably has not been born of God. Someone who has the divine life in him as a seed cannot lie habitually. However, due to weakness a child of God may lie in a particular circumstance. But because he is a child of God, he will not lie habitually. Instead of practicing sin, those who are children of God practice righteousness habitually.

In 3:4 John says that sin is lawlessness. Lawlessness is to have no law, to be without law. This does not mean to be without the Mosaic law (see Rom. 5:13), because sin was already in the world before the Mosaic law was given. Without law here denotes without, or not under, the ruling principle of God over man. To practice lawlessness is to live a life outside of and not under God's ruling principle over man. Hence, lawlessness is sin, or reciprocally, sin is lawlessness.

Christ Manifested to Take Away Sins

Verse 5 says, "And you know that that One was manifested that He might take away sins; and sin is not in Him." The Greek word for "take away" here is the same as that used in John 1:29. There Christ as the Lamb of God takes away the sin of the world, the sin which came into the world through Adam (Rom 5:12). Here He takes away sins, which are committed by all men. John 1 and Romans 5 deal with sin itself that dwells in men (Rom. 7:17-18). This chapter deals with the fruits of sin, that is, the committing of sins in men's daily life. Both are taken away by Christ.

In that One who takes away both sin and sins, there is no sin. Hence, He did not know sin (2 Cor. 5:21), He did no sin (1 Pet. 2:22), and He was without sin (Heb. 4:15). This qualified Him to take away both the indwelling sin and the sins committed in men's daily life.

Not Sinning Habitually

In verse 6 John continues, "Everyone who abides in Him does not sin; everyone who sins has not seen Him nor known Him." To abide in Him is to remain in the fellowship of the divine life and to walk in the divine light (1:2-3, 6-7).

The words "does not sin" mean not to sin habitually. This is also a condition of the life that abides in the Lord. It does not mean that the children of God do not commit sin at all; they may commit sin occasionally. It means that the regenerated believers who have the divine life and live by it do not practice sin. Their character and habit is not to sin, but to abide in the Lord.

Abiding in the Lord is a believer's living; sinning is a sinner's life. In this verse John says that everyone who practices sin, living a sinful life, has not seen Him or known Him. Not to have seen or known the Lord is not to have received any vision of Him or to have any realization of Him. This is the condition of an unbeliever. But if we have experienced the Lord, then we have seen Him and known Him. To see and know the Lord is to experience Him.

Living a Righteous Life

In verse 7 John says, "Little children, let no one lead you astray; he who practices righteousness is righteous, even as that One is righteous." To practice righteousness is to live a righteous life, living uprightly under God's ruling principle. This, according to the following verse, means not to practice sin, and, according to verse 4, not to practice lawlessness.

According to the context, "righteous" here equals "pure" in verse 3. To be righteous is to be pure, without any stain of sin, lawlessness, and unrighteousness, even as Christ is pure. The emphasis of the Apostle John is that as long as we are children of God having the divine life and the divine nature, we certainly will habitually live a life of righteousness.

The Devil Sinning from the Beginning

In verse 8 John goes on to say, "He who practices sin is of the Devil, because the Devil sins from the beginning. For this the Son of God was manifested, that He might undo the works of the Devil." This verse indicates that "practices sin" (v. 4) and "sins" in this book are synonymous, denoting to live in sin, to commit sin habitually. Such a life is of the Devil, whose life is one of sin and who sins habitually from the beginning. Sin is his nature, and sinning is his character.

In verse 8 the preposition "from" is used in the absolute sense, that is, from the time when the Devil began to rebel against God, attempting to overthrow God's rule.

Christ Manifested to Undo the Works of the Devil

In this verse John says that the Son of God was manifested for the purpose of undoing the works of the Devil. The Greek word translated "for this" literally means unto this, that is, to this end, for this purpose. The Devil sins continually from ancient times and begets sinners to practice sin with him. Hence, for this purpose the Son of God was manifested, that He might undo and destroy his sinful deeds—that is, condemn, through death on the cross in the flesh (Rom. 8:3), sin initiated by him, the evil one; destroy the power of sin, the sinful nature of the Devil (Heb. 2:14); and take away both sin and sins. On the cross Christ condemned sin, took away sin and sins, and destroyed the power of the Devil.

The Reason a Child of God Cannot Practice Sin

Verse 9 says, "Everyone who has been begotten of God does not practice sin, because His seed abides in him, and he cannot sin, because he has been begotten of God." To not practice sin does not mean that we do not commit sin in occasional acts; it means that we do not live in sin. A child of God may sin occasionally, but he does not practice sin habitually.

The reason a child of God does not practice sin is that "His seed abides in him, and he cannot sin, because he has been begotten of God." The seed here denotes God's life, which we received of Him when we were begotten of Him. This life, as the divine seed, abides in every regenerated believer. Hence, such a one does not practice sin and cannot sin. The words "cannot sin" in this verse mean cannot live in sin habitually. A regenerated believer may

fall into sin occasionally, but the divine life as the divine
seed in his regenerated nature will not allow him to live in
sin. This is similar to a sheep who may fall into the mud,
but whose clean life will not allow it to remain and wallow
in the mud as a swine does.

Verse 9 speaks of the habitual living of the children of
God. As God's children, we have the divine life, a life that
does not sin. Therefore, when we live by this life, we do not
practice sin. But why do we sometimes still sin? The
answer to this question is that we commit sin occasionally
because our body is still in the old creation. Our body is not
only the body created by God, but also the body that has
become the flesh because it has been poisoned and
corrupted by the Devil through sin. We still have sin in our
flesh. If we live by the spirit, that is, if we live by the divine
life in our spirit, we shall not sin. But if instead of living in
the spirit we live in the flesh or do things according to the
flesh, we are likely to commit sin.

We have two natures within us: the fallen nature in the
flesh and the new nature of the divine life in our spirit. If
we are on the alert, fellowshipping with the Lord and
living in our spirit by the divine life, we shall not sin. But
if we are careless and move and act in the flesh, there will
be much opportunity for us to sin, because the sinful
nature is still in us.

Some may argue and say, "Doesn't the Bible tell us that
he who has been begotten of God does not sin? How, then,
can you say that those who have been begotten of God
may still commit sin?" You may want to answer such a
question this way: "Yes, I have been begotten of God. But I
have been begotten of Him in my spirit, not in my body,
not in my flesh. This means that if we live in the flesh and
walk according to the flesh, we can still commit sin. But
one day our body will receive the full sonship. That will be
the redemption of the body."

We may use the word "sonized" to denote the full
sonship, that is, the redemption of our body. We have been
born of God, regenerated, in our spirit, but our body has
not yet been sonized. When the Lord Jesus comes back, our

body will be sonized. Then, according to Romans 8:23, we shall receive the full sonship, the redemption of our body. We need to realize that we have not yet been redeemed in our body. Our body has not been regenerated; it has not been born of God.

The Children of God and the Children of the Devil

In 3:10a John says, "In this the children of God and the children of the Devil are manifest." To practice sin or not, that is, to live in sin or not, is not a matter of behavior. It is a matter of whose children we are—the children of God or the children of the Devil. Hence, it is a matter of life and nature. Men, as the fallen descendants of Adam, are born children of the Devil, the evil one (John 8:44), possessing his life, partaking of his nature, and living in sin automatically and habitually. Practicing sin is their life. But the believers, who are redeemed from their fallen state and reborn in their spirit, are the children of God, possessing His life, partaking of His nature, and not living in sin. Practicing righteousness is their life. Whether one is a child of God or a child of the Devil is manifested by what he practices, righteousness or sin. A reborn believer may commit sin, and an unsaved man may do righteousness. Both are their outward behavior, not their outward living, thus not manifesting what they are in their inward life and nature.

ABIDING IN THE TRIUNE GOD ACCORDING TO THE TEACHING OF THE ANOINTING

If we would enjoy the divine life, we need to remain in the fellowship of the divine life. In order to remain in this fellowship, we need to abide in the Lord, who is the Triune God. Furthermore, if we would abide in the Triune God, we need to abide in Him according to the teaching of the divine anointing. If we do not care for the anointing, we shall lose the fellowship.

Because many Christians do not care for the anointing, they do not remain in the fellowship of the divine life.

Some do not even understand what the fellowship of the divine life is. Instead of caring for the anointing, the *chrisma*, in their spirit, they care for doctrines and theology. Because they do not care for the *chrisma* in their spirit, they are not in the fellowship of the divine life and therefore do not have the enjoyment of the divine life. But in the Lord's recovery we care for the anointing, the *chrisma*. Through this anointing we enjoy the virtues of the divine life.

LED BY THE ANOINTING
INTO THE VIRTUES OF THE DIVINE LIFE

We have seen that the first virtue of the divine life we enjoy through the anointing is the practice of righteousness or the living of a righteous life. We have a righteous nature within us, a nature that is not something of our natural man. This righteous nature, which is the nature of the divine life, is of our new man. As we take care of the inner anointing, the moving of the Triune God, we shall live habitually according to this righteous nature.

The anointing is the moving of the Triune God within us. This means that our God has become subjective to us. The Triune God—the Father, the Son, and the Spirit—is within our spirit. Day by day this processed Triune God as the anointing leads us into the virtues of the divine life, the virtues we have received through the divine birth. These virtues include living a righteous life, loving the brothers, and overcoming all negative things. To live a righteous life is to have a life that is right with God and with man. Righteousness is a matter of being right with both God and man. Therefore, to practice righteousness is to have a life that is right with God and man.

LIFE-STUDY OF FIRST JOHN

MESSAGE TWENTY-SEVEN

THE VIRTUES OF THE DIVINE BIRTH TO PRACTICE THE DIVINE LOVE

(1)

Scripture Reading: 1 John 3:10b-15

In 1 John there are three main sections: the fellowship of the divine life (1:1—2:11), the teaching of the divine anointing (2:12-27), and the virtues of the divine birth (2:28—5:21). The first portion in the third section (2:28—3:10a) is concerned with the practice of the divine righteousness. With this message we come to the second portion of this section (3:10b—5:3), a portion on the practice of the divine love. In the divine birth there is a virtue that enables us to practice the divine love.

BY THE DIVINE LIFE (AS THE DIVINE SEED) AND THE DIVINE SPIRIT

In order to practice the divine love as a virtue of the divine life, we need the divine life and the divine Spirit. The divine life is the divine seed that we all have within our regenerated spirit. In addition to the divine life that has been sown as the divine seed into our being, we also have the divine Spirit within our spirit. The divine life and the divine Spirit are the "capital" within us that enables us to practice the divine love. The divine life is the source, and the divine Spirit is the One who actually carries out the matter of loving others. The divine love is our daily living as the expression of the divine life carried out by the divine Spirit.

The divine life and the divine Spirit are basic factors for the practice of the divine love. With the divine life and by the divine Spirit, we can have a love that is divine and not merely human. This divine love in the daily living of the children of God is an evidence that we have both the divine life and the divine Spirit.

The One Not Loving His Brother Being Not of God

In 3:10b John says, "Everyone who does not practice righteousness is not out of God, and he who does not love his brother." Righteousness is the nature of God's acts; love is the nature of God's essence. What God is, is love; what God does is righteousness. Love is inward; righteousness is outward. Hence, love is a stronger manifestation that we are the children of God than righteousness. Therefore, the apostle, from this verse through verse 24, proceeds further, from righteousness to love, in the manifestation of the children of God, as a further condition of the life that abides in the Lord.

It is a serious thing for John to say that everyone who does not love his brother is not out of God. As children of God, we certainly are of God and even out of God. Because we are out of God, we surely have God's life and God's Spirit in us. Spontaneously, we live a life of loving the brothers. However, if someone does not have such a love, this is an evidence that he has neither the divine life nor the divine Spirit. Hence, there is a serious question concerning whether such a one is a child of God, born of Him. Loving the brothers is a strong evidence that we are out of God, having God's life and enjoying God's Spirit.

Loving One Another— the Message Heard from the Beginning

In verse 11 John goes on to say, "Because this is the message which you heard from the beginning, that we should love one another." The message heard from the beginning was the commandment given by the Lord in John 13:34, which is the word the believers heard and had from the beginning. In verse 11 the phrase "from the beginning" is used in the relative sense. The love spoken of here is a higher condition of the life that abides in the Lord.

Not as Cain

In verse 12 John continues, "Not as Cain, who was of the evil one and slew his brother. And for what reason did he slay him? Because his works were evil, and those of his brother righteous." "Of the evil one" equals a child of the Devil. Cain's brother Abel was of God, a child of God (v. 10). The Greek word rendered "evil one" here is *poneros*, which means pernicious, harmfully evil, affecting and influencing others to be evil and vicious. Such an evil one is Satan the Devil.

In verse 12 John uses two flesh brothers, Cain and Abel, as an illustration. Although these brothers were of the same parents, one of them became a child of God, and the other was a child of the Devil. We may find this difficult to believe. We may wonder how two brothers born of the same parents and living in the same environment could be so different, with one being the Devil's child and the other becoming God's child. Nevertheless, this was the fact. Here this fact is used as an illustration of what kind of person is a child of the Devil and what kind is a child of God. In order to know this, we should consider the case of Cain and Abel.

The fact that Cain was a child of the Devil is proved by his hating his brother and slaying him. This indicates that Cain did not have either the life of God or the Spirit of God. Why did Cain hate his brother? He hated him because he had the hating life of Satan in him. Why did Cain kill Abel? He killed him because he had in him the evil nature of Satan. What Cain had in him was the Devil's life, the Devil's nature, and an evil spirit. Abel, however, was altogether different. Today also those born of the same parents and raised in the same environment may become absolutely different. One may become a child of God and the other be a child of the Devil.

Not Marveling If the World Hates Us

Verse 13 says, "Do not marvel, brothers, if the world hates you." The "world" here refers to the people of the world. The people of the world, like Cain, are the children of the Devil (v. 10) and the components of Satan's cosmic system, the world (John 12:31). If the people of the world, which lies in the evil one, the Devil (5:19), hate the believers (the children of God), it is natural for them to do so. The situation among flesh brothers today may be the same as that between Cain and Abel. Suppose one brother is a child of Satan and the other is a child of God. Automatically, the one who is a child of the Devil will hate the one who is a child of God. Regarding this, we do not need to marvel.

Verse 13 indicates strongly that all the worldly people are children of the Devil. Only a comparatively small number, the regenerated believers, are God's children. If we live by God's life and by God's Spirit, the world will hate us. Because we and they are in two different categories, they will not be happy with us.

Knowing That We Have Passed Out of Death into Life

In 3:14 John says, "We know that we have passed out of death into life, because we love the brothers. He who does not love abides in death." Death is of the Devil, God's enemy Satan, signified by the tree of knowledge of good and evil, which brings death. Life is of God, the source of life, signified by the tree of life, which issues in life (Gen. 2:9, 16-17). Death and life are not only of these two sources, Satan and God; they are also two essences, two elements, and two spheres. To pass out of death is to pass out of the source, the essence, the element, and the sphere of death into the source, the essence, the element, and the sphere of life. This took place in us at our regeneration. We know (*oida*) this, we have the inner consciousness of this, because we love the brothers. Love (*agape*—the love of God) toward the brothers is a strong evidence of this. Faith in the Lord is the way for us to pass out of death into life; love toward the brothers is the evidence that we have passed out of death into life. To have faith is to receive the eternal life; to love is to live by the eternal life and express it.

Not loving the brothers is evidence of not living by the essence and element of the divine life and not remaining in its sphere. It is living in the essence and element of the satanic death and abiding in its sphere.

The word in 3:14 is quite similar to the word spoken by the Lord Jesus quoted by John in his Gospel: "Truly, truly, I say to you, he who hears My word and believes Him who sent Me has eternal life, and will not come into judgment, but has passed out of death into life" (5:24). John's word brings us back to the fall in the garden of Eden. After man was created, he was put before two trees: the tree of life and the tree of the knowledge of good and evil. The second tree is related to death, for in Genesis 2 Adam was told that if he ate of the tree of the knowledge of good and evil, he would die. Hence, the tree of the knowledge of good and evil is related to death. Eve and Adam ate of the fruit of the tree of knowledge. As a result, they received death into their being. In other words, they ate themselves into death. Because of the fall, mankind has been brought into death. For this reason, everyone born into Adam is born into death. This means that everyone born into Adam is born not to live, but to die. A child is born to die because, as a descendant of Adam, he is born into death.

When we repented of our sins and believed in the Lord Jesus, we were saved. Simultaneously, we were regenerated. To be regenerated actually means to receive the tree of life, from which mankind was cut off through Adam's fall. When Adam ate of the fruit of the tree of knowledge, he received death into him and lost the opportunity to receive the tree of life. But the opportunity of receiving the tree of life has been recovered through Christ's redemption. At the time we repented and believed in the Lord Jesus, that opportunity was opened to us. By repenting and believing, spontaneously we received the divine life into us, and at that very moment we passed out of death into life.

If you consider your salvation experience, you will realize that when you were saved and regenerated, you passed out of death into life. Because we all passed out of death into life when we believed in the Lord Jesus and received Him as our Savior, a great change in life followed. We began to live another life, a life of righteousness and love. It became our desire to be righteous and to love the children of God. This is not merely an outward change; it is the passing out of death into life. Therefore, when we love the brothers in the Lord, this love is an evidence that we have passed out of death into life.

If someone does not love the brothers but instead hates them, this is an evidence that this one remains in the death that came into mankind through Adam's fall. Because death entered into mankind long ago, we were born into that death. But when we repented and believed, we passed out of death into the divine life. Because we have passed out of the death of the tree of knowledge into the life of the tree of life, we have had a change and now live a life of righteousness and love.

Everyone who has been saved and regenerated can testify that he has passed out of death into life. There is no need to tell others what you were before you were saved. Simply tell them what you have become since salvation.

Because you have been saved and regenerated, your desire is to live a life that is right with God and man. You want to be right with your husband or wife, with your parents, with your children, with your relatives, neighbors, and colleagues. Your aspiration is to live a life that is right with everyone and even with everything. For example, a person who lives such a righteous life will not even mistreat an animal. As those who have received the divine life with the divine nature, a nature that is righteous, we have the aspiration to be right in every way.

This aspiration to be right with all things even extends to material things. Before they were saved, certain ones may have had the habit of kicking a chair or throwing something when they were angry. But when such a person receives the divine life with the divine nature, he does not want to be unrighteous in any matter.

Because of the fall, our natural life is not righteous. For this reason, in the natural life we are not right with others and even with things. But when we received the Lord Jesus, we received the life of the tree of life, a life with a righteous nature. Because we have received this life with the divine nature, automatically we aspire to be right with everyone and everything.

As saved and regenerated ones, we can also testify that we desire to love others. As those born of God, we want to help people and love them. When we love others, we feel happy. But we may feel sad when we miss the opportunity to help someone or to show love to him.

Love is the nature of the divine life we have received. Because the essence of God is love, the life of God has the nature of love. Love is the essence of God's nature. When we have Him as our divine life, we have the nature of this life, which is love. We Christians, the children of God, have a life that aspires to live rightly with everyone and everything and also aspires to love others. We have such an aspiration because of the divine nature within us. As we have pointed out, if someone does not live in a way that is right with everyone, everything, and every matter and does not live a life of loving others, there is a serious question whether this one has received the divine life.

The One Not Loving Abiding in Death

In 3:14 John says, "He who does not love abides in death." If we do not love others, this is an evidence that we still remain in death. In other words, it is a sign that we have not yet passed out of death into life.

Everyone Who Hates His Brother Being a Murderer

In verse 15a John goes on to say, "Everyone who hates his brother is a murderer." To the divine attributes, hatred is versus love, death versus life, darkness versus light, and lie (falsehood) versus truth. All the opposites of these divine virtues are of the evil one, the Devil.

In verse 15 murderer does not denote an actual murderer, but indicates that in spiritual ethics hating equals murdering. No actual murderer, an unsaved person, as Cain was (v. 12), has eternal life abiding in him. Since we know this, we, who have passed out of death into life and have eternal life abiding in us, should not behave as an unsaved murderer by hating our brothers in the Lord.

This section concerns the life that abides in the Lord. A believer who has eternal life, but does not abide in the Lord and let the Lord who is the eternal life abide and work in him, may hate a brother and commit other sins occasionally, but this should not be habitual.

Someone may not be an actual murderer, but he may be a murderer in principle. This means that, even though he has never murdered anyone, he may still be a murderer in principle by hating others. If we hate someone, in principle we are behaving as a murderer, even though we have not killed anyone. Therefore, we need to realize that, strictly speaking, we Christians, the children of God, should not hate anyone. On the contrary, we need to love others. The Bible even tells us to love our enemies (Matt 5:44). Because the divine life we possess is a loving life, a life that is love, we must love those who are not lovable and even those who mistreat us. There should not be anything of the element of hate in us. Love is our life and nature, and love should be our essence and living. Therefore, we must not have hatred for anyone. Today some may oppose the Lord's recovery, but we should not hate them. Instead of hating them, we should love them. If we hate those who oppose us, then in principle we are behaving as a murderer.

No Murderer Having Eternal Life Abiding in Him

In verse 15b John continues, "And you know that no murderer has eternal life abiding in him." When John says that no murderer has eternal life in him, he is not speaking of saved persons but of unsaved ones, like Cain.

After reading verse 15, some have questioned whether a believer can murder someone and still have eternal life abiding in him. When I was young in the ministry, I was asked such a question at least a few times. Some have asked if it is possible for a real believer to murder someone and, if he did, would he still have eternal life abiding in him. It is difficult to give a definite answer to such a question. It is not safe to say that it is absolutely impossible for a real believer to actually murder someone. On the other hand, it is not safe to say that it is possible for a saved person to commit murder. It is better for us to leave this matter to the Lord and not try to explain it.

In matters like this, we should not be distracted by the lust for knowledge. Someone may say, "First John 3:15 tells us that no murderer has eternal life abiding in him. I would like to know what would happen if a real believer committed murder. Would this one still have eternal life?" This kind of question is injected into our mind by the Devil. If such a thought comes to you, you should say, "Devil, don't ask me this. I am not the one to answer this question. If you want an answer to this question, ask my God. I don't know these things, and I don't want to be bothered by them. However, I do know, Devil, that I have been regenerated and have the divine life within me. I also know that I am enjoying the divine nature and that I have the very God, as the divine Spirit, living in me. Satan, I do not want to answer your questions. Get away from me!" I can testify that the Lord has been merciful to me and has given me the wisdom to handle such questions in this way. However, some brothers are confident that they are knowledgeable and capable of giving an answer to questions concerning the possibility of a believer who has eternal life committing murder. We should not have such confidence in ourselves. It is sufficient for us to see that as children of God we should not hate others. We should not behave as if we were a murderer.

We have seen that in principle hatred equals murder. It is possible for a child of God to hate someone occasionally, but no regenerated person should do this habitually. If you hate others habitually, there is a question whether you have received the divine life. This is similar to committing sin. A believer may commit sin occasionally, but he should not do this habitually. If you sin habitually, this will also raise a question as to whether you have received the divine life.

John's intention is to show us that, through the divine birth, the divine seed has been sown into our being. This seed is the divine life, and the divine life has the divine nature. Furthermore, we have received the divine Spirit to carry out whatever is in the divine life and the divine nature. Instead of trying to answer questions that are beyond our ability to answer, we need to know that we have received the divine life, that we are enjoying the divine nature of this life, and that the divine Person, God Himself as the Spirit, is within us carrying out whatever is in this divine nature. Therefore, we should live this life, abide in this One, and maintain unbroken fellowship with Him according to the inner anointing. This is the central point of John's writing.

LIFE-STUDY OF FIRST JOHN

THE VIRTUES OF THE DIVINE BIRTH
TO PRACTICE THE DIVINE LOVE

(2)

Scripture Reading: 1 John 3:14-19a

SOURCE, ESSENCE, ELEMENT, AND SPHERE

First John 3:14a says, "We know that we have passed out of death into life, because we love the brothers." In the foregoing message we saw that death is of the Devil, the source of death, and that life is of God, the source of life. Not only are death and life of these two sources, Satan and God; they are also two essences, two elements, and two spheres. To pass out of death into life is to pass out of the source, essence, element, and sphere of death into the source, essence, element, and sphere of life. This took place when we were regenerated, born of God.

We need to consider further the source, essence, element, and sphere both of death and of life. What is the difference between the essence of life and the element of life, and what is the difference between the element of life and the sphere of life? It is important for us to understand the difference between these things.

Perhaps the best way to point out the difference between source, essence, element, and sphere as applied to both life and death is to use the following illustration. Suppose a particular drink is composed of three elements: milk, tea, and sugar. Each element has its own essence. This means that with tea there is the essence, the substance, of tea. In like manner, milk and sugar each have different essences or substances. We would not say that this drink is made up of three substances. Rather, we would say that the drink is composed of three elements and that within these elements are three different essences or substances.

When we were saved, we received more than one element from God. We received life, and we also received righteousness. Both life and righteousness are mentioned in Romans 5. What elements did we have before we were saved? Before we were saved we were one with Satan, and we had the elements of sin and death. But when we were saved, we received righteousness, which is versus sin, and life, which is versus death.

On both the negative side and the positive side, we have two elements. On the negative side, we have sin and death; on the positive side, we have righteousness and life. In each of these four elements there is a certain kind of essence. The essence of life and the essence of righteousness are of one kind, and the essence of sin and the essence of death are a different kind.

Righteousness and Life

Let us now apply these matters to our experience. When we were in the element of death, we experienced the essence, the substance, of death. Again, we may use tea as an illustration. When we drink tea, what we drink is not the element of tea; we drink the essence of tea. When we received the Lord Jesus at the time we were saved and regenerated, we received two elements. However, we should not say that we received two essences. At regeneration we received the elements of life and righteousness, and now we are living in these elements. But it would not be correct to say that we received two essences and that we are now living in these essences. Having received the elements of life and righteousness, we are now enjoying and experiencing the essences of these elements. We have received the element of righteousness, and now we are enjoying the essence of this element. Likewise, we have received the element of life, and now we are experiencing the essence of this element. Before we were regenerated, we were in the elements of sin and death, and we were suffering from the working of the essence of sin and the essence of death within us. This brief word may help us to know how to apply the essence and element of righteousness and life.

As children of God, we have two divine elements— righteousness and life. Now in our daily experience we enjoy the divine righteousness and the divine life. However, strictly speaking, we enjoy the essence, the substance, of the divine righteousness and life.

Passing Out of Death into Life

We have pointed out that through regeneration we have passed out of the source, essence, element, and sphere of death into the source, essence, element, and sphere of life. Please notice the sequence: source, essence, element, and sphere. The essence follows the source, the element follows the essence, and the sphere follows the element. First we have the source. Then out of the source comes the essence. The essence forms an element, and eventually this element becomes a sphere. Therefore, regarding life, we first have the source of life. Out of this source of life comes the essence of life. The essence forms the element of life, and this element of life then becomes the sphere of life.

We may use a fountain to illustrate the difference between the source of life, the essence of life, the element of life, and the sphere of life. Water flows out of a fountain and becomes a river. The fountain is the source. We may say that H_2O is the essence of what comes out of the fountain. This essence then takes the form of water, and the flowing water becomes a river. Here we have the fountain as the source, the H_2O as the essence, the water as the element, and the river as the sphere. Therefore, in the sphere of the river we have the water as the element, and the essence of this element is H_2O. The source of it all is the fountain.

As children of God, we have received the divine life from God. God is the source, the fountain, of the divine life. The essence of the divine life is the very being of God. Hence, God's being, His essence, is the essence of the spiritual water we have received as the divine life. This life also is an element by which and in which we can live. When we live in the element of the divine life, the divine life becomes the sphere of our living. Now we are living in the sphere of the divine life, possessing the element of the divine life, and enjoying the essence of the divine life. Furthermore, as we enjoy the essence of the divine life, we are organically joined to God as the source of this life. This is the reason we say that with the divine life we have the source, the essence, the element, and the sphere.

The principle is the same with death. Before we were saved and regenerated, we were in the source, essence, element, and sphere of death. We were living in the sphere of death, possessing the element of death, and suffering the essence of death. Moreover, we were joined to Satan, the source of death. Therefore, before regeneration, we were experiencing and suffering the source, essence, element, and sphere of death.

Before we were saved, we experienced the four aspects of death. Now that we have been saved, we experience the four aspects of life. Although we have had all these aspects in our experience, we have been short of the knowledge to analyze them and the terms to describe them.

LAYING DOWN OUR LIVES
ON BEHALF OF THE BROTHERS

In 3:16 John says, "In this we have known love, that that One laid down His life on our behalf, and we ought to lay down our lives on behalf of the brothers." Literally, the Greek words for "life" and "lives" in this verse are "soul" and "souls." Hence, this verse says that Christ laid down His soul life, His *psuche* life, for us, not His divine life, His *zoe* life. For Christ to lay down His soul for us means that He laid down His human life on our behalf. Now we ought to lay down our lives on behalf of the brothers. This means that, if necessary, we should die for them. We have within us such a loving life that longs to die for others and is able to die for them. The divine life within us, the *zoe*, longs to love others and even die for them if necessary. We are able to do this because we have the divine life.

LOVING IN REALITY

In verses 17 and 18 John continues, "But whoever has the livelihood of the world and beholds his brother having need and shuts up his affections from him, how does the love of God abide in him? Little children, let us not love in word nor in tongue, but in deed and truth." The livelihood of the world in verse 17 refers to material things, to the necessities of life. In verse 18, deed is versus word, and truth versus tongue. Tongue denotes the play of vain talk. Truth denotes the reality of love. Truth denotes sincerity, in contrast with tongue, as deed with word. Truth here denotes the genuineness, the sincerity, of God as a divine virtue becoming a human virtue as an issue of the divine reality. Therefore, the truth in this verse is the reality of God becoming our virtue.

John says that we should not love the brothers merely in word or in tongue, not merely telling the saints that we love them. This is not love in truth, love in reality. To love the saints in truth or reality means to love them in the divine reality that becomes our virtue, something that is honest, faithful, sincere, and real. We should love the brothers in this way. Of course, this kind of love in truth includes a love that supplies the needy ones with material things or money when necessary. We should not love the brothers with vain words; we should love them in truth and even with our livelihood.

We should not think that to love in truth is simply to love in the human virtue of sincerity. No, here John is not speaking of the natural human virtue of sincerity. The truth here is more than human sincerity; it is the divine reality becoming our virtue. Thus, it is the expression of what God is. This means that in loving the saints we should express God.

KNOWING THAT WE ARE OF THE TRUTH

In 3:19a John goes on to say, "In this we shall know that we are of the truth." In this verse truth denotes the reality of the eternal life which we have received of God in our divine birth. Having received eternal life, we may now love the brothers by the divine love. By loving the brothers with the divine love, we know that we are of this reality.

The phrase "in this" refers to our loving the brothers in truth, in sincerity, as mentioned in verse 18. This truth is the issue of the experience of the Triune God as our reality. In this kind of love we shall know, shall have the assurance, that we are of the truth.

In verses 18 and 19 the word "truth" is used with two different denotations. In verse 18 truth denotes the human virtue of sincerity, a virtue that is the issue of the enjoyment of the Triune God as our reality. But in verse 19 truth denotes the reality of eternal life, which is something higher, deeper, and richer than our sincerity. This truth is the reality of the eternal life which we received from God in our divine birth so that we may love the brothers by this love.

DIVINE BIRTH AND ETERNAL LIFE

In this Epistle John presents deep, divine, and mysterious things. All these things are related to the divine life. However, Christians often speak of the life of God or eternal life with a very limited understanding. They do not understand the divine life in a deep, rich, and profound way. Some believers do not even realize that eternal life is an organic matter. They regard eternal life merely as an eternal blessing or as everlasting life that we shall enjoy in eternity. But even though we may have a right understanding of eternal life as something organic, our understanding of it may still be rather shallow.

We have received eternal life through our divine birth. However, when many Christians talk about everlasting life, they do not realize that eternal life is the result, the issue, the fruit, of the divine birth. In the past, many of us did not realize that eternal life came into us as a result of the divine birth. In speaking about eternal life, we may not have had the concept that it is related to the divine birth. Therefore, it is important for us to realize that eternal life has come into us through the divine birth. Apart from the divine birth, we cannot have eternal life.

We have seen that in verse 19 truth, or reality, refers to the reality of the divine life which we received in our divine birth. Therefore, this reality involves the divine life and the divine birth. Now that we have received the divine life, we can love the brothers by the divine love. Here we have the divine birth, the divine life, and the divine love. By this we see that loving the brothers is not a shallow or simple matter. On the contrary, our love for the brothers is the issue of the divine birth and the divine life.

Because we have received the divine life through the divine birth, we have the divine love with which to love the brothers. We may say that we have the spiritual capital needed to love the brothers. The divine life is our ability to love the brothers. We are well able to love the brothers because we have been born of God. Through the divine birth we have received the divine life, and the essence of this life is love. Therefore, we can love the brothers with the divine love.

If we love the brothers in sincerity, which is the issue of our enjoyment of God as reality, this will be the evidence that we are in the divine reality. It will be a confirmation of the fact that we are in the reality of the divine life, which we have received through the divine birth. By loving the brothers with the divine love, we know that we are of the divine reality.

LIFE-STUDY OF FIRST JOHN

MESSAGE TWENTY-NINE

THE VIRTUES OF THE DIVINE BIRTH TO PRACTICE THE DIVINE LOVE

(3)

Scripture Reading: 1 John 3:19-24

THE ASSURANCE THAT WE ARE IN THE REALITY

In this message we shall consider 3:19-24. In verse 19 John says, "In this we shall know that we are of the truth, and we shall persuade our heart before Him." Here "truth" denotes the reality of the divine life, which we received of God in our divine birth. We have received the divine life so that we may love the brothers by the divine love. If we love the brothers with the divine love, we shall know that we are of this reality.

John's way of writing here is not doctrinal but experiential. Apart from spiritual experience, we cannot understand what John is saying. In verses 18 and 19 John is telling us that if we love the brothers in truth, sincerity, honesty, as the outcome of our enjoyment of the Triune God, we shall have the assurance that we are in the divine reality.

PERSUADING OUR HEART BEFORE HIM

According to John's word, if we love in truth, we shall also be able to "persuade our heart before Him." The Greek word rendered "persuade" also means conciliate, convince, assure, tranquilize. To persuade our heart before God is to have a good conscience, void of offense (1 Tim. 1:5, 19; Acts 24:16), that our heart may be conciliated, convinced, assured, and tranquilized before the Lord. This is also a condition of the life that abides in the Lord. To abide in the Lord requires a tranquil heart with a conscience void of offense. This is also vital to our fellowship with God, which is covered in the first section of this Epistle. A heart disturbed by a conscience with offense frustrates our abiding in the Lord and breaks our fellowship with God.

We know from experience that if we do not love by the divine love, our heart will not be at peace. Furthermore, we shall not have peace if we are not right even with a small matter in our environment. Suppose a brother becomes upset and knocks over a chair. Certainly he does not have peace in his heart. But if instead he lives by the divine life and loves others by the divine love, he will be able to conciliate his heart, to persuade his heart before God.

When we have the assurance that we are in the divine truth, we shall be able to convince, persuade, and assure our heart and cause it to be tranquil. Otherwise, there will be turmoil within, for our heart will protest that we do not love according to the divine love. Our heart may say, "You are a child of God, but you are not living by the divine life. Why do you knock over a chair?" If we want our heart to be tranquil, we need to live by the divine life in relation to everyone and everything. Suppose, for example, that I carelessly throw something aside. I know from experience that if I do this, I will not have peace in my heart. In order for my heart to be tranquil, I need to be right with everything. Only when we live a life that is the expression of the divine reality can we cause our heart to be tranquil.

Many times we, the children of God, are not happy. Nehemiah 8:10 says, "The joy of the Lord is your strength," and Proverbs 17:22 says, "A merry heart doeth good like a medicine." Why is it that often we do not have joy within? The reason we do not have joy is that our heart is not at peace. Instead of peace, there is turmoil. The reason our heart is not tranquil is that we are not living in the divine life. But when we live in the divine life, we are in the truth, the reality. Then we can persuade, conciliate, convince, our heart and cause it to be tranquil. As a result, we shall be happy.

At the end of verse 19 John inserts the phrase "before Him." This tells us that the Lord is living with us and in us. If we do not live by the divine reality, our heart will protest. Then we shall not have a calm heart before Him. We need to remember that the Lord is living in us and that we are living before Him. Only when we live by the divine life can we persuade our heart before Him. The phrase "before Him" points to a crucial matter—that our living as children of God, and also our heart, are before Him. Therefore, we must take care to always have a tranquil heart before Him.

OUR HEART BLAMING US
AND GOD BEING GREATER THAN OUR HEART

In verse 20 John continues, "Because if our heart blames us, God is greater than our heart and knows all things." Actually it is our conscience, which is a part not only of our spirit but also of our heart, that blames us or condemns us. The conscience in our heart is the representative of God's ruling within us. If our conscience condemns us, surely God, who is greater than His representative and knows all things, will condemn us. The consciousness of such condemnation in our conscience alerts us to the danger of breaking our fellowship with God. If we attend to this, it will be a help to our fellowship with God and will keep us abiding in the Lord.

By reading the context, we can see that in verse 20 the heart actually refers to the conscience. The conscience is one of the four parts of the heart, which is composed of the mind, the emotion, the will (the three parts of the soul), and the conscience, which is part of our spirit. Our heart is influenced, directed, and controlled to a great extent by our conscience.

When our heart blames us, this means that our conscience condemns us. If we do not live by the divine reality, our conscience will check, blame, and condemn us. As a result, our heart will protest.

In verse 20 John says that God is greater than our heart; that is, God is greater than our conscience. God has

a government, and this government has a local administration within us. This local administration of God's
government is our conscience. Our conscience, therefore,
is the local government of God within us. In a sense, our
conscience is both a "law court" and "police station."
Often our conscience "arrests" us. The police station of our
conscience, which knows the law very well, may issue an
order for our "arrest." Then the police station knows when
to turn us over to the law court. We know from experience
that many times we are arrested and taken to the law
court, where we are judged and condemned. When this
happens, we need the cleansing of the precious blood of
Jesus, the Son of God. This indicates that the condemnation of the conscience spoken of in chapter three will take
us back to the cleansing mentioned in chapter one.

If our conscience blames us, arresting us and condemning us, certainly God will also condemn us, for He is
greater than our conscience and knows all things.

The Epistle of 1 John is not only on the divine
fellowship, but is also on the details of this fellowship.
Here in 3:20 we have one of the details related to the divine
fellowship. John's writing regarding this matter is profound, mysterious, divine, and detailed. In no other portion
of the holy Word do we have as many details about the
divine fellowship as we have in these verses in chapter
three of 1 John. These verses are crucial to our fellowship
with God.

In chapter one much is unveiled regarding the fellowship of the divine life. But in chapter three this fellowship
is viewed from another angle. In chapter one the angle is
that of the divine light shining within us. As a result of
this shining, we are exposed and realize that we have
sinned. But here in chapter three we have the angle of
living by the divine reality. If we do not live by the divine
reality, our conscience will protest and condemn us. That
condemnation is a sign of God's condemnation. Therefore,
we must do something to conciliate the situation, to calm
the turmoil in our heart, to cause our conscience to be at
peace with God. In order for our heart to be quiet and calm

in this way, we need to live, behave, and act in the divine reality.

If our heart condemns us for not living in the divine reality, this is a sign that God also condemns us. Therefore, we need to have an improvement in our inward condition. This does not mean, however, that we should try to improve our character or outward behavior. It means that we need to deal with our inward situation so that we may be willing to live by the divine life and in the divine reality. If we do this, we shall have the assurance that we are in the divine reality. Then we shall be able to persuade our heart, cause it to be tranquil, and enjoy peace in our conscience with God. This is related to the divine fellowship.

What John says concerning fellowship in chapter one involves the confessing of sins under the shining of the divine light and the cleansing of our sins by the blood of Christ. But in chapter three we have the protesting and blaming of our conscience within us. This is not only a matter of the divine light shining in us, upon us, and through us; it is also a matter of a cleansed, purified, and purged conscience giving us a sign that we are not right in our living, that we are not living in the divine reality. When we do not live by the divine reality, our conscience will protest and condemn us. This is a sign that God is not pleased with us and that we need an improvement of our inward condition.

BOLDNESS TOWARD GOD

In 3:21 John says, "Beloved, if our heart does not blame us, we have boldness toward God." The Greek word rendered "boldness" is *parresia*, meaning boldness of speech, confidence. We have such boldness in tranquility to contact God, to fellowship with Him, and to ask of Him, because there is no condemnation of the conscience in our heart. This preserves us in abiding in the Lord.

KNOWING GOD IN OUR HEART

Christians often talk about knowing God. However,

their concept is that of objective knowledge of a God who is great and almighty. But here the Apostle John does not teach us to know God in that kind of objective way. On the contrary, John's word here is about knowing God in a very subjective way. Some may speak about the almighty God who rules the universe, but here John speaks concerning the God who is in our heart. He does not talk about the mighty God, about the great God; instead he speaks concerning the practical God. Not only is God infinite, unlimited, and beyond our ability to comprehend; He is also small enough to be in our heart. When God becomes our experience, He is not only the One on the throne who is universally vast, but He is the One in our heart.

Some have said, "How is it possible for Christ to be in you? Christ is great, and you are small. How could you contain such a great Christ?" This kind of talk comes from the fallen human mentality. According to the teaching of the New Testament, we need to know God in the personal realm of our heart. God is known by us not in the vastness of the universe, but in the smallness of our heart.

Where do you know God? To say that you know God in the universe is to speak in a religious way. I certainly believe that God is great and almighty. But here I am burdened to point out that the concern of the New Testament is that we know the God who has come into our being, the One who dwells in our spirit and desires to spread into all the inward parts of our heart. Therefore, we need to know God in our heart.

In 3:20 John does not say that God is greater than the universe. Here John says that God is greater than our heart. This way of writing indicates that our knowledge of God must be experiential. Knowing God is a matter not of the universe but of our heart. Is your heart at peace? Is your heart tranquil? This is related to your knowing God. Some may say that they know God. But they may know Him in a religious way, in an objective way. We need to know God in our heart, in our conscience. To know God in this way is for the great, almighty, infinite God to become practical to us in our conscience. If our conscience bothers us, this means that God also has a problem with us.

I can testify that from experience I have learned to know God in my conscience. Often in my Christian life I have wondered why God cares for all the details in my daily life. For example, I know that He would bother me if I were to show a "long face" toward my wife. If I give my wife a "long face," He will trouble me in my conscience. If I argue with Him about matters like this, the God who is in my conscience will not agree with me. This is an example of the experiential way to know God.

In being known by us experientially, God is small, not infinite. A brother may argue with God; he may think that it is not right for Him to trouble his conscience regarding a certain matter. Suppose the brother says to Him, "Why does my conscience bother me concerning my wife? She is wrong, and I am right. She caused the problem, and I have been trying to avoid an argument. But she is trying to force me to say something. Why, then, does my conscience bother me about the way I feel? This isn't fair!" But no matter how much the brother may argue with Him, God will not rule in his favor. Rather, He will agree with the brother's conscience in condemning him.

If we are honest, we shall admit that sometimes we are stubborn with God. We may not be stubborn with our husband or wife or with the saints, but we may be stubborn with God. A certain brother may be kind and gentle; nevertheless, at times even such a brother may be stubborn with God. He may be subdued by his wife, but he may not be easily subdued by God. He may go for a period of time without being willing to be subdued by God regarding a particular matter. I believe that we all can testify of having been stubborn with God in this way.

The reason we have been stubborn is that we were arguing with God about something. We may have thought that we were right and that the other party was wrong, and that for this reason our conscience should not trouble us. We may have questioned why our conscience, the representative of God's government within us, would keep troubling us about that matter. Therefore, for a period of time we were stubborn with God.

I use this as an illustration of the fact that the New Testament way for us to know God is personal, detailed, and experiential. The New Testament way is to know God as the One who is in our heart. How precious is this experiential way of knowing God!

Sometimes we may wonder why God, who has billions of matters to take care of, would be concerned with a small detail in our daily living. Although God is infinite and almighty, He cares even for the small things in our life. For example, He may care about a brother's inward attitude toward his wife, something so small that it may seem it takes a divine magnifying glass to see it. Nevertheless, God cares for such a matter. We know God cares for such things because our conscience bothers us concerning them. Whenever our conscience is not tranquil, we know that we need to take care of the feeling of our conscience, which is the representative of the divine government. In this way we know God not in great matters but in small things. This way of knowing God is experiential and practical.

KEEPING HIS COMMANDMENTS AND PRACTICING THE THINGS THAT ARE PLEASING IN HIS SIGHT

In verse 22 John goes on to say, "And whatever we ask we receive from Him, because we keep His commandments and practice the things which are pleasing in His sight." Offenses in the conscience of a condemning heart are obstacles to our prayer. A conscience void of offense in a tranquil heart straightens and clears the way for our petition to God.

In verse 22 the keeping of the commandments is not the keeping of the commandments of the Mosaic law by our own endeavor and strength. It is rather a part of the believers' living as the issue of the divine life that abides in them. This is the habitual keeping of the Lord's New Testament commandments through the inner operation of the power of the divine life. This accompanies the practicing, the habitual doing, of the things which are pleasing in His sight. This is a prerequisite to God's answering our prayers, and it constitutes a condition of the life that abides in the Lord (v. 24).

In verse 22 John speaks of "the things which are pleasing in His sight." No doubt, these things are the living of a life of righteousness and love. Literally, the Greek word rendered "sight" means seeing into. This does not refer to objective sight. On the contrary, it refers to the Lord's watching over us and seeing into our situation. This indicates that the relationship between us and God is very personal.

THE COMMANDMENTS TO BELIEVE AND LOVE

In verse 23 John goes on to say, "And this is His commandment, that we should believe in the name of His Son Jesus Christ and love one another, even as He gave a commandment to us." This is a summary of the commandments in the preceding and following verses. All the commandments are summarized in two: one is to believe in the name of God's Son Jesus Christ, and the other is to love one another. The first is concerning faith; the second, love. To have faith is to receive the divine life in our relationship with the Lord; to love is to live the divine life in our relationship with the brothers. Faith touches the source of the divine life; love expresses the essence of the divine life. Both are needed for the believers to live a life that abides in the Lord.

According to the Gospel of John, faith and love are the two requirements for us to enjoy God. In order to receive God and enjoy Him, we need to believe in the Lord Jesus. We also need to love Him and love one another.

ABIDING IN HIM BY LIVING IN THE DIVINE REALITY

In verse 24 John concludes, "And he who keeps His commandments abides in Him, and He in him. And in this we know that He abides in us, by the Spirit whom He gave to us." This verse is the conclusion of this section, which begins in 2:28, on our abiding in the Lord according to the teaching of the divine anointing, as unfolded in the preceding section (2:20-27). This section reveals that abiding in the Lord is the living of the children of God by His eternal life as the divine seed, which grows in practicing the righteousness of their begetting God (2:29; 3:7, 10) and the love of their begetting Father (3:10-11, 14-23). Such an abiding and its bases—the divine birth and the divine life as the divine seed—are mysterious yet real in the Spirit.

To keep His commandments is to live a life according to the divine reality. This is what it means to keep the Lord's commandments according to this Epistle. This means that keeping His commandments is not the keeping of the Mosaic law. To keep the commandments of the Lord is to have a life according to the divine reality.

If we keep the Lord's commandments by living in the divine reality, we shall abide in Him, and He in us. We abide in the Lord; then He abides in us. Our abiding in Him is a condition for His abiding in us (John 15:4). We enjoy His abiding in us by our abiding in Him.

THE SPIRIT

The second part of verse 24 says, "And in this we know that He abides in us, by the Spirit whom He gave to us." Literally, the Greek for "by" means out of. The phrase "by the Spirit" modifies "we know."

Thus far in this Epistle the Spirit has not been referred to, though the Spirit is anonymously implied in the anointing in 2:20 and 27. Actually, the Spirit, that is, the all-inclusive compound life-giving Spirit, is the vital and crucial factor of all the mysteries unveiled in this Epistle: the divine life, the fellowship of the divine life, the divine anointing, the abiding in the Lord, the divine birth, and the divine seed. It is by this Spirit we are born of God, we receive the divine life as the divine seed in us, we have the fellowship of the divine life, we are anointed with the Triune God, and we abide in the Lord. This wonderful Spirit is given to us as the promised blessing of the New Testament (Gal. 3:14). He is given without measure by the

Christ who is above all, who inherits all, and who is to be increased universally (John 3:31-35). This Spirit and the eternal life (1 John 3:15) are the basic elements by which we live the life that abides in the Lord continually. Hence, it is by this Spirit, who witnesses assuringly with our spirit, that we are the children of God (Rom. 8:16), and that we know that the Lord of all abides in us (1 John 4:13). It is through this Spirit that we are joined to the Lord as one spirit (1 Cor. 6:17). And it is by this Spirit that we enjoy the riches of the Triune God (2 Cor. 13:14).

Chapter three of 1 John concludes with a word concerning the Spirit. This indicates that what is covered in this chapter is a matter of the all-inclusive, compound, life-giving, indwelling Spirit. In this verse John does not speak of the Spirit of God or of the Holy Spirit; he speaks of the Spirit. Whenever the New Testament mentions the Spirit, it refers to the all-inclusive compound, life-giving, indwelling Spirit. In the last chapter of the Bible, we have a word concerning the Spirit (Rev. 22:17). The Spirit is more inclusive than the Spirit of God and the Holy Spirit. The Spirit refers to the Spirit who was not yet (John 7:39) before Christ's glorification. Now since the resurrection of Christ, the Spirit is here. Therefore, we abide in the Lord and He abides in us by the Spirit whom He has given to us.

LIFE-STUDY OF FIRST JOHN

MESSAGE THIRTY

PROVING THE SPIRITS

(1)

Scripture Reading: 1 John 4:1-6

In this message we come to 4:1-6. These verses stand as a particular section. Apparently this section has nothing to do with either the preceding section or the following section. As we have seen, the preceding section is concerned with loving the brothers. The following section returns to the matter of loving the brothers. Therefore, 4:1-6 stands between two sections concerned with loving the brothers. We may wonder, then, how 4:1-6 is related to these sections.

THE NEED TO PROVE THE SPIRITS

I believe 4:1-6 is inserted for at least two reasons. The first reason is related to our need to discern the spirits. In 3:24 John speaks of the "Spirit whom He gave to us." Because the Spirit is mentioned here, John goes on to the matter of discerning, proving, trying, the spirits. There is more than one kind of spirit in the universe. Hence, we need John's warning to prove the spirits.

First John 4:1-6 is a parenthetical section warning the believers to discern the spirits that they may recognize the false prophets. This warning is related to the mention of the Spirit in the preceding verse, 3:24, the Spirit whereby we know that the Lord abides in us. A similar warning was given in 2:18-23. The expressions "every spirit" and "the spirits" in 4:1 refer either to the spirits of the prophets (1 Cor. 14:32) motivated by the Spirit of truth, or to the spirit of the false prophets actuated by the spirit of deception. Hence, there is the need to discern the spirits by

proving them to see whether they have their source out of
God. This is the reason John says in verse 1, "Beloved, do
not believe every spirit, but prove the spirits whether they
are out of God." To prove the spirits is to discern them
(1 Cor. 12:10) by putting them on trial.

NOT RECEIVING FALSE PROPHETS
AND ANTICHRISTS

I believe that a second reason for John's inserting 4:1-6
is to warn the believers that although we need to love the
brothers, we should not receive false prophets and antichrists. We should love all men, including our enemies.
However, we cannot receive a false prophet or an antichrist.

In the early years of my ministry, we found it necessary
to inoculate the saints against modernism. A number of
professors and others in the universities had been influenced by modernistic teachings concerning Christ and
the Bible. The modernists taught that Christ is not God,
that He was an illegitimate son of Mary with Joseph, that
He was a great philosopher, and that He died on the cross
not for redemption but as a martyr. Furthermore, the
modernists did not believe in the Bible. In particular, they
did not believe in the miracles recorded in the Scriptures.

When we stood up to oppose modernism, some friends
said to us, "Shouldn't we love them? Shouldn't we receive
them?" We, however, practiced John's word in his second
Epistle: "If anyone comes to you and does not bring this
teaching, do not receive him into your house, and do not
say to him, Rejoice!" (v. 10). To love a person is one thing,
but to receive one who is a false prophet or an antichrist is
an altogether different thing.

John realized that it was necessary for him, when
speaking about loving the brothers, to say a word
regarding false prophets and antichrists. We must prove
the spirits and stay away from the false prophets.
Although we need to love the brothers and even all men,
we should never receive a false prophet or an antichrist.

In 4:1 John tells us that "many false prophets have

gone out into the world." In Matthew 24:24 the false prophets differ from the false Christs. But here the false prophets are the antichrists (v. 3), those who teach heretically concerning the Person of Christ (2:18, 22-23). The "world" in 4:1 does not refer to the universe or to the earth; rather, it refers to the people, to human society on earth, who are the components of the satanic world system.

KNOWING THE SPIRIT OF GOD

In 4:2 John continues, "In this you know the Spirit of God: every spirit which confesses Jesus Christ having come in the flesh is out of God." The "spirit" here is the spirit of a genuine prophet motivated by the Holy Spirit of truth, a spirit that confesses the divine conception of Jesus, affirming that He was born as the Son of God. Every such spirit surely has its source in God; it is out of God. In this we know the Spirit of God.

Jesus was conceived of the Spirit (Matt. 1:18). To confess Jesus coming in the flesh is to confess that He was divinely conceived to be born as the Son of God (Luke 1:31-35). Since He was conceived of the Spirit to be born in the flesh, the Spirit would never deny that He has come in the flesh through divine conception.

THE MEANING OF ANTICHRIST

At this point we need to consider further the meaning of the word "antichrist." In Matthew 24:5 the Lord Jesus says, "For many shall come in My name, saying, I am the Christ, and they shall lead many astray." This verse speaks of a false Christ, someone who pretends to be Christ, in order to lead the believers astray.

In 2:26 and 3:7 John also speaks of being led astray. In this Epistle, to be led astray is to be led away from the reality of the Person of Christ, from the reality that Jesus is the Christ, the Son of God. But according to Matthew 24:5, a false Christ is one who pretends to be Christ in order to lead people astray.

In Matthew 24:23 and 24 the Lord Jesus says, "Then if

anyone says to you, Behold, here is the Christ, or, Here; do not believe it. For false Christs and false prophets shall arise and shall show great signs and wonders so as to lead astray, if possible, even the elect." These verses indicate that it is possible for even the chosen people of God to be deceived and led astray. Due to the Lord's word concerning false Christs and false prophets, there was the teaching among the believers in the early days that false Christs and false prophets would rise up.

In 1 John there are three verses concerning the antichrist. In 2:18 John says, "Young children, it is the last hour, and even as you heard that antichrist is coming, even now many antichrists have come; whereby we know that it is the last hour." Notice that in this verse the definite article is not used before "antichrist." John simply says that the believers heard that antichrist is coming and then goes on to say that many antichrists have come.

In 2:22 John again speaks concerning the antichrist: "Who is the liar if not he who is denying that Jesus is the Christ? This is the antichrist, who is denying the Father and the Son." The word "liar" indicates a false prophet. The liar, the false prophet, who denies that Jesus is the Christ, is the antichrist, the one who denies the Father and the Son.

First John 4:3 says, "And every spirit which does not confess Jesus, is not out of God; and this is the spirit of the antichrist, of which you have heard that it is coming, and now is already in the world." Like 2:22, this verse indicates that in the first Epistle of John an antichrist is a false prophet, and a false prophet is an antichrist.

In 4:3 the spirit that does not confess Jesus, is the spirit of a false prophet actuated by the spirit of deception, the spirit that does not confess Jesus coming in the flesh. This is the spirit of the errors of the Docetists (Docetes). This name was derived from the Greek *dokein*, "to seem," "to appear to be." The heretical view of the Docetists was that Jesus Christ was not a real man, but simply appeared so. According to the Docetists, Christ was merely a phantasm. Docetism was mixed up with Gnosticism, which taught that all matter was essentially evil. Hence, Docetists taught that, since Christ is holy, He could never have had the defilement of human flesh. They said that Christ's body was not real flesh and blood, but merely a deceptive, transient phantom, so that He did not suffer, die, and resurrect. Such heresy not only undermines the Lord's incarnation, but also undermines His redemption and resurrection. Docetism was a characteristic feature of the first antichristian errorists whom John had in view here and in 2 John 7. The spirit of such errorists surely does not have its source in God; it is not out of God. This is the spirit of the antichrist.

In 2 John 7 the Apostle John once again speaks concerning the antichrist: "Because many deceivers went out into the world, who do not confess Jesus Christ coming in the flesh. This is the deceiver and the antichrist." These deceivers are the liars, the false prophets, who deny that Jesus is God incarnate and in this way deny the deity of Christ. John clearly says that these deceivers are antichrists.

In the past a number of Bible teachers have used the title antichrist in a particular way. In 2 Thessalonians 2:3 and 4 Paul speaks of the man of lawlessness, "the son of destruction, who opposes and exalts himself above all that is called God or an object of worship, so that he seats himself in the temple of God, proclaiming himself that he is God." As prophesied in Daniel 7:20-21, 24-26; 8:9-12, 23-25; 9:27; and 11:36-37, this man of lawlessness will cast down the truth to the ground, change laws, destroy and corrupt many to an extraordinary degree, blaspheme God, and deceive men. Paul prophesied of the coming of this man of lawlessness.

In Revelation 13 we have two beasts: the first beast from the sea and the second beast from the earth. The second beast is the false prophet, who works for the first beast: "He exercises all the authority of the first beast in his sight, and he causes the earth and those who dwell in it to worship the first beast, whose death stroke was healed" (v. 12). The first beast will be the last Caesar of the restored kingdom of the Roman Empire, and the second beast, the false prophet, will work for him.

Because of these prophecies, many Bible teachers have applied the title "antichrist" to the coming man of lawlessness, the one who will exalt himself above God and cause himself to be worshipped and who will oppose and persecute Christians and Jews. He is also identified with the first beast in Revelation 13. It certainly is not wrong to apply the title antichrist to this person.

DIFFERENT INTERPRETATIONS
OF THE COMING OF ANTICHRIST

However, regarding the coming antichrist, Bible teachers have followed different interpretations. For instance, in his reference Bible, Dr. Scofield says that the antichrist will be the second beast in Revelation 13, the beast from the earth: "The 'many antichrists' precede and prepare the way for *the* Antichrist, who is 'the Beast out of the earth' of Rev. 13:11-17, and the 'false prophet' of Rev. 16:13; 19:20; 20:10. He is the last ecclesiastical head, as the Beast of Rev. 13:1-8 is the last civil head. For purposes of persecution he is permitted to exercise the autocratic power of the emperor-Beast." In contrast to Scofield's understanding, other Bible teachers say that the first beast of Revelation 13 will be the antichrist and that the second beast will be the false prophet. But Scofield says that the second beast, the false prophet, will be the antichrist. This means that Dr. Scofield says that the false prophet will be the antichrist.

The New Scofield Reference Bible in its note offers a somewhat different interpretation: "Many identify the 'beast coming up out of the earth' as the Antichrist.... If the 'beast coming up out of the earth' (vv. 11-17) is the Antichrist, he is the same as the 'false prophet' of 16:13; 19:20; 20:10. Because the word 'antichrist' is never directly applied to him, however, some have considered the term 'antichrist,' defined in the sense *against Christ*, as applying to the first beast (vv. 1-10), who is the political ruler." It is clear, therefore, that Bible teachers have different interpretations in the matter of to whom the title "antichrist" should be applied.

We have considered this matter in order to point out that there will not be just one antichrist. I do not think that any Bible teacher would dare to say that only the coming man of lawlessness, the son of destruction, is the antichrist. We should not be so definite as to teach that there will be only one antichrist and that before the coming of this one there will not be any other antichrists. But due to traditional teachings, many Christians have the concept that only one person will be *the* antichrist.

Bible teachers often speak about *the* antichrist, giving the impression that antichrist is a proper noun referring only to one person. However, according to John's use of this term in 2:18, 22; 4:3; and 2 John 7, this is a general title, a title referring to a category of persons. It is not a unique, proper title referring to one particular person. Therefore, the title "antichrist" is different from the title "Christ," for there is only one Christ and anyone who claims to be Christ is either a false Christ or an antichrist. But we should not use the word antichrist as if it were a proper noun.

Regarding this, translators of the Bible hold different opinions. For example, in his translation Wuest capitalizes antichrist, thus making it a proper noun. The Berkeley version does the same thing. However, J. N. Darby does not capitalize this word in his New Translation. Likewise, the word antichrist is not capitalized in the King James Version, the American Standard Version, or in the New American Standard Version.

It is not scriptural to say that there will be only one antichrist. But it is also wrong to say that the man of lawlessness, the son of destruction who exalts himself above all that is called God, is not an antichrist. That person should definitely be regarded as an antichrist.

In Matthew 24 the false prophets are of one category, and the false Christs are of another category. In Matthew 24:24 the Lord Jesus clearly speaks of both false Christs and false prophets. But in John's Epistles the false prophets are antichrists. As we have pointed out, some Bible teachers say that the first beast in Revelation 13 will be the antichrist. But Scofield and others say that the second beast, the false prophet, will be the antichrist. According to Scofield's interpretation, the antichrist is in the same category as the false prophets.

What conclusion should we draw from all these considerations? Should we regard the false prophets and the antichrists as two different categories? In a sense, we may understand them as two distinct categories. Eventually, however, the false prophets and the false Christs are all *anti*-Christ, against Christ, and hence are all antichrists. In the following message we shall consider the principle of antichrist.

LIFE-STUDY OF FIRST JOHN

MESSAGE THIRTY-ONE

THE PRINCIPLE OF ANTICHRIST

Scripture Reading: 1 John 2:18, 22; 4:3; 2 John 7

There are four verses in his Epistles where the Apostle John speaks of antichrist. In 2:18 he says that many antichrists have come; in 2:22, that the antichrist, the liar, is one who denies the Father and the Son; in 4:3, that the spirit of the antichrist does not confess Jesus; and 2 John 7, that the deceivers who have gone out into the world are antichrists. In these four verses we can see that there is a principle of antichrist.

What is an antichrist in principle? In order to answer this question, let us consider 2:18, "Young children, it is the last hour, and even as you heard that antichrist is coming, even now many antichrists have come; whereby we know that it is the last hour." This verse implies a principle. Anyone who practices this principle is in the category of antichrist.

During the time of the apostles, there was much talk about the coming antichrist. John refers to this when he tells those who received this Epistle that they "heard that antichrist is coming." Then he immediately goes on to say that many antichrists have come. The fact that there have been many antichrists implies a principle, the principle of antichrist.

DENYING WHAT CHRIST IS

In 2:22 we can see more clearly what the principle of antichrist is: "Who is the liar if not he who is denying that Jesus is the Christ? This is the antichrist, who is denying the Father and the Son." I would call your attention to the word "denying" used twice in this verse. This verse speaks of denying that Jesus is the Christ and also of denying the Father and the Son. Here we have the principle of antichrist. The principle of antichrist is to deny what Christ is. What principle must one follow in order to be an antichrist? He must follow the principle of denying what Christ is. Jesus is the Christ, Christ is the Son of God, and the Son of God is the embodiment of the Father. To deny any aspect of this truth is to deny something of what Christ is and thereby to follow the principle of antichrist.

The principle of antichrist is to deny something of Christ's Person. According to 2:22, the antichrist denies that Jesus is the Christ. As we have seen, this was the heresy of Cerinthus, who separated the earthly man Jesus from the heavenly Christ. (He considered Jesus the son of Joseph and Mary.) Cerinthus also taught that after Jesus was baptized, Christ as a dove descended upon Him, but left Jesus at the end of His ministry so that Jesus suffered on the cross and rose from the dead, while Christ remained separated as a spiritual being. Cerinthus, therefore, denied that Jesus is the Christ. As verse 22 indicates, this is also to deny the Father and the Son. When the two sentences in verse 22 are put together, we can see clearly that to deny Christ is to deny the Father and the Son. Because Cerinthus denied that Jesus is the Christ and thereby denied the Father and the Son, he was an antichrist. This is an illustration of the principle of antichrist. What makes a person an antichrist, at least in principle, is that he denies some aspect of what Christ is.

AGAINST CHRIST AND REPLACING CHRIST

The Greek prefix *anti* has two main meanings. First, it means against; second, it means in place of, or instead of. This indicates that an antichrist is against Christ and also replaces Christ with something else. To be an antichrist is, on the one hand, to be against Christ; on the other hand, it is also to have something instead of Christ, something that replaces Christ. By this we see that the principle of antichrist involves denying what Christ is. This is to be anti-Christ, against Christ. Of course, whenever someone denies what Christ is, automatically that person will replace Christ with something else. Hence, an antichrist is both against Christ and is one who replaces Christ.

We may use the modernists as an illustration of denying Christ and replacing Christ. Modernists deny that Christ is the Redeemer. They do not believe that Christ died on the cross for our sins. Instead, they claim that Christ was persecuted for His teachings and was put to death because of His teachings and died on the cross as a martyr. It is clear that modernists deny that Christ is the Redeemer who died on the cross for our sins. First, they deny this aspect of Christ's Person. Then they go on to replace the Redeemer with a martyr. In this way, they have a martyr in place of the Redeemer. This is to have something instead of Christ as the result of denying what Christ is.

We must be careful never to deny anything of what Christ is. We should never deny any part, any aspect, or any item of Christ's Person. To deny any aspect of Christ's Person is to practice the principle of antichrist. Some who hear this may say, "I certainly am not an antichrist, for I am not against Christ." One may not be against Christ or deny Christ consciously. But unconsciously we may deny some aspect of Christ's Person and then replace this aspect with something else.

THE ETERNAL FATHER
AND THE LIFE-GIVING SPIRIT

Some condemn us for teaching that, according to the Scriptures, Christ is all-inclusive, for teaching that He is God, the Son, the Father, and the Spirit. Second Corinthians 3:17 clearly says, "The Lord is the Spirit." A confirming verse is 1 Corinthians 15:45b, "The last Adam became a life-giving Spirit." Furthermore, Isaiah 9:6 says that a child is born to us and that a Son is given to us, and that His name is called the everlasting Father, or, according to the Hebrew, the Father of eternity. Here we see that the Son is called the eternal Father. These verses reveal that Christ is the Spirit and also the eternal Father.

Several years ago some opposing ones held a meeting to

discuss how to deal with our so-called heretical teaching concerning the Triune God. In that meeting the following remarks were made: "Isaiah 9:6: For unto us a child is born, unto us a son is given: and the government shall be upon his shoulder: and his name shall be called Wonderful, Counselor, The mighty God, The everlasting Father, The Prince of Peace. There Jesus is called the Father. Right? So He's the Father. That's what it says. That's Isaiah 9:6. Now we don't normally say this because tradition is involved here." These critics admitted that, because of their tradition, they normally do not say that Christ is the Father. I am glad that in the midst of the opposers' criticism there was an honest word admitting that according to Isaiah 9:6, Jesus is the Father, even though they do not normally say this because it involves the matter of tradition. By this we can see that regarding this matter they care more for tradition than for what the divine revelation actually says. However, we follow the pure Word of God. According to the Scriptures, the Son is called the eternal Father, and Christ the Lord is the Spirit who gives life.

It was in 1933 that I first began to realize that Christ is the Spirit. For more than seven years I had been under the teaching of the Brethren. They taught that the Father, the Son, and the Holy Spirit are three separate Persons. This teaching that I inherited from the Brethren no doubt corresponds to common traditional teaching. I came into the church life in 1932, and I went to Shanghai to be with Brother Nee in 1933. One day the church in Shanghai invited an itinerant Chinese preacher, who was working with the China Inland Mission, to speak in one of the meetings. In his message he strongly emphasized the point that we should not think that the Lord Jesus is separate from the Spirit. Instead, Christ and the Spirit are one. To this, Brother Nee, who was sitting at the back of the meeting hall, said a loud "Amen." Brother Nee's response surprised me. After the meeting Brother Nee and I talked about the message. In that conversation Brother Nee said to me, "Witness, we all must know that Christ is the Spirit, and this must be our message." Then I began to study this matter carefully. The more I studied the Word, the more convinced I became that today Christ and the Spirit are one.

Concerning certain aspects of Christ's Person, many believers follow tradition and neglect the revelation of the Bible. If we are fair, we shall realize that Isaiah 9:6 says that the Son is called the Father and that 2 Corinthians 3:17 and 1 Corinthians 15:45b reveal that Christ is the life-giving Spirit. To deny that Christ is the eternal Father or that He is the life-giving Spirit is to be anti these aspects of His Person. In this sense, to make such a denial is to follow the principle of antichrist, which is to deny something of what Christ is.

THE CREATOR AND THE CREATURE

We see further aspects of Christ's Person in chapter one of Colossians. According to Colossians 1:15, Christ is the Firstborn of all creation, and according to verse 18, He is the Firstborn from among the dead. As the Firstborn of all creation, Christ is the first among God's creatures, just as the Firstborn from among the dead means that He is the first One in resurrection. However, some Bible teachers will admit that Christ is the first One in resurrection, but they will not say that Christ is the first One in God's creation. It is absurd to say that Christ is first in resurrection, but not first in creation. The title "Firstborn" is used twice in the same chapter, referring to Christ being the Firstborn in God's creation and also in resurrection. Traditional theology admits that Christ is first in resurrection, but not that Christ is first in God's creation.

Some teachers and theologians will not say that Christ is a creature. They claim that it is impossible for Christ, the very God, the Creator, to be a creature. Nevertheless, with respect to His humanity Christ certainly is a creature. The Bible clearly and definitely says that Christ partook of flesh and blood (Heb. 2:14). Christ became a man possessing blood and flesh. Is it not true that man is a creature? Is it not true that blood and flesh are elements of creation?

Certainly humanity, flesh, and blood are all created things. Actually, to say that Christ is not a creature is almost equal to saying that Christ did not come in the flesh, as is condemned in 1 John 4.

Some of those who deny that Christ is a creature have a good intention. Their intention is to uphold the deity of Christ. According to their understanding, to say that Christ is a creature is to take away His deity and His status as the Creator, the almighty God. In principle, this is what the Docetists did. The heretical view of the Docetists was that Jesus Christ was not a real man, but simply appeared to be a man in the flesh. They taught that since Christ is holy, He could never have had the defilement of human flesh. Therefore, they taught that His body was not real flesh and blood, but merely a transient phantom. Holding to the concept that matter is inherently evil, the Docetists denied that Christ came in the flesh. Even if the Docetists had a good intention, they nonetheless followed the principle of antichrist because they denied something of what Christ is.

No matter what a person's intention may be, whether it is good or evil, as long as he denies any aspect of Christ's Person, he is following the principle of antichrist, although he may be doing so unconsciously. Someone may have the good intention of exalting Christ as the almighty Creator. Having this intention, he may not be willing to say that Christ is a creature. Nevertheless, the Bible reveals that with respect to His humanity, which surely is something created, Christ is a creature. Furthermore, according to the New Testament, Christ today is still a man. However, some Christians do not believe that Christ is now sitting on the throne in the heavens as a man. Jesus Christ is both God and man. Because He is both God and man, He is both the Creator and a creature.

Those who follow traditional theology often deny three aspects of what Christ is. They deny that Christ is the Spirit, they deny that Christ is the Father, and they deny that Christ is the first among the creatures. Since the principle of antichrist is to deny some aspect of what

Christ is, to deny any of these three aspects is to practice this principle, although it may be done unconsciously and unintentionally.

If we understand what the principle of antichrist is, we shall realize that certain Bible teachers unconsciously follow this principle. According to the Epistles of 1 and 2 John, anyone who denies any item of Christ's Person is following the principle of antichrist. May we be impressed with the fact that the principle of antichrist is first to deny something of what Christ is and then to replace Christ with something else.

LIFE-STUDY OF FIRST JOHN

EXPERIENCING AND ENJOYING
THE ALL-INCLUSIVE SPIRIT

Scripture Reading: 1 John 4:1-6

Our burden in the Lord's recovery is to minister the Triune God as life and everything to us so that we may enjoy all that He is. Concerning this, we stand on the shoulders of the great teachers of the Bible who have gone before us. We have learned much from the experiences of others. We have studied church history, biographies, and the most important writings of the great teachers from the early centuries until the present. All this has been very helpful to us. Of course, we have also studied the Bible for ourselves. Therefore, we surely know where we are, and we have the assurance regarding the accuracy of whatever the Lord has led us to say in the ministry.

GOD'S INTENTION

As the result of many years' experience and study, we have come to see that, according to the entire revelation in the Bible, God's intention is to work Himself into us so that He may be our life and that we may live by Him to be His expression. This is God's intention. In order for God to accomplish this intention, it is necessary for Him to be triune. Apart from being triune, that is, without being the Father, the Son, and the Spirit, God would not have a way to work Himself into us. In order to work Himself into us, God must first impart Himself to us, dispense Himself into us. If He could not do this, He could not work Himself into us to be our life. It would be impossible for the Triune God to be our life if He remained merely as the One outside of us in whom we believe, whom we worship, and for whom we work. In order for God to be our life, He must dispense

Himself into us, and in order for this dispensing to be carried out, God must be the Father, the Son, and the Spirit.

THE SON COMING IN THE NAME OF THE FATHER
AND WITH THE FATHER

God created man in His own image for the purpose of dispensing Himself into man so that man may become His expression. God's purpose in creating man was that man would be His container enjoying Him as life in order to express Him. Man, however, became fallen. After man fell, God Himself became a man. It was God the Son, not God the Father or God the Spirit, who became a man. Nevertheless, the Son came in the name of the Father and with the Father. Many Christians emphasize only that the Son came and neglect the fact that the Son came in the name of the Father and with the Father. Some theologians have even said that when the Son of God came, the Father was left in the heavens. In contrast to this natural, human concept, the New Testament reveals that when the Son came, He never left the Father. The Lord Jesus said clearly that He was not alone, for the Father was with Him. In John 8:29 He said, "He who sent Me is with Me; He has not left Me alone." In John 16:32 the Lord said, "Behold, an hour is coming and has come, when you shall be scattered each to his own, and shall leave Me alone; and I am not alone, because the Father is with Me." During His life on earth, the Father was with Him. Hence, when the Son came to be a man, He lived as a man in the name of the Father and with the Father.

The Lord Jesus even said that, while He was on earth as a man, He was in the Father and the Father was in Him. In John 10:38 He said, "Though you do not believe Me, believe the works, that you may know and believe that the Father is in Me and I in the Father." Then in John 14:10 and 11 He said, in response to Philip's request that He show them the Father, "Do you not believe that I am in the Father, and the Father is in Me? The words which I speak to you, I do not speak from Myself; but the Father who abides in Me, He does His works. Believe Me that I am in the Father and the Father in Me." This is a matter not only of the coexistence of the Father and the Son, but also of the coinherence of the Father and the Son. This means that the Father and the Son exist in each other. Therefore, the Father and the Son coexist in the way of coinherence. Because the Son came with the Father and in the name of the Father and because He coexists in the way of co-inherence with the Father, He is called the eternal Father (Isa. 9:6). We cannot analyze this or systematize it. Instead of trying to analyze or systematize the Triune God, we should simply accept the facts as revealed in the Bible.

Have you ever heard that when the Son came, He came in the name of the Father and with the Father? As we have said already, some Christians have the impression that when the Son of God came, He came by Himself, leaving the Father on the throne. These Christians have not been taught according to the Scriptures that when the Son of God came as a man, He came with the Father. The Father was in Him, and He was in the Father. This was the reason He could say that He was never alone, for the Father was with Him, even at the time of His persecu-tion. As we have pointed out from the Gospel of John, the Father was with the Son in the way of coinherence.

Those under the influence of traditional theology may still think that when the Son of God came, He left the Father on the throne. According to this concept, while the Son was living in Nazareth and while He was carrying out His ministry, the Father was on the throne in the heavens watching Him. What is revealed concerning the Father and the Son in the Gospel of John is very different. John 1:1 says, "In the beginning was the Word, and the Word was with God, and the Word was God." By this we see not only that Christ, the Word, was with God, but that He is God. According to John 1:14, the Word became flesh; that is, Christ became a man, God incarnate. In His teaching and preaching the Lord affirmed that He came in the name of the Father and with the Father. He also told both the Jewish religionists and His disciples that He was not alone, for the Father was always with Him. Furthermore, He revealed to His disciples that He is in the Father and the Father is in Him. Therefore, it is altogether inaccurate to say that when the Son came, He left the Father on the throne.

A REVELATION OF THE SON WITH THE FATHER

When the Son was on earth, He lived in the Father, and the Father lived in Him. The Son never spoke His own word; He spoke the Father's word. The Son never did His own work; He did the Father's work. The Son never sought His own glory; He sought the Father's glory. What we have in the Gospel of John, therefore, is a revelation of the Son with the Father. Hence, Isaiah 9:6 says that the Son given to us is called the eternal Father. John 3:16 says that God so loved the world that He gave His only begotten Son. Yes, God gave His Son to us; yet the name of His Son is called the eternal Father! Some have tried to explain Isaiah 9:6 by saying that the Son is only called the Father but actually is not the Father. How ridiculous! The Son came with the Father and in the name of the Father; He also lived in the Father, and the Father lived in Him. Here we have both the Son and the Father, for we have the Son with the Father. Of course, there is still a distinction between the Son and the Father. But although there is a distinction between the Son and the Father, the Gospel of John clearly reveals that the Son is in the Father and that the Father is in the Son. This is the reason the Son could say, "I and the Father are one" (John 10:30).

THE SPIRIT AS THE REALITY OF THE SON

After the Son died on the cross and was buried, in resurrection He became the life-giving Spirit. This means that the Father is in the Son and that the Son became the life-giving Spirit. This is the Spirit spoken of in John 7:39; "But this He said concerning the Spirit, whom those who believed in Him were about to receive; for the Spirit was not yet, because Jesus was not yet glorified." Now when we preach the gospel concerning Christ the Son and people believe in Him and call on His name, they receive not only the Son, but also the Father and the Spirit, for all three are one. The Son came with the Father, and the Spirit comes not only with the Son but as the reality of the Son with the Father. We need to be clear that the Son came with the Father and the Spirit came not only with the Son but as the reality of the Son. Furthermore, all three—the Father, the Son, and the Spirit—coinhere. This is the Triune God—the Father, the Son, and the Spirit as the one God— as revealed in the Bible.

THE TRIUNE GOD DWELLING IN US
AS THE ANOINTING

When the Triune God reaches us today, He comes as the Spirit. The moving of this Spirit is the anointing within (1 John 2:27). The Triune God dwells in us as the all-inclusive, compound, life-giving Spirit, and this Spirit is the ointment moving within. We do not have merely one third of the Triune God; that is, we do not have the Holy Spirit apart from the Son and the Father. We should not have the concept that one third of the Triune God is in us and that the other two thirds are in the heavens. The entire Triune God—the Spirit as the reality of the Son with the Father—dwells in us as the anointing oil. Furthermore, He is not dormant within us; rather, He is living, moving, acting. This is the anointing, which is the Triune God as the all-inclusive Spirit moving in us to saturate us with God's essence. First this Spirit is life to us, and then He becomes everything to us, including our nature, constituent, virtues, attributes, power, wisdom, righteousness, sanctification, redemption, kindness, humility.

What we have been speaking in this message is the central view of the entire divine revelation according to the sixty-six books of the Bible. Concerning this matter, the first Epistle of John is the continuation of the Gospel of John. The Gospel of John reveals that Christ has come to accomplish everything for God's economy, and now He is ready for us to receive Him by believing in Him. After we receive Him, we should love Him, and through His love we should love the brothers. The first Epistle of John tells us how to enjoy the Triune God, who is the divine life to us. We enjoy Him by remaining, abiding, dwelling, in the divine fellowship. As long as we stay in this fellowship, we shall enjoy the Triune God as love and light. The Triune God is within us for our enjoyment.

HERESIES CONCERNING CHRIST'S PERSON

When John wrote his first Epistle, there were certain heretical teachings regarding the Person of Christ. One of these heresies claimed that Jesus was not Christ. This heresy denied the deity of Jesus. Such a heretical teaching nullifies the enjoyment of the Triune God.

Another heresy concerning Christ's Person claimed that Christ was God, but denied that He became flesh. According to this heresy, Christ was God, but He was not a man. Due to the influence of Gnosticism, those who taught this heresy said that matter is inherently evil. Then these heretics went on to say that Christ as the holy God could not possibly have become flesh. Therefore, they claimed that Christ's physical body was merely a phantasm. This means that they did not believe that He had an actual material body. This heresy also eliminates the enjoyment of the all-inclusive Christ.

In the second section of this Epistle (2:12-27), John tells the "little children" (2:12) that they have an anointing from the Holy One (2:20) and that this anointing teaches them concerning all things (2:27). John seems to be saying, "The anointing is the moving and saturating of the Triune God within you. This inner anointing teaches you all things concerning the Triune God. Do not listen to Cerinthus and his followers or to the Docetists. They are false prophets." Moreover, these false prophets were antichrists (2:18, 22; 4:3), for they were anti some aspect of Christ. They have a spirit which does not have its source in God, which is not out of God: "And every spirit which does not confess Jesus, is not out of God; and this is the spirit of the antichrist, of which you have heard that it is coming, and now is already in the world" (4:3).

As we pointed out in foregoing messages, there is more than one antichrist. Antichrist is anyone who is anti something of Christ. To be an antichrist is to be against Christ and to replace Christ with something else.

THE SUBTLETY OF THE ENEMY
IN DENYING THE ALL-INCLUSIVENESS OF CHRIST

In the first century Satan in his subtlety used the Cerinthians and the Docetists to frustrate Christians from the enjoyment of the Triune God and even to cut them off from this enjoyment. By the time of the Council of Nicea (A.D. 325) doctrine that seemed to be orthodox concerning the Triune God had been established. The Nicean Creed is commonly considered a statement of orthodox doctrine. However, this creed actually is not complete concerning the Person of Christ. This creed does not indicate clearly that the Son came in the name of the Father and with the Father and even is called the eternal Father. Neither does this creed make it clear that the Son in His resurrection became the life-giving Spirit. Moreover, this creed does not say that the Spirit of God eventually consummates in the seven Spirits. In addition, the Nicean Creed does not have a clear statement concerning Christ as the Firstborn of God's creation. By this we can see that only the Bible is complete. No creed is complete.

In his subtlety Satan, the enemy, tries to cut off certain basic items of what Christ is in His Person. Hence, those who follow the creeds and traditional teaching may emphasize only that Jesus Christ is the Son of God incarnate. They may not see that Christ is also the Father, the Spirit, and the Firstborn of God's creation. The effect of this subtlety is to present a Christ who is not all-inclusive. But the Christ revealed in the Bible is all-inclusive. He is God, and He is man. He is the Son, the Father, and the Spirit. He is also the Creator and the Firstborn of the creatures. According to the Bible, Christ is still a man, and He has a spiritual body that can be touched (John 20:27). Today the Christ who is on the throne in the heavens still has a human nature (Matt. 26:64; Acts 7:56).

Christ is the first in God's old creation and also the first in resurrection, that is, in God's new creation (Col. 1:15, 18). This all-inclusive One is our power, wisdom, righteousness, sanctification, redemption, life, life supply, and all our human virtues, including kindness, humility, patience, and meekness. This wonderful One is our enjoyment, our feast, our new moon, our Sabbath, our food, our drink, and our clothing. Truly, the Christ revealed in the Bible is all-inclusive.

Because we minister the all-inclusiveness of Christ as revealed in the Bible, some falsely accuse us of teaching pantheism. They claim that we teach that everything is God. This accusation is utterly false, and we repudiate it. However, we are not fighting for doctrine but for the enjoyment of the all-inclusive Christ.

EXPERIENCING AND ENJOYING THE TRIUNE GOD

We have seen that one subtlety of the enemy is to deny certain aspects of Christ and thereby restrict Him and make Him no longer all-inclusive. Another subtlety is to deny that the Triune God is subjective to us for experience and enjoyment and to present the divine Trinity merely as an objective doctrine for religion. The religion of many Christians is based on the creeds. In certain denominations the Apostles' Creed is recited in their services every week. Many of those who recite the creed have no experience of the Triune God. To them, the divine Trinity is merely a belief in doctrine. But the Bible reveals that the Triune God is not merely the object of our faith; He is subjective to us, dwelling in us to be our life and life supply. Daily, even hourly, we need to experience Him and enjoy Him in this way. This is confirmed by the word concerning the enjoyment of the Triune God in 2 Corinthians 13:14.

The Bible reveals clearly that the Triune God, after passing through the process of incarnation, human living, crucifixion, resurrection, and ascension, has consummated in the all-inclusive Spirit, who has come to dwell in our spirit. Hallelujah for the wonderful all-inclusive Spirit dwelling in our human spirit! Our spirit may be a small organ, but this Spirit nonetheless dwells in it.

A human being can be compared to a transistor radio. Such a radio has a receiving apparatus that enables it to receive radio waves. When the radio is tuned properly, it will play music. We may say that we human beings are like transistor radios, and that the receiving apparatus is our human spirit. When our receiver is properly tuned, we enjoy heavenly music. This is an illustration of the enjoyment of the Triune God, who is now the life-giving Spirit dwelling in our regenerated human spirit. This is the reason we stress the importance of the human spirit. It is by our spirit that we touch, enjoy, and experience the all-inclusive Spirit.

According to the Scriptures, we testify strongly that our Lord today is not merely a part of the Triune God—He is the embodiment of the entire Triune God, the Son with the Father and as the Spirit. In our experience today, He is the Spirit as the reality of the Son with the Father to be our life for our enjoyment. Realizing that He is such a wonderful One, we do not care for dead doctrines, vain religion, or meaningless rituals. Our concern is to have the daily experience and enjoyment of the Triune God.

LIFE-STUDY OF FIRST JOHN

MESSAGE THIRTY-THREE

PROVING THE SPIRITS

(2)

Scripture Reading: 1 John 4:1-6

DIFFERENT TEACHINGS AND DIFFERENT SPIRITS

In 4:1 John says, "Beloved, do not believe every spirit, but prove the spirits whether they are out of God, because many false prophets have gone out into the world." This verse tells us clearly to prove, discern, the spirits. We should not think that a particular teaching simply comes from the teaching one himself. No, every teaching, whether right or wrong, comes by a spirit. As there are different teachings, there are also different spirits. Hence, we need to test the spirits to see whether they have their source in God, whether they are out of God. In verse 2 John says that every spirit which confesses that Jesus Christ has come in the flesh is out of God. But in verse 3 he says that every spirit which does not confess Jesus is not out of God, for this is the spirit of the antichrist.

The expressions "every spirit" in verses 2 and 3 and "the spirits" in verse 1 refer either to the spirit of the prophets (1 Cor. 14:32) motivated by the Spirit of truth, or to the spirit of the false prophets actuated by the spirit of deception. Every prophet, whether a real prophet or a false one, has his own spirit. When a real prophet speaks, with his spirit there is the motivating of the Spirit of God. But when a false prophet speaks, his spirit is activated by another spirit, by a spirit of deception. Hence, there is the need to discern the spirits by proving them to see whether they are out of God.

We should not think that teaching is merely a matter of

the mind and the mouth. With every kind of speaking, every kind of teaching, the spirit of the speaker either is motivated by the Spirit of God or is actuated by a spirit of deception. This means that the speaking of any kind of doctrine always comes from a certain kind of spirit, either from the spirit of a genuine prophet motivated by the Spirit of God or from the spirit of a false prophet actuated by an evil spirit.

CONFESSING THAT JESUS CHRIST HAS COME IN THE FLESH

According to 4:2, the discernment of spirits is based upon whether or not a spirit confesses that Jesus Christ has come in the flesh. Because the spirit of a genuine prophet is motivated by the Holy Spirit of truth, this spirit will confess the divine conception of Jesus and affirm that He was born as the Son of God. Every such spirit is surely out of God.

The word "flesh" in 4:2 is very important. As human beings, we were all born of flesh to be flesh (John 3:6a). Thus every human being is flesh. To confess Jesus Christ coming in the flesh is to confess that He was divinely conceived to be born as the Son of God (Luke 1:31-35). This is marvelous! Christ is God incarnate to become a man through holy conception. He did not have a human father, for He was conceived of the Holy Spirit. His conception is holy because it was carried out by the Holy Spirit. Although He was conceived of the Holy Spirit, this conception took place in the womb of a virgin. Therefore, He, the very God, became a man in the flesh. Contrary to the false teaching of the Docetists, His body was not a phantasm. Rather, He had a real body, a physical body that was solid in its substance. He was conceived of the Holy Spirit; He became flesh and was born of the virgin Mary. Because He was conceived of the Spirit to be born in the flesh, the Spirit would never deny that He has come in the flesh through divine conception.

Anyone who denies that Jesus Christ has come in the flesh denies that He was conceived of the Holy Spirit.

Furthermore, anyone who rejects Jesus Christ coming in the flesh rejects His humanity and His human living. Such a one also rejects Christ's redemption. If Christ had not become a genuine man, He could not have had human blood to shed for the redemption of human beings. If He had not become flesh through the conception of the Holy Spirit in the womb of the virgin Mary, He never could have been our Substitute to be crucified to bear our judgment before God. Therefore, to deny that Jesus Christ has come in the flesh is to deny His holy conception, His incarnation, His birth, His humanity, His human living, and also His redemption. The New Testament makes it emphatically clear that Christ's redemption was accomplished in His human body and by the shedding of His blood.

Anyone who rejects Christ's incarnation and thereby rejects His redemption also denies Christ's resurrection. If Christ had never passed through death, it would not have been possible for Him to enter into resurrection.

Denying that Jesus Christ has come in the flesh is a great heresy. This heretical teaching makes it impossible to have the enjoyment of the Trinity. According to the revelation of the Trinity in the New Testament, the Son came in the flesh with the Father and in the name of the Father. The Son was crucified, and in resurrection He became the life-giving Spirit. Therefore, we have the Spirit as the reality of the Son with the Father. This includes incarnation, human living, redemption by the shedding of human blood, death in a human body, burial, and resurrection. All these are components, constituents, of our enjoyment of the Triune God. If anyone denies Christ's incarnation, that one denies Christ's holy birth, humanity, human living, redemption through crucifixion, and resurrection. This utterly annuls the enjoyment of the genuine Trinity. Knowing the seriousness of this matter, John included 4:1-6 in his Epistle as a warning to the believers concerning the need to prove the spirits.

THE TRIUNE GOD IN THE BELIEVERS

In 4:4 John continues, "You are out of God, little

children, and you have overcome them, because greater is
He who is in you than he who is in the world." The
believers are "out of God" because they have been begotten
of God (4:7; 2:29; 3:9).

In verse 4 those who have been overcome are the false
prophets (v. 1), the antichrists (v. 3), those who taught
heresy concerning Christ's Person. The believers have
overcome them by abiding in the truth concerning Christ's
deity and concerning His humanity through divine conception, according to the teaching of the divine anointing
(2:27).

In verse 4, John tells the believers that He who is in
them is greater than he who is in the world. The One in the
believers is the Triune God, who dwells in the believers as
the all-inclusive, life-giving, anointing Spirit, and who
strengthens us from within with all the rich elements of
the Triune God (Eph. 3:16-19). Such a One is much greater
and stronger than Satan, the evil spirit.

The words "he who is in the world" refer to Satan, the
fallen angel. Satan usurps fallen mankind as the evil spirit
and operates in evil persons, who are the components of
his world system. Such a one is less than the Triune God
and weaker than He is.

THE FALSE PROPHETS AND THE WORLD SYSTEM

In verse 5 John goes on to say, "They are out of the
world; therefore they speak out of the world, and the world
hears them." In this verse "they" denotes the false
prophets, the antichrists. Both the heretics and the
heresies concerning Christ's Person have their source in
the satanic world system. Hence, the people who are the
components of this evil system listen to them and follow
them.

KNOWING THE SPIRIT OF TRUTH AND
THE SPIRIT OF DECEPTION

In verse 6 John concludes,   "We are out of God: he who
knows God hears us; he who is not out of God does not

hear us. From this we know the Spirit of truth and the spirit of deception." The apostles, the believers, and the truth which they believe and teach concerning Christ have their source in God; they are out of God. Hence, the God-knowing people, who have been begotten of God (v. 7), listen to us and stay with us. The worldlings are not out of God because they have not been begotten of God. Hence, they do not listen to us.

Literally, the Greek words rendered "from this" in verse 6 mean "out of this." "This" refers to what has been mentioned in verses 5 and 6. From the fact that the heretics and what they speak out from their spirit, actuated by the spirit of deception, are out from the world, and that we and what we speak out from our spirit, motivated by the Spirit of truth, are out from God, we know the Spirit of truth and the spirit of deception. This implies that the Holy Spirit of truth is one with our truth-speaking spirit, and that the evil spirit of deception is one with the heretics' deception-speaking spirit.

In verse 6 John speaks of both the Spirit of truth and the spirit of deception. The Spirit of truth is the Holy Spirit, the Spirit of reality (John 14:17; 15:26; 16:13). The spirit of deception is Satan, the evil spirit, the spirit of falsehood (Eph. 2:2). The word "truth" in 4:6 denotes the divine reality revealed in the New Testament, especially here concerning the divine incarnation of the Lord Jesus, which the Spirit of God testifies (1 John 4:2). This reality is in contrast to the deception of the evil spirit, the spirit of the antichrist that denies the divine incarnation of Jesus (v. 3).

PRACTICING THE PRINCIPLE OF ANTICHRIST

In a foregoing message we pointed out that the principle of antichrist is to deny some aspect of Christ's Person and replace it with something other than Christ. If someone denies an aspect of Christ revealed in the Scriptures, that one is following the principle of antichrist, although what he is doing may be done unconsciously and unintentionally. Likewise, if someone replaces an aspect of

Christ with something that is not of Christ, he is also practicing the principle of antichrist.

The teaching among today's Christians follows this principle, at least to some extent. For instance, the traditional teaching concerning the Trinity is not complete. Moreover, this teaching makes the Trinity an objective doctrine that has very little to do with Christian experience. Some teach that the One who dwells in us is only the Spirit, representing the Son and the Father, who are in the heavens. These are illustrations of inaccurate and incomplete teachings concerning the Trinity.

We agree with much of the traditional, fundamental teaching, as far as it goes. We surely believe that God created the entire universe and, in particular, man in His image; that man sinned and became fallen; that God so loved the world that He sent His Son to be our Savior and Redeemer to die on the cross for our sins; that Christ, the Son of God, resurrected from the dead and ascended to the heavens, where He is now the Lord; that the Holy Spirit has been sent to convince people, to move in them, and to help them repent and believe in the Lord Jesus; and that the Holy Spirit enables us to behave in a way that glorifies the name of God. Although all this is correct, there is nothing here concerning the enjoyment and experience of the entire Triune God.

When I was with the Brethren, from 1 John I was taught to love others. I was told that God is love and that a Christian should imitate God by loving others. However, I was not taught that this very God who is love abides in me and that He wants to impart Himself into my being and saturate me with Himself so that I may enjoy Him inwardly as love. Neither was I taught that this love should saturate me until it becomes the love with which I love others. From the way I was taught, I understood that God is on the throne and that this God is love. As He looks down upon us, He loves everyone, and now He commands us, His children, to love others. But I did not realize that my love should have anything to do with His love. Rather, His love was presented as an example for me to imitate.

The two kinds of love had nothing to do with each other.

The revelation concerning love in 1 John is very different. John tells us that God is love. The very God who is love abides in us, and we abide in Him. According to 3:24, "we know that He abides in us, by the Spirit whom He gave to us." This Spirit keeps us in an organic union with the very God who is love, causing this God to become our life and even our being. Furthermore, this Spirit is saturating us with the substance of the God who is love. Eventually, the fibers of our being will be constituted of the loving essence of God. This means that the divine love becomes us. Then spontaneously we love others. However, we do not love them by our own love; we love them by God as our love. What a great difference between this kind of love and the love that is simply a human attempt to imitate the love of God!

What many Christians have today is for the most part an objective religion with teachings and regulations. Often the believers are advised and encouraged to do good. However, this teaching is not related to the divine life, which is actually the Triune God within us. In this sense, much of the teaching among today's Christians is in the principle of antichrist, although unintentionally, either in denying certain aspects of Christ or in replacing Christ with other things.

All the virtues in our human living should be Christ Himself as the embodiment of the Triune God expressed from within us. Christ should be our love, humility, kindness, meekness, patience. Can you see that the teaching to improve our behavior and character leads to a replacement of the living Christ who dwells within us? Paul could say, "To me to live is Christ" (Phil. 1:21). Christ was Paul's love, meekness, patience, and humility. Christ was every aspect of Paul's human virtues. By this we see that we should not have anything of ourselves in place of Christ. If we replace Christ with something of our own behavior and character, we are practicing the principle of antichrist in the sense of allowing certain things to replace Christ Himself.

We all need to apply this word to ourselves and be on the alert lest in any way we follow the principle of antichrist. If we deny an aspect of Christ's Person, we are against Him, anti Him. If we have something in our daily living that replaces Christ, we also are against Christ, anti Christ. To be anti Christ is both to be against Christ and to replace Christ with something else. If we replace Christ with our own good character and behavior, we are practicing the principle of antichrist. In a practical way, we are against the anointing, anti the moving, working, and saturating of the Triune God within us. Instead of being anti the anointing, we must live according to the anointing. Otherwise, we shall be against Christ or we shall replace Christ with something else.

Do you realize that we may follow the principle of antichrist in our daily living? We may replace Christ with things of our culture and our natural life. The Chinese may replace Christ with their ethics; the Japanese, with their way of being mysterious; the Americans, with their kind of frankness; the northern Europeans, with their conservatism. Whatever our race or culture may be, we may replace Christ with our culture or with our way of having our daily life according to our culture. To replace Christ in this way is to practice the principle of antichrist.

The Epistle of 1 John is on the fellowship of the divine life. This means that this Epistle is concerned with the enjoyment and experience of the Triune God. The divine fellowship is a matter of enjoying the divine Trinity, for the divine life is actually the Triune God Himself. Hence, when we speak of the fellowship of the divine life, we actually mean the experience and enjoyment of the Triune God. We have seen that this fellowship, this enjoyment, is carried out by the anointing within us (2:27). The anointing is the moving, the working, of the Triune God in us to saturate us with Himself and make Him everything to us. I believe that this thought was in the heart of the Apostle John as he was writing this book.

On the one hand, traditional theology may deny certain aspects of what Christ is. On the other hand, this theology may make the Triune God mostly a doctrine that is not related to our daily Christian life. Therefore, this theology may be according to the principle of antichrist in that it either denies something of what Christ is or replaces Christ with something else. Christ may be replaced with religion, culture, improved character, or good behavior. Those who hold to traditional theological teaching may not even believe that Christ dwells in the believers. They may believe only that the Holy Spirit is a power to inspire us that we may do good. But this kind of theology has nothing to do with God's essence wrought into our being to become our daily enjoyment and experience. By this we can see that much of today's theology is in the principle of antichrist.

But what is the situation with us? Perhaps doctrinally we do not deny anything of Christ's Person. But in our daily life we may replace Christ with many natural, religious, cultural, and ethical things. We may replace Christ with our thinking and habits, with our cultural standards, with our religious tradition, and with our ethical concepts, none of which has anything to do with the anointing. In this sense, we may be according to the principle of antichrist. Although we are not against Christ, we may be anti Christ in the sense of replacing Christ with other things, even the good things of religion, culture, and ethics.

We need to repent for replacing Christ with other things. We need to repent for having a daily living that is in the principle of antichrist, that allows culture, religion, ethics, and natural concepts to replace Christ. We need to pray, "Lord, save us, rescue us, and deliver us from all replacements. Lord, bring us back to Your anointing. We don't want to be anti Christ in any way. We don't want to be anti the anointing. Lord, we want to live and walk in, with, through, and by the anointing. We want to live and walk by the moving, working, and saturating of the Triune God within us." This is the revelation of the Bible, and this is also our burden in the Lord's recovery today.

LIFE-STUDY OF FIRST JOHN

THE VIRTUES OF THE DIVINE BIRTH
TO PRACTICE THE DIVINE LOVE

(4)

Scripture Reading: 1 John 4:7-15

First John 4:1-6 is a parenthetical section in which the believers are warned to discern the spirits. This means that 4:7 is the direct continuation of 3:24. First John 4:7-21 is an extension of the section from 2:28 through 3:24, stressing further the brotherly love, already covered in 3:10-24, as a higher condition of the life that abides in the Lord.

GOD—THE SOURCE OF LOVE

In 4:7 John says, "Beloved, let us love one another, because love is out of God, and everyone who loves has been begotten of God and knows God." Here John says that love is out of God. This indicates that when we love others, our love must be something that comes out of God. Our love for the brothers should not be something out of ourselves; it should be the love that is out of God. The believers, who have been begotten of God and know God, love one another habitually with the love which is out of God as the expression of God.

The Divine Birth as the Basic Factor
of Brotherly Love

In verse 7 John says that everyone who loves has been begotten of God. The apostle's emphasis here is still the divine birth, through which the divine life has been imparted into the believers, the life that affords them the life-ability to know God. This divine birth is the basic factor of brotherly love as a higher condition of the life that abides in the Lord. We have seen that John's writings emphasize the divine birth (3:9; 4:7; 5:1, 4, 18; John 1:12-13), which is our regeneration (John 3:3, 5). Through the divine birth we have received the divine life, which is the eternal life (1 John 1:2), as the divine seed sown into our being (3:9). Out of this seed all the riches of the divine life grow from within us. It is by this that we abide in the Triune God and live the divine life in our human living. The divine birth, therefore, is the basis of our Christian life.

Knowing God by the Divine Life

According to John's word in 4:7, everyone who loves not only has been begotten of God, but also knows God. This knowing is by the divine life (John 17:3) received from the divine birth. The word "knows" here also implies experience and enjoyment. We cannot know God without experiencing and enjoying Him. This indicates that this knowing is an experiential knowing, not an objective knowledge of God. We know God because we have experienced Him and are enjoying Him.

KNOWING GOD AS LOVE

In verse 8 John goes on to say, "He who does not love has not known God, because God is love." Not to know God means not to experience Him or enjoy Him. If you have experienced and enjoyed God, who is love, surely love will come forth from you.

He who has not known God does not have the knowing ability of the divine life received from the divine birth. Such a one, who has not been begotten of God and does not have God as his life, does not love with God as his love, since he does not know God as love.

In this book John twice tells us that God is love (4:8, 16). This Epistle first says that God is light (1:5), and then that God is love. Love as the nature of God's essence is the source of grace, and light as the nature of God's expression is the source of truth. When the divine love appears to us it becomes grace, and when the divine light shines upon us it becomes truth. Both of these were manifested in this way in John's Gospel. We received both grace and truth there through the manifestation of the Son (John 1:14, 16-17). Now in his Epistle we come in the Son to the Father and touch the sources of both grace and truth. These sources, love and light, are God the Father Himself for our deeper and finer enjoyment in the fellowship of the divine life with the Father in the Son (1:3-7) by our abiding in Him (2:5, 27-28; 3:6, 24).

The expression "God is love," like "God is light" (1:5) and "God is Spirit" (John 4:24), is used in a predicative sense, not in a metaphoric sense. In His nature God is Spirit, love, and light. Spirit denotes the nature of God's Person; love, the nature of God's essence; and light, the nature of God's expression. Both love and light are related to God as life, which life is of the Spirit (Rom. 8:2). God, Spirit, and life are actually one. God is Spirit, and Spirit is life. Within this life are love and light. We have seen that when the divine love appears to us, it becomes grace, and when the divine light shines upon us, it becomes truth. The Gospel of John reveals that the Lord Jesus has brought grace and truth to us so that we may have the divine life (John 3:14-16). The Epistle of 1 John reveals that the fellowship of the divine life brings us to the sources of grace and truth, which are the divine love and the divine light. In John's Gospel it was God in the Son coming to us as grace and truth that we may become His children (John 1:12-13); in his Epistle it is we the children, in the fellowship of the Father's life, coming to the Father to participate in His love and light. This is further and deeper in the experience of the divine life. After receiving the divine life in John's Gospel by believing in the Son, we should go on to enjoy this life in his Epistle through the fellowship of this life.

THE LOVE OF GOD MANIFESTED TO US

In 4:9 John goes on to say, "In this the love of God was manifested to us, that God has sent His Son, the only begotten, into the world that we might live through Him." In this verse we see God's intention and goal in sending the Son: God sent the Son so that we might live through Him. Living through the Son implies having the divine life. If we did not have life through Him, we could not live through Him. Therefore, living through the Son implies that we have received Him as our life. God sent His Son, and we have received Him as life. Now we live through Him.

In verse 9 John says that in this the love of God was manifested to us. Literally, the Greek words rendered "to us" are "in us," that is, in our case, or, in regard to us. In that God has sent His Son into the world that we might live through Him, the higher and nobler love of God was manifested to us.

GOD SENDING HIS SON
THAT WE MIGHT LIVE THROUGH HIM

In 4:9 John says that God sent His Son, the only begotten, into the world. As in 1 Timothy 1:15, the "world" here refers to fallen mankind, whom God so loved that, by making them alive through His Son with His own life (John 3:16), they may become His children (John 1:12-13).

We have seen that in verse 9 John tells us that God sent His Son into the world that we might live through Him. We, the fallen people, are not only sinful in nature and conduct (Rom. 7:17-18; 1:28-32), but also dead in our spirit (Eph. 2:1, 5; Col. 2:13). God sent His Son into the world not only to be a propitiation concerning our sins that we might be forgiven (1 John 4:10), but also to be life to us that we may live through Him. In the love of God, the Son of God saves us not only from our sins by His blood (Eph. 1:7; Rev. 1:5), but also from our death by His life (1 John 3:14-15; John 5:24). He is not only the Lamb of God who takes away our sins (John 1:29); He is also the Son of God who gives us eternal life (John 3:36). He died for our sins (1 Cor. 15:3) that we might have eternal life in Him (John 3:14-16) and live through Him (John 6:57; 14:19). In this the love of God, which is His essence, has been manifested.

A PROPITIATION CONCERNING OUR SINS

In 4:10 John says, "In this is love, not that we have

loved God, but that He loved us, and sent His Son a propitiation concerning our sins." The word "this" refers to the following fact: not that we have loved God, but that He loved us, and sent His Son a propitiation concerning our sins. In this fact is the higher and nobler love of God.

The word "propitiation" indicates that the Lord Jesus Christ offered Himself to God as a sacrifice for our sins (Heb. 9:28), not only for our redemption but also for God's satisfaction. Through His vicarious death and in Him as our Substitute, God is satisfied and appeased. Hence, He is the propitiation between God and us.

In 4:9 we see that God sent His Son in order that we might live through Him. In 4:10 we see that God sent His Son a propitiation concerning our sins. If we consider these verses together, we shall see that God's sending His Son a propitiation concerning our sins is not the goal. Rather, this is a procedure for arriving at the goal, and the goal is that we may have life and live through the Son. Therefore, God sent His Son a propitiation for us with the intention that through His Son we may have life and live.

LOVING ONE ANOTHER AND MANIFESTING GOD

In 4:11 John continues, "Beloved, if God has so loved us, we also ought to love one another." This is to love with the love of God as He loved us.

First John 4:12 says, "No one has ever beheld God; if we love one another, God abides in us, and His love is perfected in us." The word "beheld" indicates that if we love one another with the love of God as He loved us, we express Him in His essence, so that others may behold Him in us in what He essentially is.

No one has ever beheld God, that is, seen God. But if we love one another with God as love, we shall manifest God. Because God is manifested in our love for one another, others will be able to see God in this love.

In verse 12 John says that if we love one another, God abides in us. To love one another is a condition of our abiding in God (4:13), and our abiding in God is a condition of His abiding in us (John 15:4). Hence, when we

love one another, God abides in us, and His love is
perfectly manifested in us.

"The love of God" in 2:5 is God's love within us toward
Him, with which we love Him. "His love" in 4:12 is God's
love within us toward one another, with which we love one
another. This indicates that we should take God's love as
our love to love Him and to love one another.

GOD'S LOVE PERFECTED IN US

In verse 12 John also speaks of God's love being
perfected in us. The love of God is perfected already in God
Himself, but now this love needs to be perfected in us. This
requires that the love of God become our experience. If the
love of God remains in God, it will be perfected in God
Himself. But when this love becomes our experience and
enjoyment, it will be perfected in us. The love that is
already perfected in God needs to be perfected in us
through our enjoyment of this love.

The Greek word translated "perfected" in 4:12 is
teleioo, which means to complete, to accomplish, to finish.
The love of God is perfect and complete in Him. However, in us it needs to be perfected and completed in its
manifestation. It has been manifested to us in God's
sending His Son to be both a propitiation and life to us
(4:9-10). Yet, if we do not love one another with this love as
it was manifested to us, that is, if we do not express it by
loving one another with it as God did to us, it is not
perfectly and completely manifested. The love of God is
perfected and completed in its manifestation when we
express it in our living by habitually loving one another
with it. Our living in the love of God toward one another is
its perfection and completion in its manifestation in us.
Thus, others can behold God manifested in His love-
essence in our living in His love.

KNOWING THAT WE ABIDE IN HIM
AND HE IN US

In 4:13 John says, "In this we know that we abide in
Him and He in us, that He has given us of His Spirit." The

words "in this" mean in the fact that God has given us of His Spirit we know that we abide in Him and He in us. The Spirit whom God has given to dwell in us (James 4:5; Rom. 8:9, 11) is the witness in our spirit (Rom. 8:16) that we dwell in God and He in us. The abiding Spirit, that is, the indwelling Spirit, is the element and sphere of the mutual abiding, the mutual indwelling, of us and God. By Him we are assured that we and God are one, abiding in one another, indwelling each other mutually. This is evidenced by our living, a living that habitually expresses His love.

In verse 13 John indicates that we may know that we abide in God. To abide in God is to dwell in Him, remaining in our fellowship with Him, that we may experience and enjoy His abiding in us. This is to practice our oneness with God according to the divine anointing (2:27) by a living that practices His righteousness and His love. It is all by the operation of the all-inclusive compound Spirit, who dwells in our spirit and who is the basic element of the divine anointing.

GOD GIVING US OF HIS SPIRIT

In verse 13 John also says that God "has given us of His Spirit." In Greek "of" literally means out of. God has given us out of His Spirit. This closely resembles and repeats the word in 3:24, which proves that this does not mean that God has given us something, such as the various gifts in 1 Corinthians 12:4, of His Spirit, but that His Spirit Himself is the all-inclusive gift (Acts 2:38). "Out of His Spirit" is an expression which implies that the Spirit of God, whom He has given to us, is bountiful and without measure (Phil. 1:19; John 3:34). By such a bountiful immeasurable Spirit we know with full assurance that we are one with God and that we abide in Him and He in us.

GOD'S LOVE BECOMING OUR CONSTITUTION

As we consider 4:11-13, we see that we should never teach the saints to love with their own natural love, with the love that is something apart from God Himself. On the contrary, we all need to see that God abides in us, and we abide in Him. This is a matter of coinherence, of mingling, of organic union. God is not only in us; He abides in us, dwells in us. Through this mingling, this organic union, He becomes us, and we become Him. Therefore, since God is love, this love becomes our constitution. Because we become what He is, our love for others will actually be God Himself. We love others with God as love. Because God abides in us and we abide in Him, we love with God Himself as love.

GOD SENDING HIS SON
AS THE SAVIOR OF THE WORLD

In 4:14 John continues, "And we have beheld and testify that the Father has sent the Son as Savior of the world." As in 4:9 and John 3:16, "world" here denotes fallen mankind.

The Father's sending of the Son to be our Savior is an external act, that through our confessing of the Son He may abide in us and we in Him (4:15). The apostles have beheld and testify this. This is the outward testimony. In addition to this, God's internal act toward us is the sending of His Spirit to dwell in us as inward evidence that we abide in Him and He in us (4:13).

In 4:9, 10, and 14 the Apostle John says three times that God has sent His Son. God sent the Son that we might live through Him; He sent the Son a propitiation concerning our sins; and He sent the Son as Savior of the world.

CONFESSING THAT JESUS IS THE SON OF GOD

In 4:15 John says, "Whoever shall confess that Jesus is the Son of God, God abides in him, and he in God." God the Father sent His Son to be the Savior of the world with the purpose that men may believe in Him by confessing that Jesus is the Son of God, so that God may abide in them and they in God. But the heretical Cerinthians did not confess this. Hence, they did not have God abiding in them, nor did they abide in God. But whoever confesses that Jesus is the Son of God, God abides in him and he in

God. He becomes one with God in the divine life and nature.

We may have expected John to say that whoever confesses that Jesus is the Son of God has the forgiveness of sins, or has eternal life. However, here John says that whoever confesses that Jesus is the Son of God, God abides in him and he in God. We should use this verse in preaching the gospel. We should tell people that if they believe in the Lord and confess that Jesus is the Son of God, they will be forgiven of their sins and will be saved. We should also tell them that if they confess that Jesus is the Son of God, God will come into them and abide in them, and they will be able to abide in God. This is the highest preaching of the gospel. Have you ever preached the gospel in this way? In our preaching of the gospel let us tell people that if they believe in the Lord Jesus, confessing that He is the Son of God, God will come into them to abide in them, and they will abide in God.

LIFE-STUDY OF FIRST JOHN

THE VIRTUES OF THE DIVINE BIRTH TO PRACTICE THE DIVINE LOVE

(5)

Scripture Reading: 1 John 4:16—5:3

In this message we shall consider 4:16—5:3, the last message on the virtues of the divine birth to practice the divine love.

KNOWING AND BELIEVING

In 4:16 John says, "And we have known and have believed the love which God has in us. God is love, and he who abides in love abides in God, and God abides in him." Here John says that we have known and believed the love which God has in us. This love is God's love in sending the Son to be our Savior (4:14).

It is significant that in 4:16 John puts the word "known" before "believed." As we pointed out in the foregoing message, this knowing involves experience and enjoyment. The fact that according to 4:16 we know and then believe indicates that first we experience and enjoy, and then we believe. However, our concept may be that first we believe, and then experience. However, if we do not have much experience and enjoyment of God's love, we shall not be able to believe this love very much. But after we enjoy it and experience it, we surely believe the love which God has in us.

The words "in us" mean in our case, or in regard to us. Therefore, we have known and believed the love which God has in regard to us.

In 4:16 John again says, "God is love." That God is love

has been manifested in His sending His Son to be our Savior and life (4:9-10,14).

ABIDING IN GOD

In 4:16 John says that he who abides in love abides in God, and God abides in him. To abide in love is to live a life that loves others habitually with the love which is God Himself so that He may be expressed in us. To abide in God is to live a life which is God Himself as our inward content and outward expression so that we may be absolutely one with Him. God abides in us to be our life inwardly and our living outwardly. Thus, He may be one with us in a practical way.

In 4:16 we see that there is an organic union between us and God. This organic union is indicated by the word "in." It is interesting that John does not say that God is love and that he who abides in God abides in love. Instead, he says that he who abides in love abides in God. To us, the former may seem more logical. But the latter is more practical and real. To say that we abide in God when we abide in love means that the very love in which we abide is God Himself. This indicates that the love that we have toward others should be God Himself. If we abide in the love which is God Himself, we then abide in God, and God abides in us.

BOLDNESS IN THE DAY OF JUDGMENT

In verse 17 John continues, "In this has love been perfected with us, that we may have boldness in the day of the judgment, because even as that One is, so also are we in this world." In our abiding in the love which is God Himself (v. 16) the love of God is perfected in us, that is, perfectly manifested in us, that we may have boldness without fear (v. 18) in the day of judgment.

In verse 17 John speaks of the love of God being perfected with us. The word "perfected" is a translation of the Greek word *teleioo*, to complete, to accomplish, to finish. The love of God itself is perfect and complete in Himself, but it still needs to be perfected in us. In order for

God's love to be perfected in us, we need to experience this love. In our experience the love of God is perfected.

John says that if the love of God is perfected in us, we may have boldness in the day of judgment. The Greek word for "boldness" is *parresia*, meaning boldness of speech, confidence. In 3:21 boldness is for us to contact God in fellowship with Him. In 4:17 the boldness is for us to face the judgment at the judgment seat of Christ (2 Cor. 5:10) at His coming back (1 Cor. 3:13; 4:5; 2 Tim. 4:8). The judgment at the judgment seat of Christ will not be for eternal perdition or eternal salvation, but rather will be for reward or punishment. If we love the brothers with God as love, we shall have boldness in the day when Christ judges His believers at His judgment seat.

In 4:17 John indicates that "as that One is, so also are we in this world." As in 3:3 and 7, "that One" refers to Christ. He lived in this world a life of God as love, and now He is our life so that we may live the same life of love in this world and be the same as He is now.

As in 4:1, "world" does not refer to the universe or the earth, but to human society on the earth, to the people, who are the components of the satanic world system.

NO FEAR IN LOVE

In verse 18 John goes on to say, "There is no fear in love, but perfect love casts our fear, because fear has punishment, and he who fears has not been perfected in love." A literal translation of the first part of this verse would be, "Fear is not in the love." "Fear" does not refer to the fear of offending God and being judged by Him (1 Pet. 1:17; Heb. 12:28), but to the fear that we *have* offended God and will be judged by Him. "Love" refers to the perfected love mentioned in the preceding verse, the love of God with which we love others. Perfect love is the love that has been perfected in us by our loving others with the love of God. Such love casts out fear and causes us to have no fear of being punished by the Lord at His coming back (Luke 12:46-47).

In 4:18 John tells us that he who fears has not been

perfected in love. This means that the one who fears has not lived in the love of God so that it could be perfectly manifested in him.

First, John says in 4:12 and 17 that God's love needs to be perfected in us. Then in 4:18 he speaks of being perfected in love. This indicates that we and the divine love are mingled. When love is perfected in us, we are perfected in love, for we become the love, and the love becomes us.

LOVING BECAUSE GOD FIRST LOVED US

Verse 19 says, "We love, because He first loved us." God first loved us in that He has infused us with His love and generated within us the love with which we love Him and love the brothers (v. 20). First John 4:20 says, "If anyone says, I love God, and hates his brother, he is a liar; for he who does not love his brother whom he has seen, cannot love God whom he has not seen." He who hates a brother habitually proves that he is not abiding in the divine love nor in the divine light (2:9-11). When we abide in the Lord, we abide both in the divine love and in the divine light. We do not hate the brothers but love them habitually, living the divine life in the divine light and the divine love.

In 4:21 John says, "And this commandment we have from Him, that he who loves God love his brother also." The commandment here is the commandment of brotherly love (2:7-11; John 13:34). It is possible to summarize John's writing here in a simple way: God is love, and if we abide in Him, we shall love the brothers with Him as our love. This is John's basic thought in these verses.

A TRIANGULAR LOVE

In 5:1 John goes on to say, "Everyone who believes that Jesus is the Christ has been begotten of God, and everyone who loves Him who begets, loves him who has been begotten of Him." The Gnostics and Cerinthians did not believe in the identity of Jesus and the Christ. Hence, they were not the children of God, begotten of God. But whoever believes that the Man Jesus is the Christ, God incarnate,

(John 1:1, 14; 20:31), has been begotten of God and has become a child of God (John 1:12-13). Such a one loves God the Father who has begotten him and also loves the brother who has been begotten of the same Father. This explains, confirms, and strengthens the word in the preceding verses (1 John 4:20-21).

In 5:1 we have an indication that brotherly love is actually a triangular love, that is, a love that involves three parties. As a child of God born of Him, we surely love our Father, the One who has begotten us. Then according to 5:1, if we love the begetting Father, we shall also love those who have been begotten of Him. Here we have a triangular love, a love involving God, ourselves, and those born of God. This triangular love is in the organic union with the very God who is love.

John emphasizes the divine birth (5:1; 2:29; 3:9; 4:7; 5:1, 4, 18). How is it possible for us to love God and to love others? This is possible only because we have had the divine birth. We have been born of God, begotten of Him, and because of this birth we are able to love others. As we have pointed out, this is a triangular love. Therefore, the triangular love is related to the divine birth. Everyone who believes that Jesus is the Christ has been begotten of God. Now we love not only the One who has begotten us, our begetting Father, but also the ones begotten of Him. This is the triangular love related to the divine birth as revealed in 5:1.

LOVING GOD AND PRACTICING HIS COMMANDMENTS

In 5:2 John continues, "In this we know that we love the children of God, whenever we love God and practice His commandments." Loving God and practicing His commandments are the prerequisite of our loving the children of God. This is based upon the divine birth and the divine life.

In 5:2 John speaks of practicing the Lord's commandments. The Greek word rendered "practice" is *poieo*, a word that denotes doing things habitually and continually by abiding in the things; hence, it is used in this Epistle in the sense of practice. This word is used in 1:6; 2:17, 29; 3:4 (twice), 7, 8, 9, 10, 22; and here in 5:2.

Verse 3 is the conclusion of this section: "For this is the love of God, that we keep His commandments; and His commandments are not burdensome." The Greek word for love here is *agape*, denoting the love which is higher and nobler than *phileo*. Only *agape* with its verb forms is used in this Epistle for love. "The love of God" here denotes our love toward God, which is generated by His love within us.

In 5:3 John says that the love of God is that we keep His commandments, commandments that are not burdensome. Keeping the commandments of God constitutes our love toward Him and is an evidence that we love Him. Literally, the Greek word for "burdensome" means heavy. To the divine life with its capability, the commandments of God are not heavy.

LOVE AS THE OUTCOME OF THE ENJOYMENT OF THE TRIUNE GOD AS THE ALL-INCLUSIVE SPIRIT

In all these verses John is actually speaking concerning the issue of the fellowship of the divine life. When we are in the fellowship of the divine life, that is, in the enjoyment of the Triune God, this enjoyment will have a certain issue or outcome. The outcome of the enjoyment of the Triune God is the divine love. When we enjoy the Triune God, this enjoyment issues in the divine love. Such a result will certainly come out of this enjoyment. With this divine love we spontaneously love others. In particular, we love all those who are organically related to our begetting Father. We have been begotten of this Father, and many others also have been begotten of Him. If we enjoy Him, the result will be that we love all His children. Therefore, loving the brothers is the issue of enjoying the Triune God.

The Triune God as revealed in this Epistle is not only life, light, and love; He is also the all-inclusive Spirit. This Spirit dwells in us and moves in us so that we may enjoy the Triune God. As we enjoy the Triune God, His essence becomes our being. As a result, we have life, light, and love, and we live by this life and in this light and love.

Spontaneously, we live a life that loves the children of God. This is John's thought in this Epistle.

However, when we read 1 John, we may not have this understanding of loving the brothers. We may see only that we are told that God is love and that we are charged to love one another. Then in a natural, religious, and ethical way we may try to love others, imitating God's love. In our nature as human beings there is the tendency to love in this way. But this kind of love may be ethical, natural, and even cultural.

Many have been taught to love others and to be kind to them. Many Christians, of course, are under the influence of such teaching. But these Christians may not see the matter of the anointing in this Epistle. They may not realize that within them there is a divine moving, working, and saturating. They may emphasize teaching, but they may fail to emphasize the inner anointing. The word "anointing" is a key word in this Epistle. This word implies that today the Triune God is the compound ointment moving within us. This ointment includes the process through which the Triune God has passed: incarnation, human living, crucifixion, resurrection, and ascension. All the steps of this process are the ingredients of this compound ointment.

The anointing is the function of this ointment. This means that the function of this ointment is to anoint us with the Triune God. Therefore, the anointing anoints us with the Father, the Son, the Spirit, incarnation, humanity, human living, crucifixion, resurrection, and ascension. Hence, when we are anointed by the moving of the all-inclusive Spirit within us, we are anointed with all these elements. This means that the different elements of the compound ointment are anointed into our being. Just as the elements of paint are applied to something that is painted, so the elements of the divine paint, the all-inclusive Spirit, are imparted to our being.

As indicated by the word anointing, the teaching of the Apostle John in this book is very subjective and is related to our organic union with the Triune God. Whereas many

Christians today emphasize objective doctrine, God's economy, His dispensation, emphasizes the anointing. The anointing within us is saturating us with all that the Triune God is, with all that He has done, and with all that He has obtained and attained.

Although 1 John presents a subjective revelation, those who are preoccupied with doctrine, creeds, and objective belief neglect the subjective revelation, and even condemn us for teaching it. Our teaching concerning the anointing may be different from traditional teaching, but it is definitely scriptural. Even if this teaching is different from the traditional teaching, it is not different from what is revealed in the Bible.

Now that we have covered this Epistle from 1:1 to 5:3, we can see that what is revealed in this book is altogether related to the anointing. We need to remember what the anointing is. The anointing is the moving, the working, the saturating, of the processed Triune God within us to be our life, our life supply, our enjoyment, and our everything. This anointing, which is fully realized in the fellowship of the divine life, is the subject of this Epistle.

LIFE-STUDY OF FIRST JOHN

MESSAGE THIRTY-SIX

THE VIRTUES OF THE DIVINE BIRTH
TO OVERCOME THE WORLD, DEATH, SIN, THE DEVIL,
AND THE IDOLS

(1)

Scripture Reading: 1 John 5:4-13

In 2:28—5:21 we see the virtues of the divine birth. First, in 2:28—3:10a we have the practice of the divine righteousness. Then in 3:10b—5:3 we have the practice of the divine love. In order to practice the divine righteousness we need a basis, and this basis is the divine birth. We also need a means. This means is the divine life. Through abiding in the divine fellowship according to the divine anointing, we have the practice of the divine righteousness. In order to practice the divine love, we need the divine life as the divine seed, and we also need the divine Spirit (3:10b-24). Then we need the proving of the spirits (4:1-6), and we also need God as the supreme love and the bountiful Spirit (4:7—5:3).

God's economy is to work Himself into us. For this, we need to be born of Him; that is, we need the divine birth. This divine birth brings into us the divine life with the divine nature. As those who have been born of God, we now have the Triune God moving and working within us as the anointing. Day by day we need to abide, dwell, in the enjoyment of the Triune God according to this anointing. I hope that we all shall be deeply impressed with the fact that the Triune God is working Himself into our being. We have Him as the divine life with the divine nature moving and working in us as the divine anointing. Now we simply need to dwell in Him according to this divine anointing.

In this message we shall begin to consider the virtues of the divine birth to overcome the world, death, sin, the Devil, and the idols (5:4-21). Our overcoming of these negative things is not by ourselves, by what we are, or by what we can do, but by the eternal life in the Son. Surely the overcoming of the world, death, sin, the Devil, and idols is a virtue of the divine birth. First John 5:4-13, which we shall consider in this message, reveals that it is by the eternal life in the Son that we may have the practical experience of overcoming these five categories of negative things.

OUR SPIRIT REGENERATED
WITH THE DIVINE LIFE

In 5:4 John says, "Because everything that has been begotten of God overcomes the world; and this is the victory which overcame the world—our faith." The word "everything" refers to every person who has been begotten of God. Yet such an expression should refer especially to the part that has been regenerated with the divine life, that is, the spirit of the regenerated person (John 3:6). The regenerated spirit of the believer does not practice sin (1 John 3:9), and it overcomes the world. His divine birth with the divine life is the basic factor of such victorious living.

Both John's Gospel and Epistle stress the divine birth (John 1:13; 3:3, 5; 1 John 2:29; 3:9; 4:7; 5:1, 4, 18), through which the divine life is imparted into the believers in Christ (John 3:15-16, 36; 1 John 5:11-12). This divine birth that brings in the divine life is the basic factor of all the mysteries concerning the divine life, such as the fellowship of the divine life (1:3-7), the anointing of the divine Trinity (2:20-27), the abiding in the Lord, (2:28—3:24), and the divine living that practices the divine truth (1:6), the divine will (2:17), the divine righteousness (2:29; 3:7), and divine love (3:10, 22-23; 5:1-3) to express the divine Person (4:12). The divine birth with the divine life is also the basic factor of this section, from 5:4 through 5:21. It assures the God-begotten believers, giving them confidence in the ability and virtue of the divine life.

Since regenerated believers have the capability of the divine life to overcome the world, the powerful satanic world system, the commandments of God are not heavy or burdensome to them (5:3).

Regeneration takes place definitely and particularly in our spirit. John 3:6 says that that which is born of the Spirit is spirit. This indicates that regeneration takes place in our spirit. Because our spirit has been regenerated, it cannot sin. On the contrary, our spirit can overcome all negative things.

Our spirit has been regenerated with the divine life. This means that the divine life has been imparted or infused into our spirit. However, our body has not been regenerated, and our soul still remains without the life of God. For this reason, once we have been regenerated in our spirit, we should dwell in the divine life so that it may have free course to spread into our soul. The spreading of the divine life from our regenerated spirit into our soul produces a metabolic change in our being, a change which is called transformation in the New Testament. By this we see that after regeneration in our spirit, we need the divine life to saturate our soul in order to cause the transformation of our inner being, the metabolic change of our soul. Eventually, the time will come when our body will be transfigured by the power of the divine life into a glorious body.

As human beings we have three parts: the spirit, the soul, and the body. In God's salvation there are three steps: regeneration, transformation, and transfiguration. Regeneration took place in our spirit when we believed in the Lord Jesus. Now if we abide in the fellowship of the divine life, this will open the way for the divine life to spread into our soul and to transform the parts of our inward being. When the Lord Jesus comes back, He will transfigure our bodies. Then we shall be fully in the divine life and in the divine glory.

Today both our soul and body give us trouble. If we do

not abide in the fellowship of the divine life, our body and soul will give us a difficult time. Praise the Lord for the hope that our troublesome body will be transfigured! We also thank the Lord for the transformation that is taking place in our soul. All believers have experienced regeneration, the initial step of God's salvation. Through regeneration, the divine birth, we received the divine life, the eternal life, which is in the Son. Actually, this eternal life is the Son Himself.

THE REGENERATED SPIRIT
OVERCOMING THE WORLD

According to 5:4, everything that has been begotten of God overcomes the world. We have seen that "everything" points to the human spirit. Therefore, it is the regenerated human spirit that overcomes the world. Regarding overcoming the world, we should not trust in our own ability or effort. From experience I can testify that we need to trust our spirit. Our spirit is well able to overcome Satan and the world, the evil system. But in ourselves we cannot overcome the world. When we exercise our spirit, stay in our spirit, and walk by our spirit, we shall see that our spirit has the life ability to overcome all negative things. This is why we need to exercise our spirit to have fellowship with the Lord and pray concerning the enjoyment of the Lord. We also need to exercise our spirit to call on the Lord's name and to pray-read the Word. This exercise stirs up the ability in our spirit to overcome the world.

It is the divine life in our spirit that has the ability to overcome the evil, satanic world. We are surrounded by temptations. What can overcome them? The divine life in our spirit can overcome temptation. We all need to see that our spirit is mingled with the divine life and is the organ that can overcome the world.

OUR FAITH

In 5:4b John says, "And this is the victory which overcame the world—our faith." This is the faith that believes that Jesus is the Son of God (5:5) that we may be begotten of God and have His divine life, by which we are enabled to overcome the Satan-organized-and-usurped world.

Actually, our trust should not be in our faith itself. The faith by itself does not overcome the world. Our faith brings us into an organic union, and it is this organic union, not the faith directly, that overcomes the world. We may use switching on electrical current as an illustration. The act of switching on is not the power itself. It is the means by which appliances are brought into union with electricity. In a similar way, we may say that faith is the means for us to "switch on" to the Triune God. By believing in the Lord Jesus, we are brought into organic union with the Triune God; we "switch on" to Him. This union, produced by faith, then overcomes the world.

HE WHO BELIEVES
THAT JESUS IS THE SON OF GOD

In 5:5 John continues, "And who is he who overcomes the world but he who believes that Jesus is the Son of God?" Such a believer is one who has been begotten of God and has received the divine life (John 1:12-13; 3:16). The divine life empowers him to overcome the evil world energized by Satan. Such believers are in contrast to the Gnostics and Cerinthians, who were not this kind of believer, but remained the pitiful victims of the evil satanic system. But our believing that Jesus is the Son of God brings us into an organic union with the Son, who is the embodiment of the Triune God. It is this organic union with the Triune God in the Son that overcomes the world.

THE WATER, THE BLOOD, AND THE SPIRIT

In 5:6 John goes on to say, "This is He who came through water and blood, Jesus Christ; not in the water only, but in the water and in the blood; and the Spirit is He who testifies, because the Spirit is the truth." He, Jesus Christ, came as the Son of God so that we may be born of

God and have the divine life (John 10:10; 20:31). It is in His Son that God gives us eternal life (1 John 5: 11-13). Jesus, the Man of Nazareth, was testified to be the Son of God by the water He went through in His baptism (Matt. 3:16-17; John 1:31), by the blood He shed on the cross (John 19:31-35; Matt. 27:50-54), and also by the Spirit He gave not by measure (John 1:32-34; 3:34). By these three, God has testified that Jesus is His Son given to us (1 John 5:7-10) so that in Him we may receive His eternal life by believing in His name (5:11-13; John 3:16, 36; 20:31). The water of baptism terminates people of the old creation by burying them; the blood shed on the cross redeems those whom God has chosen from among the old creation; and the Spirit, who is the truth, the reality in life (Rom. 8:2), germinates those whom God has redeemed out of the old creation by regenerating them with the divine life. Thus they are born of God and become His children (John 3:5, 15; 1:12-13) to live a life that practices the truth (1 John 1:6), the will of God (2:17), the righteousness of God (2:29), and the love of God (3:10-11) for His expression.

In 5:6 John says that the Spirit testifies because the Spirit is the truth. The Spirit, who is the truth, the reality (John 14:16-17; 15:26), testifies that Jesus is the Son of God, in whom is the eternal life. By thus testifying, He imparts the Son of God into us to be our life (Col. 3:4). In verse 6 truth denotes the reality of all that Christ is as the Son of God (John 16:12-15).

Verses 7 and 8 say, "Because there are three who testify, the Spirit and the water and the blood, and the three are for the one." "For the one" also means unto the one, that is, unto the one thing, the one point or purpose in their testimony.

First John 5:6-8 says that God testified that Jesus Christ is the Son of God. God testified this in three steps: by water, by the blood, and by the Spirit. The water refers to the baptism of the Lord Jesus. According to the record of the four Gospels, immediately after the Lord came up from the water, the heavens were opened and a voice declared that He is God's beloved Son. That was God's testimony that Jesus Christ is His Son, the testimony by water, by baptism. Three and a half years later, the Lord Jesus died on the cross, shedding His blood. Someone standing near the cross testified, after the Lord died, that He was God's Son. That was the testimony of God by blood concerning Jesus Christ being the Son of God. Following this, we have the testimony of the Spirit. In resurrection Christ became a life-giving Spirit.

If we read 5:6 carefully, we shall see that the Lord Jesus came through water and through blood, but we are not told that He came through the Spirit. Then in verses 7 and 8 we are told clearly that there are three who testify, and that these three are the Spirit, the water, and the blood. Christ came through the water, through the blood, and as the Spirit. Of course, He did not come as the water or as the blood, but eventually, in resurrection, He came as the Spirit. Furthermore, according to verse 6, Christ came in the water and in the blood. But this verse does not say that He came in the Spirit. Concerning the Spirit, this verse has the thought of being, for we are told, "The Spirit *is* He who testifies." Therefore, we need to see clearly that Christ came through the water, through the blood, and as the Spirit.

The phrase "through water and blood" refers to the baptism at the beginning of His ministry and to crucifixion at the end of His ministry. After this, in resurrection Christ became the life-giving Spirit, and thus He came as the Spirit. The Son of God came through water and through blood, that is, through His baptism and through His crucifixion. We may also say that He came in the water and in the blood. Then He came not through the Spirit nor in the Spirit, but as the Spirit.

The water of baptism terminates the old creation, and the blood shed on the cross redeems whatever God has chosen of the old creation. Then the Spirit comes to germinate what God has chosen and redeemed. Therefore, here we have termination, redemption, and germination. As the old creation, we have been terminated. But as God's chosen ones we were first redeemed and then germinated to be the new creation. This new creation is a composition of God's children.

By these three steps of termination, redemption, and germination, Jesus Christ has not only been testified as the Son of God, but has also entered into us. Through the water of His baptism, through the blood of His cross, and as the Spirit, Christ has been testified as the Son of God. By these three steps He has also come into our spirit. This means that by termination, redemption, and germination, Christ is now within us. Hallelujah, we are a terminated, redeemed, and germinated people! We are no longer the old creation; we are the new creation with the new birth and a new life. Because we are the children of God, we have the life ability to overcome the world and all negative things.

THE TESTIMONY OF GOD

In 5:9 John goes on to say, "If we receive the testimony of men, the testimony of God is greater; because this is the testimony of God that He has testified concerning His Son." The testimony of God here is the testimony by water, blood, and the Spirit that Jesus is the Son of God. This testimony is greater than that of men.

Verse 10 says, "He who believes in the Son of God has the testimony in himself. He who does not believe God has made Him a liar, because he has not believed in the testimony which God has testified concerning His Son." God testified concerning His Son that we may believe in His Son and have His divine life. If we believe in His Son, we receive and have His testimony in ourselves. Otherwise, we do not believe what He has testified and make Him a liar.

ETERNAL LIFE IN THE SON

In 5:11 and 12 John continues, "And this is the testimony, that God gave to us eternal life, and this life is in His Son. He who has the Son has the life; he who does not have the Son of God does not have the life." The testimony of God is not only that Jesus is His Son, but also that He gives to us eternal life, which is in His Son. His

Son is the means to give us His eternal life, which is His goal with us. Because the life is in the Son (John 1:4) and the Son is the life (John 11:25; 14:6; Col. 3:4), the Son and the life are one, inseparable.

If we have the Son of God, we have eternal life, because eternal life is in the Son. We may say that the Son is a container of eternal life. When we receive the Son by believing in Him, we have eternal life.

We may say that eternal life, the divine life, is the "capital" of our Christian life. Actually, this eternal life is the Son, and the Son is the embodiment of the Triune God. By this we see that eternal life is the Triune God. Now the Triune God is moving and working within us as the anointing. This anointing is also the moving of eternal life. Eternal life is not a thing; it is a Person who is the embodiment of the Triune God. Now this Person is moving within us to anoint us with Himself, that is, with eternal life and with the essence of this life, which is the Triune God. The Triune God is the content, the essence, of eternal life. Therefore, when eternal life anoints us, it anoints us with the Triune God. This gives us the basis and the means to live a life that practices the divine righteousness, practices the divine love, and overcomes the world, death, sin, the Devil, and idols.

Confucius taught that the highest learning was to cultivate and develop what he called the bright virtue. But God's New Testament economy teaches that eternal life is the embodiment of the Triune God and that this life is anointing us with the essence of the Triune God. Eventually, through continuous anointing, we shall become the same in life and nature as the Triune God, in that His essence will become ours, making us the same as He. Then we shall live a life full of righteousness and love, a life that spontaneously overcomes the world, death, sin, the Devil, and idols. There is no need for us to try to live such a life. As long as we dwell in the fellowship of eternal life according to the anointing, we shall spontaneously practice righteousness and love and simultaneously overcome all negative things.

KNOWING THAT WE HAVE ETERNAL LIFE

In 5:13 John says, "I write these things to you that you may know that you have eternal life, to you who believe in the name of the Son of God." The written words of the Scriptures are the assurance to the believers, who believe in the name of the Son of God, that they have eternal life. Our believing to receive eternal life is the fact; the words of the Holy Writings are the assurance concerning this fact. They are the title deed of our eternal salvation. We are assured and have the pledge by them that because we believe in the name of the Son of God we have eternal life.

The word of the Bible is the pledge of eternal life. The Bible is also the title deed of our salvation. This is why the Bible is called a covenant or testament. We not only have the fact of eternal life; we also have the pledge, the guarantee, the title deed, to prove that we have eternal life. Praise the Lord that we have salvation and eternal life and also the title deed to prove it!

LIFE-STUDY OF FIRST JOHN

THE VIRTUES OF THE DIVINE BIRTH
TO OVERCOME THE WORLD, DEATH, SIN, THE DEVIL,
AND THE IDOLS

(2)

Scripture Reading: 1 John 5:14-17

In this message we shall consider 5:14-17.

THE DIVINE FELLOWSHIP

Verse 14 says, "And this is the boldness which we have toward Him, that if we ask anything according to His will, He hears us." The word "and" at the beginning of this verse is important. Without this word, we may think that 5:14-17 is a section separate from the foregoing section and having nothing to do with it. We may also think that what the writer covers in verse 14 comes in suddenly. Actually, however, according to spiritual facts, what John speaks of in verse 14 is not a surprise. Rather, it is a spontaneous outflow from the preceding verses.

First John 5:4-13 shows us that we have received eternal life, as mentioned in 1:1-2. Then verses 14 through 17 tell us how we pray in the fellowship of eternal life, as mentioned in 1:3-7. The first seven verses of chapter one indicate that we have received eternal life, and out of this eternal life we have fellowship with the apostles and also with the Father and the Son. The principle is the same in 5:4-17. In 5:4-13 we have received eternal life, and in 5:14-17 we are in the fellowship of this life. Of course, the word "fellowship" is not here. These verses speak of prayer. When we pray by the divine life, we are in the fellowship of the divine life. Therefore, these verses in fact refer to the divine fellowship.

ETERNAL LIFE OVERCOMING DEATH

The word "and" at the beginning of verse 14 connects the life in 5:4-13 to the fellowship in 5:14-17. In the former section we have received eternal life, and we have the written word as the assurance of this. Now John uses what he has written in 5:4-13 as a basis to show us that this eternal life can overcome death. We have received eternal life, and this life has been testified, proved, and pledged within us. Now John intends to point out that eternal life overcomes death.

Perhaps you regarded 5:14-17 as verses concerning our prayer and God's answer to our prayer. Actually, John's intention in these verses is to show us that the eternal life within us can overcome death both in ourselves and in other members of the church. Eternal life swallows up death within us and death within other members.

In the church life we do not live alone. Because the church is the Body, we live with the fellow members of the Body. Since we are in the Body, we are members with the other fellow members. Eternal life not only takes care of our own need; it also takes care of the need of the fellow members around us. It overcomes death within us, and it overcomes death within our brothers. Especially, it overcomes death in those who are weak or who have problems.

Weakness is related to death, and problems come from death. As long as there are problems in the church life, this is an indicator that there is death among those in the church. Therefore, we need eternal life to overcome, to swallow up, this death. If you are stronger and a fellow member is weaker, then you may become the one to supply the life from within you to the weaker one in order to swallow up the death within him.

Now we can understand why verse 14 begins with "and." Let us read verses 13 and 14a again: "I write these things to you that you may know that you have eternal life, to you who believe in the name of the Son of God. And this is the boldness which we have toward Him." Apparently, the first part of verse 14 is not fitting or logical. But if we touch the burden in the writer's spirit, we shall see that his intention is to show us not only that we have eternal life, but also that this eternal life within us overcomes death and swallows it up.

ASKING ACCORDING TO GOD'S WILL

In verse 14 John says, "This is the boldness which we have toward Him, that if we ask anything according to His will, He hears us." Here "boldness" refers to the boldness we have for our prayer in fellowship with God. Based upon the fact that we have received eternal life through the divine birth by believing in the Son of God, we can pray, in the fellowship of eternal life, by contacting God, in the boldness of a conscience void of offense (Acts 24:16), according to His will, with the assurance that He will hear us.

This verse speaks of asking according to God's will, not according to our desire, preference, or way. But how can we know that the thing we are asking is according to His will? A person who asks according to God's will is one who has been regenerated, who has the divine life, and who is in the fellowship of the divine life. As we saw in chapter three, such a person will have a conscience void of offense. This means that his heart does not blame him, for while he is in the fellowship of the divine life, he has a conscience without offense. As long as we abide in the fellowship of the divine life, our conscience will surely be without offense. Then we shall be able to pray, to ask, according to God's will. By this we see that a person who prays in the fellowship of the divine life is truly one with the Lord. It is in this way that we know God's will: by being one with Him, by abiding in Him, and by remaining in the fellowship of the divine life.

The prayer that is according to the will of God indicates that the praying one is abiding in the fellowship of the divine life and is also abiding in the Lord Himself. Such a believer is one with the Lord. This makes it possible to have boldness toward God. When we are in the fellowship of the divine life and our conscience is without offense, we have peace with God, and we also have boldness to pray, not according to our feeling, but according to His will. Because we pray according to His will, He hears us.

KNOWING THAT WE HAVE THE REQUESTS

In 5:15 John goes on to say, "And if we know that He hears us in whatever we ask, we know that we have the requests which we have asked from Him." This knowing is based upon the fact that after having received the divine life, we abide in the Lord and are one with Him in our prayer to God in His name (John 15:7, 16; 16:23-24). Based upon the fact that we have received the divine life through the divine birth, we may abide in the Lord and be one with Him in our prayer. Because we are one with the Lord in prayer, we pray in His name. By this we know that He hears us in whatever we ask. Our asking is not in ourselves according to our mind, but in the Lord according to God's will. Therefore, we know that we have the requests which we have asked from Him.

ASKING AND GIVING LIFE

In verse 16 John comes to his point in this section: "If anyone sees his brother sinning a sin not unto death, he shall ask and he will give life to him, to those sinning not unto death. There is sin unto death; I do not say that he should make request concerning that." Literally, the Greek word rendered "unto" in this verse means toward. Here John is saying that if anyone sees his brother, someone close to him in the Lord, sinning a sin not unto death, he should ask concerning that one. The word "ask" here must refer to a prayer made when we are abiding in fellowship with God.

No doubt, "he shall ask" refers to the one who sees his brother sinning a sin not unto death. But to whom does "he will give life" refer? There is a problem with the second "he" in this verse. Some translations capitalize the second "he" and thereby make it refer to the Lord. Actually, in both cases "he" refers to the same person, that is, to the one who sees his brother sinning and who asks concerning him.

The subject of "will give life" is still he, the subject of the first predicate "shall ask." This indicates that the asker will give life to the one asked for. This does not mean that the asker has life of himself and can give life by himself to others. It means such an asker, who is abiding in the Lord, who is one with the Lord, and who is asking in one spirit with the Lord (1 Cor. 6:17), becomes the means through which God's life-giving Spirit can give life to the one he asks for. This is a matter of life-imparting in the fellowship of the divine life. To be one who can give life to others, we must abide in the divine life and walk, live, and have our being in the divine life. In James 5:14-16 the prayer is for healing; here the prayer is for life-imparting.

The vital point here is that if we would pray for a brother according to what is described in verse 16, we need to be one with the Lord. We must abide in the Lord and ask in one spirit with Him. Because we are so one with the Lord, we can become the means, the channel, through which God's life-giving Spirit can impart life to the one for whom we ask. This imparting of life takes place in the fellowship of the divine life.

Undoubtedly, "life" in verse 16 refers to spiritual life imparted into the one asked for through the prayer of the asker. However, according to the context, this spiritual life will also rescue the physical body of the one asked for from the danger of suffering death because of his sinning (see James 5:15).

SIN UNTO DEATH

Concerning "sin unto death," Bible teachers have different interpretations. Some say that it refers to the sin of the antichrists in denying that Jesus is the Christ (2:22), a sin which keeps them in death forever. But, according to the context of this verse, sin unto death is related to a sinning brother, not to an antichrist or any other unbeliever. Since this section, 5:14-17, is related to prayer in the fellowship of eternal life covered in 1:3—2:11, whatever it deals with must be related to the matter of the fellowship of the divine life. In the fellowship of the divine life there is the governmental dealing of God according to the spiritual condition of each of His children. In God's governmental dealing, some of His children may be destined to physical death in this age due to a certain sin, and others may also be destined to physical death due to other sins. The situation is like that of Ananias and his wife Sapphira, who were dealt with by physical death because of their lying to the Holy Spirit (Acts 5:1-11). The situation also is like that of the Corinthian believers, who were dealt with by a similar judgment because of their not discerning the body (1 Cor. 11:29-30). This was typified by God's dealing with the children of Israel in the wilderness (1 Cor. 10:5-11). All of them, except Caleb and Joshua, were judged by God with physical death due to certain sins. God's governmental dealing is severe. Miriam, Aaron, and even Moses were not spared from this kind of dealing due to certain failures of theirs (Num. 12:1-15; 20:1, 12, 22-29; Deut. 1:37; 3:26-27; 32:48-52). The punishment of God's governmental dealing with His children is not at all related to eternal perdition. Rather, it is a dispensational dealing according to the divine government, which is related to our fellowship with God and with one another. Whether a sin is unto death or not depends on God's judgment according to each one's position and condition in the house of God. In any case, for the children of God to sin is a serious matter. Sin may be judged by God with physical death in this age! Concerning such a sin unto death, the apostle does not say that we should make request.

In verse 17 John goes on to say, "All unrighteousness is sin, and there is sin not unto death." Every wrongdoing, everything that is not just or righteous, is sin.

We have pointed out that in God's governmental dealing, for some saints a particular sin may be unto death. But for other saints the same sin may not be unto death. In verse 16 John says, "There is sin unto death," and in verse 17 he says, "There is sin not unto death." Furthermore, John seems to imply in verse 16 that the praying one may know whether or not a brother is sinning a sin unto death, for we are to ask only concerning a sin that is not unto death. This raises the very important question of how we can know whether or not a certain sin is unto death. This is a deep matter, and we shall consider it in some detail in the next message.

LIFE-STUDY OF FIRST JOHN

MESSAGE THIRTY-EIGHT

THE VIRTUES OF THE DIVINE BIRTH TO OVERCOME THE WORLD, DEATH, SIN, THE DEVIL, AND THE IDOLS

(3)

Scripture Reading: 1 John 5:14-17

KNOWING THAT A PARTICULAR SIN IS UNTO DEATH

In 5:16 and 17 John says, "If anyone sees his brother sinning a sin not unto death, he shall ask and he will give life to him, to those sinning not unto death. There is sin unto death; I do not say that he should make request concerning that. All unrighteousness is sin, and there is sin not unto death." These verses indicate that if we see a brother sinning a sin not unto death, we should ask concerning that one and give life to him. But how can we know if a particular sin is unto death? Suppose a brother has sinned and also has become ill. If we do not know whether or not this sin is unto death, how shall we be able to make request concerning the situation?

We have seen that 5:14-17 is related to prayer in the fellowship of eternal life. In the fellowship of the divine life there is the governmental dealing of God according to the spiritual condition of each of His children. In God's governmental dealing, some of His children may be destined to physical death in this age due to a certain sin, and others may be destined to physical death due to other sins. Whether a sin is unto death or not depends on God's judgment according to each one's position and condition in the house of God.

Although we may be clear concerning this matter in

principle, how are we to discern whether or not a particular brother has sinned unto death? In order to have this kind of discernment, we need to be a person who is absolutely one with the Lord. Actually, only the Lord Himself knows whether a certain sin is unto death. Therefore, if we are not one with the Lord, we cannot know whether or not a brother has sinned unto death. However, if we are deeply one with the Lord, if we abide in the Lord, and if we are one spirit with Him, spontaneously we shall know whether or not a particular sin is unto death. There will be no need for us to try to know this matter.

THE CASE OF MOSES

We should not think that a particular sin is serious and is unto death and that another sin is not serious and is not unto death. Consider the case of Moses in Numbers 20. Moses was provoked, and as a result he did something that was not according to God's will: he struck the rock a second time. Striking the rock twice was against God's basic principle. The rock typifies Christ, and God had no intention for Christ to be smitten twice. The first time Moses struck the rock according to God's word (Exo. 17:1-6). But the second time that Moses struck the rock was not according to God's word. God told Moses to speak to the rock. But, being provoked, Moses struck it a second time. Due to that mistake, Moses, although he was so close to God, was not allowed to enter into the good land: "And the Lord spake unto Moses and Aaron, Because ye believed me not, to sanctify me in the eyes of the children of Israel, therefore ye shall not bring this congregation into the land which I have given them" (Num. 20:12). According to Deuteronomy 32:48-52, the Lord told Moses to go up to the mountain and die because he and Aaron had trespassed against the Lord "among the children of Israel at the waters of Meribah-Kadesh, in the wilderness of Zin; because ye sanctified me not in the midst of the children of Israel" (v. 51). We may think that Moses made only a small mistake. But according to God's governmental dealing, it was a sin unto death. The case of Moses illustrates the fact that in ourselves we are not qualified or able to discern what kind of sin is unto death. We can have such discernment only when we are absolutely one with the Lord.

LIFE-IMPARTING IN THE FELLOWSHIP OF THE DIVINE LIFE

What is described in 5:14-17 concerning the life-giving petition can be experienced only by those who are deep in the Lord. In verse 14 John speaks of prayer that is according to God's will. In order to pray this kind of prayer, we must be one with the Lord. If we are deeply one with Him, we shall know His will, and we shall also know the situation of the one who is sinning. Because this one is our brother, someone very close to us in the Lord, we shall know his real situation before the Lord. This matter is deep.

If you are one with the Lord and know a sinning brother's condition and situation before the Lord, you will then know the Lord's will and be able to pray according to His will. Because you know the Lord's will, you will also know whether or not this brother will die because of his sin.

These verses indicate that we who have eternal life can pass this life on to others. This means that we can be a channel through which eternal life is supplied to others. We can be a channel for eternal life to flow out of us and into others. Verse 16 refers to this. In this verse the one who asks is also the one who gives life to the sinning brother. This indicates that the one who asks will give life to the one concerning whom he asks. The asker, who is abiding in the Lord, who is one with the Lord, and who is asking in one spirit with the Lord, becomes the means through which God's life-giving Spirit can give life to the one for whom he asks. This is a matter of life-imparting in the fellowship of the divine life.

Notice that in verse 16 John speaks of someone seeing "his brother" sinning. The words "his brother" point to a brother who is close to him, someone who is so close to him that he is a part of him. If you have a brother close to you in this way and do not know whether this brother will die because of his sin, then you are not deep in the Lord. If you are truly deep in the Lord and are one with Him, as you consider the brother's situation, you will enter into the Lord's heart and know His will. You will know whether this brother, who is so intimate to you, will die because of his sin. Then you will know how to pray for him. You will know whether or not to pray for him to be forgiven and healed. If this brother's sin is unto death, you will realize that you should not pray to impart life into him. Instead, you may be burdened to pray for him from another angle.

My burden in this message is to show you that the eternal life within us is real and practical. On the one hand, we can enjoy this eternal life within us. On the other hand, we can pass on this eternal life to others. We can be a channel for eternal life to flow out from us, or through us, to others. However, the experience of being a channel for eternal life to flow out to others is a deep matter. This cannot be done in a superficial way. If we would be a channel for eternal life to flow out to others, we must be deep in the Lord, and we must know the Lord's heart by being in His heart. If we have entered into the Lord to such a degree, spontaneously we shall know the Lord's will concerning a brother close to us who has sinned. Because we know the Lord's will concerning the brother's situation, we shall know how to pray for him.

TESTIMONY OF PERSONAL EXPERIENCE

Although I do not claim to be so deep in the Lord, I can testify that through the years I have known some cases of brothers who sinned unto death. A certain brother, who was very close to me, fell into a certain kind of sin. During the course of fellowship with the Lord, I had the deep sense that the Lord would take this brother away. I realized that this brother would die because of his sin, and eventually he did die for this reason. I prayed for this brother. First, I had the intention to pray for his healing. But the Spirit within me prohibited me from praying in that way. How do

I know that I was prohibited by the Spirit to pray for this brother's healing? I knew because as I was praying for him, I had the anointing within me. But when I was about to pray for his healing, the anointing stopped. It was in this way I realized I should not pray for that brother's healing. Simultaneously, I began to understand that probably the Lord would not heal him, that he would probably die as a result of his sin. Then with much anointing from the Lord, I prayed for this brother from another angle. I prayed for the Lord to comfort him and his wife and to care for his family.

In some cases, when I tried to pray for the healing of such a brother, I was rebuked by the Lord. The Lord said to me, "You are praying according to your own wish. This brother is close to you, and you love him and want him to live longer. You are praying not according to the will of God, but according to your own desire." Knowing that I could not continue to pray in that way, I came to realize that the Lord would probably take the brother away. This has been my experience with some cases in the past.

In 5:14-17 John shows us that eternal life is practical and can be experienced by us in a deep way. In these verses we see the need to live in the divine life to such an extent that we are absolutely one with the Lord. Then as we pray we shall know whether or not there is the anointing in our prayer. If there is the anointing, we should go on to pray for a brother according to the anointing. But if there is no anointing, we may be praying in ourselves. When we have these experiences, we know that eternal life is real and practical.

THE PROBLEM OF SIN

The Epistle of 1 John is on the fellowship of the divine life. Chapters one, three, and five indicate strongly that sin is a problem to us. In chapter one sin and sins are dealt with. According to this chapter, sin damages our fellowship in the divine life.

In chapter three John says that he who practices sin is of the Devil (v. 8), and that everyone who has been

begotten of God does not practice sin (v. 9). Then in verse
20 John says that if our heart blames us, God is greater
than our heart and knows all things. In verse 21 he goes on
to say that if our heart does not blame us, we have
boldness toward God. For our heart to blame us means
that we are wrong in some way. This indicates that sin
causes trouble to our conscience. Therefore, we need to
have our conscience void of offense.

In chapter five we see something even more serious
regarding sin. Sin not only interrupts our fellowship and
causes our conscience to have no peace; sin may even
cause physical death. According to the human concept, it
may seem insignificant to come to the Lord's table
without discerning the Lord's body (1 Cor. 11:29). Actually,
it is extremely serious to come to the Lord's table with a
divisive spirit and thereby fail to discern the body. Because
many of the believers at Corinth failed to discern the body,
some became weak. That was a warning. Some who did
not pay attention to this warning became ill. Eventually,
those who would not heed even that warning died. In our
opinion, they might not have committed a gross sin.
Nevertheless, from the point of view of God's government,
certain of the Corinthians committed a sin unto death.

Sins, failures, mistakes, and trespasses may be viewed
from different angles. From the human point of view,
certain mistakes may seem minor. But from God's point of
view, especially from the perspective of His government,
certain matters which are not serious in our sight are very
serious indeed. For example, according to God's government, Moses made a great mistake. In the sight of the
Israelites, what he did was minor. However, Moses made a
serious mistake in relation to God's government. By this
we see that it makes a difference from what angle
someone's sin or failure is viewed.

I definitely do not have the intention of frightening
anyone. I simply want to point out the truth concerning
the seriousness of sin.

If you study the situation of those who have rebelled
against the church, you will see that to oppose the church,

to try to damage the church, or to rebel against the authority of the church is a very serious matter. At least, such rebellion causes great loss to one's spiritual life. In more than fifty years' experience in the church life, I have never seen anyone who was not right with the church who continued to enjoy spiritual blessing as he should. If someone does not want to go along with the church, it is better for that one not to be involved with the church. But as soon as someone touches the church in a negative way, that person will suffer loss. In saying this I am not pronouncing a curse on anyone. On the contrary, I am simply being faithful to speak the truth. History proves that it is not a profit for anyone to seek to damage the church or rebel against it.

I would urge all the saints, especially the young brothers and sisters, never to be negligent or careless concerning sin. Never think that sin is an insignificant matter. We all should stay away from sinful things. Sin causes our fellowship to be broken, it causes us to have no peace in our conscience, and it may even cause the loss of physical life. If sin does not lead to one's physical death, it will certainly cause spiritual death. Therefore, let us learn to fear God regarding sin.

May we also learn to become deep in fellowship with the Lord. If we are deep in our fellowship with the Lord, we shall be those who are in the Lord's heart and know His will both concerning ourselves and concerning the fellow members of the Body. Then we shall be able to help those around us and even impart life to them out of the Lord and by the Holy Spirit. This means that we shall be able to be a channel for the divine life to flow out of us and into our fellow members.

Recently I was asked if all sickness is due to sin. As we consider human experience and spiritual experience, we must say that not all sickness is due to sin. Here I would emphasize the fact that by the Lord's mercy and grace, we are His children possessing His life and enjoying His nature. Now we need to be careful about everything related to our daily living: eating, drinking, contacting people, spending money. If we are careful concerning all things, then we shall do our part to be preserved from becoming sick or weak. In every way—spiritually, psychologically, physically, and materially—we need to be proper with God and man. In particular, we should not willingly and knowingly do anything that is against the Lord. It is extremely serious knowingly to go against the Lord.

LIFE-STUDY OF FIRST JOHN

MESSAGE THIRTY-NINE

THE VIRTUES OF THE DIVINE BIRTH TO OVERCOME THE WORLD, DEATH, SIN, THE DEVIL, AND THE IDOLS

(4)

Scripture Reading: 1 John 5:18-21

Before we consider 5:18-21, I would like to say a further word concerning the life-giving petition in 5:14-17. In 5:14-17 there is the indication not only that we have eternal life and enjoy it, but also that we can minister this life to others. This means that we can give eternal life to others. Regarding this matter, John's thought is deep. Although the thought here is deep, the matter is very practical in our Christian life. If we enjoy eternal life and experience it, surely we shall be able to channel this life to others. We shall be able to minister eternal life to other members of the Body.

In 5:16 John says that there is sin unto death and that we should not make request concerning it. We have pointed out that under God's governmental dealing a certain sin may be unto death. But this matter of sin unto death should not distract us from the basic thought in these verses of ministering eternal life to others. This section implies that we can channel eternal life out from within ourselves into others. You should not try to know whether or not someone will be healed or whether or not a particular sin is unto death. Instead, you should simply recognize that the saints around you, as fellow members in the Body, all need eternal life to be channeled out from within you into them.

We need to minister life to others. We can minister life to the saints by praying with them or by having fellowship with them. Sometimes we may minister life to a brother simply by visiting him without saying much to him. Our contact with him ministers life to him. As long as we are present with this brother, life comes out of our being and flows into him. From 5:14-17 we need to see that we have eternal life and that we may experience and enjoy this life and then minister it to others.

THE DIVINE BIRTH

In 5:18-21 we have a strong conclusion to the Epistle of 1 John. In this conclusion John once again emphasizes the divine birth (v. 18). As we have pointed out, this book is structured with the divine birth, divine life, divine fellowship, the divine anointing, and all the virtues that come out of the divine birth. I hope that we all shall have a deep impression concerning the divine birth, concerning the fact that we have been begotten of God. We also need to be deeply impressed concerning the divine life, which has been sown as the divine seed into our being; the divine fellowship, for us to enjoy the riches of the divine life; the divine anointing, by which we abide in the Lord and have fellowship with Him; and all the virtues that proceed from the divine birth. Concerning these matters, we should not have mere knowledge; we need to touch the depth of the reality of these things in this Epistle.

In 5:18 John says, "We know that everyone who has been begotten of God does not sin, but he who is begotten of God keeps himself, and the evil one does not touch him." In order to avoid sinning, which not only interrupts the fellowship of the divine life (1:6-10), but also may even bring in physical death (5:16-17), the apostle stresses here again, with the assurance of the capability of the divine life, our divine birth, which is the basis of the victorious life. This basic fact does not allow us, the regenerated ones, to practice sin (3:9), that is, to live in sin (Rom. 6:2).

A REGENERATED ONE
KEEPING HIMSELF FROM SINNING

In 5:18 John tells us something that is closely related to

our Christian life. He says that everyone who has been begotten of God does not sin. Then he says that he who is begotten of God keeps himself, and the evil one does not touch him. Here we have a thought that has not previously been introduced—the thought that regenerated persons can keep themselves from sinning.

Some teachers say that "he" in 5:18 refers to Christ, who was begotten of God and keeps the regenerated one, based upon John 17:15. But the phrase "begotten of God" in this clause, as a repetition of that in the preceding clause, should be the logical and determining factor that "he" refers still to the regenerated believer. A regenerated believer (especially his regenerated spirit, which is born of the Spirit of God—John 3:6), keeps himself from living in sin, and the evil one does not touch him, especially his regenerated spirit. His divine birth with the divine life in his spirit is the basic factor of such a safeguard.

This understanding of the pronoun "he" in 5:18 is supported by John's word in 5:4: "Because everything that has been begotten of God overcomes the world." Strictly speaking, this verse refers to our regenerated spirit. It is this regenerated spirit that keeps us from sinning.

As we have indicated, some translators say that "he" in 5:18 refers to the Lord Jesus and should be rendered "He." According to this understanding, Christ has been begotten of God, and He keeps us. But as the result of much study and according to our experience, we have come to understand that the pronoun "he" refers to the person who has been begotten of God. This is indicated by the fact that "begotten of God" is used twice in this verse. First, we are told that everyone who has been begotten of God does not sin, and then that he who is begotten of God keeps himself. It is not logical to say that in the first case "begotten of God" refers to a regenerated believer and that in the second case this phrase refers to Christ. In 5:18 "he" refers to a regenerated person, a person who has been begotten of God and who thereby keeps himself from sinning. The word "keeps" means to guard by watchful care.

NOT TOUCHED BY THE EVIL ONE

In 5:18 John says that the evil one does not touch the one who has been begotten of God and who keeps himself. Here "touch" means to grasp, to lay hold of, for doing harm and fulfilling evil purposes. The Greek word rendered "evil one" is *poneros.* This word differs from *kakos,* which refers to an essentially worthless and wicked character, and also differs from *sapros* which indicates worthlessness and corruption, degeneracy from original virtue. The Greek word *poneros* means pernicious, harmfully evil, affecting and influencing others to be evil and vicious. Such an evil one is Satan the Devil, in whom the whole world lies (v. 19).

At least one version says, "The evil one cannot touch him," instead of, "The evil one does not touch him." To say that the evil one cannot touch you is different from saying that the evil one does not touch you. The correct translation is, "The evil one does not touch him." The thought here is not that the evil one is not able to touch us; the thought is that the evil one does not touch us. Here John is saying that as long as we abide in our regenerated spirit, this spirit will keep us from sinning, and the evil one does not touch us. He knows that if he tries to touch us when we are abiding in our regenerated spirit, he will be wasting his time. Hence, the thought here is not that the evil one cannot touch us, but that he does not touch us when we are in spirit.

We know from experience that when we are in the flesh, forgetting our regenerated spirit, we become prey to the evil one, even a "delicious dish" for him to eat. At such a time, the evil one may say, "Oh, here is something good for me to eat." The evil one will not only touch us—he will swallow us. But when we are in our regenerated spirit, he will not waste his time with us.

The thought in 5:18 is that we have been born of God and have the divine life. This divine birth took place in our regenerated spirit, and now the divine life is in our regenerated spirit. Therefore, we should simply stay in our regenerated spirit. Regeneration with the divine birth and the divine life keeps us from sin, failure, and defilement. When we stay in our regenerated spirit, Satan knows that there is no way for him to touch us, and he will not try to touch us.

If we consider the entire Epistle, we shall realize that the Apostle John is trying to impress us with the fact that we have been born of God. We have had a divine birth, and we possess the divine life. A specific part of our being—our spirit—has been regenerated with the divine life. Now we have a safeguard: our regenerated spirit with the divine life. As long as we stay in our regenerated spirit, we are in a refuge, a place of protection and safeguard, and the evil one does not touch us.

THE WHOLE WORLD LYING IN THE EVIL ONE

In 5:19 John goes on to say, "We know that we are of God, and the whole world lies in the evil one." Literally, the Greek word for "of" here means out of, out from. Since we have been begotten of God, we are out of Him, out from Him, possessing His life and partaking of His nature. By this we are separated unto God from the satanic world which lies in the evil one.

In 5:19 John says that the whole world lies in the evil one. The whole world comprises the satanic world system (2:15) and the people of the world, the fallen human race (4:1). For the whole world to lie in the evil one means that it remains passively in the sphere of the evil one's influence, under his usurpation and manipulation. While the believers are living and moving actively by the life of God, the whole world is lying passively under the usurping and manipulating hand of Satan, the evil one. This is especially true of the people of the world. Whereas we are out of God, belong to God, and are one with God, the world lies in the evil one and belongs to the Devil. The people in the world do not have their own freedom. Rather, they are under the Devil's control and manipulation.

We may use surgery as an illustration of how the whole world is lying in the evil one. During surgery a patient lies passively on the operating table, and the surgeon performs the operation. The patient is fully under the surgeon's control. The whole world today is like this in relation to Satan. Satan is an evil "surgeon," and the people of the world are the "patients" lying on his "operating table." Praise the Lord that we are of God and have a relationship in life with Him!

THE SON OF GOD COMING
AND GIVING US AN UNDERSTANDING

In verse 20 John continues, "And we know that the Son of God has come, and has given us an understanding that we might know Him who is true; and we are in Him who is true, in His Son Jesus Christ. This is the true God and eternal life." The word "come" here indicates that the Son of God has come through incarnation to bring God to us as grace and reality (John 1:14) that we may have the divine life, as revealed in John's Gospel, to partake of God as love and light, as unveiled in this Epistle.

In 5:20 John says that the Son of God has given us an understanding so that we may know Him who is true, or know the true One. This understanding is the faculty of our mind enlightened and empowered by the Spirit of reality (John 16:12-15) to apprehend the divine reality in our regenerated spirit. In this verse to "know" is the ability of the divine life to know the true God (John 17:3) in our regenerated spirit (Eph. 1:17) through our renewed mind, enlightened by the Spirit of reality.

The understanding spoken of in verse 20 involves our mind, our spirit, and the Spirit of reality. According to our natural being, our spirit is deadened, and our mind is darkened. Hence, in our natural being we do not have the ability to know God. How can someone with a deadened spirit and a darkened mind know the invisible God? This is impossible.

The Lord Jesus, the Son of God, has come and has given us an understanding that we might know the genuine and real God. He has come to us by the steps of incarnation, crucifixion, and resurrection. He accomplished redemption for us, and when we repented and believed in Him, we received Him. Now that we have believed in Him and received Him, our sins have been forgiven, our darkened mind has been enlightened, and our deadened spirit has been enlivened. Furthermore, the Spirit of reality, who is the Spirit of revelation, has come into our being. This means that the Spirit of reality has been added to our quickened spirit and has shined into our mind to enlighten it. Now we have an enlightened mind and a quickened spirit with the Spirit of reality, who reveals spiritual reality to us. As a result, surely we have an understanding and are able to know the true One. Before we were saved, we did not have this understanding. But the Son of God has come to us and has given us this understanding so that we may know God.

THE ABILITY TO KNOW GOD

In John 17:2 and 3 we see that eternal life has the ability to know God: "Even as You gave Him authority over all flesh, that He may give eternal life to all whom You have given Him. And this is eternal life, that they may know You, the only true God, and Him whom You have sent, Jesus Christ." Eternal life is divine life with a special function—to know God. In order to know God, the divine Person, we need the divine life.

Because as believers we have been born of the divine life, we are able to know God. In order to know a certain living thing, you need to have the life of that thing. For example, a dog cannot know human beings, because a dog does not have a human life. It takes human life to know human beings. The principle is the same with knowing God. The Lord has given us eternal life, the divine life, the life of God. The life of God certainly is able to know God. Therefore, the life of God, which has been given to us, has the ability to know God and the things of God.

In 5:20 John speaks of knowing the true One. Here the word "know" actually means experience, enjoy, and possess. Therefore, to know the true One is to experience, enjoy, and possess the true One. In this universe only God

Himself is the true One. We need God's life in order to experience, enjoy, and possess Him.

This Epistle reveals clearly that we have received the divine life, for we have been born of Him. Just as a child can know his father because he has the father's life, so we can know God because we have God's life. Having the divine life, we have the ability to know God. Because we have the life of God, we are able to experience God, enjoy God, and possess God.

The Son of God has come through incarnation and through death and resurrection and has given us an understanding, the ability to know the true God. This understanding includes our enlightened mind, our quickened spirit, and the revealing Holy Spirit. Because our mind has been enlightened, our spirit has been enlivened, and the Spirit of reality dwells in us, we have the ability to know God, the ability to experience, enjoy, and possess the true One.

LIFE-STUDY OF FIRST JOHN

THE VIRTUES OF THE DIVINE BIRTH
TO OVERCOME THE WORLD, DEATH, SIN, THE DEVIL,
AND THE IDOLS

(5)

Scripture Reading: 1 John 5:18-21

In 5:20 John says, "And we know that the Son of God has come, and has given us an understanding that we might know Him who is true; and we are in Him who is true, in His Son Jesus Christ. This is the true God and eternal life." The Son of God, who has come to us in incarnation and through death and resurrection, has given us the understanding, the ability, to know the true God. This understanding, this knowing ability, includes our enlightened mind, our enlivened spirit, and the Spirit of reality. Now we have the ability to know God. As we have pointed out, to know God is to experience Him, enjoy Him, and possess Him.

THE TRUE ONE

In 5:20 John twice speaks of "Him who is true." A better translation would be "the true One." To speak of God simply as God may be to speak in a rather objective way. However, the term "the true One" is subjective; it refers to God becoming subjective to us. In this verse, the God who is objective becomes the true One in our life and experience.

What is the meaning of the expression "the true One"? In particular, what does the word "true" mean? Here the Greek word translated "true " is *alethinos*, genuine, real (an adjective akin to *aletheia*, truth, verity, reality—John 1:14; 14:6, 17), opposite of false and counterfeit. Actually, the true One is the reality. The Son of God has given us an understanding so that we may know—that is, experience, enjoy, and possess—this divine reality. Therefore, to know the true One means to know the reality by experiencing, enjoying, and possessing this reality.

First John 5:20 indicates that God has become our reality in our experience. The Son of God has come through incarnation and through death and resurrection and has given us an understanding so that we may experience, enjoy, and possess the reality, which is God Himself. Now the God who once was objective to us has become our subjective reality.

In 5:20 John says that we are in the true One. We not only know the true God; we are also in Him. We not only have the knowledge of Him; we are in an organic union with Him. We are one with Him organically.

When John says that we are in the true One, He is making a crucial point. Not only do we know the true One, and not only do we experience, enjoy, and possess Him as the reality, but we are in this reality. We are in the true One.

IN THE TRUE ONE, IN HIS SON JESUS CHRIST

In 5:20 John says, "We are in Him who is true, in His Son Jesus Christ." To be in the true God is to be in His Son Jesus Christ. Since Jesus Christ as the Son of God is the very embodiment of God (Col. 2:9), to be in Him is to be in the true God. This indicates that Jesus Christ the Son of God is the true God.

Let us consider in more detail John's word "we are in Him who is true, in His Son Jesus Christ." Notice that there is a comma after the word "true." In the original Greek text there is no punctuation at all. Hence, translators differ concerning whether or not a comma should be placed after "true."

Moreover, there is a question whether the phrase "in His Son Jesus Christ" is in apposition to "in Him who is true," or is an adverbial phrase. Some interpreters say that this phrase is in apposition; others say that it functions like an adverb. If this phrase is in apposition to "in Him who is true," the meaning would be that to be in the true One is equal to being in His Son Jesus Christ. If "in His Son Jesus Christ" is an adverb, then this phrase indicates that we are in the true One by being in His Son Jesus Christ.

Grammatically speaking, it may be preferable to say that "in His Son Jesus Christ" is not in apposition to the foregoing phrase, but is a modifier describing how we are in the true One. In this case, the meaning is that we are in the true One because we are in His Son Jesus Christ. In other words, we are in the true One by being in Jesus Christ. The reason we need to consider this matter is that it is vital to our spiritual experience.

After much study, I have come to the conclusion that either way we understand the function of the phrase "in His Son Jesus Christ," the outcome is the same. Whether this phrase is in apposition to the foregoing phrase or is a modifier, the result is the same. If the latter phrase is in apposition to the former, the meaning is that to be in the true One is equal to being in His Son Jesus Christ. This would also indicate that the true One and Jesus Christ are one in the way of coinherence. Therefore, to be in the Son is spontaneously to be in the true One. If "in His Son Jesus Christ" is a modifier, the meaning is that we are in the true One by being in His Son Jesus Christ. How are we in the true One? We are in Him by being in His Son Jesus Christ.

If we consider this matter carefully, we shall see that in both ways of understanding these phrases, the meaning is actually the same. Whether we say that to be in the true One is to be in His Son Jesus Christ, or we are in the true One by virtue of being in Jesus Christ, the outcome is the same.

THE TRUE GOD AND ETERNAL LIFE

Let us now go on to consider the last part of verse 20: "This is the true God and eternal life." "This" refers to the God who has come through incarnation and has given us

the ability to know Him as the genuine God and be one
with Him organically in His Son Jesus Christ. All this is
the genuine and real God and eternal life to us. This
genuine and real God is eternal life to us so that we may
partake of Him as everything for our regenerated being.

We need to pay special attention to the word "this." In
5:20 John does not say "He is"; he says "This is." This is
the correct translation of the Greek. Furthermore, John
uses the word "this" to refer both to the true God and to
eternal life. By this we see that the true God and eternal
life are one.

We have seen that we are in the true One and in His
Son Jesus Christ. Doctrinally, the true One and His Son
Jesus Christ may be considered two. But when we are in
the true One and in Jesus Christ experientially, They are
one. For this reason John uses "this" to refer both to the
true One and to His Son Jesus Christ.

For someone who is not in the true One and Jesus
Christ, They are two. But when we are in Them experientially, They are one. We have seen that to be in the true
One is to be in His Son Jesus Christ. This means that in
our experience of being in Them, They are one.

Moreover, when we are in the true One and Jesus
Christ, They are our true God and also our eternal life.
First, John speaks of the true One and His Son Jesus
Christ, and then he speaks of the true God. Here there may
be some distinction between the true One and the true God.
When we are in the true One and His Son Jesus Christ, the
true One is called the true God, and His Son Jesus Christ is
called eternal life. This means that first They are the true
One and His Son Jesus Christ. But when we are in Them,
They become the true God and eternal life.

We need a clear understanding of what "this" in 5:20
refers to. The word "this" refers to the very God who has
become experiential to us through our being in Him. No
longer are we outside of this God. Rather, we are in this
God, and we are in the true One, in His Son Jesus Christ.
Because we are in Them, God and Jesus Christ are no
longer objective to us, and in our experience They are no

longer two. When we are in Them, They become one to us. Therefore, John says that "this" is the true God, and "this" is eternal life. Who is "this"? "This" is the very God and the very Jesus Christ in whom we are. We may also say that "this" includes the condition of our being in God and Jesus Christ. Hence, the true God and eternal life include our being in the true One and His Son Jesus Christ.

We are in the true One and in Jesus Christ. Now in our experience this true One becomes the true God, and Jesus Christ becomes eternal life. Where are we now? Are we outside the true God and outside eternal life? No, we are in the true God and in eternal life. The word "this" includes this fact of our being in the true God and eternal life. Hallelujah, this is the true God and eternal life, and we are in this God and in this life! We know that we are in the true God and in eternal life because we are in the true One and in His Son Jesus Christ.

Verse 20 says that the Son of God has come and has given us an understanding so that we may know the true One, and we are in the true One, which means that we are in His Son Jesus Christ. When we are in the true One and Jesus Christ, *this*, including the fact that we are in Them, is the true God.

If we are not in God, we cannot say from experience that to us He is true. Of course, He would still be true in Himself, but we could not testify that in us He is true. But since we are in the true One, to us He is the true God. Furthermore, Christ is eternal life to us. If we were not in Him, Christ would still be eternal life in Himself, but He would not be eternal life to us. Because we are now in Him, to us Jesus Christ is eternal life.

Verse 20 indicates strongly that we are now experiencing the true God, and we are experiencing Him by being in Him. We experience, enjoy, and possess Him by being in Him. This, to us, is the true God and eternal life.

In verse 20 we have the crucial conclusion of the entire Epistle of 1 John. This Epistle reveals that now we are truly one with the Triune God, and He becomes true, real,

to us. He becomes reality and life to us because we are in
Him.

GUARDING OURSELVES FROM IDOLS

In verse 21 John goes on to conclude "Little children,
guard yourselves from idols." The word "guard" means to
garrison ourselves against attacks from without, like the
assaults of the heresies. "Idols" refers to the heretical
substitutes, brought in by the Gnostics and Cerinthians,
for the true God, as revealed in this Epistle and in John's
Gospel and referred to in the preceding verse. Idols here
also refer to anything that replaces the real God. We as
genuine children of the genuine God should be on the alert
to guard ourselves from these heretical substitutes and all
vain replacements of our genuine and real God, with whom
we are organically one and who is eternal life to us. This is
the aged apostle's word of warning to all his little children
as a conclusion of his Epistle.

According to John's understanding, an idol is anything
that replaces, is a substitute for, the subjective God, the
God whom we have experienced and whom we are still
experiencing. Through this enlightenment, we are able to
understand 5:18-21 in a very experiential way.

Before we were saved, we were outside of God. God was
true in Himself, but we could not say in our experience that
He was true to us. But after we believed in the Lord Jesus,
we entered into God. Therefore, 5:20 says not only that we
know the true One, but also that we are in the true One. We
have seen that to be in the true One means that we are in
His Son Jesus Christ. Because we are in God, He now
experientially becomes true to us. Likewise, because we are
in Jesus Christ, He becomes experientially true to us. Due
to our experience of God and Christ by being in God and in
Christ, we can say that this is the true God and eternal life.

The word "this" in 5:20 implies that God, Jesus Christ,
and eternal life are one. In doctrine, there may be a
distinction between God, Christ, and eternal life, but in our
experience they are one. When we are in God and in Jesus
Christ and when we experience eternal life, we find that all

these are one. Therefore, John concludes verse 20 by saying, "This is the true God and eternal life." This sentence is not merely the conclusion of verse 20; it is actually the conclusion of the entire book. What this Epistle reveals is the true God and eternal life.

John's last word, in 5:21, is the charge to guard ourselves from idols. Anything that is a substitute or replacement for the true God and eternal life is an idol. We need to live, walk, and have our being in this God and in this life. If we do not live in the true God and eternal life, then we shall have a substitute for the true God, and this substitute will be an idol.

THE BASIC AND SUBSTANTIAL ELEMENT OF JOHN'S MENDING MINISTRY

The center of the revelation in this Epistle is the divine fellowship of the divine life, the fellowship between the children of God and their Father God, who is not only the source of the divine life, but also light and love as the source of the enjoyment of the divine life (1:1-7). To enjoy the divine life we need to abide in its fellowship according to the divine anointing (2:12-28; 3:24), based upon the divine birth with the divine seed for its development (2:29—3:10). This divine birth was carried out by three means: the terminating water, the redeeming blood, and the germinating Spirit (5:1-13). By these we have been born of God to be His children, possessing His divine life and partaking of His divine nature (2:29—3:1). He is now indwelling us through His Spirit (3:24; 4:4, 13) to be our life and life supply that we may grow with His divine element unto His likeness at His manifestation (3:1-2).

To abide in the divine fellowship of the divine life, that is, to abide in the Lord (2:6; 3:6), is to enjoy all His divine riches. By such abiding, we walk in the divine light (1:5-7) and practice the truth, righteousness, love, the will of God, and His commandments (1:6; 2:29, 5; 3:10-11; 2:17; 5:2) by the divine life received through the divine birth (2:29; 4:7).

To preserve this abiding in the divine fellowship, three main negative things need to be dealt with. The first is sin, which is lawlessness and unrighteousness (1:7—2:6; 3:4-10; 5:16-18). The second is the world, which is composed of the lust of the flesh, the lust of the eyes, and the vainglory of this life (2:15-17; 4:3-5; 5:4-5, 19). The last is idols, which are the heretical substitutes for the genuine God and the vain replacements of the real God (5:21). These three categories of exceedingly evil things are weapons used by the evil one, the Devil, to frustrate, harm, and, if possible, even annihilate our abiding in the divine fellowship. The safeguard against his evil doing is our divine birth with the divine life (5:18), and, based upon the fact that the Son of God has through His death on the cross destroyed the works of the Devil (3:8), we overcome him by the word of God that abides in us (2:14). In virtue of our divine birth, we also overcome his evil world by our faith in the Son of God (5:4-5). Moreover, our divine birth with the divine seed sown into our inner being enables us not to live habitually in sin (3:9; 5:18), because Christ has taken away sins through His death in the flesh (3:5). In case we sin occasionally, we have our Paraclete as our propitiation to care for our case before our Father God (2:1-2), and the Son's everlasting efficacious blood cleanses us (1:7). Such a revelation is the basic and substantial element of the apostle's mending ministry.

LIFE-STUDY OF SECOND JOHN

MESSAGE ONE

THE WALK IN TRUTH AND LOVE

Scripture Reading: 2 John 1-6

THE SUBJECT OF THE EPISTLE

The subject of this book is the prohibition of participation in heresy. John speaks of heresy in verse 7: "Because many deceivers went out into the world, who do not confess Jesus Christ coming in the flesh. This is the deceiver and the antichrist." Certain heretics denied that Jesus is the Christ (1 John 2:22), and others denied the Son, not confessing that Jesus is the Son of God (1 John 2:23). Cerinthus, who denied that Jesus is the Christ, was a heretic. The Docetists and the Gnostics also taught heresy concerning the Person of Christ.

The Epistle of 2 John prohibits us from participating in any heretical teaching concerning Christ's Person. In verse 10 the Apostle John says, "If anyone comes to you and does not bring this teaching, do not receive him into your house, and do not say to him, Rejoice!" As in verse 9, the "teaching" here is the teaching concerning the deity of Christ, especially regarding His incarnation by divine conception. In this Epistle John warns us not to receive anyone who denies the truth concerning Christ's deity and incarnation.

INTRODUCTION

Loving in Truth for the Truth

In verse 1 John says, "The elder to the chosen lady and to her children, whom I love in truth, and not only I, but also all those who have known the truth." The Apostle John, like Peter, was also an elder in the church in

Jerusalem before its destruction in A.D. 70 (Gal. 2:9; 1 Pet. 5:1). According to history, after returning from exile, John stayed in Ephesus to care for the churches in Asia. Thus he was probably also an elder in the church at Ephesus, where he wrote this Epistle.

John addresses this Epistle to the "chosen lady and to her children." The Greek word rendered "lady" is *kuria*, the feminine form of *kurios*, lord, master. There are different interpretations of the word here. The most preferable is that it refers to a Christian sister of some prominence in the church, as "co-chosen" in 1 Peter 5:13 does. *Kuria* may have been her name, since it was a common name at that time. According to some accounts, she lived near Ephesus, and her sister (in v. 13) lived in Ephesus, where the church was under John's care. There was a church in her locality meeting in her home.

In verse 1 John speaks of loving in truth. According to John's usage of the word truth, especially in his Gospel, the first instance of "truth" in this verse denotes the revealed divine reality—the Triune God dispensed into man in the Son Jesus Christ—becoming man's genuineness and sincerity, to live a life that corresponds to the divine light (John 3:19-21) and to worship God, as God seeks, according to what He is (John 4:23-24). This is the virtue of God (Rom. 3:7; 15:8) becoming our virtue, by which we love the believers. This is the genuineness, truthfulness, sincerity, honesty, trustworthiness, and faithfulness of God as a divine virtue and of man as a human virtue (Mark 12:14; 2 Cor. 11:10; Phil. 1:18; 1 John 3:18), and as an issue of the divine reality (3 John 1). In such truth, the Apostle John, who lived in the divine reality of the Trinity, loved the one to whom he wrote. This is the denotation of the first usage of "truth" in this verse.

Simply speaking, the first usage of truth in verse 1 denotes sincerity, and John is speaking of loving in sincerity. However, the meaning of sincerity here is not simple. Usually, when we speak of sincerity, we understand sincerity to be merely a human virtue. But here sincerity is more than a human virtue. The human virtue in which the Apostle John loved the one who received this Epistle was the issue of the divine reality that he enjoyed.

What is the divine reality enjoyed by John? This reality is the Triune God. The writer of this Epistle enjoyed the Triune God in the Son as his divine reality. Out of the enjoyment of this reality, which is the Triune God in Christ, issued sincerity. This sincerity, or faithfulness, actually is a virtue of God. When we enjoy God as our reality, His divine virtue becomes our human virtue, and this human virtue is sincerity, faithfulness.

This understanding of loving in truth is based upon what is revealed in John's first Epistle. In that Epistle John indicates that we should love one another by God Himself as love. God is love (1 John 4:8, 16). As we enjoy God as love, out of this love issues a love with which we love others. When we love others with the love that issues from our enjoyment of God as love, our love will be in sincerity. This sincerity is not our human virtue; rather, it is the issue of our enjoyment of the divine reality.

As we consider what John means in verse 1 by loving in truth, we are reminded that it is not a superficial matter to know the Bible. In particular, it is not sufficient to know the Epistles of John in a superficial way. Only when we get into the depths of these Epistles can we know the meaning of the writer.

In verse 1 John speaks of "all those who have known the truth." Here John refers to those who not only have received Christ by believing that He is both God and man, but who also have fully known the truth concerning the Person of Christ.

At the end of verse 1 John again uses the word truth. Here truth denotes the divine reality of the gospel, especially concerning the Person of Christ as revealed in John's Gospel and first Epistle. (See note 6[6] in 1 John 1.) The divine reality of the gospel here especially includes the fact that Christ is both God and man, having deity and humanity, possessing both the divine nature and the human nature, to express God in human life and to accomplish redemption with divine power in human flesh

for fallen human beings, so that He may impart the divine
life into them and bring them into an organic union with
God. The second and third Epistles of John stress this
truth. The second warns the faithful believers against
receiving those who do not abide in this truth—in the
teaching concerning Christ. The third encourages the
believers to receive and help those who work for this
truth.

In verse 2 John goes on to say, "Because of the truth
which abides in us and shall be with us forever." The
Apostle John, in his Gospel and first Epistle, inoculated
the believers with his mending ministry concerning the
revelation of the Person of Christ against the heresies
regarding Christ's deity and humanity. Because of such
an inoculating truth, he and all those who had known
this truth loved those who were faithful to this truth.

In verse 2 John says that the truth abides in us and
will be with us forever. In verse 1 he tells us that he and
all those who have known the truth love in truth the one
to whom this Epistle was written. In verse 2 John uses
the word truth with the same meaning as that of the second usage in verse 1, that is, to denote the divine reality
of the gospel, especially concerning the Person of Christ.
This divine reality, which actually is the Triune God,
abides in us now and will be with us for eternity.

Grace, Mercy, and Peace in Truth and Love

In verse 3 John says, "Grace, mercy, peace shall be with
us from God the Father and from Jesus Christ, the Son of
the Father, in truth and love." Truth here refers to the divine
reality of the gospel, especially concerning the Person of
Christ, who expressed God and accomplished His purpose.
Love refers to the expression of the believers in loving one
another through receiving and knowing the truth. These two
matters are the basic structure of this Epistle. In love and
truth, grace, mercy, and peace will be with us.

The apostle greets and blesses the believers with grace,
mercy, and peace based upon the existence among them of

the two crucial matters of truth and love. When we walk in the truth (v. 4) and love one another (v. 5), we enjoy the divine grace, mercy, and peace.

If truth and love do not exist among the believers, there is no way for them to enjoy grace, mercy, and peace from God the Father and from Jesus Christ. Grace, mercy, and peace can be unto us only when the basic factors of truth and love are present. Therefore, this Epistle emphasizes truth and love. All of us need to live a life of truth and love.

THE WALK IN TRUTH AND LOVE

In Truth

In verses 4 through 6 John speaks concerning the walk in truth and love. Verse 4 says, "I rejoiced greatly that I have found some of your children walking in truth, even as we received commandment from the Father." The truth concerning the Person of Christ is the basic and central element of John's mending ministry. When he found the children of the faithful believer walking in truth, he rejoiced greatly (3 John 3-4).

In verse 4 John uses the word "walking." As in 1 John 1:7, where John speaks of walking in the light, the word "walk" means to live, behave, and have our being. The truth concerning the Person of Christ should not only be our belief; it should also be our living.

Once again, truth here denotes the divine reality, especially concerning the Person of Christ. The Father commands us to walk in this reality, that is, in the realization of the divine fact that Jesus Christ is the Son of God (see Matt. 17:5), that we may honor the Son as the Father desires (John 5:23).

The Father commands us to walk in the truth, in the reality. He commands us to walk in the realization of the divine fact that Jesus Christ is the Son of God. If we walk in this reality, we shall honor the Son according to the Father's desire.

In Love

In verses 5 and 6 John goes on to say, "And now I ask

you, lady, not as writing a new commandment to you, but that which we have had from the beginning, that we should love one another. And this is love, that we walk according to His commandments. This is the commandment, even as you heard from the beginning, that you should walk in it." The phrase "from the beginning" is found a number of times in John's writings. In some instances this phrase is used in the absolute sense (1 John 1:1; 3:8), but here in verses 5 and 6, as elsewhere (John 15:27; 1 John 2:7), it is used in the relative sense.

The commandment referred to in verses 5 and 6 is the commandment given by the Son that we should love one another (John 13:34). The Father commands us to walk in the truth to honor the Son, and the Son commands us to love one another to express Him.

LIFE-STUDY OF SECOND JOHN

NOT PARTICIPATING IN HERESY

Scripture Reading: 2 John 7-13

In this message we shall consider verses 7 through 13 of 2 John.

DECEIVERS AND ANTICHRISTS

Verse 7 says, "Because many deceivers went out into the world, who do not confess Jesus Christ coming in the flesh. This is the deceiver and the antichrist." The deceivers mentioned here were heretics, like the Cerinthians, the false prophets (1 John 4:1).

These deceivers do not confess Jesus Christ coming in the flesh. This means that they do not confess that Jesus is God incarnate. Thus, they deny the deity of Christ. Jesus was conceived of the Spirit (Matt. 1:18). To confess Jesus coming in the flesh is to confess that, as the Son of God, He was divinely conceived to be born in the flesh (Luke 1:31-35). The deceivers, the false prophets, would not make such a confession.

In verse 7 John says that those who do not confess Jesus coming in the flesh are not only deceivers but also antichrists. We have seen that an antichrist differs from a false Christ (Matt. 24:5, 24). A false Christ is one who pretends deceivingly to be the Christ, whereas an antichrist is one who denies Christ's deity, denying that Jesus is the Christ, that is, denying the Father and the Son by denying that Jesus is the Son of God (1 John 2:22), not confessing that He has come in the flesh through the divine conception of the Holy Spirit (1 John 4:2-3). Whoever denies the Person of Christ is an antichrist.

RECEIVING A FULL REWARD

In verse 8 John goes on to say, "Look to yourselves that

you do not lose the things which we wrought, but that you may receive a full reward." Here "look to yourselves" means watch yourselves, watch for yourselves, and "lose" means destroy, ruin.

In verse 8 John speaks of not losing the things which we wrought. The things which the apostles wrought are the things of the truth concerning Christ, which the apostles ministered and imparted to the believers. To be influenced by the heresies regarding the Person of Christ is to lose, destroy, and ruin the precious things concerning the Person of Christ which the apostles had wrought into the believers. Here the apostle warns the believers to watch for themselves lest they be influenced by the heresies and lose the things of the truth.

In verse 8 John also indicates that the believers "may receive a full reward." According to the context, expecially verse 9, the full reward must be the Father and the Son as the full enjoyment to the faithful believers, who abide in the truth concerning the Person of Christ and do not deviate from it by the influence of the heresies regarding Christ. This interpretation is justified by the fact that there is no indication this reward will be given in the future, as the rewards mentioned in Matthew 5:12; 16:27; 1 Corinthians 3:8, 13-14; Hebrews 10:35-36; Revelation 11:18; and 22:12. If we are not led astray by the heresies, but abide faithfully in the truth concerning the wonderful and all-inclusive Christ who is both God and man, both our Creator and Redeemer, we shall enjoy in Him the Triune God to the fullest extent as our full reward, even today on earth.

If we lose the precious things wrought into us by the apostles, this means that we do not abide in the truth. Then we shall miss the enjoyment of the Father and the Son. But if we stay in the truth, we shall receive a full reward, a reward that is actually the enjoyment of the Father and the Son. Praise the Lord that such a reward is in view waiting to be enjoyed by us! To enjoy this reward, we need to remain, abide, in the divine truth concerning Jesus Christ, the Son of God. Those, like today's modernists, who do not abide in this truth certainly do not have this enjoyment. For them, there is no reward of the Father and the Son as their enjoyment. If you contact them, you will find them spiritually starved and dry.

GOING BEYOND AND NOT ABIDING IN THE TEACHING OF CHRIST

In verse 9 John continues, "Everyone who goes beyond and does not abide in the teaching of Christ, does not have God; he who abides in the teaching, this one has both the Father and the Son." Literally, the Greek word translated "goes beyond" means to lead forward (in a negative sense), that is, to go further than what is right, to advance beyond the limit of orthodox teaching concerning Christ. This is contrasted with abiding in the teaching of Christ. The Cerinthian Gnostics, who boasted of their supposedly advanced thinking concerning the teaching of Christ, had such a practice. They went beyond the teaching of the divine conception of Christ, thus denying the deity of Christ. Consequently they could not have God in salvation and in life.

The modernists today go beyond and do not abide in the teaching of Christ. They also claim to be advanced in their thinking. According to them, it is out of date to say that Christ is God, that He was born of a virgin through divine conception, that He died on the cross for our sins, and that He was resurrected both physically and spiritually. Denying this truth concerning Christ, the modernists claim to be advanced in their philosophical thought. In principle, they follow the way of the Cerinthian Gnostics.

In verse 9 John speaks of not abiding in the teaching of Christ. This is not the teaching by Christ, but the teaching concerning Christ, that is, the truth concerning the deity of Christ, especially regarding His incarnation by divine conception.

HAVING THE FATHER AND THE SON

According to verse 9, the one who goes beyond and does not abide in the teaching of Christ, does not have God. But he who abides in the teaching of Christ has both the Father and the Son. To "have God" is to "have both the Father and the Son." It is through the process of incarnation that God has been dispensed to us in the Son with the Father (1 John 2:23) for our enjoyment and reality (John 1:1, 14). In the incarnated God we have the Son in His redemption and the Father in His life. We are thus redeemed and regenerated to be one with God organically so that we may partake of and enjoy Him in salvation and in life. Hence, to deny the incarnation is to reject this divine enjoyment; but to abide in the truth of incarnation is to have God, as the Father and the Son, for our portion in the eternal salvation and in the divine life.

This point in verse 9 concerning having both the Father and the Son has helped me to interpret the full reward spoken of in verse 8. The full reward is to have both the Father and the Son for our enjoyment. Today's modernists, like the ancient Gnostics, do not have the Father and the Son, for they do not abide in the teaching of Christ.

NOT SHARING IN HERETICAL WORKS

In verse 10 John goes on to say, "If anyone comes to you and does not bring this teaching, do not receive him into your house, and do not say to him, Rejoice!" Concerning the teaching of Christ, we should not only teach this as a theory, but also bring it as a reality. Wherever we go, we should bring this reality, the reality of what the all-inclusive Christ is. Some of the young people may have an opportunity to present to their parents this reality, which is a wonderful treasure.

In verse 10 the pronoun "him" refers to a heretic, an antichrist (v. 7; 1 John 2:22), a false prophet (1 John 4:1), who denies the divine conception and deity of Christ, as today's modernists do. Such a one we must reject, not receiving him into our house or greeting him. Thus, we shall not have any contact with him or share in his heresy, heresy that is blasphemous to God and contagious like leprosy.

We should not receive anyone who does not bring with

him the teaching of Christ. Do not think that because we are told to love others, we should receive a heretic. Concerning this, love does not avail. John says clearly that we should not receive an antichrist, a false prophet, into our house, and we should not even say to him, "Rejoice!"

The Greek word for rejoice is *chairein*, be happy, rejoice, hail; it is used for greeting or farewell. Instead of telling false prophets to rejoice, we should tell them to weep because they do not have the enjoyment of the Triune God. The point here is that we should have nothing to do with such persons and with their contagious heresy.

In verse 11 John says, "For he who says to him, Rejoice, shares in his evil works." Just as bringing to others the divine truth of the wonderful Christ is an excellent deed (Rom. 10:15), so spreading the satanic heresy, which defiles the glorious deity of Christ, is an evil work. It is a blasphemy and abomination to God! It is also a damage and curse to men. No believer in Christ and child of God should have any share in this evil. Even to greet such an evil one is prohibited. A severe and clear separation from this evil should be maintained.

The New Testament is very strong in the matter of not receiving one who denies the Person of Christ. Even though the second Epistle of John is an Epistle about loving one another, here John prohibits us from sharing, participating, in heresy. We should not have any contact with heretics, false prophets. We should not receive them, and we should not greet them. They are lepers, and this leprosy is contagious. Therefore, we should have nothing to do with them.

JOHN'S CONCLUSION IN THIS EPISTLE

Hope of Closer Fellowship for More Joy

In verses 12 and 13 we have the conclusion of this Epistle. In verse 12 John expresses the hope of closer fellowship for more joy: "Having many things to write to you, I do not want to do so with paper and ink, but I am hoping to be with you and to speak mouth to mouth, that

our joy may be made full." Here the apostle expresses his
desire for a deeper and richer fellowship with the church
member for fullness of joy in the enjoyment of the divine
life (1 John 1:2-4).

On the one hand, John's writing is divine; on the other
hand, he is very human in his behavior. We see this
humanness in verse 12, where John expresses his hope for
fellowship that He describes as mouth to mouth.

Greeting in the Endearing Care

In verse 13 John says, "The children of your chosen
sister greet you." This indicates what an intimate fellowship with the church members and what an endearing care
for them the aged elder had.

We have pointed out that the sister to whom this Epistle
was written may have lived near Ephesus and that her
sister lived in Ephesus, where there was a church under
John's care. In this Epistle John greets the one who
received this Epistle on behalf of the children of her chosen
sister. That she was not included in the greeting may
indicate that she was deceased. However, her children were
still in the church at Ephesus under John's care. In this
verse we can see the endearing care of the Apostle John for
the saints.

THE DIVINE REALITY

The three Epistles of John are arranged in a good
sequence. No doubt, the writing of the second Epistle was
based upon the first. In the first Epistle of John we see
what the divine truth is.

In 1975 I gave a series of messages on the seven
mysteries in 1 John: the mystery of the divine life, the
mystery of the divine fellowship, the mystery of the
abiding, the mystery of the anointing, the mystery of the
divine birth, the mystery of the divine seed, and the
mystery of the water, the blood, and the Spirit. Recently, I
have been deeply impressed with the divine reality in
John's first Epistle. The central factor in 1 John is the
divine reality. This reality is actually the Triune God. The

divine reality is the Triune God not merely in theology or doctrine; this reality is the Triune God in our experience, that is, the Triune God dispensed into us for our enjoyment. This is the divine reality in 1 John.

The Enjoyment of the Triune God

If you review the messages given in the Life-study of 1 John, you will see that in those messages the divine reality is ministered to you. Of course, in those messages there is ministered to us the eternal life, the fellowship of the divine life, the abiding in the Lord, the anointing, the divine birth, the divine seed, and the water, the blood, and the Spirit. When all these divine factors are put together, what we have is the enjoyment of the Triune God. Hence, the Triune God is the reality, the truth, we are enjoying. What are we doing day by day in the Christian life? We are enjoying the Triune God. If you were to ask me what I have been doing for more than fifty years, I would answer that I have been enjoying the Father, the Son, and the Spirit. As a result of my enjoyment of the Triune God, I have been burdened to share this enjoyment with others. However, because of the influence of traditional teaching, certain ones are not open to hear about the enjoyment of the Triune God.

People everywhere need to hear of the divine reality in the Epistle of 1 John. Do you not believe that this is what others, including religious leaders and Bible teachers, need today? Some recite the Apostles' Creed in their services every week, yet they are not saved and do not have any experience of the Triune God. We thank the Lord for opening to us the Epistle of 1 John, a book that contains course after course for our spiritual nourishment. Oh, what riches of our Triune God are revealed in this Epistle for our experience and enjoyment!

The True God Becoming Our Experience

According to 1 John 5:20, we not only experience and enjoy the Triune God, but we are in Him: "And we know that the Son of God has come, and has given us an understanding that we might know Him who is true; and we are in Him who is true, in His Son Jesus Christ. This is the true God and eternal life." We have pointed out that a better translation of "Him who is true" would be "the true One." Actually, the Greek simply says "the true." Only our Triune God is true; everything and everyone else is false. John tells us that we are in the True, in His Son Jesus Christ. No longer are we outside the True, and no longer are we outside His Son Jesus Christ.

In the second part of 1 John 5:20, John goes on to say, "This is the true God and eternal life." The true God becomes our experience as eternal life. This is the basic factor of John's first Epistle.

In 1 John we have the enjoyment of the Triune God as eternal life. Because we are in the true God, He contains us. When we are in the true God, He becomes eternal life to us.

In 1 John 5:20 we have the true One, Jesus Christ, the true God, and eternal life. In John's concept all these are one. However, in doctrine they are four: the true One, His Son Jesus Christ, the true God, and eternal life. But in our experience they are one. When we are in the true One, we are in His Son Jesus Christ. Then the true One becomes our God, and His Son Jesus Christ becomes eternal life to us. This eternal life is actually the true God. Furthermore, because the true God is real to us, in our experience He becomes our eternal life. This is the true God and eternal life.

Sincerity as the Issue of the Enjoyment of the Divine Reality

John's second Epistle is based upon the truth revealed in his first Epistle. Second John 1 says, "The elder to the chosen lady and to her children, whom I love in truth, and not only I, but also all those who have known the truth." In the foregoing message we pointed out that the first instance of "truth" in this verse denotes the revealed divine reality—the Triune God dispensed into man in the Son Jesus Christ—becoming man's genuineness and sincerity. This sincerity is the issue of the enjoyment of the

divine reality. Hence, when John says that he loves in
truth, he is saying that he loves in a sincerity that is the
issue of the divine reality. We have also seen that the
second usage of truth in this verse denotes the divine
reality of the gospel, especially concerning the Person of
Christ. This is "the truth which abides in us and shall be
with us forever" (v. 2). These verses are simple, but their
implication is profound. The entire first Epistle of John is
needed for the explanation of the first two verses of his
second Epistle.

Walking in Truth and Love

After speaking concerning truth in verses 1 through 3,
John goes on to tell us in verses 4 through 6 that we need
to walk in truth and love. Truth is the reality of the
Trinity, and love is the expression of this reality. When we
walk in truth, we walk in the divine reality we enjoy daily.
Love is the expression of this reality. As we walk in the
divine reality, spontaneously we love others. This love is
the expression of the divine reality we enjoy day by day.
Because of this reality and love, grace, mercy, and peace
are with us (v. 3). Praise the Lord that we may walk in the
divine reality and in the divine expression!

LIFE-STUDY OF THIRD JOHN

HOSPITALITY TO THE TRAVELING WORKERS

Scripture Reading: 3 John 1-8

The subject of the Epistle of 3 John is encouragement to the fellow workers in the truth. In this message we shall consider 3 John 1-8. Verses 1 through 4 are the introduction, and verses 5 through 8 speak of hospitality to traveling workers.

INTRODUCTION

Loving in Truth

The beginning of 3 John is similar to that of 2 John. In verse 1 the Apostle John says, "The elder to Gaius the beloved, whom I love in truth." Like Peter, John was an elder in the church at Jerusalem before its destruction in A.D. 70. According to history, after returning from exile, John stayed in Ephesus to care for the churches in Asia. Probably he was an elder in the church at Ephesus, where he wrote this Epistle.

The Epistle of 3 John is addressed to "Gaius the beloved." This is not the Gaius of Macedonia (Acts 19:29), the Gaius of Derbe (Acts 20:4), nor the Gaius of Corinth (1 Cor. 1:14; Rom. 16:23), but another with the name of Gaius, a name that was very common at the time. According to the contents of this Epistle, Gaius must have been an outstanding brother in the church.

In verse 1 John speaks of loving Gaius in truth. Here "truth" denotes the revealed divine reality—the Triune God dispensed into man in the Son Jesus Christ—becoming man's genuineness and sincerity, to live a life that corresponds to the divine light (John 3:19-21) and to worship God, as God seeks, according to what He is (John

4:23-24). This is the virtue of God (Rom. 3:7; 15:8) becoming our virtue, by which we love the believers. In such truth, the Apostle John, who lived in the divine reality of the Trinity, loved Gaius the beloved.

Prospering in All Things and in Health

In verse 2 John says, "Beloved, concerning all things I wish that you may prosper and be in health, even as your soul prospers." According to the context of this verse, "all things" refer to external and material things. Probably the word "wish" is used in the sense of prayer. Literally, the Greek word for "prosper" here means to have a good journey, to go on well, that is, to succeed in reaching a desired end; thus, to prosper. "Health" here is bodily health, as in Luke 5:31; 7:10; and 15:27.

In verse 2 John speaks of the soul prospering. Man is of three parts: spirit, soul, and body (1 Thes. 5:23). The soul is the mediating organ between the body and the spirit, possessing self-consciousness, that man may have his personality. The soul is contained in the body and is the vessel to contain the spirit. With the believer, God as the Spirit dwells in his regenerated spirit (Rom. 8:9, 16) and spreads from his spirit to saturate his soul, that it may be transformed to express Him (Rom. 12:2; 2 Cor. 3:18). This is the prosperity of the believer's soul. When our soul is occupied and directed by the Spirit of God through our spirit to direct and use our body for God's purposes, it prospers. The apostle wishes that the one who receives his Epistle, who is a beloved brother, outstanding in such prosperity of his soul, may prosper in all things and in bodily health, just as his soul prospers in the divine life.

Our body may prosper in health, and our living may prosper in many material things. However, our soul needs to prosper in the divine life. What, then, is the prosperity of our soul? The prosperity of our soul is the spreading of the divine life into the soul. Through regeneration the divine life has been imparted to our spirit. Now from our spirit this life needs to spread into our soul. If this takes place, our soul will prosper by the spreading of the divine life into it. I hope that we all shall pursue this so that we will have adequate experience of the prospering of our soul through the spreading of the divine life into it.

The beloved brother Gaius was prospering in his soul. The Apostle John wished that this brother would not only prosper in his soul, but also prosper in material things and that he would be in health. This greeting here is particular; it is unique in the entire Bible.

The New Testament is a book on spiritual prosperity, not on material things or bodily health. Nevertheless, John, who writes concerning divine things, wished that the one who received this letter would prosper in bodily health and even in material things.

Walking in Truth

In verse 3 John goes on to say, "For I rejoiced greatly at the brothers coming and testifying to your truth, even as you walk in truth." The truth concerning the Person of Christ is the basic and central element of John's mending ministry. When he found that his children were walking in truth (v. 4), he rejoiced greatly. To walk in truth means that the Triune God becomes our enjoyment in reality. Therefore, our daily walk is the walk in truth, which is the reality of the Triune God enjoyed by us.

In verse 3 John speaks of "your truth." "Your truth" is the truth concerning Christ, especially His deity, by the revelation of which the recipient's way of life is determined and to which the recipient holds as his fundamental belief. The thought here is deep. John's thought is that the objective truth becomes ours. Hence, the truth becomes subjective to us in our daily walk. This truth is the reality of Christ's deity. Our life is determined and shaped by the revelation of this truth. This means that we live, walk, and behave in the divine reality of the Triune God, who is our enjoyment. This enjoyment shapes our walk, our way of life. This indicates that our way of life is determined, shaped, molded by what we believe concerning the Person of Christ and by what we have seen and enjoyed of this reality. This truth is actually the Triune God becoming our enjoyment.

We believe that the Triune God became a man and lived on earth, died on the cross for our redemption, and in resurrection became a life-giving Spirit. Now this life-giving Spirit is the consummation of the Triune God. This Spirit is the consummation of all that the Father is and of all that the Son is as a person possessing divinity and humanity. Christ the Son is the very God and also a real man, who has accomplished redemption and is now the Life-giver, the life-imparting Spirit. We believe this, and this belief now shapes, determines, molds, our way of life. This is what it means to walk in truth.

The philosophy a person holds will determine his way of life. What a person believes will always shape his living. We Christians walk in the divine truth. This means that our way of life is determined, shaped, molded, by the divine reality—the Triune God Himself—which we enjoy.

In verse 3 John says to Gaius, "Even as you walk in truth." The one who receives this word not only holds to the truth, but also walks and lives in the truth. The truth concerning the Person of Christ should not only be our belief, but should also be our living, a living that testifies to our belief. The truth in which we walk, therefore, becomes our truth in our daily life.

In verse 4 John continues, "I have no greater joy than these things, that I hear that my children are walking in the truth." As in 2 John 4, "truth" here is the divine reality, especially concerning the Person of Christ as revealed in John's Gospel and first Epistle, that is, that Christ is both God and man, having both deity and humanity, possessing both the divine nature and the human nature, to express God in human life and to accomplish redemption with divine power in human flesh for fallen human beings so that He may impart the divine life into them and bring them into an organic union with God. The second and third Epistles of John emphasize this truth. The second warns the faithful believers against receiving those who do not abide in this truth, and the

third encourages the believers to receive and help those
who work for it.

JOHN'S CONCERN IN HIS EPISTLES

Both 2 John and 3 John are based on 1 John. Both 2
and 3 John indicate that we need to live in truth and walk
in truth. The difference is that in 2 John there is the
prohibition of participating in heresy, of participating in
any teaching that is against this truth. We must stay away
from any teaching or any person who is against the reality
of the Triune God. But in 3 John there is the encouragement to help the fellow workers in the truth. We need to
join ourselves to anyone who works for the divine reality
of the Triune God that we are enjoying, and we need to do
whatever we can to promote this work. Hence, in 2 John
there is a negative attitude toward heresy and in 3 John, a
positive attitude toward the work for the truth. Whether
our attitude should be negative or positive depends on
whether the particular situation is for the divine reality or
against it.

The concern of the Apostle John in writing his three
Epistles was the enjoyment of the Triune God. This is also
our concern today. Among believers there is a great lack of
the divine reality and hardly any enjoyment of the Triune
God. Instead of the enjoyment of the Triune God, Christians have religion with doctrines, creeds, rituals, and
practices. Using a phrase from John Bunyan's *Pilgrim's
Progress*, we may say that, as a whole, today's religion is a
"vanity fair." Whereas John Bunyan used this term to
describe the world, we use it to describe religion. Instead of
reality and the enjoyment of the Triune God, with religion
there is all manner of vanity. We, however, need to be
careful not to merely talk about truth, reality, without
having the genuine experience of the divine reality.

What is the truth, the divine reality, that John talks
about in his Epistles? This reality is the Father in the Son,
and the Son as the Spirit dispensed into God's chosen,
redeemed, and regenerated people so that they may enjoy
Him as life, life supply, and everything in the new creation

life. Actually, this truth, this reality, is the enjoyment of
the Triune God. The Father in the Son became a man, who
died on the cross to accomplish redemption and resurrected
to become the life-giving Spirit. Now He can dispense
Himself into His chosen people so that they may have Him
for their enjoyment and also as their life, life supply, and
everything they need for the life of the new creation. This
is the divine reality as revealed in the Epistles of John.

Many Christians today do not pay attention to this
divine reality. Instead, to them everything concerning God
and salvation is objective. They have only an objective
God, objective Savior, objective redemption, objective
salvation, objective justification, and objective reconciliation. They may believe many fundamental doctrines, but
all these doctrines are merely objective and are used to
form a religion. In the spiritual lexicon of these Christians
there is no such word as enjoyment.

The Bible reveals that God is our enjoyment and He is
food to us. According to the pure Word, God is edible (John
6:57). After the creation of man, we have the tree of life.
Then in God's redemption and salvation as typified by the
history of Israel, we see the eating of the Passover lamb
with the unleavened bread. After the children of Israel
entered the wilderness, they daily ate manna, which is a
type of Christ. Although certain Christians realize that
manna is a type of Christ, they do not realize that the Lord
Jesus is edible. In chapter six of the Gospel of John the
Lord Jesus reveals that He is the bread of life and that we
need to eat Him. Furthermore, we remember Him at His
table by eating and drinking Him.

The Lord Jesus established the table by taking bread,
blessing it, passing it on to the disciples, and telling them
to eat it. He charged them to do this in remembrance of
Him. This indicates that the Lord's way for us to remember
Him is not by kneeling or prostrating ourselves. Rather,
what honors Him is that we remember Him by eating Him.
The principle is the same with the drinking of the cup.

It is vital that we all see what the divine reality is. The
divine Trinity should become our subjective enjoyment.

This is the divine reality, and this is what has been neglected by Christians today. Therefore, in the Lord's recovery we have been charged by the Lord to pay full attention to this matter.

In the recovery we should not have the words "reality" and "truth" as mere terms. If we have only terms, then we are still in the realm of doctrine, although it may be doctrine of a higher standard and more complete truth. We all need to see that the truth, the reality, is the divine Person—the Father, the Son, and the Spirit—becoming our enjoyment and even our constituent.

In both 2 and 3 John the Apostle John speaks of loving in the truth. In 2 John 1 he also says that those who have known the truth also love the receiver of the Epistle in truth, because of the truth which abides in us and will be with us forever (2 John 2). Furthermore, both in 2 John 4 and in 3 John 3 and 4 John is happy to see that his children are walking in the truth, that they are walking in the enjoyment of the Triune God. The reason we love others is that we enjoy the Triune God and that the Triune God enjoyed by us is love. Because we enjoy the Triune God, love flows out of us to others. Because we take into us the God who is love, because we "eat" God as love, we become love. Concerning this matter, we are reminded of the saying, "You are what you eat." The result of eating God is that we love others in truth.

Beginning in the first century, distractions and replacements of the divine reality began to creep in. Among Christians today there are a great many replacements, substitutes, for Christ. Many have Christ only in name.

In order to experience and enjoy the Triune God in a practical way, we need to see that He is the Spirit dwelling in our regenerated spirit. This Spirit is the all-inclusive, compound, life-giving Spirit, who is the consummation of the processed Triune God. This Spirit may be considered the "extract" of the Triune God. Just as the extracts of certain substances used as medicine or for cooking may be quite strong, so the Spirit as the extract of the Triune God is very strong. Today our God is the Spirit in our spirit. If we turn to our spirit, stay in our spirit, and exercise our spirit to call on the name of the Lord and pray-read the Word, we shall enjoy the Triune God. Then this enjoyment will change us, transform us, and shape our way of life.

HOSPITALITY TO THE TRAVELING WORKERS

Given Faithfully in Love, and Worthily of God

In verses 5 and 6 John goes on to say, "Beloved, you do faithfully in whatever you may have wrought for the brothers, and this for strangers, who testified to your love before the church, whom you will do well to send forward worthily of God." Here John speaks concerning hospitality to traveling workers. In verse 5 "whatever" refers to the hospitality afforded (as taught by Paul in Romans 12:13 and Hebrews 13:2), the receiving of the brothers (3 John 10) who traveled for the gospel and the ministry of the Word. The word "this" also indicates hospitality rendered to those brothers who went out for the sake of the truth. Because those brothers were not acquainted with Gaius, the one who received this Epistle, they were strangers to him.

In verse 6 John says that these traveling brothers, who were mostly strangers to Gaius, unacquainted with him, testified to his love before the church. This was in the past and was in the church where the apostle was. Then John continues by saying that Gaius will do well to send them forward worthily of God. This indicates something to be done in the future. The apostle on the one hand praises Gaius for what he has done in receiving the traveling brothers in the past; on the other hand, he encourages him to send them forward in the future. In particular, John encourages Gaius to send them forward worthily of God, that is, in a manner worthy of God.

Here "worthily" modifies "send forward." The sending forward should be in a manner that matches God, who is generous. This indicates that the sending forward must be with generosity.

By the Fellow Workers in the Truth

In verses 7 and 8 John indicates that by rendering hospitality to the traveling brothers, we may become fellow workers with those who go out for the sake of the truth. Verse 7 says, "For on behalf of the Name they went out, taking nothing from the Gentiles." The Name here is the exalted and glorious Name of the wonderful Christ (Phil. 2:9; Acts 5:41; James 2:7). Since the time of the Lord's ascension, there has never been a name on earth above that of Jesus.

In verse 7 John says that the traveling workers for the truth take nothing from the Gentiles. The Gentiles, pagans, have nothing to do with God's move on earth to carry out His economy. It is a shame and even an insult to God for anyone who works for God's New Testament economy to receive help for God's work, especially financial support, from unbelievers. In the apostle's time, the brothers who worked for God took nothing from the pagans. Therefore, the apostle encourages the believers to support this work for God's economy.

In verse 8 John concludes, "We therefore ought to support such, that we may become fellow workers in the truth." The Greek word translated "support" is *hupolambano*, made up of two words: *hupo*, under, and *lambano*, to take; hence, to take up from underneath, that is, to undertake, to sustain, to support. We, the believers including the apostle, ought to support and undertake for the need of the brothers who work for God in His divine truth and who take nothing from the Gentiles. If we support the traveling workers, we participate in the work and thereby become fellow workers in the truth.

In verse 8 "truth" denotes the revealed divine reality as the contents of the New Testament according to the apostles' teaching concerning the divine Trinity, especially the Person of the Lord Jesus, for God's economy. All the apostles and faithful brothers worked for this.

LIFE-STUDY OF THIRD JOHN

MESSAGE TWO

IMITATION NOT OF THE EVIL BUT OF THE GOOD

Scripture Reading: 3 John 9-14

In the foregoing message we pointed out that the subject of this Epistle is encouragement to fellow workers in the truth. Verses 1 through 4 are the introduction and speak of loving in truth (v. 1), prospering in all things and in health (v. 2), and walking in truth (vv. 3-4). Then verses 5 through 8 go on to speak of hospitality to traveling workers. In this message we shall consider verses 9 through 14.

THE SELF-EXALTING
AND DOMINEERING DIOTREPHES—
AN EVIL EXAMPLE

In 3 John 9-12 John gives two examples: the negative example of Diotrephes (v. 9) and the positive example of Demetrius (v. 12). In verse 9 John says, "I wrote something to the church, but Diotrephes, who loves to be first among them, does not receive us." The church here is the church of which Gaius was a member.

The name Diotrephes is made up of *Dios* (from the name of Zeus, who was the chief of the gods in the Greek pantheon) and *trepho*, to nourish; hence, Zeus-nourished. This indicates that Diotrephes as a professing Christian never dropped his pagan name. This was contrary to the practice of the early believers, who took a Christian name at their baptism. According to history, Diotrephes advocated the Gnostic heresy, which blasphemes the Person of Christ.

John says that Diotrephes loved to be first among those in the church and did not receive the apostle. This means that Diotrephes did not receive him hospitably.

Diotrephes' loving to be first was against the words of the Lord Jesus in Matthew 20:25-27 and 23:8-11, which places all His believers on the same level, that of brothers. In 2 John 9 the Cerinthian Gnostics took the lead to advance in doctrine beyond the teaching concerning Christ. Here in 3 John 9 is one who was under the influence of Gnostic heretical doctrine, loving to be the first in the church. The problem of Gnostic doctrine was one of intellectual arrogance; the problem of loving to be first was one of self-exaltation in action. These two evils are sharp weapons used by God's enemy, Satan, to execute his evil plot against God's economy. One damages the believers' faith in the divine reality: the other frustrates their work in God's move.

The principle was the same both with the Cerinthian Gnostics in their desire to be advanced in doctrine and with Diotrephes' love to be first; they wanted to be above others. The Cerinthians wanted to be above others in advanced thought, and Diotrephes wanted to be first. Today's modernists can be compared to the Cerinthians in their desire to have a higher, more advanced, philosophy. The modernists may think that the general belief among Christians is too low. Therefore, they desire to be above others in thought or philosophy. The desire to be above others and the desire to be first are both instances of pride and arrogance, and both were issues of heresy.

Among Christians today these two problems still exist. The first problem, the desire to be above others in thought, is related to doctrine. The second problem, the love of being first, is related to practice. In doctrine many desire to be advanced, to go beyond others. In practice, many love to be first. Such a love leads even to the desire to be a "pope." Sometimes this evil principle creeps into the church life. For example, in standing up to give a testimony we may want to say something advanced, something that goes beyond what others can say. Furthermore, in the church life we may also desire to be first. Even in a small service group, we may want to be the first, the head. This is in principle the evil spirit of Diotrephes.

Diotrephes was influenced by the Gnostics, and he advocated, promoted, Gnosticism. In this we see the subtlety of the enemy in trying to annul the enjoyment of the Triune God. Satan in his subtlety seeks either to distract us from the enjoyment of the Triune God, to cut us off from this enjoyment, or even to destroy it altogether. Consider the situation among believers today with respect to the enjoyment of the Triune God. Even the teaching of the Bible is utilized by the enemy to keep believers away from the proper enjoyment of the Triune God. Concerning this matter, a battle is raging, and we are fighting for the truth. We are not fighting for doctrine; we are fighting for the reality, which is the enjoyment of the Triune God.

As we go on to read 3 John 10, we see how domineering the evil Diotrephes was: "Therefore, if I come, I will bring to remembrance his works which he does, babbling against us with evil words; and not being satisfied with these, neither does he receive the brothers, and those intending to do so he forbids and casts them out of the church." The Greek word translated "babbling," *phluareo*, comes from *phluo*, to boil over, to bubble up, to overflow with words, to talk idly; hence, to babble, to talk folly or nonsense.

The babbling of Diotrephes was with "evil words." The Greek word for "evil" here is *poneros,* which denotes something pernicious. *Poneros* differs from *kakos* which refers to an essentially worthless and wicked character; it differs as well from *sapros*, which indicates worthlessness and corruption, degeneracy from original virtue. The word *poneros* denotes something pernicious, harmfully evil, that affects and influences others to be evil and vicious.

In verse 11 John goes on to say, "Beloved, do not imitate the evil, but the good. He who does good is of God; he who does evil has not seen God." Here the Greek word rendered "evil" is *kakos*, worthless, wicked, depraved. "Does good" comes from the Greek *agathopoieo* (of the root *agathos*, good), to be a well-doer (as a favor or a duty), practicing good; hence, to do good.

In this verse John says that he who does good is "of God." Literally, the Greek word for "of" means out of, out from. Because we have been begotten of God, we are out from Him, possessing His life and partaking of His nature. God is the source of good. A well-doer, a doer of good, is one who has his source in God; that is, he is one who is out from God.

In verse 11 John tells us that he who does evil has not seen God. The Greek word rendered "does evil" is *kako-poieo* (of the root *kakos*, worthless), to be an evildoer, practicing evil; hence, to do evil. An evildoer not only is not out of God, but has not even seen God. This means that he has not enjoyed God or experienced Him.

In verse 11 to see God actually means to enjoy God and experience Him. We cannot see God without enjoying Him, and we cannot know God without experiencing Him. Seeing and knowing God are a matter of enjoying and experiencing Him.

Recently I have been encouraged by many of the testimonies given by young saints in the meetings. These testimonies indicate that these young saints are enjoying God and experiencing Him. This also indicates that they have seen God and have known Him. Without seeing and knowing God, without enjoying and experiencing Him, they could not give such testimonies. Our testimonies indicate whether or not we are enjoying and experiencing God. As we have pointed out, our enjoyment of God is our seeing of Him, and our experience of God is our knowing of Him.

THE WELL-REPORTED DEMETRIUS—A GOOD EXAMPLE

In verse 12 John goes on to say, "To Demetrius testimony has been borne by all, and by the truth itself; and we also testify, and you know that our testimony is true." Demetrius, who may have been one of the traveling brothers working for the Lord (vv. 5-8), may have been also the bearer of this Epistle to Gaius. Hence, a favorable and strong commendation of him by the writer was needed.

John says in verse 12 that to Demetrius testimony has been borne by all. The word "all" indicates many saints in different churches. John's word indicates that Demetrius must have been a brother working among the churches, and thus was well known.

John also says that testimony has been borne to Demetrius "by the truth itself." This is the revealed truth of God, as the reality of the essence of the Christian faith, which is the divine rule for the walk of all believers and by which the believers' walk is determined. Thus, it gives a good testimony to him who walks in it, as it did to Demetrius.

Finally, in verse 12 John says, "We also testify, and you know that our testimony is true." The "we" here denotes the Apostle John and his associates. The Greek word for "true" is *alethes* (an adjective akin to *aletheia*), genuine, real; hence, true.

THE CONCLUSION OF THIS EPISTLE

In verses 13 and 14, as the conclusion, John expresses the hope of closer fellowship (vv. 13-14a) and extends mutual greetings (v. 14b): "I had many things to write to you, but I do not want to write to you with ink and pen; but I hope to see you shortly, and we will speak mouth to mouth. Peace to you. The friends greet you. Greet the friends by name." Here we see that the apostle expresses his desire for a deeper and richer fellowship with Gaius for fullness of joy in the enjoyment of the divine life (1 John 1:2-4).

THE UNDERLYING THOUGHT IN JOHN'S EPISTLES

In the Epistles of John there is an underlying thought. This thought is related to the fact that at the time these Epistles were written certain heresies concerning the Person of Christ had crept in. The effect of these heretical teachings was to annul the saints' enjoyment of the Triune God. This enjoyment has a focal point: God becoming man, and this God-man accomplishing redemption and in resurrection becoming the life-giving Spirit.

In order to see that this underlying thought is in fact found in John's Epistles, let us review a number of points.

In his first Epistle John says that God sent His Son a propitiation concerning our sins (4:10). John also says that God sent His Son, the only begotten, into the world that we may live through Him and also that the Son may be the Savior of the world. (4:9, 14). In 3:8 John says that "the Son of God was manifested, that He might undo the works of the Devil."

God's sending His Son implies incarnation. In what way did God send His Son? God sent His Son through incarnation. Now we need to go on to ask what incarnation is. Incarnation is the Son coming with the Father and by the Spirit to become a man. According to the New Testament, the Lord Jesus was conceived of the Spirit and came with the Father. By this we see that the Trinity is involved with the incarnation. The issue of the incarnation, in which the Trinity was involved, was a wonderful Man by the name of Jesus. Therefore, the incarnation was not an act merely of the Son, not an act that had nothing to do with the Father or the Spirit. Rather, when the Son was incarnated, He came with the Father and by the Spirit. Hence, the Three of the Trinity—the Father, the Son, and the Spirit—all participated in the incarnation.

As God incarnate, the Lord Jesus lived on earth for thirty-three and a half years. Then He went to the cross and died for our redemption. In resurrection He became the life-giving Spirit.

In the Epistles of John the truth includes all these crucial matters concerning Christ's incarnation, human living, crucifixion, and resurrection. This means that the truth in these Epistles implies divinity, humanity, incarnation, crucifixion, redemption, and resurrection. This truth implies all that the Triune God is, all that He has done, and all that He has obtained and attained. This all-inclusive reality is the truth that is the basic structure of John's Epistles.

We have seen that the enemy brought in different heresies concerning the Person of Christ. The intention of the enemy was to distract people from the truth or confuse them with respect to the truth, with the result that the saints' enjoyment of the Triune God would be destroyed.

John wrote his three Epistles to combat the work of the enemy. These Epistles reveal one main point, and this point is that the divine truth should become our reality, life, and living, that this truth should be kept in the divine fellowship, and that this truth should be applied to our entire being in everything and in every way. This is the picture portrayed in these Epistles.

We all must see the picture of the divine reality presented by John in his Epistles. This is a picture of the Triune God becoming our enjoyment through incarnation, human living, crucifixion, resurrection, and ascension. Whoever is against this enjoyment is a false prophet, a deceiver, an antichrist. But whoever is for the enjoyment of the Triune God is an honest and faithful worker for the truth, and we should be joined to that one and participate in his work. Anything that replaces this divine reality, is a substitute for it, is an idol, and we should garrison ourselves against it. We need to guard ourselves, keep ourselves, from all idols, from all substitutes for the divine reality. If we see this vision, we shall be clear concerning the situation of today's religion, and we shall also be clear concerning our burden in the Lord's recovery.

LIFE-STUDY OF JUDE

MESSAGE ONE

CONTENDING FOR THE FAITH

Scripture Reading: Jude 1-7

With this message we begin the life-study of the book of Jude. The subject of Jude is contending for the faith. In verse 3 Jude entreats us to "contend for the faith once for all delivered to the saints." In this message we shall cover the first seven verses of this Epistle.

INTRODUCTION

Verses 1 and 2 are the introduction to the book of Jude. In these verses Jude says, "Jude, a slave of Jesus Christ, and brother of James, to those who are called, beloved in God the Father and kept by Jesus Christ: mercy to you and peace and love be multiplied." Both Jude and James were brothers of the Lord Jesus in the flesh (Matt. 13:55). James was one of the apostles (Gal. 1:19) and one of the elders in Jerusalem (Acts 15:2, 13; 21:18), reputed with Peter and John to be a pillar of the church (Gal. 2:9). He also wrote the Epistle of James (James 1:1). Jude was not listed among the twelve, nor are we told that he was an elder in a church. Nevertheless, he wrote this Epistle, a short yet excellent book.

According to verse 1, this book is addressed to "those who are called, beloved in God the Father and kept by Jesus Christ." The Greek word rendered "by" may also be translated "for." "By" denotes the strength and means of keeping; "for" denotes the purpose and object of keeping. All the believers have been given to the Lord by the Father (John 17:6), and they are being kept for Him and by Him.

Many Bible teachers believe that this Epistle, like 1 and 2 Peter, was written to Jewish believers in Christ. In Jude's words, these believers were called, beloved in God the Father, and kept by Jesus Christ.

In verse 2 Jude says, "Mercy to you and peace and love be multiplied." The fact that mercy is mentioned instead of grace in this greeting may be due to the church's degradation and apostasy (see vv. 21-22). In 1 and 2 Timothy Paul includes God's mercy in his opening greeting. God's mercy reaches farther than His grace. In the degraded situation of the churches, God's mercy is needed.

As sinners, we were in a pitiful situation. But God's mercy reached us and brought us out of that situation and qualified us to receive His grace. In principle, grace requires that we be in a somewhat good condition. However, because mercy reaches farther than grace, it is able to reach those who are in a most pitiful condition.

CONTENDING FOR THE FAITH

Verse 3 says, "Beloved, using all diligence to write to you concerning our common salvation, I found it necessary to write to you, entreating you to contend for the faith once for all delivered to the saints." Here Jude speaks of our common salvation. This is general salvation, which is common to and held by all believers, like the common faith (Titus 1:4).

Some Christians misapply Jude's word about contending for the faith. They think that to contend for the faith means to contend for matters such as baptism and foot washing. Some argue concerning head covering or about the kind of bread used in the Lord's table. However, the faith in verse 3 does not refer to such matters.

The faith in this verse is not subjective; it is objective. It does not refer to our believing, but refers to our belief, to what we believe. The faith denotes the contents of the New Testament as our faith (Acts 6:7; 1 Tim. 1:19; 3:9; 4:1; 5:8; 6:10, 21; 2 Tim. 2:18; 3:8; 4:7; Titus 1:13), in which we believe for our common salvation. This faith, not any doctrine, has been delivered once for all to the saints. For this faith we should contend (1 Tim. 6:12).

In the Old Testament God gave Abraham a promise. Later, through Moses God gave the law to the children of Israel. In the Gospel of John we are told that when the Lord Jesus came, grace came (1:17). Here we have three important matters: promise, law, and grace. Some Bible teachers speak of the dispensation of promise, the dispensation of law, and the dispensation of grace.

In order to understand the truth in the New Testament, we need to see that God first gave a promise to Abraham. We may say that this promise was on the "main track" of God's dealing with man. But because of the ignorance and unbelief of God's chosen people, it was necessary for God to give the law to the children of Israel. In the book of Galatians Paul likens the law to Hagar, Abraham's concubine, not to Sarah, Abraham's wife (Gal. 4:21-25). This means that Hagar was a type, or prefigure, of the law. Hence, the position of the law is not that of the wife, but that of a concubine. Now in the New Testament God gives faith instead of the law.

With the faith given by God there is both a subjective side and an objective side. The subjective side concerns our believing, and the objective side concerns the things we believe. In verse 3 the faith does not denote our ability to believe; rather, it refers to what we believe. Hence, the faith refers to the contents of the New Testament.

Peter tells us in his second Epistle that like precious faith has been allotted to us (2 Pet. 1:1). This faith is subjective and refers to the faith that is within us. This differs from the faith in Jude 3, for the faith here is objective.

The faith in the objective sense is equal to the contents of God's will given to us in the New Testament. The law includes the contents of the Ten Commandments and all the subordinate ordinances. The law was given in the Old Testament, but what God gives in the New Testament is the faith that includes all the items of God's new will. This will even includes the Triune God. However, it does not include such matters as head covering, foot washing, or methods of baptism. Nevertheless, some believers contend for such things, thinking that they are contending for the faith. But that is not the correct understanding of what Jude means by contending for the faith once for all delivered to the saints.

To contend for the faith is to contend for the basic and crucial matters of God's new will. One of these basic matters is Christ's death for our redemption.

Suppose a modernist tells you that Jesus died on the cross not for redemption, but because He was a martyr and sacrificed Himself for His teachings. This understanding of the death of Christ is heretical. It is contrary to one of the main items of God's new will. We need to contend for the truth concerning Christ's redemption.

Many years ago in China we contended for the truth of redemption when we fought against the book *For Sinners Only*, a book which claims that a sinner can be favored by God or saved apart from the blood of Jesus. The Bible clearly says that without the shedding of blood there is no forgiveness of sins (Heb. 9:22). We fought against that heretical book and inoculated the believers against its modernistic teachings.

We thank the Lord that in this country today many fundamental Bible teachers are also fighting against heretical, modernistic teachings. This is to contend for the faith once for all delivered to the saints. This faith has been delivered to the saints once for all, and what we need to do now is to contend for it.

THE HERESIES OF THE APOSTATES

In verse 4 Jude goes on to say, "For certain men have crept in unnoticed, who of old have been written of beforehand for this judgment, ungodly men, perverting the grace of our God into licentiousness, and denying our only Master and Lord, Jesus Christ." Verses 4 through 19 of Jude are in close parallel with chapter two of 2 Peter. This indicates that the Epistle of Jude was written in the time of the church's apostasy and degradation.

In verse 4 Jude says that certain men have "crept in unnoticed." Literally the Greek means to get in by the side, or slip in by a side door. We may compare this with "secretly bring in" in 2 Peter 2:1. As the enemy crept in to sow tares among the wheat (see Matt. 13), the apostates have crept in unnoticed.

The words "this judgment" refer to the judgment of the creeping in unnoticed of the apostates, the judgment unfolded in the following verses. Judgment here is the condemnation for punishment, and it refers to being condemned to be punished.

Here Jude speaks of ungodly men, who pervert the grace of God into licentiousness and deny our Master and Lord, Jesus Christ. The evil of these heretical apostates is twofold: perverting the grace of God into wantonness, that is, into the abuse of freedom (see Gal. 5:13; 1 Pet. 2:16), and denying the headship and lordship of the Lord. These two go together. Turning the grace of God into an abused freedom for wantonness requires denying the Lord's rule and authority.

HISTORICAL EXAMPLES OF
THE LORD'S JUDGMENT UPON APOSTASY
The Children of Israel

In verses 5 through 7 Jude gives some historical examples of the Lord's judgment upon apostasy. The first example is that of the children of Israel: "But I intend to remind you, though you know all things once for all, that the Lord, having saved a people out of the land of Egypt, afterward destroyed those who did not believe" (v. 5). There was apostasy among those who were led out of the land of Egypt. This means that the unbelieving children of Israel became apostates. In this verse Jude tells us that the Lord destroyed those who did not believe.

The Angels Who Did Not
Keep Their Own Principality

Verse 6 says, "And angels who did not keep their own principality, but abandoned their own dwelling place, He has kept in eternal bonds under gloom for the judgment of the great day." The angels here are the same as those in

2 Peter 2:4; they are the "sons of God" in Genesis 6. The Greek word translated "principality" is *arche*. This word means the beginning of power, the first place of authority; hence, original dignity in a high position. The fallen angels did not keep their original dignity and position, but abandoned their own dwelling place, which is in heaven, to come to earth at Noah's time to commit fornication with the daughters of men (Gen. 6:2; 1 Pet. 3:19). The "gloom" is the gloomy pits of Tartarus (2 Pet. 2:4), and the judgment of the great day will probably be the final judgment of the great white throne.

Sodom and Gomorrah

In verse 7 Jude continues, "As Sodom and Gomorrah and the cities around them, who in like manner with these gave themselves over to fornication and went after other flesh, are set forth as an example, undergoing the penalty of eternal fire." The word "as" here is important and means in the same manner as. This word proves that the angels in the preceding verse are the sons of God in Genesis 6:2, who committed fornication with strange flesh and were condemned by God for the judgment of the great day, for immediately following that was the judgment on Sodom, Gomorrah, and the cities around them. The relative pronoun "who" in verse 7 refers to Sodom, Gomorrah, and the cities around them.

The phrase "in like manner" means in the manner of committing fornication with strange flesh, as the fallen angels did. The fallen angels committed fornication with another race, which to them was strange flesh. The Sodomites indulged their lusts with males (Rom. 1:27; Lev. 18:22), with flesh different from and strange to what God ordained by the nature of His creation for human marriage (Gen. 2:18-24). In verse 7 "other flesh" denotes flesh that is strange or different, and "these" refers to the fornicating angels in the preceding verse.

If we compare Jude with 2 Peter, we shall see that these two Epistles cover many of the same points. This indicates that the apostles and early teachers must have had fellowship regarding these matters. Otherwise, how could Peter and Jude have written in a way that is so similar? These two brothers, both of whom had a Jewish background and bore the responsibility to sound the trumpet for the New Testament truths, condemned the same things and emphasized the fact that anyone who takes the way of apostasy will suffer God's judgment.

It is extremely serious to deny the Lord's Person and His redemptive work. Certain modernists who deny the Lord in this way have suffered God's judgment even in their lifetime. When the Oxford movement, or Buchmanism, was active in China, some modernists were so bold as to say that Jesus Christ was not the Son of God born of a virgin, but was the illegitimate son of Mary. This is not only heretical; it is blasphemous. What blasphemy it is to claim that our Lord Jesus Christ was the illegitimate son of Mary! Eventually, some of those who taught such heretical and blasphemous things did not have a good end in life. Not only will they be judged by God in the future—they were judged by God during their lifetime. As a result, the ending of their life was not at all good.

We need to learn from the books of Jude and 2 Peter to fear God and to be very careful concerning the Lord's Person and His redemptive work. Because we live in a perverted age, the young people especially need to be on the alert. We all must have a basic understanding of the Word of God. This will protect us. As Peter says, the Word will be a lamp shining within us (2 Pet. 1:19). Then if we come in contact with apostates and heretics, we will know that their teaching concerning the Person of Christ and His redemptive work is false and blasphemous, and we will not listen to them. Because we fought against modernism when we were in China, the Christians there were protected. Of course, other Christians were also faithful to fight against heretical teachings. Today we all need to be faithful to contend for the faith once for all delivered to the saints.

LIFE-STUDY OF JUDE

EVILS OF THE APOSTATES AND THEIR PUNISHMENT UNDER THE LORD'S JUDGMENT

Scripture Reading: Jude 8-19

In the foregoing message we saw that the subject of the Epistle of Jude is contending for the faith. Jude charges us to contend for the faith, and then he goes on to speak concerning apostasy (v. 4). In verses 5 through 7 he gives some historical examples of the Lord's judgment upon apostasy. Now in verses 8 through 19 he points out the evils of the apostates and their punishment under the Lord's judgment. Let us consider these verses one by one and pay attention to certain crucial points.

DESPISING LORDSHIP

Verse 8 says, "Yet in like manner these dreamers also defile the flesh and despise lordship and revile dignities." The ungodly men spoken of in verse 4 are dreamers, bearing the name of Christians yet doing things as in dreams, such things as perverting the grace of God into licentiousness to defile their flesh and denying Jesus Christ as our only Master and Lord, despising His lordship and reviling the authorities in His heavenly government.

According to what we have observed throughout the years, those who deny the Lord Jesus and refuse to believe the holy Word eventually cast off the feeling in their conscience. In Paul's words, their conscience has been seared (1 Tim. 4:2) and does not function properly. As a result, they may become unclean and immoral. Once a person's conscience has become seared, he no longer has a protection or safeguard.

The apostates defile the flesh, despise lordship, and

revile dignities because they do not care for God's government. Having no regard for God's authority, they are altogether lawless. They despise lordship; that is, they despise the lordship of Christ, which is the center of the divine government, dominion, and authority (Acts 2:36; Eph. 1:21; Col. 1:16). They also revile dignities, which probably refer to both angels and men in power and authority.

In verse 9 Jude continues, "But Michael the archangel, when disputing with the Devil, arguing concerning the body of Moses, did not dare to bring a reviling judgment against him, but said, The Lord rebuke you." The body of Moses was buried by the Lord in a valley in the land of Moab, in a place known by no man (Deut. 34:6). It must have been purposely done in this manner by the Lord. When Moses and Elijah appeared with Christ on the mount of transfiguration (Matt. 17:3), Moses must have been manifested in his body, which was kept by the Lord and resurrected. Probably, in view of this, the Devil attempted to do something to his body, and the archangel argued with him concerning this. The reference in 2 Peter 2:11 is general, but this is a definite case, concerning the body of Moses.

Jude points out that Michael did not bring a reviling judgment against the Devil, but said, "The Lord rebuke you." This indicates that, in the Lord's heavenly government, the Devil, Satan, was even higher than the archangel Michael. God appointed and set him so (Ezek. 28:14). In any case, Satan was under the Lord. Therefore, Michael said to him, "The Lord rebuke you." Michael kept his position in the order of divine authority.

REVILING WHAT THEY DO NOT KNOW

Verse 10 says, "But these revile whatever they do not know; and whatever they understand naturally, as animals without reason, in these they are being corrupted." The first mention of the word "these" in verse 10 refers to the dreamers in verse 8. In Greek the word "know" here denotes a deeper sensing of invisible things, and the word for "understand" denotes a superficial realization of visible objects. We need both an understanding of visible things and a knowing of invisible things.

The Greek word rendered "naturally" also means instinctively. These dreamers revile what they do not know, things which they should know; and what they understand they understand naturally, instinctively, without reason, as animals of instinct. They do not exercise the deeper and higher knowledge of man with reason, including the consciousness of man's conscience. What they practice is the shallow and base instinctive understanding, like that of animals without human reason. By behaving this way they are being corrupted or destroyed.

THE WAY OF CAIN, THE ERROR OF BALAAM, AND THE REBELLION OF KORAH

Verse 11 says, "Woe to them! Because they have gone in the way of Cain, and poured themselves out in the error of Balaam for reward, and perished in the rebellion of Korah." Here Jude refers to the way of Cain, the error of Balaam, and the rebellion of Korah. The way of Cain is the way of serving God religiously after one's own will and rejecting heretically the redemption by blood required and ordained by God. Those who follow the way of Cain are according to the flesh and envy God's true people because of their faithful testimony to God (Gen. 4:2-8).

Today some so-called Christians follow the way of Cain in that they serve God according to their own will. Because they like to do things a certain way, they do them that way. This is to serve God religiously after one's own will.

We have pointed out that Cain rejected redemption by blood as required by God, and he was also envious of his brother, Abel. Abel was a true child of God, and his testimony was faithful to God and accepted by Him. God was pleased with Abel's offering. But Cain envied his brother to such an extent that he killed him. In principle, this has happened throughout the last nineteen centuries. The ones accepted by God suffer at the hands of those who serve God religiously according to their own will.

In verse 11 Jude says that the apostates have "poured themselves out in the error of Balaam for reward." For the apostates to pour themselves out in this way means that they gave themselves up to this error, rushed headlong into it, ran riotously into it.

The error of Balaam is the error of teaching wrong doctrine for reward, although the one teaching knows that it is contrary to the truth and against the people of God. The error of Balaam also involves abusing the influence of certain gifts to lead the people of God astray from the pure worship of the Lord to idolatrous worship (Num. 22:7, 21; 31:16; Rev. 2:14). Balaam knew that what he taught was against God's truth and against His people, and he knowingly taught it for gain.

Today certain Bible teachers and preachers have fallen into the error of Balaam. Some of these know the deeper truths of the Word. However, fearing the loss of financial support, they do not dare to teach these truths. For example, in 1963 I had a pleasant fellowship with a particular preacher. He told me that he knew the truth concerning the church. But he said that he could not teach this truth, because if he did so, his organization would lose financial support. This indicates that he taught only those things that would enable him to receive financial support. At least to some extent, he practiced the error of Balaam.

If we know the truth, we should teach it and preach it at any cost. But if we dare not teach and preach the truth because we fear loss or because we desire financial gain, we are practicing the error of Balaam. What a shame that certain preachers do not preach the truth because they fear the loss of financial support! In principle, this is the error of Balaam.

In verse 11 Jude also speaks of those who perished in the rebellion of Korah. The Greek word translated "rebellion" here literally means contradiction, speaking against. The rebellion of Korah was a rebellion against God's deputy authority in His government and His word spoken by His deputy (like Moses). This brings in destruction (Num. 16:1-40).

Moses was God's deputy in authority and also in the speaking of His word. But Korah and two hundred fifty others rebelled against Moses' authority and speaking. Actually, this authority and speaking were of God, not of Moses. Moses' authority was God's authority, and his speaking was God's speaking. Nevertheless, Korah and his group rebelled against this. As a result, Korah and those with him suffered a serious judgment: the earth opened and swallowed them all.

We know from history that God always speaks through a deputy authority. To rebel against this authority and speaking is, in principle, to be in the rebellion of Korah.

HIDDEN REEFS

In verse 12 Jude goes on to say, "These are hidden reefs in your love feasts, feasting together with you without fear, shepherds that feed themselves, waterless clouds, carried along by winds, autumn trees without fruit, having died twice, rooted up; wild waves of the sea, foaming out their own shames, wandering stars, for whom the gloom of darkness has been kept for eternity." The Greek word translated "hidden reefs," *spilades*, originally meant a rock. It may allude here to a sunken rock with the sea over it (Darby); hence, hidden rocks. The Greek word *spiloi* for "spots" in 2 Peter 2:13 is very close to *spilades;* hence, some translations render this spots. Actually, these two words refer to two different things. The spots are defects on the surface of precious stones; the hidden rocks are at the bottom of the water. The early heretics were not only spots on the surface but also hidden rocks at the bottom, both of which were a damage to the believers in Christ.

The love feasts mentioned in verse 12 were feasts of love motivated by God's love (*agape*—1 John 4:10-11, 21). In the early days the believers were accustomed to eating together in love for fellowship and worship (Acts 2:46). This kind of feasting was joined to the Lord's supper (1 Cor. 11:20-21, 33) and called a love feast.

Jude calls the apostates "shepherds that feed themselves." The pleasure-seeking heretics (2 Pet. 2:13) pretend to be shepherds, but at the love feasts they only fed themselves, having no concern for others. To others, they were waterless clouds, having no life supply to render.

TREES WITHOUT FRUIT

These heretics are also called "autumn trees without fruit, having died twice, rooted up." Autumn is a season for reaping fruit. The self-seeking apostates seem to be fruit trees in season, but they have no fruit to satisfy others. They have died twice, not only outwardly in appearance as most trees do in autumn, but also inwardly in nature. They are thoroughly dead; they should be uprooted.

WILD WAVES AND WANDERING STARS

In verse 13 Jude goes on to speak of the heretics as "wild waves of the sea, foaming out their own shames, wandering stars, for whom the gloom of darkness has been kept for eternity." Shepherds, clouds, trees, and stars are positive figures in biblical metaphor, but hidden reefs, waves, and the sea are negative. These apostates are false shepherds, empty clouds, dead trees, and wandering stars. They are hidden reefs and wild, raging waves of the sea, foaming out, without restraint, their own shame. The metaphor of wandering stars indicates that the erratic teachers, the apostates, are not solidly fixed in the unchanging truths of the heavenly revelation, but are wandering about among God's star-like people (Dan. 12:3; Phil. 2:15). Their destiny will be the gloom of darkness, which has been kept for them for eternity.

THE LORD COMING WITH MYRIADS OF SAINTS

In verse 14 Jude continues, "And Enoch, the seventh from Adam, prophesied also of these, saying: Behold, the Lord came with myriads of His saints." The coming of the Lord spoken of here must be the appearing of the Lord's *parousia* (coming), as mentioned in 2 Thessalonians 2:8; Matthew 24:27, 30; and Zechariah 14:4-5. The Greek words rendered "myriads of His saints" may also be translated

"His holy myriads." These myriads probably include, as in Zechariah 14:5, the saints (1 Thes. 3:13) and the angels (Matt. 16:27; 25:31; Mark 8:38).

Different opinions may be held concerning the myriads of the saints, or the holy myriads, in verse 14. Some may claim that the saints here are angels, and others may say that these saints are believers. According to the Scriptures, when the Lord Jesus comes back to judge all persons and things, He will come both with the holy angels and with the holy believers. In His sight, both these angels and believers are holy ones. When the Lord Jesus comes back, He will come with His angels and with the overcomers. The overcomers will make up Christ's bride, who will also be His army. Therefore, the Lord will come with these saints and angels to fight against Antichrist and his army.

JUDGMENT UPON THE UNGODLY

We see from verse 15 that the Lord will come "to execute judgment against all, and to convict all the ungodly concerning all their ungodly works which they have done in an ungodly way, and concerning all the hard things which ungodly sinners have spoken against Him." The Lord's coming will be to carry out God's governmental judgment, and by this judgment all the ungodly ones will be dealt with.

In verse 15 Jude uses the word "ungodly" four times. He speaks of the ungodly and their ungodly works which they have done in an ungodly way. He also mentions the hard things which ungodly sinners have spoken against the Lord. All this will be judged by the Lord at His coming.

In verse 16 Jude says that these ungodly ones are murmurers and complainers. They go on according to their own lusts, their mouths speak great swelling things, and they admire persons for the sake of advantage. Then in verses 17 and 18 Jude reminds the believers of the words spoken by the apostles of the Lord Jesus Christ that in the last time there will be mockers going on according to their ungodly lusts.

NOT HAVING SPIRIT

In verse 19 Jude says, "These are those who make separations, soulish, not having spirit." The Greek word translated "soulish" is *psychikos*, the adjective form of *psyche*, which means soul. "The *psyche* (soul) is the center of the personal being, the 'I' of each individual. It is in each man bound to the spirit, man's higher part, and to the body, man's lower part; drawn upwards by the one, downwards by the other. He who gives himself up to the lower appetites, is *fleshy;* he who by communion of his *spirit* with God's Spirit is employed in the higher aims of his being, is *spiritual.* He who rests midway, thinking only of self and self's interest, whether animal or intellectual, is the *psychikos*, the selfish *(soulish)* man, the man in whom the spirit is sunk and degraded into subordination to the subordinate *psyche* (soul)" (Alford).

In verse 19 Jude speaks of the apostates as "not having spirit." This is the human spirit, not the Spirit of God. The apostates are devoid of spirit. They "have not indeed ceased to have a spirit, as a part of their own tripartite nature (1 Thes. 5:23), but they have ceased to possess it in any worthy sense: it is degraded beneath and under the power of the *psyche* (soul), the personal life, so as to have no real vitality of its own" (Alford). They do not care for their spirit or use it. They do not contact God by their spirit in communion with the Spirit of God; neither do they live and walk in their spirit. They have been drawn downward by their flesh and have become fleshy, so that they have lost the consciousness of their conscience and become animals without reason (Jude 10).

LIFE-STUDY OF JUDE

CHARGES TO THE BELIEVERS

Scripture Reading: Jude 20-25

In verses 20 through 23 Jude gives certain charges to the believers. In verses 20 and 21 he charges the believers to build themselves up in the holy faith and to live in the Triune God. Then in verses 22 and 23 he charges the believers to care for others with mercy in fear.

BUILDING OURSELVES UP
IN OUR MOST HOLY FAITH

In verse 20 Jude says, "But you, beloved, building up yourselves in your most holy faith, praying in the Holy Spirit." The faith here is objective faith and refers to the precious things of the New Testament in which we believe for our salvation in Christ. On the foundation of this holy faith and in the sphere of it, through praying in the Holy Spirit, we build up ourselves. The truth of the faith in our apprehension and the Holy Spirit through our prayer are necessary for our building up. Both the faith and the Spirit are holy.

It is correct to say that faith in verse 20 is objective faith. However, we need to realize that this objective faith produces subjective faith. Faith first refers to the truth contained in the Word of God and conveyed by the Word. The written word of God in the Bible and the spoken word in the genuine and proper preaching and teaching contain the truth and convey the truth to us. By truth we mean the reality of what God is, the reality of the process through which God has passed, and the reality of what He has accomplished, attained, and obtained. Hence, truth as reality includes all the facts concerning what God is, what God has passed through, what God has accomplished, and

what God has attained and obtained. All this is revealed in
the New Testament. We may read about this in the Bible,
or we may hear it through someone's preaching and
teaching. But in either case this reality is contained in the
holy Word and conveyed by the Word to us.

As we listen to the word that contains the truth, the
Spirit of Christ works within us. The Spirit of Christ
always works according to the Word and with the Word.
This means that the Spirit of Christ cooperates with the
Word. As a result of this cooperation, eventually in our
experience there is a "click," like that made by the shutter
of a camera, and the "scene" of what is contained in the
Word is impressed on our spirit and becomes our faith. As
we pointed out in the Life-study of 2 Peter, this is the faith
allotted to us as our portion from God (2 Pet. 1:1), and this
portion is nothing less than the New Testament inheritance.

This faith is both objective and subjective. As we build
ourselves up in our most holy faith, we build ourselves up
in a faith that is not only objective but especially
subjective. The subjective faith comes out of the objective
faith. In other words, faith implies both what we believe in
and also our believing. This is the most holy faith.

This faith is not something of ourselves. In ourselves we
do not have such a faith. The most holy faith is a great
blessing given to us from God, of God, and even with God.
When this faith comes into us, it comes with God, with all
that God is, with all that God has passed through, with all
that God has accomplished in Christ and through the
Spirit, and with all that God has obtained and attained.
All this comes into us with God in this faith. As long as we
have this faith, we have the processed God, redemption,
regeneration, the divine life, and all things related to life
and godliness. We are also positioned and privileged to
partake of the divine nature and enjoy it. Therefore, once
we have this faith, we have everything. Now we need to
build ourselves up in this holy faith.

With what materials do we build ourselves up in our
holy faith? The answer is that this faith is both the

materials with which we build and also the base or
foundation on which we build. If we do not have faith, we
do not have the materials, and we do not have the base, the
foundation, on which to build. This means that without
faith we have nothing to build on and nothing to build
with. As believers, we build ourselves up with the content
of our most holy faith, and we build ourselves up on this
faith as a foundation. Praise the Lord that we have such a
faith!

The Chinese version of the Bible translates the Greek
word for faith in verse 20 with a word that means "the true
word." Faith in this verse surely implies the true word, for
faith is produced out of the contents of the true word, God's
revelation. The word of God's revelation contains the
divine reality of God's being, process, redemptive work,
accomplishment, and attainment, and this word conveys
all this divine reality into us. When we hear the words
concerning this reality, the Holy Spirit works within us in
a way that corresponds to these words. The outcome is
faith.

Although faith implies the true word, it implies much
more than this. According to the New Testament, faith is
all-inclusive. As long as we have faith, we have all the
divine things. Therefore, with these divine things as the
material and foundation, we may build ourselves up in our
most holy faith.

To build ourselves up in the faith does not mean to build
ourselves up with theological doctrines or biblical knowledge. Mere doctrine or knowledge is too objective and also
empty. But truth as the reality of the holy Word is not
empty. This truth is the content of the most holy faith.
Therefore, with this content we have something real and
solid with which and on which to build.

The building up in the most holy faith is not indi-
vidualistic; rather, this building is a corporate matter. Jude
is speaking to the believers corporately when he charges
them to build up themselves in their most holy faith. If we
would build up ourselves in the faith, we must do it in a
corporate way; that is, we must do it in the Body, in the

church life. Apart from the church life, we cannot build
ourselves up in the faith. Outside the church life, there is
not such a building. Actually, to build up ourselves in the
most holy faith is to build up the Body of Christ.

PRAYING IN THE HOLY SPIRIT

According to verse 20, if we would build up ourselves in
our most holy faith, we need to pray in the Holy Spirit.
Faith is related to the Word, and in the Holy Spirit we have
life. In this verse the Holy Spirit mainly refers to life, not
to power. However, some Christians today understand the
Holy Spirit mainly in terms of power. In Romans 8:2 Paul
speaks of the Holy Spirit as the Spirit of life. From
experience we know that praying in the Holy Spirit is
much more a matter of life than a matter of power. When
we pray we may not sense power; however, we often have
the sense of life. Life is more precious than power.

Regarding praying in the Holy Spirit, Pentecostal
people may relate this more to power than to life because
their emphasis is on power instead of on life. There is a
great difference between emphasizing life and emphasizing power. Actually, real spiritual power comes from
spiritual life.

Genuine power is a matter of life. We may use seeds as
an illustration. Seeds of every kind are small. I have never
seen a seed as large as a baseball. But although a seed is
small, it is dynamic and full of life. Because a seed is full of
life, it is powerful. After you sow a seed in the ground, it
sprouts and grows into a plant or tree. Although the
sprouts may be very tender, they have the power to break
through the soil. This power comes from the life in the
seed. In a similar way, building ourselves up by praying in
the Holy Spirit is mainly a matter of life.

KEEPING OURSELVES IN THE LOVE OF GOD

In verse 21 Jude says, "Keep yourselves in the love of
God, awaiting the mercy of our Lord Jesus Christ unto
eternal life." We should keep ourselves in the love of God
by building up ourselves in the holy faith and praying in

the Holy Spirit. In this way we should await and look for the mercy of our Lord so that we may not only enjoy eternal life in this age, but also inherit it for eternity (Matt. 19:29).

The way to keep ourselves in the love of God is by building ourselves up in our most holy faith and praying in the Holy Spirit. If we do not build up ourselves in the faith and if we do not pray in the Holy Spirit, it will be easy for us to depart from the love of God. Actually, the words "in the love of God" mean in the enjoyment of the love of God. Here Jude does not speak of the love of God in an objective way; he speaks of the love of God in a subjective way, in the way of enjoying this love. Hour after hour, we need to enjoy the love of God. We should be in the love of God not only objectively but also subjectively. We need to keep ourselves always in the enjoyment of God's love by building ourselves up and by praying. Building up ourselves is related to the holy Word, and praying is related to the Holy Spirit. Therefore, if we have the Word applied to us and the Spirit working within us, we shall be kept in the enjoyment of God's love as we await the mercy of our Lord Jesus Christ unto eternal life.

In verses 20 and 21 Jude not only charges the believers to build themselves up in the holy faith, but also charges them to live in the Triune God. The entire blessed Trinity is employed and enjoyed by the believers by their praying in the Holy Spirit, keeping themselves in the love of God, and awaiting the mercy of our Lord unto eternal life. In these verses we have the Spirit, God the Father, and the Son, our Lord Jesus Christ. We need to pray in the Holy Spirit, keep ourselves in the love of God, and await the mercy of the Lord Jesus Christ. Therefore, in these verses we definitely have the Triune God.

According to Jude 20 and 21, we need to live in the Triune God. But how can we live in the Triune God? We live in the Triune God by praying in the Holy Spirit, keeping ourselves in the love of God, and awaiting the mercy of the Lord Jesus.

It is significant that, once again, Jude speaks of mercy

and not of grace. Peter emphasizes grace, but Jude emphasizes mercy. In verse 2 of this Epistle Jude says, "Mercy to you and peace and love be multiplied." We have pointed out that mercy reaches further than grace does. While we are praying in the Spirit and keeping ourselves in the love of God, we should await further mercy from the Lord.

UNTO ETERNAL LIFE

Jude concludes verse 21 with the words "unto eternal life." Here the word "unto" means issuing in or resulting in. The enjoyment and inheritance of eternal life, the life of God, is the goal of our spiritual seeking. Because we aim at this goal, we want to be kept in the love of God and await the mercy of our Lord.

Jude is not saying that we do not yet have eternal life. Neither is he saying that if we keep praying in the Holy Spirit and remain in the love of God, awaiting the mercy of the Lord we shall eventually have eternal life. Rather, Jude is saying that praying in the Holy Spirit, keeping ourselves in the love of the Father, and waiting for the mercy of the Lord issue in the present enjoyment of eternal life. We already have eternal life in us. However, if we do not pray in the Holy Spirit, keep ourselves in the love of the Father, and wait for the mercy of the Lord, we shall not enjoy this eternal life. But when we do all these things, the eternal life within us becomes our enjoyment.

Furthermore, although we have eternal life, our measure of this life may be somewhat limited. But if we pray in the Spirit, keep ourselves in the Father's love, and wait for the Son's mercy, the eternal life in us will grow in measure. Therefore, "unto eternal life" means not only unto the enjoyment of eternal life, but also unto the growth, the increase of the measure, of eternal life. To experience this is to live in the Triune God.

CARING FOR OTHERS WITH MERCY AND FEAR

In verses 22 and 23 Jude goes on to point out that as we live in the Triune God we need to care for others with mercy and fear. Verse 22 says, "And have mercy on some who are wavering." The Greek here may be rendered "convict some who are disputing." The word for wavering also means doubting. When we live in the Triune God, we shall have a genuine concern for others. We shall care for those who are younger and weaker and for those who are wavering. But if we do not live in the Triune God, we shall not have this care for weaker ones.

In verse 23 Jude continues, "Save them, snatching them out of the fire; on others have mercy in fear, hating even the garment spotted from the flesh." Jude's word concerning snatching them out of the fire is probably adopted from Zechariah 3:2. The fire here is the fire of God's holiness for His judgment (Matt. 3:10, 12; 5:22). According to this word, we should seek to save others and snatch them out of the fire.

In this verse Jude charges us to have mercy in fear, hating the garments spotted from the flesh. While we are having mercy on others, we should be in fear of the awful contagion of sin, hating even the things spotted by the lust of the flesh.

As we exercise mercy on others, we need to be in fear lest we be influenced by them. Sinfulness is contagious. If we are not in fear as we show mercy to others, we may become contaminated with their "germs." For example, suppose you want to help someone who is involved in an unclean or worldly practice. If you are not careful, instead of helping that one, you may become contaminated and eventually join him in that very practice. Therefore, in order not to be contaminated, we need to have mercy on others in fear.

As we show mercy on others in fear, we need to hate the garment spotted from the flesh. Now we see that in showing mercy upon weak ones we need to fear and we need to hate. These weak ones may be in a pitiful state, and we surely need to show mercy to them. But at the same time we need a holy fear and a holy hatred, a holy fear of being contaminated by sinful things and a holy hatred of these things.

CONCLUSION

In verses 24 and 25 we have the conclusion of this Epistle. Verse 24 says, "But to Him who is able to guard you from stumbling, and to set you before His glory without blemish in exultation." In this concluding phrase, the writer indicates clearly that although he has charged the believers to endeavor in the things mentioned in verses 20 through 23, yet only God our Savior is able to guard them from stumbling and to set them before His glory without blemish in exultation. Glory here is the glory of the great God and our Savior, Christ Jesus, which will be manifested at His appearing (Titus 2:13; 1 Pet. 4:13) and in which He will come (Luke 9:26). The preposition "in" here means in the element of, and "exultation" signifies the exuberance of triumphant joy (Alford).

In verse 25 Jude concludes, "To the only God our Savior, through Jesus Christ our Lord, be glory, majesty, might, and authority before all time, and now, and unto all eternity. Amen." The only *God* is our Savior, and the *Man* Jesus Christ is our Lord. To such a Savior, through such a Lord, be glory, majesty, might, and authority throughout all ages. Glory is the expression in splendor; majesty, the greatness in honor; might, the strength in power; and authority, the power in ruling. Therefore, to the only God and our Savior be expression in splendor, greatness in honor, strength in power, and power in ruling. In Jude's words this is "before all time, and now, and unto all eternity." Before all time refers to eternity past; now, to the present age; and unto all eternity, to eternity future. Therefore, it is from eternity past, through time, unto eternity future.

LIFE-STUDY OF JUDE

MESSAGE FOUR

THE BASIC STRUCTURE
OF THE EPISTLES OF PETER AND JUDE

(1)

Scripture Reading: 1 Pet. 1:2-3, 11; 2:1-3, 9; 3:4; 4:14; 5:10;
2 Pet. 1:14; 3:18; Jude 3, 20-21

In this message I would like to give a further word
concerning the central thought of the Epistles of Peter and
Jude.

It is very surprising, even astounding, that an unedu-
cated fisherman from Galilee such as Peter could write the
two Epistles of 1 and 2 Peter. In his writings Peter
embraces all the matters of God's eternal economy, the
same matters that Paul covers in his Epistles. Paul, of
course, was highly educated. He had been trained in the
Scriptures of the Old Testament, and he also had been
educated in Greek and Roman culture. Peter, however, did
not have this learning. Nevertheless, he wrote his two
Epistles in a marvelous way.

Peter even used certain terms and expressions that Paul
did not use. For example, Peter speaks about being
partakers of the divine nature (2 Pet. 1:4). This profound
expression cannot be found in the writings of Paul. Not
only does Peter use deep and profound expressions, but in
his Epistles he also covers a number of significant details.
In quantity Peter wrote much less than Paul wrote, but in
certain points he may be richer than Paul. Therefore, we
need to spend adequate time to study the two Epistles of
Peter to see the crucial points and the details.

THE TRIUNE GOD AS OUR PORTION

The first basic matter covered by Peter in his writings is

the Triune God. Peter indicates that the God in whom we believe is the Triune God. In the opening words of Peter's first Epistle we can see the Triune God: "According to the foreknowledge of God the Father, in sanctification of the Spirit, unto obedience and sprinkling of the blood of Jesus Christ" (v. 2). Here we have the foreknowledge of God the Father, the sanctification of the Spirit, and the obedience and sprinkling of the blood of Jesus Christ. God the Father has regenerated us (1 Pet. 1:3), Christ has accomplished redemption with His precious blood, and the Spirit applies God's full salvation to His chosen people. Here we see the Triune God in the accomplishment of full salvation.

Peter also unveils to us the fact that this Triune God is our portion. This fact is indicated by the word "partakers" in 2 Peter 1:4. According to this verse, we have become partakers of the divine nature. This indicates that the Triune God is now our portion. If God were not our portion, we could not partake of His nature.

THE MEANS FOR US TO PARTAKE OF GOD

In his writings Peter also reveals the way for us to partake of the Triune God as our portion. The way involves the hidden man of the heart, and this hidden man is our spirit (1 Pet. 3:4). In his Epistles Paul has much to say concerning our spirit, but he does not use the expression "the hidden man of the heart." This hidden man, our human spirit, is the means by which we enjoy the Triune God as our portion.

Although Peter speaks of God's Spirit only a few times, his terminology is marvelous. In 1 Peter 4:14 he says, "If you are reproached in the name of Christ, you are blessed, because the Spirit of glory and of God rests upon you." Literally, the Greek here means "the Spirit of glory and that of God." The Spirit of glory is the Spirit of God. Peter also speaks concerning the Spirit of Christ (1 Pet. 1:11). Our human spirit as the hidden man of the heart and God's Spirit as the Spirit of glory and as the Spirit of Christ are the means for us to partake of God as our portion.

THE TRIUNE GOD PROCESSED
TO BECOME OUR ENJOYMENT

We have pointed out that the Epistles of Peter are on the subject of God's government, in particular on God's governmental dealings through judgment. This is the central subject of these two books. Nevertheless, the structure of 1 and 2 Peter is the Triune God, who has been processed to become our portion so that we may participate in Him, partake of Him, and enjoy Him through His Spirit, who is the Spirit of Christ and the Spirit of glory, and by the exercise of our spirit.

I encourage you to study all the details in the Epistles of Peter. However, as you study these details, do not be distracted from the central thought and the basic structure of God's holy writings in general and the Epistles of Peter in particular. The basic structure is the Triune God who has been processed to become our all-inclusive portion. We enjoy Him by exercising our spirit to cooperate with and respond to the divine Spirit. We should never forget this basic structure or be distracted from it. If we hold firmly to the basic thought and the basic structure as we study all the other points in the writings of Peter, we shall be enriched and we shall experience the Triune God in a very rich, absolute, and detailed way.

The three Epistles of 1 and 2 Peter and Jude cover many points. But the basic structure of these Epistles is the Triune God operating on His elect that they may be brought into the full enjoyment of the Triune God. Both Peter and Jude indicate strongly that the Triune God has passed through a process in order to do many things for us and to become everything to us that we may partake of Him for our enjoyment.

THE TRIUNE GOD BECOMING OUR GRACE

Peter begins his first Epistle with a word concerning the threefold operation of the Triune God upon His chosen people to bring them into the participation and enjoyment of Himself. At the beginning of his second Epistle Peter speaks concerning the divine provision. He tells us that the divine power has granted us and even imparted to us all things related to life and godliness in order that we may partake of the divine nature. Furthermore, according to chapter one of 2 Peter, the divine provision gives us not only the divine life but also the divine light (v. 19).

At the end of his first Epistle Peter says, "But the God of all grace, who called you into His eternal glory in Christ, after you have suffered a little while, will Himself perfect, establish, strengthen, and ground you" (5:10). Here Peter indicates that we shall be grounded in God Himself. Then at the end of his second Epistle Peter says, "But grow in grace and the knowledge of our Lord and Savior Jesus Christ" (3:18). Here the knowledge of our Lord is equal to the truth, the reality of all that He is. Therefore, in this verse Peter charges us to grow in grace and in truth, reality. Although Peter covers many matters in his Epistles, the basic structure of his writings is the Triune God becoming our grace that we may enjoy Him, grow in life, and through the growth in life be perfected, established, strengthened, and grounded in the Triune God.

As we study the details of the Epistles of Peter and Jude, we need to remember that all the detailed points help us to solve our problems so that we may be brought back to the enjoyment of the Triune God. Therefore, we should not consider the details in a detached way. Every point is a help in solving our problems so that we would not be distracted further from the enjoyment of the Triune God, but instead be brought back to this enjoyment.

CONTENDING FOR THE FAITH
AND LIVING IN THE TRIUNE GOD

Toward the beginning of his Epistle Jude charges us to contend for the faith: "Beloved, using all diligence to write to you concerning our common salvation, I found it necessary to write to you, entreating you to contend for the faith once for all delivered to the saints" (v. 3). We have seen that the faith is the New Testament inheritance substantiated to us and realized by us. We pointed out in the Life-study of 2 Peter that this inheritance is actually the Triune God processed to be our portion.

Toward the end of his Epistle Jude says, "But you, beloved, building up yourselves in your most holy faith, praying in the Holy Spirit, keep yourselves in the love of God, awaiting the mercy of our Lord Jesus Christ unto eternal life" (vv. 20-21). Jude's word concerning building up ourselves in our most holy faith is equal to Peter's word about being built up a spiritual house, into a holy priesthood (1 Pet. 2:5). Then Jude goes on to speak of living in the Triune God. This is indicated by Jude's word concerning praying in the Holy Spirit, keeping ourselves in the love of God, and awaiting the mercy of our Lord Jesus Christ.

UNTO ETERNAL LIFE

Jude ends verse 21 with the words "unto eternal life." Here "unto" means issuing in or resulting in. This phrase indicates the enjoyment of the Triune God. Eternal life is the Triune God, and "unto eternal life" indicates the full enjoyment of what the Triune God is.

A WORD OF REMINDER

We need to be impressed with the fact that these three Epistles were written with a basic structure, and this structure is the Triune God processed to become the all-inclusive life-giving Spirit for our enjoyment. This structure is according to God's economy, and it corresponds fully to what is unveiled in Paul's writings. I hope that this word will serve as a reminder to you. When you consider the matters of God's government and the historic examples of His dealing in His judgment, you should not be distracted by these matters. Instead, these things should bring you back to the basic structure of these Epistles—the Triune God as our full enjoyment. Futhermore, you need to take care of your spirit as the hidden man of the heart and realize that the divine Spirit, the Spirit of glory and the Spirit of Christ, is within you. Then you will enjoy the

Triune God and express Him as godliness, which will consummate in glory.

CHOSEN FOR GOD'S PURPOSE

In the first one and a half chapters of 1 Peter we have a clear picture of how God in eternity past selected us according to His foreknowledge to be His chosen people. Praise Him that out of the billions of human beings He has selected us! God selected us for a purpose, and this purpose is that God would put Himself into us as our life so that we may grow with Him into a building, His dwelling place. This building is God's house, the place where He houses Himself. Furthermore, this building becomes God's expression to "tell out the virtues of Him" as the One who has called us out of darkness into His marvelous light (1 Pet. 2:9). To tell out God's virtues is to express what He is. This is God's purpose. This is also God's goal.

If God would fulfill His purpose and reach His goal, He needs to apply to us what He decided in eternity past. In order to do this, it is necessary for God to be the Spirit. It is the Spirit who applies to us what God has decided. Moreover, because His chosen people had become fallen, it became necessary for God to accomplish redemption. Hence, God came in the Person of the Son to accomplish redemption. The Lord Jesus shed His blood so that we may be sprinkled and redeemed to God.

In 1 Peter we see that the Spirit applies God's decision to us, the Son redeems us, and the Father regenerates us. For this reason, Peter says, "Blessed be the God and Father of our Lord Jesus Christ, who according to His great mercy has regenerated us unto a living hope through the resurrection of Jesus Christ from among the dead" (1 Pet. 1:3). This means that God entered into us as the divine life containing the divine "genes" to regenerate us. Now that we have been regenerated, we may taste that the Lord is good (1 Pet. 2:3).

THE RESULT OF TASTING THE LORD

As a result of tasting the Lord, we have the desire to put

away our natural being. Therefore, in 1 Peter 2:1 Peter speaks of "putting away all malice and all guile and hypocrisies and envyings and all evil speakings." Here Peter mentions five matters: malice, guile, hypocrisies, envyings, and evil speakings. Malice issues in guile, guile is related to hypocrisy and envy, and the result is evil speaking. Those who have malice will also have guile. This guile will cause them to pretend and to become envious of others. As a result of this envy, they will speak evil concerning others.

In Romans 1 Paul lists more than thirty items related to sinful mankind. But here Peter uses five items to express the total situation of fallen man. No doubt, Peter's word in 2:1 was written according to his experience in the church life.

After we have been regenerated and have tasted that the Lord is good, we shall certainly want to put away these five negative things. We shall want to put away all malice, for we shall not agree with malice in any way. Simultaneously, we shall have a love for the Word of God and an appetite to take in the Word as our nourishment. Peter speaks of this in 2:2 : "As newborn babes, long for the guileless milk of the word, that by it you may grow unto salvation." Having been born through regeneration (1:3, 23), the believers become babes who can grow in life by being nourished with the spiritual milk, the guileless milk, of the Word. This growth is for God's building. To grow is a matter of life and in life. We receive the divine life through regeneration, and now we need to grow in this life and with this life by being nourished with the milk conveyed in the Word of God.

I can testify that after I was saved I had a deep longing for the Word of God and a desire to be nourished through the Word. However, I was led astray by the desire to know the Bible. Instead of being guided to the central focus of the divine revelation, I was distracted by others to the pursuit of biblical knowledge. For a number of years, I met with a group of believers who were famous for their knowledge of the Bible. These believers often spoke about

God's foreknowledge and selection and about Christ as the precious stone rejected by man but chosen by God. They also warned us concerning God's judgment beginning from His own household, and they taught concerning the mighty hand of God. We were exhorted to subject ourselves under the mighty hand of God. Although this teaching was good, it did not help me to see God's purpose. I heard a number of teachings based upon the Epistles of Peter, but I did not see God's goal, and I did not know what God is seeking. I was distracted from the central focus of the divine revelation by good Bible knowledge.

Eventually in His mercy the Lord caused me to see the basic structure of the Epistles of Peter and Jude. In particular, I began to see the matters of growth, transformation, and building. Growth in life is unto transformation, and transformation is for the building.

In the Epistles of Peter and Jude we can see God's economy. In these Epistles we also see God's purpose and goal. God's purpose was formed in eternity past, and God's goal will be attained in full in eternity future. God's goal is to have His building as His expression, and He is reaching this goal through our growth in the divine life.

LIFE-STUDY OF JUDE

MESSAGE FIVE

THE BASIC STRUCTURE
OF THE EPISTLES OF PETER AND JUDE

(2)

Scripture Reading: 1 Pet. 1:2-4, 11, 18-19, 22-23; 2:2, 5; 5:10; 2 Pet. 3:15-16, 18; Jude 20-21

In this message I would like to give a further word concerning the basic structure of the Epistles of Peter and Jude.

THE OPERATION OF THE TRIUNE GOD

In 1 Peter 1:2 and 3 we can see the operation of the Triune God: "According to the foreknowledge of God the Father, in sanctification of the Spirit, unto obedience and sprinkling of the blood of Jesus Christ: Grace to you and peace be multiplied. Blessed be the God and Father of our Lord Jesus Christ, who according to His great mercy has regenerated us unto a living hope through the resurrection of Jesus Christ from among the dead." In these verses we have the foreknowledge of God the Father, the sanctification of the Spirit, and the obedience and sprinkling of the blood of Jesus Christ. Here we have the Triune God— the Father, the Spirit, and Jesus Christ, the Son. In verse 3 Peter also tells us that the Father has regenerated us unto a living hope through Christ's resurrection. Here again we see the Father's operation. The Father not only chose us in eternity, but in time He also regenerated us. In verse 2 Peter says that the Spirit sanctifies us, applying to us what the Father decided concerning us in eternity past. Then in verse 11 Peter speaks concerning the witness of the Spirit of Christ in the prophets of the Old Testament. In verses 18 and 19 Peter says, "Knowing that you were redeemed not with corruptible things, with silver or gold, from your vain manner of life handed down from your fathers, but with precious blood, as of a lamb without blemish and without spot, the blood of Christ." Now that we have been redeemed with Christ's precious blood, we need to have our souls purified by obedience to the truth unto unfeigned brotherly love (v. 22). This purification of the soul is based upon the Father's regeneration. We have been regenerated by the Father with an incorruptible seed, a seed that is the living and abiding word of God (v. 23).

As we consider chapter one of 1 Peter as a whole, we can see that this chapter reveals the operation of the Triune God. Here we have the Father's regeneration, the Spirit's sanctification, the blood of Christ, the incorruptible seed, the living hope, and also the inheritance kept for us in the heavens (v. 4). In this chapter we have not only the basic structure of the first Epistle of Peter, but we also have the basic structure of our Christian life. The Christian life is constructed of all the items related to the operation of the Triune God.

THE TWO TREES

The basic structure of the Christian life revealed in 1 Peter 1 is something far different from our natural concept. In our natural mind we do not have the kind of thought presented in 1 Peter 1. Our natural thought is to do good, to love others, to worship God, and to work for God. This concept is religious and traditional.

A person who is far from God may not care for God at all. But once such a person repents and begins to care for God, he will immediately have the desire to do good in order to glorify God. He will also have the desire to be more considerate of others. He may even decide to give a tenth of his income to the Lord. Although these things are good, they are religious, traditional, and natural.

You may have heard many messages telling you that the Triune God has been processed to become the life-giving Spirit in order to be everything to you. But in your daily life you may not care for the processed Triune God.

Instead, you may try to be a good husband or wife and a good parent. In your effort to improve yourself, you may not have the realization that you are not living the Triune God, that you are not one with the life-giving Spirit. Instead of putting into practice the word concerning being one spirit with the Lord in your daily living, your desire may be to be victorious or to improve yourself.

The reason we fail to put into practice what we have heard is related to the tree of the knowledge of good and evil. In our fallen being there is the tendency toward this tree. The thought of doing good belongs to the tree of the knowledge of good and evil. Before you repented and believed in the Lord, you may have had the knowledge of evil. But now that you are a believer, you may turn to the knowledge of good. However, the knowledge of both good and evil are of the same tree.

Throughout my years in the ministry, I have come to realize that although the saints may listen to messages on the Triune God as life, in their daily living they care for the tree of the knowledge of good and evil. But whenever we come back to the Triune God as the life-giving Spirit, we are immediately feeding on the tree of life.

TWO SOURCES

There are only two sources in this universe—God and Satan. After God created man, He placed him in front of two trees signifying these two sources. God is signified by the tree of life, and Satan is signified by the tree of the knowledge of good and evil. God is the source of life. If we contact Him, we contact life. Satan is the source of death. If we contact him, we contact death. Therefore, God clearly told Adam not to eat of the tree of the knowledge of good and evil, for the result of eating that tree is death. God's intention was that man would contact Him in order to receive life. If we contact the tree of knowledge instead of the tree of life, we shall contact death. God's intention is that man would contact Him to receive life. But in the fall Adam turned to Satan, the other source.

Satan is not honest or straightforward. Rather, Satan

wears a cloak and pretends to be something he is not. For example, when he first appeared to Adam, he appeared in the form of a serpent. Satan lurks behind the knowledge of good and evil. The result of the knowledge of either good or evil is death.

Today unbelievers and many times believers as well are under death because they daily contact the good aspect of the tree of the knowledge of good and evil. In religion, people are taught to know what is good and what is evil, and to do good and stay away from evil. This kind of teaching is common among Christians today. However, this teaching is natural and religious, and according to our fallen nature.

In the Bible we have two sources, two lines, and two results. First we have the tree of life, the line of life, and the New Jerusalem. The tree of life will be found in the New Jerusalem. Without the tree of life, the New Jerusalem would not have any enjoyment. The unique enjoyment in the New Jerusalem will be the tree of life.

Then in the Bible we have the second source and the second line: the tree of the knowledge of good and evil and the line of death. The result of this source and line is the lake of fire.

We need to have our eyes opened to see the tree of life in the Bible. Many Christians read the Bible, but they cannot see the tree of life. Because this is mysterious, unless our eyes are opened we shall not be able to see it.

The crucial point in what we have been saying concerning the tree of life and the tree of the knowledge of good and evil is that the structure of the Christian life as revealed in chapter one of 1 Peter is very different from our natural concept, which is according to the knowledge of good and evil. I am very happy to see that, according to 1 Peter 1, the basic structure of this Epistle, and of the entire Christian life, is the Triune God.

THE ENJOYMENT AND INCREASE OF ETERNAL LIFE

In verses 20 and 21 Jude says, "But you, beloved, building up yourselves in your most holy faith, praying in the Holy Spirit, keep yourselves in the love of God, awaiting the mercy of our Lord Jesus Christ unto eternal life." In these verses we have the Triune God for our experience with a view to eternal life. First, Jude charges us to pray in the Holy Spirit. Then he tells us to keep ourselves in the love of God as we await the mercy of our Lord Jesus Christ. This is "unto eternal life," that is, unto the enjoyment and increase of eternal life.

When I was young, I could not understand what Jude meant by the words "unto eternal life." Someone might say that this means to go to heaven and enjoy everlasting blessing. However, this interpretation does not satisfy us. Apparently these words indicate that we do not yet have eternal life, that eternal life is something that we shall have in the future. But this is not the meaning. John 3:16 tells us that whoever believes in the Son of God has eternal life. When we believe in Christ, we receive eternal life. Since we already have eternal life, what does it mean to say that we are awaiting the mercy of our Lord Jesus Christ unto eternal life? Yes, we already have eternal life within us, but we may not enjoy this life very much. Some Christians enjoy eternal life hardly at all. They do not even know that it is possible to have the enjoyment of eternal life. Furthermore, we may not have the increase of eternal life. God has given us eternal life with the intention that we would enjoy this life and that it would increase within us forever. Therefore, the words "unto eternal life" mean unto the enjoyment and increase of eternal life now and in eternity.

THE TRIUNE GOD AS OUR PORTION, ENJOYMENT, AND EXPERIENCE

According to Jude 20 and 21, we need to pray in the Holy Spirit, keep ourselves in the love of God, and wait for the mercy of Jesus Christ so that we may have the enjoyment and increase of eternal life forever. This is a description of the experience of the Triune God.

Chapter one of 1 Peter and the Epistle of Jude both speak concerning the Triune God. Peter's word concerning the Triune God is profound, and Jude's word is somewhat simple. We may say that Jude gives a word to "elementary students," and Peter gives a word to "graduate students." However, many Christians are not even able to understand Jude's elementary word concerning the experience of the Triune God. We thank the Lord that He has enlightened us to see the meaning both of Peter's word in chapter one of his first Epistle and Jude's word toward the end of his Epistle. In both 1 Peter and Jude we see that the Triune God is to be our portion, enjoyment, and experience.

THE CENTRAL FOCUS

In our study of the Epistles of 1 and 2 Peter and Jude we need to see the central focus of these books. Although the subject of 1 and 2 Peter is God's government, especially His government shown in His judgment, this is not the central focus of these books. Neither is the divine government the basic structure of the Epistles of Peter. What is the focus of these Epistles? What is their basic structure? In order not to be distracted by the many precious matters in 1 and 2 Peter, we need clear answers to these questions.

In 1 Peter actually only one and a half chapters are crucial in relation to life. These one and a half chapters include all of chapter one and the first eleven verses of chapter two. In addition, we need to regard Peter's word in 5:10 as crucial. In this verse Peter says, "But the God of all grace, who called you into His eternal glory in Christ, after you have suffered a little while, will Himself perfect, establish, strengthen, and ground you." We have a similar situation in the Epistle of 2 Peter. In this book the first half of the first chapter and the last verse of the last chapter are crucial in relation to life. In these vital portions of 1 and 2 Peter we have the central focus of these Epistles.

A Simple Sketch of 1 Peter 1

In chapter one of 1 Peter we see the operation of the Triune God for His full salvation. In verse 2 we see the foreknowledge of God the Father, the sanctification of the

Spirit, and the sprinkling of the blood of Jesus Christ. This verse reveals the Father's foreknowledge, the Son's redemption, and the Spirit's application. This is the operation of the Triune God to carry out God's full salvation. In verse 3 Peter says that the Father has regenerated us unto a living hope. The full salvation of God is composed of three elements: the Father's regeneration, the Son's redemption, and the Spirit's application. When we experience this salvation, we have a life that is characterized by holiness and love. We are holy in our manner of life, and we love the brothers. Therefore, holiness and love are the issue of God's full salvation. Furthermore, in this salvation there is a seed, the incorruptible seed, which is the living and abiding word of God. This is a simple sketch of chapter one of 1 Peter.

Growth, Transformation, and Building

Let us now go on to consider 1 Peter 2:1-11. Having been regenerated, we are now newborn babes longing for the guileless milk of the word so that by it we may grow unto salvation (v. 2). In chapter one we see that we have been regenerated and that the full salvation of God is our portion. Now we need to partake of and enjoy this salvation. For this, we need to feed on the milk of the word.

By feeding on the guileless milk of the word and by growing unto salvation, we shall be transformed into precious stones. Therefore, Peter refers to the believers as living stones (v. 5). These stones are for the building up of a spiritual house, and this house is a holy priesthood: "You yourselves also, as living stones, are being built up a spiritual house, into a holy priesthood, to offer up spiritual sacrifices acceptable to God through Jesus Christ" (v. 5). On the one hand, this spiritual house is God's dwelling place; on the other hand, it is something that tells forth the virtues of God, that expresses what God is.

This spiritual house, of course, is a corporate matter. We are being built up together in a corporate way to afford God a dwelling place and to tell forth God's virtue, that is, to express Him.

Caring for the "Heart" of These Epistles

In these two portions of 1 Peter, including 5:10, we have the central focus of this book. We need to be fully captured by this focus. Then we shall not be in danger of being distracted from this focus as we pay attention to the other matters in this book.

We may compare the central focus of 1 Peter to the heart in the human body. We should not take care of the other members of the body at the cost of damaging our heart. We may lose a toe, an arm, or a leg and still live. But we cannot live without a heart. In a similar way, we need to care for the "heart," the central focus, of 1 Peter.

The heart of this book is the operation of the Triune God to carry out His threefold salvation, which includes regeneration, redemption, and application. We have become God's children through regeneration, and now we need to feed on His word in order to grow unto full salvation. Then we shall be transformed in order to be built together to provide God a dwelling place and to be His expression. For this purpose, the God of all grace will perfect, establish, strengthen, and ground us. Furthermore, according to 2 Peter 3:18, we need to grow in God's grace and in the knowledge of Him. This is the focus of 1 and 2 Peter and the focus of the book of Jude.

NOT DISTRACTED FROM THE BASIC STRUCTURE

This central focus is also the basic structure of these Epistles. In the books of 1 and 2 Peter and Jude there are many matters, but not all of these matters are part of the basic structure. We may use a physical building as an illustration. The basic structure of the meeting hall in Anaheim consists of steel beams and columns. Many things can be removed from this building without affecting its basic structure. However, the beams and columns cannot be taken out of the building without destroying the basic structure. Just as the meeting hall in Anaheim has a basic structure, so there is a basic structure to the Epistles of 1 and 2 Peter and Jude.

My concern is that the saints may be distracted from this basic structure by the various matters covered in these books. I am not saying that we should not pay attention to these matters. We need to pay attention to them and even emphasize them, but in doing so we must be certain that we have not been distracted from the basic structure of these writings. This basic structure is the Triune God operating to accomplish a threefold salvation so that we may be regenerated, that we may feed on His word, and that we may grow, be transformed, and be built up in order that He may have a dwelling place and that we may express Him.

This basic thought can also be seen in the Epistles of Paul. For this reason, Peter says, "Even as also our beloved brother Paul, according to the wisdom given to him, wrote to you, as also in all his letters, speaking in them concerning these things" (2 Pet. 3:15-16). Paul also reveals that we may feed on the Lord and grow in order to be built up into a spiritual house so that God may have a corporate expression. Therefore, these two apostles ministered the same thing, but with somewhat different terminology. Both Peter and Paul had the same focus. I hope that none of us in the Lord's recovery will be distracted from the central focus and the basic structure of the apostles' ministry revealed in the New Testament.